CORPORATE SOCIAL RESPONSIBILITY AND SMEs

The world's people and their leaders face a complex and multifaceted set of 'eco-social questions'. As the productivity of humanity increases, the negative external environmental effects of production and consumption patterns become increasingly problematic and threaten human welfare. As the regulating power of national and international governments is limited, this challenge has generated a strong interest in the corporate social responsibility (CSR) of companies. Firms find it increasingly important to meet the expectations of stakeholders with respect to the company's contribution to profit, planet, and people.

The primary aim of this book is to introduce the reader to the impacts and drivers of CSR, with a special focus on small and medium-sized enterprises (SMEs). Research into the social and environmental impacts of CSR is rare. This is a serious gap because if CSR were to fail to have favourable social and environmental impacts on society, the whole concept may become redundant. If societal impacts of CSR are substantial, it is important to know the drivers of CSR. This book considers (1) factors internal to the company, (2) the competitive environment of the company, (3) institutions external to the company, and (4) how the impacts of institutions are mediated or moderated by company internal factors.

This book will fill this gap by estimating various types of models that integrate the external and internal factors driving CSR and its impacts on environment, innovation, and reputation, making it a valuable resource for researchers, academics, and students in the fields of business management and CSR.

Johan J. Graafland is Professor in Economics, Business, and Ethics at Tilburg University, The Netherlands, and Fellow of the Tilburg Sustainability Center.

Routledge Studies in Management, Organizations and Society

This series presents innovative work grounded in new realities, addressing issues crucial to an understanding of the contemporary world. This is the world of organized societies, where boundaries between formal and informal, public and private, local and global organizations have been displaced or have vanished, along with other nineteenth century dichotomies and oppositions. Management, apart from becoming a specialized profession for a growing number of people, is an everyday activity for most members of modern societies.

Similarly, at the level of enquiry, culture and technology, and literature and economics, can no longer be conceived as isolated intellectual fields; conventional canons and established mainstreams are contested. *Management, Organizations and Society* addresses these contemporary dynamics of transformation in a manner that transcends disciplinary boundaries, with books that will appeal to researchers, students and practitioners alike.

Recent titles in this series include:

Reputation Management and Family Business
Zdzisława Dacko-Pikiewicz

Governance and Business Models for Sustainable Capitalism
Atle Midttun

Corporate Social Responsibility and SMEs
Impacts and Institutional Drivers
Johan J. Graafland

For a full list of available titles please visit: www.routledge.com

CORPORATE SOCIAL RESPONSIBILITY AND SMEs

Impacts and Institutional Drivers

Johan J. Graafland

Routledge
Taylor & Francis Group
NEW YORK AND LONDON

Cover image: © Getty Images

First published 2022
by Routledge
605 Third Avenue, New York, NY 10158

and by Routledge
2 Park Square, Milton Park, Abingdon, Oxon, OX14 4RN

Routledge is an imprint of the Taylor & Francis Group, an informa business

Library of Congress Cataloging-in-Publication Data
Names: Graafland, J. J., author.
Title: Corporate social responsibility and SMEs : impacts and institutional drivers / Johan J. Graafland.
Description: 1 Edition. | New York, NY : Routledge, 2022. | Series: Routledge studies in management, organizations and society | Includes bibliographical references and index.
Identifiers: LCCN 2021037243 (print) | LCCN 2021037244 (ebook) | ISBN 9781032106717 (hardback) | ISBN 9781032106724 (paperback) | ISBN 9781003216483 (ebook)
Subjects: LCSH: Social responsibility of business. | Small business.
Classification: LCC HD60 .G6923 2022 (print) | LCC HD60 (ebook) | DDC 658.4/08—dc23
LC record available at https://lccn.loc.gov/2021037243
LC ebook record available at https://lccn.loc.gov/2021037244

ISBN: 978-1-032-10671-7 (hbk)
ISBN: 978-1-032-10672-4 (pbk)
ISBN: 978-1-003-21648-3 (ebk)

DOI: 10.4324/9781003216483

CONTENTS

FIGURES

TABLES

ABOUT THE AUTHOR

Johan J. Graafland (1960) is Full Professor of Economics, Business, and Ethics at Tilburg University, The Netherlands, since 2000 and is Fellow of Tilburg Sustainability Center. He is a member of the Department of Economics at the Faculty of Economics and Business Administration, Philosophy at the Faculty of Humanities, and Theology at Tilburg University. He studied economics at Erasmus University, Rotterdam, and theology at Utrecht University. His research focuses on economic ethics, business ethics, CSR, and the relationship between economics and religion. From 2017 until 2021, Johan J. Graafland led a large multidisciplinary research of a consortium of Tilburg University, Radboud University, Erasmus University, and the Vrije Universiteit on the research project 'What good markets are good for'. He has published seven books and about 70 articles in peer-reviewed journals. He teaches the courses Philosophy of Economics and Economic Ethics, History of Economic Thought, Christianity in Dialogue with Social Economic World, and Corporate Social Responsibility at Tilburg University. His work has attracted over 3000 ISI citations.

PREFACE

The market system has generated welfare and economic growth. However, increasing income inequalities, depletion of the natural environment, the financial crisis in 2008, and the current Covid crisis have led to an intense debate about the negative side effects of markets. As the regulating power of national and international governments is limited, this challenge has generated a strong interest in the corporate social responsibility (CSR) of companies.

Research has shown that CSR is potentially a promising mechanism to foster sustainable development because there is some evidence that the financial performance of companies is positively related to CSR. However, if CSR is really a 'business case', why is sustainable development so challenging, and why do governments put so much stress on stimulating CSR? This begs the question of how companies can be motivated to CSR.

The primary aim of this monograph is to introduce the reader to the impacts and institutional drivers of CSR, with a special focus on small and medium-sized enterprises (SMEs). Although the effects of CSR on financial performance have been well researched, research into the social and environmental impacts of CSR is very rare. This is a serious gap because if CSR were to fail to have favourable social and environmental impacts on society, the whole concept may become redundant. A second type of question concerns the drivers of CSR. In this book, we consider three types of drivers: factors internal to the company, the competitive environment of the company, and institutions external to the company. We particularly focus on the impacts and drivers of CSR of SMEs. A focus on SMEs is important because small businesses collectively account for up to 70% of industrial pollution worldwide.

Fourteen chapters (e.g. Chapters 2, 3, 5, 7, 8, and 10–18) are based on academic articles published previously in various scientific journals. The unpublished chapters (Chapters 1, 4, 6, 9, 19, and 20) fill some of the gaps that remained after the published articles. The added value of bringing together this material in one volume and combining it with unpublished academic work is that the book presents a complete framework of the impacts and drivers of CSR of SMEs, in which the individual chapters are embedded. In this way, the book gives an integrative account of the impacts and drivers of CSR rather than isolated mechanisms described in the individual articles. The integrated analysis makes the book more apt for educational purposes than the individual papers.

The book will be used as a textbook in a master's course on CSR. The course aims to inspire master's students in management to develop new ideas on the mechanisms that explain the links between the fundamental causes and outcomes of CSR. Access to the data used in the analysis in the various chapters will provide students with material for exercises.

ACKNOWLEDGEMENTS

At the start of this book, I want to thank my colleagues who co-authored some of the articles published in this book: Frank de Bakker (Chapter 14), Lans Bovenberg (Chapter 15), Reyer Gerlagh (Chapter 16), Niels Noorderhaven (Chapters 9, 11, and 17), and Hugo Smid (Chapters 2 and 13). Working together with them substantially improved the quality of these papers and was always great fun for me.

I also keep good memories to the IMPACT research team of the European FP7 programme (SSH-2009–2.1.3), headed by Regine Barth, that provided the starting point for this study.

Furthermore, I want to thank the European Union and ING bank for financing the surveys in 2011 and 2014, respectively, and CentERdata (particularly Marije Oudejans) for programming and sending out the surveys.

Finally, the Templeton World Charity Foundation Inc. is greatly acknowledged for providing me financial assistance for the research project 'What good markets are good for' that allowed me to devote a substantial part of my time on research in the relationship between free market institutions and CSR during 2017–2020.

1 INTRODUCTION

1.1 Introduction

Today, the world's people and their leaders face a complex and multifaceted set of 'eco-social questions'. As the productivity of humanity increases, the negative external environmental effects of production and consumption patterns become increasingly problematic and threaten the human welfare. As the regulating power of national and international governments is limited, this challenge has generated a strong interest in corporate social responsibility (CSR) of companies. Firms find it increasingly important to meet the expectations of stakeholders with respect to the company's contribution to profit, planet, and people. This interaction between companies and various stakeholders constitutes a third mechanism that supplements the shortcomings of the market mechanism and government regulation in serving the well-being of the society.

What Does CSR Mean?

This book analyses the impacts and drivers of CSR. Based on a study of 37 definitions, Dahlsrud (2008) identifies five common dimensions of CSR: the economic, social, environmental, stakeholder, and voluntariness dimensions. These elements are nicely illustrated by the well-known definition of CSR by the European Commission (2001): 'Corporate social responsibility refers to a concept whereby companies integrate social and environmental concerns in their business operations and in their interaction with their stakeholders on a voluntary basis.' The economic dimension links to the *P* of profit in Elkington's triple bottom line (Elkington, 1997) and refers to the profitability and other economic dimensions of welfare, such as innovations and the resulting employment opportunities

DOI: 10.4324/9781003216483-1

for society. The social dimension (the *P* of people) is concerned with the ability of a firm to contribute to a better society, including respect of civil and human rights, abolition of world poverty, and better working conditions for employees. The environmental dimension refers to the *P* of planet and relates to the natural environment and natural resources. The stakeholder element means that the three dimensions – economic, social, and environmental – are important for various types of stakeholders who are affected by the corporate behaviour of the firm. The voluntary dimension reflects that CSR mostly concerns actions that go beyond the legal obligations of the organization.

The concept of CSR is closely related to the concept of corporate social performance (CSP). This concept distinguishes CSR policies, CSR implementation, and their impacts (Carroll, 1979). One of the most influential, parsimonious, and yet comprehensive conceptualizations of CSP is Wood's CSP model (Wood, 1991, 2010). In her model, Wood synthesizes the various previous attempts to model CSP. Wood defines CSP as 'a business organization's configuration of principles of social responsibility, processes of social responsiveness, and policies, programs and observable outcomes as they relate to the firm's societal relationships' (Wood, 1991: 693). Wood's model thus consists of three main parts. The first part concerns the principles of social and environmental responsibility, which includes the motivations for companies to be involved in CSR. The second part refers to the processes of social responsiveness, including environmental assessments, stakeholder management, and issues management. The third part includes implementation of CSR through programmes and the impacts of CSR in terms of the effects on stakeholders and society. By analysing the motives, implementation, and impacts of CSR, this book links to all three parts of Wood's model.

Link between CSR and Financial Performance

Research has shown that CSR is potentially a promising mechanism to foster sustainable development because there is some evidence that the financial performance of companies is positively related to CSR (Orlitzky, 2001; Van Beurden and Gössling, 2008; Margolis et al., 2007). In a well-known meta-analysis of 52 empirical studies, Orlitzky et al. (2003) found that CSR is significantly correlated with corporate financial performance (CFP). The causation seems to be that CSR and CFP mutually affect each other through a virtuous circle: financially successful companies spend more to CSR because they can afford it but CSR also helps them become more successful.

1.2 Gaps in our Knowledge of CSR

The empirical indications of a positive relationship between CSR and CFP would suggest that the market provides companies incentives to engage in CSR and contribute to sustainable development. However, there remain several important questions that need to be answered before we can conclude that relying on CSR will effectively meet the eco-social challenges that the world faces in the long run.

CSR of Small- and Medium-Sized Enterprises

First, current research into corporate environmental responsibility is often limited to large companies. As far as small and medium-sized enterprises (SMEs) are concerned, large-scale empirical research is rare. SMEs (defined by the EU as firms with fewer than 250 employees and with a turnover of less than €50 million or a balance sheet of less than € 43 million) account for more than 98% of EU firms and for 67% of EU-19 employment (European Commission, 2012). A focus on SMEs is important because small businesses collectively account for up to 70% of industrial pollution worldwide. There are several reasons to expect systematic differences between large and small companies. As small firms are less visible to the public and the media, the reputational significance of CSR will be weaker for SMEs than for large companies, making investment in CSR less rewarding for them. Furthermore, because SMEs operate on a smaller scale, the costs involved with the development and implementation of CSR programmes are relatively large. Moreover, as small firms face more intense competition on their output markets than large firms, their profit rates will be lower. Large companies will therefore have more slack resources that can be invested to obtain long-term gains from CSR. Lack of money and lag of time are among the most frequent reasons for SMEs for not being involved with CSR (ENSR, 2001). This raises important questions, such as how much SMEs engage in CSR and how SMEs can be encouraged to contribute to meeting the environmental challenges the world faces. As large-scale empirical research on the drivers and impacts of CSR of SMEs is very scarce, these questions are still insufficiently answered.

A main reason for the lack of large-scale empirical research of CSR by SMEs is lack of data. In this book, we fill this gap by using a large database of 5,205 SMEs from twelve European countries (Denmark, Finland, Sweden, The Netherlands, Germany, France, Austria, Hungary, Poland, Italy, Spain, and the UK), which will be used throughout the book for empirical testing. The data stem from a large survey, which the author conducted in 2011 and repeated in 2014 (8,838 observations in total). The survey consisted of 130 questions that surveyed the institutional and economic drivers of CSR, the implementation of CSR policies and programmes, and their impacts. The survey document was translated from English into the languages of the 12 countries in which the companies were located. This survey, which was financed by the European Union, provides a unique means of testing the research questions addressed in this volume on a consistent data base.[1]

Impacts of CSR

More and more companies now employ various kinds of CSR instruments, such as codes of conduct, ISO certifications, and stakeholder dialogue. But the impacts of these instruments in terms of the realization of social and environmental goals are uncertain. Therefore Banerjee (2008) argues that CSR initiatives are really nothing more than window dressing. Whereas the triple bottom line approach calls on companies to weigh the effects on stakeholders and the environment alongside profit, in practice companies have co-opted it and shifted towards a business ethics agenda that supports rather than questions business practices and only adopted CSR insofar it can be aligned to narrow strategic interests (Marens, 2008).

Whereas the various models of CSP conceptualizes CSR policies, CSR implementation, and their impacts, there are relatively few empirical studies that analyse the causal relationship between these three elements. Part I of the book addresses this research gap by analysing the incidence of decoupling, defined as the divergence between implementation of CSR instruments and CSR impacts. By studying the relationship between CSR implementation and their impacts, we can identify if CSR is merely ceremonial or if it really creates substantial impacts. Because of limited empirical evidence, it remains uncertain to what extent the implementation of CSR really leads to impacts. This is a serious gap in the field of CSR research because if CSR would fail to have favourable social and environmental impacts on society, the whole concept may become redundant.

Another type of impact of CSR concerns innovation. Literature has recognized that CSR may be of strategic value because it contributes to innovation. Several researchers claim that CSR can stimulate innovation (Porter and Kramer, 2006; Frondel et al., 2007; Clausen and Loew, 2009; Wagner, 2007b; Bocquet et al., 2011). One of the reasons is that CSR attracts highly qualified people who foster innovation in general (Turban and Greening, 1997). With its focus on sensitivity to industrial and societal needs, CSR represents an approach that supports innovation (Midtun, 2007). However, innovation may also reversely impact CSR. Innovation frequently is a condition for bringing about the changes required for the realization of CSR (Shrivastava, 1995; McWilliams and Siegel, 2000; Scholtens, 2008). Hence, innovation could be seen as a factor stimulating CSR and R&D intensity (an indicator of innovation at the firm level) has indeed been shown to lead to CSR (Padgett and Galan, 2009). This two-way causation suggests that innovation and CSR can form a virtuous circle. Still, the empirical evidence of a virtuous circle between CSR and innovation remains weak, particularly for SMEs.

Drivers of CSR

A third gap in our knowledge of CSR concerns other drivers than financial performance. As discussed earlier, some researches indicate that companies may be interested in CSR in terms of the 'business case', as CSR might improve financial performance and innovation. However, if CSR is really a 'business case', why is sustainable development so challenging and governments put so much stress on stimulating CSR? If CSR is in a company's own interest, we would expect that companies take responsibility for the society's welfare by developing CSR initiatives that contribute to the three dimensions of value creation outlined earlier. Social and environmental challenges that the world faces would be solved in a natural way by the market, provided that companies devise rational strategies that guarantee their economic success. In reality, the data indicate that, although companies have increased their CSR strengths between 1991 and 2005, this was more than countered by a rise in the number of CSR concerns, which means that the average (net) CSR decreased (Lougee and Wallace, 2008). Apparently, CSR is not always a 'business case'.

Indeed, the empirical evidence of a positive link between CSR and CFP is not undisputed. Some studies found a neutral or negative relationship between CSR and CFP (Jones and Wicks, 1999; McWilliams and Siegel, 2000). This also holds more specifically for the environmental dimension of CSR. For example, Filbeck and Gorman (2004) and Telle (2006) did not find a positive relationship between environmental and financial performance, rather the opposite. The latter conclusion is supported by Cañón-de-Francia and Garcés-Ayerbe (2009), who found that the relationship between ISO 14001 certification and the market value of companies is negative for less-polluting and less-internationalized companies. The argument that companies care about CSR because it increases the company's financial performance therefore seems too superficial, particular in the case of SMEs.

A study into other drivers than financial performance to explain the CSR of SMEs more thoroughly is therefore warranted. If the influence of CSR on profitability is ambiguous, one wonders why companies would take up a proactive attitude towards CSR. What factors other than the profit motive stimulate companies to engage in CSR? In this book, we consider two types of drivers of CSR: factors that are internal to the company and factors that are external to the company.

Internal drivers include motives of business-owners and managers to engage in CSR. Research into the motives for enterprises engaging in CSR other than strategic motives to ensure the financial success of the firm is still considered embryonic (Campbell, 2007). The main strategic reasons to engage in CSR are enhancement of reputation, meeting pressures from governmental and civil pressure groups, strengthening the competitive advantage of a firm, and the potential retention of employees (Whitehouse, 2006). Within the boundary condition of maintaining or enhancing profitability, stakeholder expectations are satisfied as much as possible. However, there are indications that other motives matter as well, particularly in the case of SMEs. ENSR (2001) found that ethical reasons, improved relations with community and public authorities, and customer loyalty are the most important motives of CSR for SMEs in Europe. Graafland and Van de Ven (2006) and Basu and Palazzo (2008) found that ethical motivation is a stronger driver of CSR of SMEs than the financial motive.

Research into CSR has recently also become more focused on external drivers, such as competitive landscape and national and global institutions (Aguilera and Jackson, 2003; Campbell, 2007; Matten and Moon, 2008; Brammer, Jackson et al., 2012). The concept of institutions has been famously defined by North (1991: 97) as 'the humanly devised constraints that structure political, economic and social interactions'.[2] National and international institutions shape corporate decisions by giving rise to different competitive environments that affect the behaviour of important external stakeholders of the company.[3] Other studies have conceptualized CSR as resulting from a combination of internal and external factors (Delmas and Toffel, 2004; Aguilera et al., 2007; Brown et al., 2010; Delmas and Burbano, 2011). This type of literature provides more insight into the interaction between the internal and external drivers of CSR. Differences in the internal environment can explain why firms exposed to very similar external contexts differ with regard to their CSR. When researchers only focus on external factors, there is insufficient consideration for differences in CSR at the individual company level given the external environment. On the other hand, studies that only consider internal factors ignore contextual factors that might also influence and explain CSR. Because of the fragmented character of the available empirical studies, there is little knowledge about how external conditions interact with the internal factors driving CSR, particularly for SMEs. The empirical validity of the theoretical models that aim to integrate institutional theory with a perspective of the internal factors that drive CSR therefore remains very fragile. As the links between external and internal factors remain a black box from an empirical point of view, policy advises based on integrative theoretical models of the company are still ill founded.

For modelling the interaction between the external and internal factors of CSR, this book uses two types of models: mediation models and moderation models. Mediation models give insight into how an independent variable affects the dependent variable by changing an intermediate variable, the so-called mediator. In the frameworks used in this book, the independent variable is an external factor of CSR, whereas the mediator is an internal driver of CSR that is affected by this external factor and, in turn, has an effect on CSR. The external factor thus influences CSR indirectly through changing the internal factor. The mediation model consists of three relations (see Figure 1.1). Relation (a) explains how the internal factor is affected by the external factor, and relation (b) explains how CSR is affected by the internal factor. Relation (c) depicts a possible direct effect of the external factor on CSR. The total effect of the external factor on CSR is equal to the sum of the direct effect (c) plus the indirect effect defined as the multiplication of relation (a) and (b) (e.g. a * b).

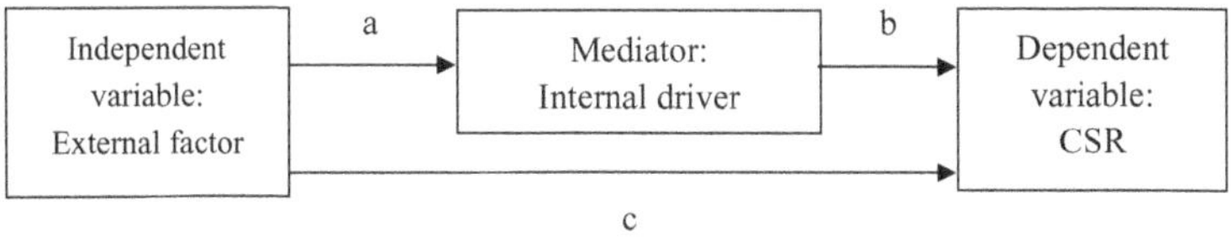

FIGURE 1.1 Mediation model

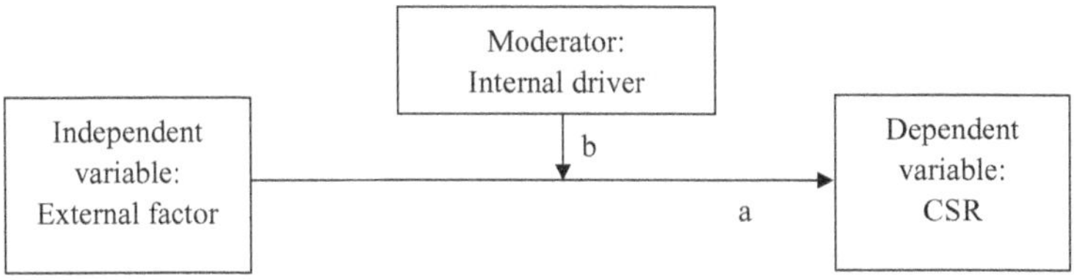

FIGURE 1.2 Moderation model

Moderation models explain when an independent variable affects a dependent variable (relation (a) in Figure 1.2). The strength of this effect depends on the level of a third variable, the so-called moderator (relation (b) in Figure 1.2). In our book, we use the moderation model to explain how the effect of an external driver on CSR may depend on the level of an internal driver.

1.3 Purpose and Structure of the Book

In this book, we aim to fill these gaps by various studies that analyse the impacts of CSR and the interactive influences of external with internal drivers of CSR using a large sample of European companies that includes large companies as well as SMEs. The overall framework of the study is depicted in Figure 1.3.

The reader will gain insight into:

1. The impacts of the use of CSR instruments on environmental performance (EP), innovation, and reputation (Part I);
2. How CSR is affected by internal factors (e.g. intrinsic motivations, ownership structure, the gender composition of management, and the business culture of the company) (Part II);
3. The effects of the competitive environment (e.g. intensity of price competition and technological competition) on CSR and how these influences are mediated or moderated by company internal factors (Part III);
4. The effects of external institutions on CSR (e.g. CSR monitoring by NGOs and media, free market institutions, and government regulation) and how these influences are mediated or moderated by company internal factors (Part IV).

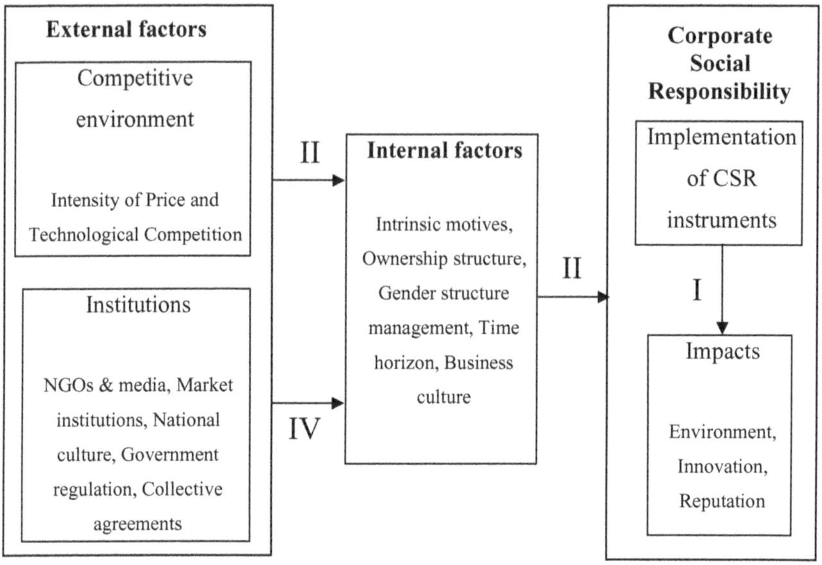

FIGURE 1.3 Overall framework

These insights will help to develop effective policy and management strategies that improve the social and EP of SMEs. Here we describe the content of each part in more detail.

Part I: Impacts of CSR

Part I studies the impacts of CSR on environmental outcomes, innovation of companies, and their reputation.

Much literature on CSR suggests that formal management tools to manage environmental impacts, such as environmental reporting or ISO 14001 certification, are not suitable for SMEs. Other studies, however, argue that using some form of formalization helps SMEs to improve environmental management. Chapter 2 studies empirically the effects of relatively simple formal management tools in the form of SMEs using targets for environmental impacts. The test results show ample support for a positive impact of target setting on environmental outcomes. Since only 25% of SMEs use targets, there is scope for substantial improvement in environmental impacts if all SMEs were to implement this relatively simple process step.

In academic literature, it is argued that the adoption of ISO 14001 certification is symbolic, aiming to improve an enterprise's public image, without substantial favourable environmental impacts. However, previous research has neglected possible mediators through which ISO 14001 may have a positive indirect influence on environmental outcomes. Chapter 3 conjectures that ISO 14001 certification stimulates participation in external environmental networks, and that such networks generate favourable effects on the EP of their participants. This mediation channel seems particularly relevant for SMEs. They often lack knowledge of how to handle the increasingly complex issue of EP and can receive guidance about managing these processes from other parties in the network. Test results confirm that participation in networks – through cooperation in the supply chain and partnerships with training institutes or local organizations – mediates the impact of ISO 14001 certification on the environmental outcomes of SMEs. Based on these results, we conclude that promotion of ISO 14001 certification among SMEs is particularly useful if combined with participation in external networks that facilitate its implementation.

As discussed earlier, literature has argued that CSR has a favourable impact on innovation. Empirical verification of this causal relationship is, however, challenging because of potential reverse causality. Some recent studies have used instrumental variables to identify a causal impact of stakeholder orientation on innovation. However, this research is limited to publicly traded companies and cannot be held to be representative of SMEs. In Chapter 4, we test the CSR–innovation link on a sample of SMEs. Using instrumental variables, CSR is found to have a significant causal effect on innovation.

CSR is not only believed to improve a company's innovation, but also its reputation. However, CSR may also put reputation at risk by making the company a more attractive target for activists' campaigns. Test results in Chapter 5 show that CSR increases the future probability that an SME is monitored by local non-governmental organizations (NGOs) and that this increases the criticism on the SME's CSR. The results imply that SMEs that implement CSR only halfheartedly are more vulnerable to public criticism than SMEs that do not engage in CSR at all.

Part II: Internal Drivers of CSR

Part II of the book focuses on the internal factors driving CSR, including intrinsic and extrinsic motivations, ownership structures, gender structure of management, and business culture.

Motivation (i.e. the reason upon which one acts) is an important antecedent to behaviour (Treviño et al., 2006). Companies may have different motives for actively pursuing CSR. Literature often distinguishes extrinsic or strategic motives (market demand, regulation or reputation) from intrinsic motives (moral duty or pleasure) (Muller and Kolk, 2010; Aguilera et al., 2007; Child and Tsai, 2005; Lindenberg, 2001; Weaver et al., 1999). Previous research on the motives of CSR has produced mixed results. Chapter 6 studies the relevance of both types of motives and shows that CSR is more driven by intrinsic than by extrinsic motives. Both intrinsic and extrinsic motivation increase with company size.

An important internal institution driving CSR is the ownership structure of companies. Recent theoretical research suggests, however, that the relationship between family business ownership and EP is contingent. Chapter 7 makes two contributions to this literature. First, we conjecture that the relationship between family business ownership and CSR is weaker for large firms than for small firms. Second, we surmise that the involvement of family members in management moderates the relationship between family business ownership and CSR in a non-linear way. Test results support both hypotheses. The difference in CSR between family owned and non-family-owned enterprises is largest for small companies managed by a combination of family and non-family members.

CSR may also be related to the gender structure of management. The literature on the relationship between gender diversity in management and CSR of large companies has produced mixed results. Whether and how gender diversity stimulates the CSR of SMEs has not yet been researched. In Chapter 8, we hypothesize that having more women in management positions improves the CSR of SMEs because this encourages the use of relational management instruments. Small business literature has shown this type of instrument to be more effective in improving the CSR of SMEs than bureaucratic management instruments. Test results support this hypothesis. However, the effect is non-linear and CSR reaches its maximum when the proportion of women managers is 54%.

Chapter 9 investigates the influence of business culture on CSR. While the relationship between business culture and innovation at the firm level has been established in the academic literature, very little research has been done into the relationship between business culture and CSR. Using the competing values framework for organizational culture, we hypothesize that an open systems business culture fosters CSR. Test results support this hypothesis and show that an open systems business culture that combines a flexibility orientation and external focus is most conducive to CSR.

Part III: Impacts of Competition on CSR

In Part III of the book, we research how competitive conditions affect CSR and how these relationships are mediated by factors internal to the company.

Chapter 10 studies the relationships between the intensity of price competition, the firm's time horizon, and EP. More intense price competition may discourage EP by inducing short-termism in companies. The test results show that price competition shortens the time horizon that companies apply in strategic decisions and that a (long) time horizon increases their EP. However, the total negative effect of the intensity of price competition on EP is rather small in absolute terms.

Besides price competition, companies also compete on innovation (Bengtsson, 1998; Vickers, 1995). In the free market perspective of the Neo Austrian School of economic thought, economic growth does not result from price competition but rather from the competition in innovation in new consumer goods, new technologies, sources of supply, and new types of organizational structures (Schumpeter, 1976). Companies that operate in markets that compete on technology may be particularly interested in the innovation-enabling potential of CSR. Academic literature has proposed various motives for firms to engage in CSR but no attention has been paid to innovation as a motive. In Chapter 11, we explore the role of this motive and hypothesize that it is particularly important for companies facing intensive technological competition. Test results show that the innovation motive mediates the relationship between the intensity of technological competition and CSR and is the most (second most) important motive for environmental (social) CSR.

Competition in technology may not only stimulate the innovation motive but also affect the intrinsic motivations towards CSR. Chapter 12 investigates the theoretical and empirical relevance of this so-called motivation crowding effect for owner-managers' intrinsic motivation towards CSR. Motivation crowding theory has argued that external pressures enforce (crowd in) intrinsic motivation if these pressures are perceived as supportive. Based on this theory, we conjecture that a competitive environment that is characterized by a high intensity of competition on technology will crowd in intrinsic CSR motivation if owner-managers believe that CSR increases the innovative capability of their company. The test results support this hypothesis.

Part IV : Institutional Drivers of CSR

In Part IV, we address the external institutional drivers of CSR and how they interact with factors internal to the company.

Whereas social licence pressure is held as a strong motive for the CSR of large enterprises, it is argued in academic literature that it will not sufficiently motivate SMEs. We conjecture, however, that social licence pressure may also be important for SMEs because of the strong embeddedness of SMEs in their local communities, but large-scale empirical studies supporting this hypothesis are still lacking. Chapter 13 shows that social licence pressures significantly affect the EP of micro, small, and medium-sized enterprises directly as well as indirectly through mediation by the perceived market benefits of CSR. In all cases, the social licence pressure provides a stronger stimulus to improving EP than the motive to comply with government regulation.

Chapter 14 studies the crowding effects of non-governmental organizations (NGOs) and media pressure on intrinsic motivations towards CSR. We surmise that the monitoring of CSR by NGOs and media may influence the intrinsic motivations of managers positively as well as negatively and that the perceived financial benefits of CSR mediate this relationship. Test results show that NGOs and media pressures increase the financial benefits of CSR that, in turn, crowd in intrinsic motivation. These findings emphasize the important role of NGOs and media. By increasing transparency in the marketplace, they not only strengthen the business case for CSR but also intrinsic motivations in corporations.

Besides competition in innovation and NGOs and media pressure, intrinsic motivations towards CSR may also be affected by government regulations. Previous literature did not test how governmental regulation affects CSR motivation. Empirical evidence of motivation crowding by government regulations is therefore still lacking. Chapter 15 fills this research gap and shows that government regulation enhances EP directly but harms it indirectly by crowding out the intrinsic and extrinsic motivations of business leaders. Only if business leaders have low intrinsic CSR motivation, government regulation stimulates the EP, because crowding-out effects are absent in that case.

Chapters 16 and 17 study the influence of free market institutions on CSR as measured by economic freedom. The effect of free market institutions on firms' CSR is still unconcluded. In Chapter 16, we conjecture that the effects are conditional on a firm's internal motivation. Test results show clear support that the effects of economic freedom and intrinsic motivation on corporate EP interact with each other. These findings explain the ambiguous results of previous empirical studies at the aggregate level.

Studies trying to explain international differences in CSR tend to focus on either regulative institutional or cultural factors. In Chapter 17, we propose that the influence of both types on CSR interact. More specifically, we theorize that free market institutions only have a positive influence on CSR practices in societies with a culture of long-term orientation. Test results confirm this expectation. This finding exemplifies the importance for international comparative research of exploring the interactive effects of institutions and cultures.

Part IV concludes with a study in Chapter 18 into the relationship between collective agreements and CSR. More specifically, we research the impact of collective agreements on female management and job opportunities of employees from disadvantaged groups (e.g. migrants, people with disabilities, and long-term unemployed). We find that collective agreements stimulate the female presence in board and executive positions and the inflow of employees from disadvantaged groups. Moreover, female management further enforces job opportunities of disadvantaged workers. Countries with high coverage of collective agreements therefore, directly as well as indirectly, through female management foster integration of employees from disadvantaged groups into the labour market.

Part V: Integration and Management Lessons

Chapter 19 gives an overview of the hypotheses and empirical results of Parts I–IV and explores the interactions between the different parts of the overall framework presented in Figure 1.3. We use the integrated framework to explain CSR differences between large and small companies and how these are mediated by internal factors, competitive environment, and external institutions. Chapter 20 summarizes the policy and management implications of this study.

Notes

1 For more details of the survey questions, see Appendix 1.
2 In his definition, North includes both so-called regulative or formal institutions, which refer to rules, laws and constitutions created and codified by the polity, as well as so-called normative or informal institutions, which consist of (mostly uncodified) norms of behaviour, taboos, traditions, convention, and self-imposed codes of conduct. For North, informal institutions are part of culture. Culture refers to decision-making heuristics, which typically manifest themselves as values, beliefs, or social norms. Or, in the words of Guiso et al. (2006: 23) 'those customary beliefs and values that ethnic, religious, and social groups transmit fairly unchanged from generation to generation'.
3 There is a discussion if organizations are also institutions, because North (1990) made a distinction between institutions and organizations. In his view, institutions are the rules of the game and organizations and their entrepreneurs are the players. Therefore, it seems that North is saying that organizations are not institutions. But North does not actually write this. In saying that 'organizations are players', he is making an abstraction rather than defining organizations in this way. Organizations involve structures or networks, and these cannot function without rules of communication, membership, or sovereignty. The unavoidable existence of rules within organizations means that even by North's own definition, organizations must be regarded as a type of institution (Hodgson, 2006).

PART I

Impacts of Corporate Social Responsibility

2

ENVIRONMENTAL IMPACTS OF FORMAL MANAGEMENT INSTRUMENTS*

2.1 Introduction

CSR, and environmental management in particular, has long been perceived as being the province of large companies and not necessarily well adapted to the world of SMEs (European Commission, 2007). However, Hillary (2000) estimated that SMEs collectively account for up to 70% of industrial pollution worldwide. Hence, it is evidently important to study the CSR of SMEs. The question of whether CSR contributes to the environmental impacts of SMEs, such as a reduction of energy consumption and waste disposal, has rarely been adequately addressed. Few empirical studies considered the environmental impacts of the CSR of SMEs. For example, Friedman and Miles (2001) and Ammenberg and Hjelm (2003) found that the establishment of an environmental management system (EMS) in Britain and Sweden, respectively, resulted in environmental improvements. Surveying environmental managers in Spanish hotels, Armas-Cruz (2011) found that environmental management improves both commercial and EP. However, these studies are based on a limited number of case studies of SMEs in specific countries and sectors, and further research into the impacts of CSR is in need of a much larger dataset to test if these findings apply more generally. In this chapter, we used a large dataset consisting of 5,205 companies from 12 European countries to assess the environmental impacts of the CSR of SMEs.

Many studies suggest that formal environmental management instruments, such as public environmental reports, audits, and EMSs, are not suitable for SMEs. Fassin (2008) argued that the way large companies deal with CSR cannot be simply transposed to SMEs as they are less bureaucratic and often need to solve problems on a day-to-day basis (Battaglia et al., 2010). In addition, Tilley (2000) argued that SMEs tend to govern their businesses in a less systematic way than

DOI: 10.4324/9781003216483-3

larger companies as they have limited resources and have difficulties in identifying a clear environmental vision to build on. Tilley (1999) argued that outsiders often regard the environmental impacts of SMEs as negligible compared to those of large companies and therefore do not urge them to communicate their impacts, making formal reporting for SMEs less relevant. Generally speaking, SMEs can be regarded as being more embedded in the local environment. Because of this characteristic, Spence et al. (2003) and Perrini (2006) argued that studies into SME's environmental management can be better based on the concept of social capital, rather than on stakeholder theory. Welford and Frost (2006) concluded that the main challenge for the future is moving away from an inspection and auditing mentality and towards capacity building on the ground and creating longer term trusting relationships down the supply chain.

However, not formalizing CSR at all may also result in suboptimal environmental management practices by SMEs. It can be argued that relatively simple formal instruments, such as using targets for environmental improvements, will help managers of SMEs to provide a systematic framework for tracking and communicating issues. Formalization improves the quality of internal management and cost efficiency (Hillary, 2004; Zorpas, 2010) and stimulates the environmental awareness of employees and internal communication (Ammenberg and Hjelm, 2003; Rao et al., 2009; Zorpas, 2010).

The research question that we address in this chapter is therefore to what extent simple formal management instruments as target setting are used by SMEs to improve their environmental impacts and how effective these instruments are compared with an informal way of managing environmental issues or full-fledged management systems such as ISO 14001.

In the following section, we introduce the conceptual framework and the hypothesis of this study. We then describe the methodology and present the results of the empirical analysis. The last section summarizes the main findings.

2.2 Conceptual Framework

Large companies often use formal management instruments to improve their environmental impacts (e.g. ISO 14001 and EMAS (Eco Management and Audit System EMAS)). However, these management systems are less applicable to SMEs. SMEs are not just miniature versions of large companies, but are often considered as having distinctive characteristics (see Table 2.1 for an overview).

Due to the informal and diversified nature of SMEs, many studies supposed that formal environmental management instruments, such as public environmental reporting, auditing, and environmental management programmes, are not suitable for SMEs, and that SMEs should stick to informal management. However, not formalizing CSR implies that it is difficult to hold the company accountable for its CSR achievements. The tools of sustainability management assist managers

TABLE 2.1 Reasons for (not using) formal management instruments by SMEs

Reasons for not using formal measures by SMEs	*References*
SMEs are embedded in informal and local social network	Tilley (2000), Spence et al. (2003), Murillo and Lozano (2006), Perrini (2006), Battisti and Perry (2011), Baden et al. (2011)
Limited time, expertise, and finances for environmental management	Tilley (2000), Spence et al. (2003); Lepoutre and Heene (2006), Perrini (2006), Studer et al. (2006), Welford and Frost (2006), Russo and Tencati (2009)
No separation of ownership and control	Dewhurst and Thomas (2003), Beaver and Prince (2004), Lepoutre and Heene (2006), Murillo and Lozano (2006), Revell and Blackburn (2007), Aragón-Correa et al. (2008), Revell et al. (2010)
Reasons for using formal measures by SMEs	*References*
Cooperation in industrial cluster	Battaglia et al. (2010)
Quality of internal management and cost efficiency	Hillary (2004), Zorpas (2010)
Environmental awareness of employees and internal communication	Ammenberg and Hjelm (2003), Rao et al. (2009), Zorpas (2010)
Organizational learning and innovation	Stewart and Gapp (2014)
Systematic and continuous implementation	Jones (1999), Leroy et al. (2013)
Reducing value-action gap	Perez-Sanchez et al. (2003), Cassells and Lewis (2011), Tilley (1999), Studer et al. (2006), Gadenne et al. (2009), Revell et al. (2010)

in monitoring and evaluating internal developments while simultaneously engaging in a dialogue with external stakeholders on sustainable development issues (Perrini and Tencati, 2006). This can lead to organizational efficiencies and to internal cost savings in the long run, even for SMEs. Furthermore, formal procedures can help in making employees and other stakeholders more aware of CSR (Ammenberg and Hjelm, 2003). By creating feedback channels, they will foster organizational learning and innovativeness (Stewart and Gapp, 2014). Furthermore, the owner-directors, on whom CSR often depends in SMEs, can be erratic in their implementation of CSR and therefore not realize the full potential of the company. Using formal management tools can therefore improve the internal management of CSR by making CSR less dependent upon the subjective judgments of its director (Studer et al., 2006).

Balancing the disadvantages of costly, fully-fledged management systems for SMEs on the one hand, and the advantages of using some formal environmental management instruments on the other, we hypothesize that the use of relatively simple formal management instruments fosters improvements in environmental impacts. Whereas fully-fledged formal systems, such as public environmental reporting or ISO 14001 certification, may not fit the context of SMEs, small process steps will raise the quality of the environmental management of SMEs without necessarily incurring high bureaucratic costs. We therefore focus on a relatively simple procedure: setting targets for environmental impacts. Target setting is a proven management instrument for initiating change and improvement that is also feasible for small companies (Palmer and Van der Vorst, 1997). When appropriate, targets can be defined in quantitative terms (e.g. reduce energy consumption by 10%) or refer to qualitative objectives (e.g. build a bund wall to contain spills). Whereas reducing energy, water, and waste may be considered low hanging fruits, targets on environmental conditions of suppliers represent a more ambitious strategic form of EP because it involves other stakeholders. The establishment of voluntary targets is an essential first step. It requires the identification and specification of concrete, measurable performance indicators and a commitment to management plans that specify how much they can be improved (Hummels and Karssing, 2007).

Our framework thus posits the following hypothesis:

> *Hypothesis 2.1 Formalization of environmental management by the use of targets reinforces the effects of informal efforts to improve the environmental impacts of SMEs.*

Informal efforts refer to all kinds of practical actions to improve environmental impacts. For example, ICT companies can take all kinds of practical measures to reduce the energy consumption of their main operations. These actions are often not formalized into policy statements or environmental programmes, as in large companies, but limited to making an effort to act appropriately (Fassin, 2008).

2.3 Methodology

The data were taken from the survey conducted in 2011.[1] Table 2.2 reports the descriptive statistics of the measures that are used in the empirical analysis. We distinguish five environmental issues: energy consumption, use of renewable energy, water consumption, disposal of waste, and recycling of waste. In order to measure informal efforts, respondents were asked to indicate for each environmental issue whether their enterprise actively improves it. The response was measured by a three-point scale ranging from 0 (no effort), 0.5 (incidental effort) to 1 (continuous effort). The use of targets is measured by a binary scale (0: no; 1: yes). Environmental impacts are measured by a seven-point scale for the change in

TABLE 2.2 Measures[a]

	Variables	*Mean*
Informal efforts	Reduction in energy consumption and increase in use of renewable energy (91)	0.62
	Reduction in water consumption (92)	0.56
	Reduction in waste disposal and increase in waste recycling (93)	0.72
Use of targets	Reduction in energy consumption and increase in use of renewable energy (96)	0.26
	Reduction in water consumption (97)	0.20
	Reduction in waste disposal and increase in waste recycling (98)	0.29
Environmental impacts	Growth in energy consumption (102)	−0.46
	Increase in % renewable energy (103)	0.19
	Growth in water consumption (104)	−0.35
	Growth in waste disposal (105)	−0.38
	Increase in % recycling of waste (106)	0.36
Number of companies as a share of all companies that	Reduced energy consumption	0.38
	Increased % renewable energy	0.16
	Reduced water consumption	0.28
	Reduced waste disposal	0.32
	Increased % recycling of waste	0.30

a The numbers in brackets refer to the numbers of the survey questions in Appendix 1.

the respective variable between 2007 and 2010. Besides this seven-point scale, we also used binary scales for companies that improved their environmental impacts. In this way, we can test whether formal instruments increase the chance that companies improve their environmental impacts.

Improvements in environmental impacts may result from several causes: companies' own voluntary initiatives, collective voluntary initiatives in the supply chain and/or industry, legally enforced requirements, or market pressure. In order to test to what extent the changes in EP are voluntary (one of the five dimensions of CSR) rather than initiated because of direct regulation or market pressure, we asked the respondents of companies that improved their environmental impacts to indicate for each aspect which of the four aforementioned causes contributed *most* to the improvement on that aspect. The results are reported in Table 2.3. Most SMEs indicate that the improvements are due to their own voluntary initiatives. This illustrates that the voluntary dimension is very relevant for our sample.

In order to test the influence of the use of targets as a stand-alone measure, we control for the use of the ISO 14001 management system as the use of targets may be a part of a larger management system. Table 2.4 shows that small companies relatively more often use (informal) efforts to improve their environmental impacts. If they use targets, these are often applied independently from a larger

TABLE 2.3 Reasons for improvement in environmental impacts (% of respondents)

	Voluntary measures own company	*Collective initiatives industry*	*Legal requirements*	*Market pressure*
Energy consumption	74	5	11	11
Renewable energy	67	7	17	8
Water consumption	76	5	12	7
Waste disposal	72	6	15	7
Recycling of waste	70	6	17	6

TABLE 2.4 Effort and targets for energy consumption, ISO 14001, and company size[a]

	Micro (≤10)	*Small (11–50)*	*Medium (51–250)*	*Large (>250)*
Effort (mean score)	0.56	0.61	0.66	0.77
Use of targets (%)	15	23	29	39
ISO 14001 (%)	4	10	20	41

a Company size is measured in number of employees (in full time equivalents)

management system. In contrast, large companies are more likely to use an ISO 14001 programme. This supports the notion of our conceptual framework that small companies differ from large companies and more often only use informal measures or small process steps than fully-fledged management systems to improve their environmental impacts.

2.4 Results

Tables 2.5 and 2.6 report the estimation results of the multiple regression analysis.

Table 2.5 shows that for all four environmental aspects both putting more effort into a certain environmental issue and targeting significantly improve its impacts. The empirical analysis thus supports the hypothesis of our conceptual framework that formal measures reinforce environmental impacts. In addition, ISO 14001 certification significantly improves environmental impacts.

Table 2.6 shows that if we use binary logistic regression analysis, we find that informal efforts, targeting, and ISO 14001 all significantly increase the odds that companies decrease their energy consumption, water consumption or waste disposal and increase the use of renewable energy and recycling of waste.

If we combine the estimated unstandardized coefficients reported in Table 2.5 with the average effort, use of targets, and ISO 14001 certification as reported in Tables 2.2 and 2.3, we can calculate the maximum improvement in environmental impacts if all companies were to put continuous effort, target their environmental impacts, or apply an ISO 14001 system. Table 2.7 shows that if all companies

TABLE 2.5 Results of multiple regression analysis[a]

	Energy consumption	*Water consumption*	*Waste disposal*	*Recycling of waste*
Effort	−0.49***	−0.44***	−0.35***	0.22***
Use of targets	−0.26***	−0.32***	−0.23***	0.09*
ISO 14001	−0.18**	−0.11*	−0.19***	0.19**

a Unstandardized coefficients; * $p < 0.05$; ** $p < 0.01$; *** $p < 0.001$; $N = 5{,}205$. Controlled for company size, sector, regional, and inverse Mill's ratio.

TABLE 2.6 Binary logistic regression analysis of companies that improved environmental impacts[a]

	Renewable energy	*Energy consumption*	*Water consumption*	*Waste disposal*	*Recycling*
Effort	1.78***	1.21***	1.58***	1.15***	1.05***
Use of targets	0.28**	0.38***	0.61***	0.46***	0.31***
ISO 14001	0.30**	0.41***	0.26**	0.39***	0.38***

a Unstandardized coefficients; * $p < 0.05$; ** $p < 0.01$; *** $p < 0.001$; $N = 5{,}205$. Controlled for company size, sector, regional, and inverse Mill's ratio.

TABLE 2.7 Impact multipliers[a]

	100% effort	*100% use of targets*	*100% ISO 14001*	*Total*
Energy consumption	−0.12	−0.13	−0.11	−0.36
Water consumption	−0.13	−0.17	−0.06	−0.36
Waste disposal	−0.06	−0.11	−0.11	−0.28
Recycling	0.04	0.04	0.11	0.19

a Measured by change in annual increase (in %).

were only to fully target their impacts (without increasing their informal efforts or introducing an ISO 14001 system), the improvement would be relatively large for energy consumption, water consumption, and waste disposal.

2.5 Conclusion

In this chapter, we have tested a conceptual framework on the environmental impacts of CSR for SMEs. Until now, the actual environmental impacts for SMEs have not been assessed on a large scale (mostly only case studies). We focused on SMEs and not on large companies, as SMEs generate the biggest part of environmental pollution in Europe. Because of their smaller size, SMEs are more embedded in their local environments, have fewer skills, and have less financial resources to devote to environmental management. Formal management instruments therefore are often regarded as inappropriate for SMEs. Nevertheless, certain process steps could help the management of environmental impacts by, for example, bringing focus, improving communication, and making the company less dependent on the subjective judgments of the owner-manager. To test this hypothesis, our framework for SMEs explicitly distinguished the use of formal process steps to foster environmental impacts from only making some unspecified 'effort'. In our empirical analyses, we make use of a unique dataset of 5,205 SMEs from 12 European countries to estimate our model.

The results show that for all environmental issues examined, targeting impacts significantly improves environmental impacts. This supports our hypothesis that simple process steps reinforce environmental impacts. This result challenges the common opinion in literature that SMEs, in contrast to large companies, should not formalize CSR because they are different in nature from large companies (see e.g. Fassin, 2008). We agree that procedures adopted by large companies, such as ISO14001, may not always fit the context of SMEs. But there are many small process steps that SMEs can take to raise the quality of environmental management in their organization, without necessarily incurring high bureaucratic costs. Even for a very small company with ten or less employees, it is fairly easy to set targets for issues such as energy or water consumption or waste disposal, without having to resort to complex and costly bureaucratic procedures. Our results show that a combination of informal and such formal instruments seems to be especially fruitful in generating impacts as it provides a more systematic framework for tracking issues, bringing focus and discipline, and creating awareness.

Notes

* An extended text of this chapter has been published in: Graafland, J., and Smid, H. (2016). Environmental impacts of SMEs and the effects of formal management instruments: Evidence from EU's largest survey. *Corporate Social Responsibility and Environmental Management*, 23: 297–307. Hugo Smid co-authored this article when he was doing PhD at Tilburg University. Hugo Smid published his dissertation (titled 'Rhetoric and realities of corporate social responsibility') in 2014. He is currently working at De Nederlandsche Bank.

1 For a description of the survey questions, see Appendix 1. Appendix 2 describes the methodology of the survey.

3

ENVIRONMENTAL IMPACTS OF ISO 14001 AND THE MEDIATING ROLE OF NETWORKS*

3.1 Introduction

Increasingly, enterprises are using EMSs (Darnall and Sides, 2008). A widely used voluntary programme is the ISO 14001 certificate (Delmas and Montes-Sancho, 2011). However, research has cast doubt on the effectiveness of this system in improving environmental impacts (Koehler, 2007; Aravind and Christmann, 2011; Boiral, 2012). The reason that companies with ISO 14001 may not produce better environmental results than other companies might be that these companies employ this voluntary measure primarily to prevent government interventions (Maxwell et al., 2000) or to safeguard their reputation (Castka and Prajogo, 2013). As a result, the implementation of ISO 14001 could be a superficial gesture disconnected from the internal practices that could improve environmental impacts (so-called decoupling). Decoupling of programmes and outcomes could be especially relevant for SMEs. Because of the specific characteristics of these businesses, standardized management systems may not be a proper tool for SMEs (Welsh and White, 1981; Tilley, 2000; Spence et al., 2003; Perrini, 2006; Aragón-Correa et al., 2008; Battisti and Perry, 2011) and these tools may even be counterproductive (Fassin, 2008).

However, research has ignored the fact that ISO 14001 may also *indirectly* improve the environmental impacts of SMEs. One of the mechanisms that may mediate the effect of ISO 14001 on environmental impacts is the participation in external networks to foster information exchange on best environmental management practices. Some studies into the effectiveness of ISO 14001 for SMEs have referred to this mechanism but without empirically verifying whether it explains any positive effects of ISO 14001 on environmental impacts (Ammenberg and Hjelm, 2003; Darnall and Sides, 2008; Lopez-Gamero et al., 2009). The

DOI: 10.4324/9781003216483-4

aim of this chapter is therefore to analyse the following research question: Does participation in external networks mediate a positive impact for ISO 14001 on the environmental impacts of SMEs? The research is conducted on a large sample of 3,633 SMEs in 12 countries in Europe. The data are taken from the surveys conducted in 2011 and in 2014.

In the next section, we present the literature review and hypotheses. In section 3.3, we discuss the methodology. Section 3.4 describes the empirical results, followed by a conclusion.

3.2 Conceptual Framework

This section first reviews recent literature on the impacts of ISO 14001 certification on environmental impacts. Then we highlight the importance of external networks for improving the environmental impacts of SMEs. Subsequently, we will argue that ISO 14001 certification and external networks are not independent because ISO 14001 may stimulate the company to participate in external environmental networks. The section then presents a set of hypotheses, including a mediation hypothesis postulating that external networks mediate the impact of ISO 14001 on environmental impacts.

ISO 14001 and Environmental Impacts

Companies aiming to improve their environmental impacts can apply various types of standardized instruments. Standardized instruments refer to systems that provide procedures and specifications for the integration of environmental measures into an enterprise's everyday practices and are designed for all kinds of companies (Barth and Wolff, 2009). Examples are the ISO 14001 standard and the European EMAS (Eco Management and Audit Scheme) that set requirements for an EMS, the Greenhouse Gas Protocol Initiative that sets a standard for how to measure, manage, and report greenhouse gas emissions, or the Global Reporting Initiative (GRI) that provides standardized approaches and principles on social reporting.

This chapter focuses on ISO 14001. This is a global standard, open to all organizations and having a practical focus. Each year the firm has to define an environmental plan that sets targets for those areas of the business to be improved, specifying the activities it will undertake to achieve that improved performance. The environmental plan goes into the specific detail of how these actions will be implemented, such as the costs per action, which division is responsible for implementing them, and the date that the target will be reached.

But for SMEs that implement ISO 14001 certification, it cannot simply be assumed that this generates favourable environmental impacts. Institutional theory states that companies are more likely to decouple implementation from impacts if they experience a tension between gaining social legitimacy from their stakeholders and pressure to maintain internal efficiency (Davis, 2005). By showing that they qualify for ISO 14001, companies may obtain legitimacy from external stakeholders (Martín-de Castro et al., 2017). But, at the same time, discretion over how the enterprise improves its environmental impacts provides room for symbolic policies generating sufficient internal flexibility to avoid measures that might be too costly (David et al., 2007). As a result, the environmental impacts may be disconnected from ISO 14001. This kind of decoupling is invited by the absence of mechanisms to monitor the environmental impacts of most companies (and particularly SMEs) (Ogawa and Scribner, 2002). Several empirical studies on corporate social outcomes indeed showed that managers, when responding to external pressures, tend to adopt formal measures that have little impact on core processes (Weaver et al., 1999). Jamali (2010) also found that most companies respond in a symbolic way to strong pressure, adapting their formal structures to signal coherence with external expectations, but then barely changing their internal processes so as to avoid incurring costs.

Decoupling may be particularly relevant for ISO 14001 as it merely indicates the enterprise has a well-documented and consistent EMS (Oliveira et al., 2010). The system does not require that the degree of control over environmental impacts is revealed. When scrutinizing the documents provided by organizations, ISO 14001 audits focus on procedures (Heras-Saizarbitoria et al., 2013) and not on the real environmental impact. It is therefore not surprising that many researchers have found that the use of ISO 14001 is merely symbolic (Aravind and Christmann, 2011; Boiral, 2012) and that mature adoption of ISO 14001 is associated with low improvement in environmental impacts (Testa et al., 2014). Castka and Prajogo (2013) found that ISO 14001 brings reputational benefits because NGOs and industry watchdogs accept it as evidence of a firm's environmental efforts but that this does not contribute to the substantive effect of ISO 14001. Schylander and Martinuzzi (2007) found that the desire to improve public image by credibly communicating activities that receive outside recognition is the most important motivation behind the implementation of ISO 14001. Another explanation of the limited effects of ISO 14001 is that many companies have already been applying targets long before they formalized their EMS (Steger, 2000; King et al., 2005). As a result, the instrument does not lead to substantial changes in the realization of these goals.

Nevertheless, there are also studies showing that ISO 14001 certification does improve environmental impacts for SMEs (Ferenhof et al., 2014; Nguyen and Hens, 2015). Several studies have argued that the use of ISO 14001 is an effective way of raising the quality of the environmental management of SMEs because it disciplines the enterprise to pay continuous attention to improving environmental impacts through information gathering and auditing (Seiffert, 2008; Rao et al., 2009; Parisi and Maraghini, 2010). Although the ISO 14001 standard does not establish specific performance criteria, it prescribes requirements for having an environmental policy, as well as the planning, implementation, operation, verification, corrective action, and critical analysis by management (Oliveira et al., 2016). It contributes to better internal communication and helps managers to track issues systematically, while making it easier for outsiders to check the environmental efforts and hold companies more accountable for their behaviour. Guerrero-Baena et al. (2015), who evaluated the effects of ISO 14001 certification for Spanish olive oil firms, found that ISO 14001 certification stimulates environmental awareness among employees. Nguyen and Hens (2015), who conducted a study on the influence of ISO 14001 certification in the cement industry in Vietnam, also found a significant improvement in environmental awareness in certified plants. Moreover, their analysis showed that certification has a significant positive effect on EP. Singh et al. (2015) showed that ISO 14001 significantly reduced the waste of SMEs in India. Oliveira et al. (2016) estimated that organizations having an ISO 14001 certification with full scope tend to adopt more so-called cleaner production practices, and these have been shown to be one of the most successful proactive environmental strategies (Van Hoof and Lyon, 2013). A recent case study by Wong et al. (2017) of a ISO 14001 certified coal power plant in Malaysia concluded that the company not only achieved relatively better EP but also the ISO 14001 certification induced better compliance with Malaysia's environmental rules and regulations. In line with this finding, Ferreira Rino and Salvador (2017) found that among 11 Brazilian companies, ISO 14001 certification over time led to a reduction in the number of environmental penalties imposed by the state environmental agency because it fosters a preventive culture and develops practices that deal with environmental impacts. These findings are confirmed in a study by Mazzi et al. (2016) who asked Italian practitioners of ISO 14001 certification what, in their view, are the greatest advantages of ISO 14001 certification. According to these practitioners, the main benefits of ISO 14001 certification are that it stimulates environmental competences and awareness among employees, increases compliance with legal requirements, and facilitates operational control of EP. From the information provided by this literature review, it is likely that the implementation of ISO 14001 has a positive impact on the environmental impacts of SMEs.

Networks and Environmental Impacts

Apart from standardized instruments, a number of specific, tailor-made tools exist by which businesses strive to improve their environmental impacts. Some of these non-standardized instruments are internally oriented, such as employee training (Graafland et al., 2003). Other instruments are externally oriented, such as participation in external networks to share best practices (Maon et al., 2009; Schouten and Remmé, 2006; Pirsch et al., 2006).

In research among participants in a German energy efficiency network, Wohlfarth et al. (2017) found that the companies participating in the network were mainly motivated by the need for practical knowledge and information about specific measures and technologies that would reduce energy cost. The second most important reason was decision support provided by the exchange of experiences. A further important set of reasons (with an average score of 4 on a scale from 1 to 5) concerned organization and implementation, such as gaining information about crucial aspects of planning and about difficulties in implementation. In a second survey, Wohlfarth et al. (2017) estimated the extent to which these expectations were met by the network. They did not find any significant differences between the ranking of expectations and the ranking of the extent to which those expectations had been fulfilled by the energy efficiency network. They concluded that the network was well able to meet the expectations of the participants. The majority of participants reported implementation of measures that would not have been implemented without participation in the network.

Other studies have also shown that collaboration on environmental issues leads to more positive results (Perz et al., 2010; Valentine, 2016). Cooperation with other parties is particularly appropriate for SMEs (Albino et al., 2012) as they are often part of a larger enterprise's network of suppliers or of a local network of SMEs (Battaglia et al., 2010). As small firms are more resource constrained, they must rely on external experts to provide them with appropriate solutions to environmental challenges. Cooperation and partnerships in the supply chain, or guidance from training institutes, will help bring expertise to the enterprise and provide knowledge both on technology and on how to integrate environmental concerns into the businesses. From these networks, SMEs can also learn what the most important environmental issue is to focus on (Tilley, 2000). Collaboration with suppliers or customers in the supply chain can compensate for a lack of technical capacity but also for legal and business skills that a small enterprise may lack. Supply chain management, and practices implemented along the supply chain, are an important driver of environmental impacts. Research has shown that suppliers provide SMEs with various solutions that have significant effects on environmental impacts (Arimura et al., 2008; ECEI, 2010; Darnall and Sides, 2008; Bos-Brouwers, 2010). Participation in projects with training institutes aimed at reducing environmental impact, or at anticipating the technological evolution of products or services, was also found to contribute to better environmental results (ECEI, 2010; European Commission, 2002). From all of this, it is likely that participation in external networks has a positive impact on the environmental impacts of SMEs.

ISO 14001 and External Networks

ISO 14001 and participation in external networks are probably not independent. On the basis of a literature study, Ferenhof et al. (2014) concluded that the implementation of EMS-based methods not only improves environmental impacts but also leads to better collaborative networks. Lopez-Gamero et al. (2009) also argued that the use of an EMS stimulates the development of informal information exchange channels for best management practices as well as the capacity to cooperate with external stakeholders. Similarly, on the basis of an analysis of nine U.S. studies, Darnall and Sides (2008) argued that EMSs help SMEs to establish peer networks and encourage greater collaboration among the participating firms. These networks stimulate the exchange of information on best management practices, strengthening a firm's management of their environmental capabilities. Battaglia et al. (2010) argued that cooperation with stakeholders or other enterprises in their local networks helps SMEs to overcome barriers in the implementation of formal CSR policies and practices. The cooperation makes it possible to improve results and decrease the costs of implementing CSR (European Commission, 2007). According to Ferenhof et al. (2014), the costs of implementing EMSs can be reduced by up to 50% if an enterprise uses systems of cooperation instead of implementing the scheme on an individual basis.

Ammenberg and Hjelm (2003) described an illustrative case study of SMEs in Sweden where certified EMSs generated more cooperation in peer networks. Small enterprises formed an environmental group and a network to jointly implement an EMS. Each enterprise fulfilled the requirements of ISO 14001 and had a certificate of its own but the administration was done by a central organization. This cooperation in turn improved the environmental impacts. Therefore, it could be that the importance of ISO 14001 for SMEs lies in it stimulating the formation of networks that reduce the costs of implementation and generate positive indirect impacts on environmental impacts through exchange of best practices within a firm's network.

Set of Hypotheses

On the basis of the literature review and the arguments in the previous sections, we hypothesize that (see also Figure 3.1):

Hypothesis 3.1 The implementation of ISO 14001 positively affects the environmental impacts of SMEs.

Hypothesis 3.2 Participation in external networks positively affects the environmental impacts of SMEs.

Hypothesis 3.3 ISO 14001 stimulates participation in external networks.

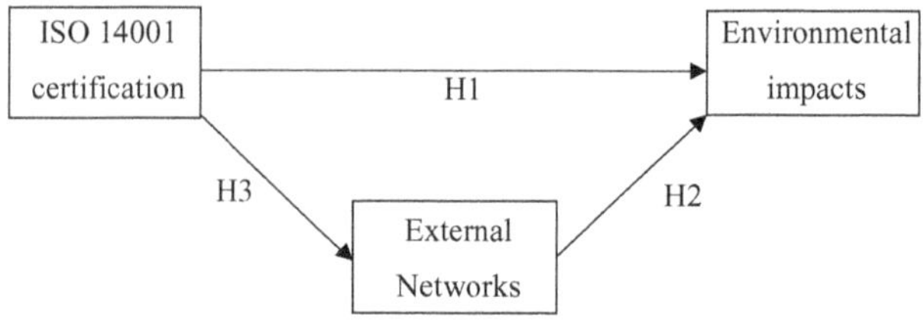

FIGURE 3.1 Conceptual framework of hypothesized relationships

The combination of Hypothesis 3.2, that participation in networks leads to better environmental impacts, and Hypothesis 3.3, that ISO 14001 stimulates participation in external networks, implies that external networks mediate the impact of ISO 14001 on environmental impacts. Hence, our final hypothesis is:

Hypothesis 3.4 External networks mediate the impact of ISO 14001 on environmental impacts.

3.3 Methodology

The data were taken from the surveys conducted in 2011 and in 2014. The survey results in 2011 were used for measuring the independent, mediating, and control variables and the survey results in 2014 for measuring the dependent variables. In this way, it can be tested if ISO 14001 and participation in external networks improve environmental impacts in later years.

ISO 14001 was measured by a three-point scale, with 0 if the enterprise is not certified for ISO 14001 at all, 0.5 if it is certified for part of the enterprise's operational sites, and 1 if it is certified for all operational sites of the enterprise. This is in line with the methodology of Oliveira et al. (2016) who distinguished those companies with ISO 14001 certification with a partial score, covering just one sector of the organization, from companies that have ISO 14001 certification with full scope.

The participation in external networks was measured by three indicators. First, companies can participate in networks in the supply chain (Bos-Brouwers, 2010; Pirsch et al., 2006; European Commission, 2007). Second, companies can develop partnerships with professional training institutes (technical schools, laboratories, etc.) in order to anticipate the technological evolution of products or services (ECEI, 2010; European Commission, 2002). Third, SMEs can participate in the local initiatives of governments and/or social organizations (Barth and Wolff, 2009). Each instrument is measured by a binary scale.

For environmental impacts, we used similar indicators as in Chapter 2 to measure the change in energy consumption, waste production, and water consumption between 2010 and 2013.

The scores for the three measures for networks were highly correlated. In addition, the various environmental impacts significantly correlate. The Cronbach's alphas (see α in Table 3.1) indicate the internal consistency of these two factors, as both meet the accepted threshold of 0.60 (Kline, 2000). These test results show that networks and outcomes measure single, unidimensional, and latent constructs.

3.4 Results

The estimation results are reported in Figure 3.2 and Table 3.2. As the mediating and independent variables are likely to be interdependent, we used structural equation modelling (SEM) in STATA (Version 14) with maximum likelihood

TABLE 3.1 Descriptive statistics of dependent and independent variables[a]

Variable	*Measure*	*Mean*	*SD*	*Year*
ISO 14001		0.10	0.28	2011
External networks	Cooperation supply chain (46)	0.26	0.44	2011
(α = 0.68)	Partnerships with training institutes (47)	0.24	0.43	2011
	Participation in local initiatives (48)	0.27	0.44	2011
Environmental impact	Reduction energy consumption (102)	0.53	1.18	2014
(α = 0.73)	Reduction in waste (104)	0.44	1.01	2014
	Reduction in water consumption (105)	0.32	0.87	2014

a * $p < 0.05$, ** $p < 0.01$, *** $p < 0.001$. The numbers in brackets refer to the number of the survey questions reported in Appendix 1.

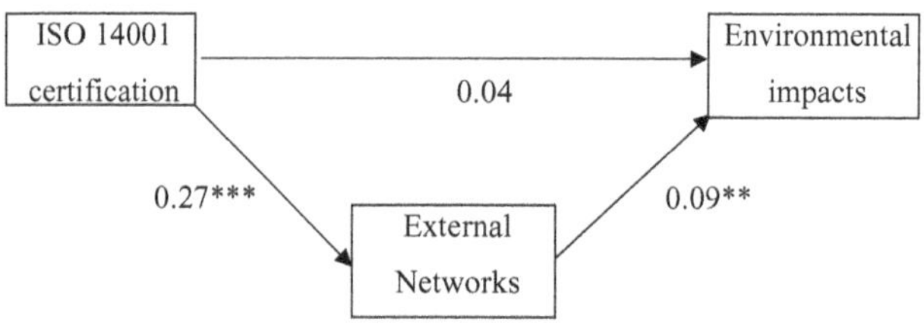

FIGURE 3.2 Estimation results of structural relations: core relationships

TABLE 3.2 Estimation results of structural equation model[a]

	External networks	*Environmental impact*
ISO 14001	0.27***	0.04
External networks		0.09**
Measurement model		
External networks		
- Cooperation supply chain		0.59***
– Partnerships with training institutes		0.63***
– Participation in local initiatives		0.69***
Ecological outcome		
- Energy		0.69***
- Waste		0.67***
- Water		0.75***

a Standardized coefficients; * $p < 0.05$ ** $p < 0.01$, and *** $p < 0.001$. Controlled for sector, region, position in the chain, intensity of price competition, age structure, skill level of employees, organizational culture, and time horizon. Global fit indices: CFI = 0.964; TLI = 0.944; RMSEA = 0.020; $R^2 = 0.205$.

with missing values as estimation technique. The structural model is simultaneously estimated with the measurement model. The model is confirmed by the global fit indices. The Comparative Fit Index (CFI), the Tucker–Lewis Index (TLI), and RMSEA measure are all acceptable (Kaplan, 2009).

TABLE 3.3 Estimation results for direct, indirect, and total effects of ISO 14001 on environmental impacts[a]

Independent variable	*Mediator*	*Dependent variable*	*Direct effect*	*Indirect effect*	*Total effect*
ISO 14001	Environmental network	Environmental impact	0.131	0.068***	0.199**

a Unstandardized coefficients; * $p < 0.05$, ** $p < 0.01$, and *** $p < 0.001$.

The estimation results show that ISO 14001 has no significant direct effect on environmental impacts, but stimulates participation in networks. Based on these results, we reject Hypothesis 3.1 and accept Hypothesis 3.3. Participation in external networks has a significant positive effect on environmental impacts, which provides support for Hypothesis 3.2.

For large samples (as in our case), a convenient method to test for mediation is by using the estimates that SEM provides for the significance of the indirect effects by way of the Wald statistic (Shrout and Bolger, 2002; Little et al., 2007). For the indirect effect from ISO 14001 on environmental impacts, this effect equals $a * b$, where a is the unstandardized coefficient of ISO 14001 in the equation of external networks and b the coefficient of external networks in the equation of environmental impacts (Preacher and Hayes, 2008). The total effect on environmental impacts is equal to the direct effect of ISO 14001 on environmental impacts and the indirect effect as mediated by environmental networks.

Table 3.3 shows that the indirect and the total effects are both significant. These results show that participation in networks positively mediates the effect of ISO 14001 on environmental impacts, which provides support for Hypothesis 3.4.

3.5 Conclusion

This chapter investigates the relationship between ISO 14001 certification, external environmental networks, and the environmental impacts of SMEs in 12 European countries. The chapter contributes to the academic literature by analysing the patterns of the impact of ISO 14001 on the environmental impacts of SMEs by distinguishing direct effects from indirect effects mediated by participation in environmental networks. Previous research has not conjectured that participation in external networks mediates the influence from ISO 14001 certification on environmental impacts, although several authors do hint at the existence of this mechanism (Ferenhof et al., 2014; Lopez-Gamero et al., 2009; Darnall and Sides, 2008; Battaglia et al., 2010; Ammenberg and Hjelm, 2003).

A second major contribution to the academic literature is that we test the mediation model on a large sample of 3,633 SMEs from 12 countries by structural equation modelling. Our test results confirm that participation in external networks mediates the relationship between ISO 14001 certification and EP.

Our study is important because it bridges two opposing positions on the effectiveness of ISO 14001 certification that are found in the literature. According to Martín-de Castro et al. (2017), the question of whether ISO 14001 certification really contributes to better EP or could be just 'greenwash' is still unanswered. On one hand, several studies found low improvements in environmental impacts from ISO 14001 certification (Jamali, 2010; Aravind and Christmann, 2011; Boiral, 2012; Testa et al., 2014; Castka and Prajogo, 2013) and that the main motive to employ ISO 14001 certification is to improve public image (Schylander and Martinuzzi, 2007). On the other hand, there are several other studies that did identify the positive effects of ISO 14001 certification on EP and suggested that it stimulates environmental awareness among employees and better compliance with environmental regulation (Ferenhof et al., 2014; Nguyen and Hens, 2015; Guerrero-Baena et al., 2015; Nguyen and Hens, 2015; Singh et al., 2015; Oliveira et al., 2016; Wong et al., 2017; Ferreira Rino and Salvador, 2017). In this debate, our analysis takes an intermediate position. Our empirical analysis corresponds to the first line of research – that ISO 14001 does not significantly improve the future environmental impacts of SMEs, as we find no direct effect from ISO 14001 certification on the growth in energy consumption, waste production, and water consumption. At the same time, our findings support the second line of research – that ISO 14001 does contribute to better EP, but we find that this influence is indirect and mediated by participation in networks.

This mediation channel seems particularly relevant for SMEs, on which we focused our sample. SMEs often lack the resources to have up to date knowledge of the increasingly complex issue of environmental impacts (Baumann-Pauly et al., 2013). They need guidance from external parties to manage such processes and ISO 14001 certification may be the trigger for the SME to collaborate with other network partners who can offer this guidance. Getting involved in external networks helps SMEs share best practices and compensates for a lack of technology and/or skills.

Note

* An extended text of this chapter has been published in: Graafland, J. (2018). Ecological impacts of the ISO 14001 certification of small and medium sized enterprises in Europe and the mediating role of networks. *Journal of Cleaner Production*, 174: 273–282.

4

IMPACTS OF CORPORATE SOCIAL RESPONSIBILITY ON INNOVATION

4.1 Introduction

Literature has recognized that CSR may be of strategic value because it contributes to innovation. Several researchers claim that CSR can stimulate innovation (Porter and Kramer, 2006; Frondel et al., 2007; Midtun, 2007; Wagner, 2007a; Surroca et al., 2010; Lioui and Sharma, 2012; Luo and Du, 2015). Still, the empirical evidence that CSR stimulates innovation remains weak. One of the problems which is encountered by this type of research is reverse causality. CSR may require the introduction of a new technique or new product attribute and it is found that these kinds of investments are positively related to innovation (Hitt et al., 1997). Product innovation is necessary for redesigning products to make them more environmentally responsible, whereas process innovation allows redesigning manufacturing processes to make them less contaminating (Christmann, 2000). Therefore, innovation frequently is a condition for bringing about the changes required for the realization of CSR (McWilliams and Siegel, 2000; King and Lenox, 2002; Scholtens, 2008; Padgett and Galan, 2009). This suggests two-way causation and indeed MacGregor and Fontrodana (2008) hypothesized that innovation and CSR can form a virtuous circle.

In a recent article, Flammer and Kacperczyk (2016) solved the causality issue by using an instrumental variable approach and found support for a causal impact of CSR (measured by stakeholder orientation) on innovation. One of the limitations of the analysis of Flammer and Kacperczyk (2016) is that their sample is limited to public traded companies. In this chapter, we test the causal effect of CSR on innovation for SMEs. SMEs make up 90% of business worldwide and account for 50–60% of employment (Jamali et al., 2008) and it is evidently important to know if the findings of Flammer and Kacperczyk also apply to SMEs. SMEs are

DOI: 10.4324/9781003216483-5

not just miniature versions of large companies, but are often thought to have distinctive characteristics (Battisti and Perry, 2011). The level playing field on which most SMEs operate means that they face severe competition which puts their profitability under pressure. Lack of time, finances, skills, and knowledge are commonly identified by SMEs as constraints to CSR (Tilley, 2000; Spence et al., 2003; Lepoutre and Heene, 2006; Studer et al., 2006; Welford and Frost, 2006; Russo and Tencati, 2009) and are also a barrier to innovation (Madrid-Guijarro et al., 2009; Hewitt-Dundas, 2006; Bergman et al., 2006; Mosey et al., 2002). SME managers tend to have a short-term horizon focusing on survival (Burt and Van der Heijden, 2003) and are less likely to carry out strategic planning (Laverty, 2004). The long-term benefits of CSR and innovation therefore often remain beyond the strategic horizon of SMEs. This raises the question whether the results of Flammer and Kacperczyk also apply to SMEs.

The research question in this chapter is therefore: Does CSR causally influence innovation of SMEs? In what follows, we first describe three hypotheses of Flammer and Kacperczyk (2016) that we test for SMEs. Next, we discuss our methodology. Then we present the test results and conclude with a summary of our results.

4.2 Conceptual Framework

CSR has been claimed to stimulate innovation, for several reasons. First, CSR helps in attracting highly qualified employees who may foster innovation (Clausen and Loew, 2009). Turban and Greening (1997) argued that CSR will enable companies to attract more intelligent, motivated, experienced, visionary, creative, and committed employees, and this will likely also foster the innovative capability of the firm. Second, Surroca et al. (2010) argued that the innovative capacity of a firm is enhanced by the quality of the relational capital of a company. Since building team morale by good relationships among employees is an important social dimension of CSR (Mandl and Dorr, 2007), CSR will strengthen the affective commitment and knowledge sharing behaviour of current employees, which in turn is a determinant of innovative performance. Third, the stakeholder orientation dimension of CSR may stimulate innovation by making the company more sensitive to industrial and societal needs (Midtun, 2007; Bocquet et al., 2011). Fourth, Flammer and Kacperczyk (2016) defended the CSR-innovation link by arguing that stakeholder orientation is likely to relieve customers and employees from short-termism. Long-term orientation will stimulate customers to be more loyal to the firm and tolerate failures of new products and encourage employees to invest more effort in risky innovation. Furthermore, stakeholder orientation will increase employees' job satisfaction, which is likely to foster employees' engagement with innovation. Fifth, Jamali et al. (2011) showed that companies that have strategic CSR partnerships with NGOs can be more capable of innovation (dependent on the social capital of the partnership). More directly, engaging in CSR may stimulate a company to perform innovations that are necessary to accomplish certain aspects of CSR (McWilliams and Siegel, 2000; Clausen and Loew, 2009; Surroca et al., 2010). For example, the adoption of an environmental programme may stimulate product innovation of environmentally friendly products or process innovation by redesigning production processes to realize CSR-related goals (e.g. reduction of energy consumption).

Based on this literature, we posit three hypotheses of which 4.2 and 4.3 are taken from Flammer and Kacperczyk (2016):

Hypothesis 4.1 The implementation of CSR instruments contributes to innovation.
Hypothesis 4.2 The positive impact of CSR instruments on innovation is greater in consumer-focused industries.
Hypothesis 4.3 The positive impact of firms' CSR instruments on innovation is greater in less eco-friendly industries.

In defence of the second hypothesis, Flammer and Kacperczyk argued that positive attitudes among consumers leading to greater demand for the firm's products provide an incentive to product innovation because the firm knows there is a market for the product. It will take more risks if consumers are committed to the company. Furthermore, stakeholder orientation may encourage consumers to act as a source of new ideas by participation in an exchange in ideas on new products.

The third hypothesis is built on the argument that stakeholder orientation will particularly encourage eco-friendly innovation as this type of innovation appeals to various stakeholders and that eco-friendly innovation matters more in industries engaged in high-polluting activities than in other industries.

4.3 Methodology

For CSR instruments, the responses from the 2011 survey were used. CSR instruments were operationalized by five management instrument measures that companies can use to improve their CSR impacts (see Table 4.1). An internal code of conduct and CSR training increase the CSR awareness of employees (Adams et al., 2001; Yu, 2009). Other instruments that are particularly relevant for SMEs are participation in CSR networks or in local CSR initiatives. As small firms are more resource constrained, they must rely on external experts for appropriate solutions to, for example, environmental challenges. Cooperation with other enterprises or NGOs will help bring expertise to the SME (Arimura et al., 2008; Bos-Brouwers, 2010). Furthermore, we included ISO 14001 certification.

Innovation was based on the responses in the 2014 survey. Innovation was measured by one question on product information ('Has your enterprise introduced new or significantly improved products or services since 2010? Exclude the simple resale of new goods and changes of a solely aesthetic nature') and one question on process information ('Has your enterprise introduced new or

TABLE 4.1 Descriptive statistics and exploratory factor analysis[a]

	Mean	*SD*	*Factor loadings*	
			CSR instruments	*Innovation*
Internal code of conduct (43)	0.48	0.50	0.61	
CSR training employees (53)	0.29	0.45	0.69	
ISO 14001 (57)	0.14	0.32	0.50	
CSR cooperation supply chain (46)	0.36	0.48	0.62	
Participation in local CSR initiatives (47)	0.41	0.49	0.55	
Position in the chain (6)	1.88	1.00		
High pollution sector	0.10	0.31		
Product innovation (123)	4.14	1.81		0.91
Process innovation (124)	4.11	1.74		0.91
Eigen value			2.08	1.39
Cronbach alpha			0.60	0.81

a The numbers in brackets refer to the numbers of the survey questions in Appendix 1.

significantly improved production or organizational processes since 2010?'), both measured on a seven-point Likert scale. The internal consistency of CSR and innovation is confirmed by exploratory factor analysis and the Cronbach's alphas, which exceed the lower limit of 0.60 (Hair et al., 1998). Based on these results, average values for CSR and innovation were used.

The position in the chain was measured by one survey question in the 2011 survey asking whether companies operate in business-to-consumer (B2C) relations or business-to-business (B2B) relations, measured on a five-point Likert scale. Furthermore, a dummy for high-polluting industries was constructed, following Flammers and Kacperczyk's definition that includes metal mining, electric utilities, chemicals, primary metals, paper, food, beverages, tobacco, and hazardous waste.

Using a lag of three years for CSR instruments in the regression analysis for innovation reduce potential simultaneity bias in the relationship between CSR instruments and innovation. But to further control for simultaneity bias, we also used IV estimation technique with two instrumental variables for CSR instruments. First, we used CSR information provided by industrial associations to the company. Institutional theory argues that business associations can educate their members on CSR (Campbell, 2007); for example, by providing information on codes of conducts. The second instrumental variable measures the degree of monitoring of the company's CSR by NGOs and/or media, which increases the probability of reputational harm for companies with low CSR. Since it is likely that these variables affect innovation only indirectly through stimulating the use of CSR instruments, we assumed that they can serve as instrumental variables for CSR instruments. The variables are measured in the 2011 survey (see survey questions 41 and 42 in Appendix 1).

Besides IV regression analysis, we also tested for predictive causality by employing Granger causality tests by including innovation measured in the 2011 survey as additional control variable. CSR instruments are said to Granger cause innovation if the lagged CSR instruments significantly affect innovation, while controlling for lagged innovation and all other control variables. An advantage of controlling for lagged innovation is that it also captures the influence of other unobserved variables driving innovation.

4.4 Results

Table 4.2 reports the results of the regression analysis. We used the bootstrap estimation procedure with 1,000 bootstrap samples to estimate the model. First, we tested the strength of the instrumental variables. Column 1 of Table 4.2 shows that CSR information of industrial associations and CSR monitoring by NGOs and media have very significant positive effects on CSR instruments (T-values are 7.03 and 7.42, respectively). Hence, they satisfy the condition that the instrumental variables must sufficiently be correlated with the independent variable.

TABLE 4.2 Regression analysis[a]

	1	*2*	*3*	*4*	*5*	*6*
	CSR instruments	*Innovation*				
Info industrial organizations	0.197** (0.001)					
Monitoring NGOs & media	0.208** (0.001)					
CSR		0.237** (0.002)	0.164** (0.001)	0.164** (0.001)	0.166** (0.001)	0.079** (0.003)
CSR * B2C				−0.011 (0.677)		
CSR * polluting					−0.004 (0.892)	
Innovation lagged						0.397** (0.001)
R^2	0.234	0.127	0.143	0.143	0.143	0.275
P value Hausman–Wu test		0.309				
P value Sargan test		0.183				
Estimation method	OLS	IV	OLS	OLS	OLS	OLS

a OLS estimated with bootstrap $N = 1{,}000$. Standardized coefficients; p-values in brackets. * $p < 0.05$; ** $p < 0.01$. Controlled for sector, country, price competition, organizational culture, time horizon, age structure, skill structure, tenure, ownership structure, and company size. Details of the control variables are reported in Appendices 1 and 2.

The IV estimation results reported in column 2 of Table 4.2 show that CSR instruments significantly stimulate innovation, thus confirming Hypothesis 4.1. The Sargan test shows that the instrumental variables pass the exogeneity requirement. Furthermore, the Hausman–Wu test shows that CSR instruments are exogenous to innovation, indicating that there is no reverse causal influence of innovation on CSR. Based on the Hausman–Wu test, omitted variable bias or other biases that result from correlation between the independent variable and the residual can also be excluded.

Since OLS is preferable to IV if there is no endogeneity, we proceeded with OLS (column 3 in Table 4.2). In comparison to the IV estimation results, the significance of CSR instruments further increases. In column 4 and 5, we added (centered) moderators for B2C and high-pollution industries but we find no support for hypotheses 4.2 and 4.3. In column 6, we controlled for lagged innovation from 2011. CSR instruments remains highly significant, showing that it Granger causes innovation.

4.5 Conclusion

In this chapter, we tested three hypotheses derived from a recent study by Flammer and Kacperczyk (2016) on the influence of CSR instruments on innovation by SMEs. It is widely recognized that SMEs have several characteristics that distinguish them from public-traded companies (Tilley, 2000; Spence et al., 2003; Burt and Van der Heijden, 2003; Laverty, 2004; Bergman et al., 2006; Lepoutre and Heene, 2006; Studer et al., 2006; Welford and Frost, 2006; Hewitt-Dundas, 2006; Russo and Tencati, 2009; Madrid-Guijarro et al., 2009; Battisti and Perry, 2011). First, SMEs often operate on a level-playing field and are subject to intensive price competition. SME managers respond to this market pressure in a reactive way rather than undertaking proactive investments in CSR or innovation. Second, because of the intensive price competition, SMEs' profitability is lower than the profitability of large public-traded firms that operate more on oligopolistic markets. As a consequence, SMEs have limited resources in the form of time, money, and human capital. They often face short-term payment problems and lack the necessary skills and capabilities to pursue CSR and innovation strategies. Third, SMEs tend to think and plan in the short term and focus on survival. Consequently, the long-term strategic benefits of CSR and its impact on innovation often remain beyond the strategic horizon of SMEs. Because of these characteristics, size might be a crucial factor for the CSR–innovation link. The findings of Flammer and Kacperczyk (2016) can therefore not be generalized to SMEs without further research.

In our study, we found confirmative evidence of the finding of Flammer and Kacperczyk (2016) that the implementation of CSR instruments has a positive, causal effect on innovation. This finding is very reassuring not only because the companies in our sample differ markedly in size (34% being micro companies with 10 or less employees) from the companies in Flammer and Kacperczyk's sample but also because we studied SMEs in Europe instead of US. Our finding thus provides a strong indication that the conclusion of Flammer and Kacperczyk that stakeholder orientation sparks innovation holds more generally.

However, our analysis does not support Flammer and Kacperczyk's finding that the CSR-innovation link is moderated by consumer-focused industries. A possible reason is that the argument of Flammer and Kacperczyk that positive attitudes among consumers provide an incentive to product innovation applies equally to SMEs operating in B2B relationships. The stimulating effect of large customers setting responsibility targets for their smaller suppliers has been widely acknowledged (Lepoutre and Heene, 2006). As the reputation of large companies with strong brands can be severely harmed by negative publicity about issues in their supply chain, they have a major interest in the CSR performance of their suppliers (Roberts, 2003). If an SME builds a strong relationship with a large business customer by meeting CSR standards that this customer applies in its supplier relationships, the SME's risks will be lower and it will have a stronger incentive to invest resources in the development of new products or processes.

In addition, moderation of the CSR-innovation link by high-pollution industries is not supported. A possible explanation is that the stakeholder orientation in SMEs is foremost directed towards the own employees and less to stakeholders with a high concern for the environment. Jamali et al. (2008) found that out of six stakeholder groups, SMEs rank employees as the most important and environment as the second-least important stakeholder group. Mandl and Dorr (2007) showed that much of the SMEs' CSR initiatives aim at stimulating engagements and building team morale of the SMEs' own employees (Mandl and Dorr, 2007). Therefore, it is likely that the social dimension (e.g. employee training, healthy working conditions, and fair reward systems) is more important than the environmental dimension of CSR for SMEs and, hence, that the innovation effects from CSR are to be found as much in labour-intensive sectors as in high-pollution sectors. As argued by Flammer and Karcperczyk's, a strong stakeholder focus on employees encourages the employee's engagement in innovation and it is likely that this mechanism also explains why we found a link between CSR instruments and innovation for SMEs. Our results that the CSR-innovation link is not moderated by consumer-focused industries or by high-pollution industries illustrate that not all findings of Flammer and Kacperczyk (2016) can be generalized to the context of SMEs.

Another interesting result is that CSR instruments appear to be exogenous to innovation. Hence, we find no evidence of a virtuous circle between CSR instruments and innovation for SMEs. This result might be explained by the analysis of Hull and Rothenberg (2008) who found that CSR and innovation are alternative ways for companies to differentiate themselves from other companies. Companies that are already innovative do not need CSR instruments to maintain or gain market share. Hence, the virtuous circle probably only holds for CSR-related innovation that improves CSR outcomes, but not for innovation in general.

5

DOES CORPORATE SOCIAL RESPONSIBILITY PUT REPUTATION AT RISK?*

5.1 Introduction

One of the advantages of engaging in CSR is that it can improve the firm's reputation (Gardberg and Fombrun, 2006; Heikkurinen, 2010; Babiak and Trendafilova, 2011; Melo and Garrido-Morgado, 2012; Lin et al., 2016). The enhanced stakeholder perceptions are a valuable resource that will lead to improved financial performance (Walker and Mercado, 2015). Environmental certifications can signal quality, mobilize trust of stakeholders, and help to differentiate the firm from competitors (Djupdal and Westhead, 2015). Moreover, CSR often effectively carries with it a kind of insurance-type protection by reducing business and corporate risks (Godfrey et al., 2009; Lin et al., 2016). For example, a strong CSR programme can help limit reputational damage if accidents happen.

While most papers look at the positive effects of CSR, a few others consider the potential negative reputational effects (Rhee and Haunschild, 2006; Wagner et al., 2009; De Vries et al., 2015). King and McDonnell (2012) challenged the insurance like capability of CSR by pointing at the so-called reputational liability effect. They argued that if activists want the maximum amount of attention in the media, it is better for them to target a firm with a good CSR reputation. Thus, by investing in CSR to improve its reputation a firm sets itself up to be targeted by activists. King and McDonnell tested this effect by relating data on boycotts that targeted publicly traded firms in the U.S to the Forbes reputation index. Their study showed that firms in the highest tier of CSR reputation have a higher chance of being boycotted.

The question is whether this reputational liability effect is also relevant for SMEs. Large companies are more visible and hence more likely to be targeted by non-governmental organizations (NGOs) (Hendry, 2006). Given their limited

DOI: 10.4324/9781003216483-6

means to gather information, it is more efficient for activists to focus on large enterprises, as they are often market leaders in their organizational field and indirectly affect the behaviour of SMEs through supplier–customer relations in the chain. Still, the reputational liability effect of CSR might also be important for SMEs. As they are embedded in their local community (Doshi et al., 2013), their CSR may be noticed by local activists in their local community and become known in local media (Fuller and Tian, 2006). King and McDonnell's finding that an increase in CSR activities makes a company a more likely target of activists' engagement, may therefore also apply to SMEs.

At present, there is no research that tested this potential negative effect of CSR for SMEs. In contrast with King and McDonnell (2012), our analysis therefore focuses on SMEs. The main research questions of this chapter are: 'What is the effect of CSR of an SME on the intensity that its CSR is monitored by external parties like activists?' and 'How does this CSR monitoring affect the SME's exposure to public criticism on its CSR?' These research questions are not only interesting for the academic community but also for the practitioners of CSR. Many SMEs may not realize that by engaging in CSR activities they might be setting themselves up to be monitored by external parties. If the reputational liability effect is also operating for SMEs, they should be careful in positioning themselves as firms that proactively pursue CSR policies to gain reputational benefits, because these benefits of CSR may easily turn into reputational liabilities.

The model is tested on a sample of 1,355 SMEs in 12 European countries that have been surveyed twice with an interval of three years. By using data for two periods, we can analyse how CSR affects CSR monitoring and criticism on CSR in later years. The content of this chapter is as follows. First, we present the conceptual model and the hypotheses. Section 5.3 describes the methodology and data. Section 5.4 presents the results of the regression analysis. Section 5.55 summarizes the main findings.

5.2 Conceptual Framework

The conceptual framework is depicted in Figure 5.1.

CSR and Monitoring

We take our starting point in social movement theory (King, 2008; Fligstein and McAdam, 2011). Social movements are group-based, coordinated attempts to change relationships among people and social institutions (Hendry, 2006). Companies require a social licence to operate, that is an ongoing acceptance of a company's operations by the surrounding civil society (Lynch-Wood and Williamson, 2007). Civil society can vary from grassroot organizations and neighbourhoods at the local level to non-governmental organizations (NGOs) at the regional, national, and international level (Dare et al., 2014). NGOs are potentially an

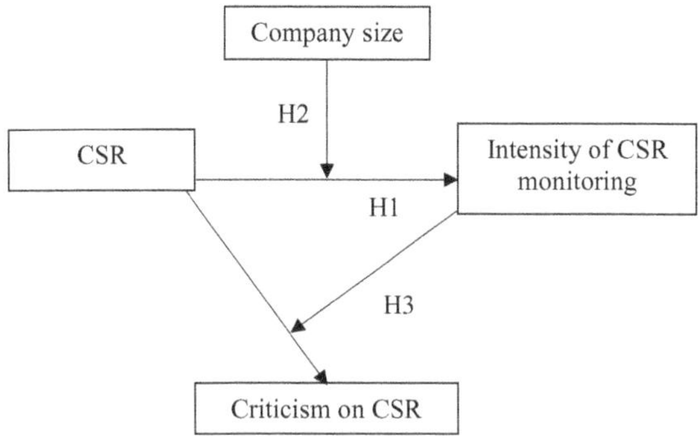

FIGURE 5.1 Conceptual framework

important stakeholder of companies. They can monitor companies and generate attention in the media about situations they find undesirable, which will reflect negatively on the public's perception about the firm.

To prevent such negative reputational effects, companies can pursue an active CSR policy to deter NGOs from damaging the reputation of the firm (Maxwell et al., 2000). Being known as a company with highly ranked CSR is believed to discourage NGOs from monitoring a firm (Klein and Harford, 2004). If a company signals that it is meeting societal expectations regarding social and EP, NGOs will have more trust in the company and be less inclined to monitor it and therefore less frequently uncover reasons to make complaints. Godfrey et al. (2009) explain that participating in CSR activities creates a form of goodwill for the firm. Analysing firm-level CSR activities and 178 negative actions against firms during 1993–2003, they found that participation in institutional CSR activities provided an 'insurance-like' protection. The policy implication of this belief would be that by taking pre-emptive actions through instituting socially responsible practices, firms can prevent becoming targets of future monitoring by NGOs. The incentive that community-level pressures provide companies to pursue CSR seems even to be stronger than CSR's direct effects on company profitability or market value (Marquis et al., 2007).

However, social movement theory has cast doubt on this belief that CSR diminishes monitoring by external parties. King and McDonnell (2012) argued that firms developing positive CSR reputations put themselves in the spotlight, thereby increasing activists' attention to the firm. To attract public attention, activists target well-known companies with a good reputation. They use the good reputation of the firm as a resource they can draw on to generate public attention as the public will pay more attention to NGOs' grievances when they make critical claims of a well-known firm (Hendry, 2006; Vogel, 2010). High reputation increases the chance that a company responds to the criticism of the NGO (Baron and Diermeier, 2007; McDonnell and King, 2013). Companies that express commitment to CSR raise expectations among their stakeholders and become obligated to uphold their commitment (Joyner and Payne, 2002). Stakeholders will react more negatively when such a firm is found to lack behind (Rhee and Haunschild, 2006; Wagner et al., 2009). Testing their model on 157 publicly traded firms that were boycotted during 1990–2005 and 471 comparable firms, King and McDonnell (2012) indeed found that firms in the highest tier of Fortune's Most Admirable Firms Index are significantly more likely to be targeted. Similarly, McDonnell et al. (2015) found that firms issuing a CSR report are significantly more open to being challenged by NGOs in the future, as the publication of CSR reports empowers external monitors by providing them with easier access to information about a firm's social activities, which makes it easier to identify areas in which the firm still needs to improve.

Based on these arguments and findings, we postulate the following hypothesis:

Hypothesis 5.1 High CSR intensifies CSR monitoring by NGOs and media.

Moderation by Company Size

Although SMEs are less visible, it can be argued that they also need a social licence from the local community. Since SMEs are highly embedded in their local community, they will be seriously harmed if local NGOs spread bad news about their CSR in the media in the local community (Doshi et al., 2013; Fuller and Tian, 2006).

Still, it is likely that the reputation liability effect is dependent on company size (Gunningham et al., 2004). Previous research has shown that SMEs are heterogeneous in nature (Brammer, Hoejmose et al., 2012). The smaller the company, the less public attention it will attract. Naming and shaming strategies are less relevant for very small companies than for medium-sized companies (Lynch-Wood and Williamson, 2007). Therefore, it is to be expected that the strength of the reputational liability effect depends positively on firm size. When a micro firm starts to upgrade its CSR, for example by participating in CSR networks in the supply chain, it will attract less attention from NGOs than when a medium-sized firm does so, because the small firm is less visible. Therefore, we propose that:

Hypothesis 5.2 Firm size positively moderates the positive influence of CSR on CSR monitoring.

CSR and Exposure to Criticism: Moderation by Monitoring

The last part of our conceptual framework concerns the relationship between CSR and the probability that a company is criticized for its (low) CSR. More and more companies have become aware that low CSR can harm economic performance by damaging their corporate reputation (Lin et al., 2016; Tang et al., 2012). However, the empirical evidence on this assumption is ambiguous, as there are also studies that do not find evidence of reputational or financial harm (Karpoff et al., 2005; Schons and Steinmeier, 2016).[1] A possible reason is that the relationship between the CSR and reputational damage is more complex and moderated by the intensity of CSR monitoring. If activists start monitoring the CSR of a company, it is more likely that they notice the controversial effects of the company's operations, which provides them with a weapon to criticize the firm and to organize actions against the firm. The likelihood that monitoring leads to identification of such controversial issues depends negatively on the CSR of the company. Hence, societal criticism on a company's CSR depends on the combination of low CSR and high intensity of monitoring. If a company is intensively monitored by external parties while its CSR is of high quality, there will be no cause for NGOs to blame the company and it is unlikely that its CSR will be criticized. But the same holds for companies with a low CSR that are not monitored, because then external stakeholders lack the information to make complaints about the company's CSR. As Reuber and Fischer (2010) argued (without testing this hypothesis), the relationship between low CSR and reputational loss is positively moderated by media coverage of the discreditable CSR. Hence, only if a low performing company is monitored by external parties, will its CSR invoke external criticism. Therefore, we expect that:

Hypothesis 5.3 The intensity of CSR monitoring moderates the influence of CSR on the exposure to criticism on the company's CSR.

5.3 Methodology

The data were taken from the surveys conducted in 2011 and in 2014. The survey results in 2011 were used for measuring the independent, mediating, and control variables and the survey results in 2014 for measuring the dependent variables.

Table 5.1 reports the descriptive statistics of the dependent and independent variables and the results of exploratory factor analysis. The dependent variable – the extent that a company's CSR is criticized – was measured by a seven-point Likert scale from 1 (not at all) to 7 (very much). The mean value of the responses shows that, on average, SMEs do not often face criticism on their CSR.

Regarding the moderating variables, the intensity of CSR monitoring was measured by a seven-point Likert scale from 1 (not at all) to 7 (very much). Table 5.1 shows that the average intensity of monitoring is higher than the extent that an SME's CSR is criticized, but it is still rather low. Company size has been measured by the number of FTEs in 2011.

The independent variable, CSR, has been measured by six concrete management instruments that firms can use to improve their CSR impacts: public code of conduct (Kaptein and Wempe, 1998); ISO 14001 certification; participation in CSR networks in the supply chain (Battaglia et al., 2010); partnerships with professional training institutes (Bos-Brouwers, 2010); dialogue with NGOs on CSR

TABLE 5.1 Descriptive statistics and factor analysis[a]

	Measurement	*Descriptive statistics*		*Year*	*Loadings*
Variable	*Description*	*Mean*	*SD*[d]		
CSR criticism	To what extent did your enterprise face complaints about your enterprise's social and/or environmental aspects? (40)	0.77	1.18	2014	
CSR monitoring	To what extent do NGOs and/or media monitor your enterprise's CSR? (42)	1.23	1.43	2014	
CSR	Public code (44)	0.20	0.40	2011	0.61
	ISO 14001 certification (57)	0.17	0.36	2011	0.52
	Active dialogue with NGOs (45)	0.18	0.39	2011	0.64
	CSR cooperation supply chain (46)	0.41	0.49	2011	0.73
	Partnerships with training institutes (47)	0.36	0.48	2011	0.68
	Participation in local CSR initiatives (48)	0.44	0.50	2011	0.74
Eigen value					2.59
Cronbach alpha					0.74

a The numbers in brackets refer to the number of the survey question reported in Appendix 1.

(Hall et al., 2015); and participation in local CSR initiatives (Barth and Wolff, 2009). These indicators were each measured by a binary scale (0: no; 1: yes). As shown in Table 5.1, all instruments load on one factor. Also the Cronbach's alpha indicates internal consistency of the CSR instruments, as it meets the accepted threshold of 0.60 (Kline, 2000). In the regression analysis, we therefore used the factor for CSR as estimated by the exploratory factor analysis as independent variable.

As social licence provides an incentive to firms to engage in CSR, CSR monitoring and CSR criticism may also reversely affect the use of CSR policies (McDonnell et al., 2015). In order to prevent simultaneity bias in the estimation results, we therefore used the 2SLS estimation technique. In the first stage, CSR was regressed on all control variables and two instrumental variables, the innovation motive to CSR and the motive to satisfy employees. Research has shown that CSR stimulates innovation (Flammer and Kacperczyk, 2016). Managers may therefore be interested in CSR to increase innovation. Furthermore, CSR may also provide personal satisfaction to the current workforce, leading to stronger commitment from employees and a more positive attitude to work and good conduct (Greening and Turban, 2000). In contrast to the reputation motive

(CSR as a means to prevent reputational damage), the innovation and employee motives for CSR are internal rather than external drivers of CSR. There is no theoretical reason that they directly affect the intensity of CSR monitoring and complaints on a company's CSR. The innovation motive was measured in the 2011 survey by survey question 22 and the employee motive by survey question 26 (see Appendix 1). In the second stage, we used the estimated predicted value of CSR to construct the interaction terms and used them, together with the predicted value of CSR, as explanatory variables in the regression analysis of CSR monitoring and CSR criticism.

5.4 Results

Table 5.2 presents the outcomes of the multivariate regression. First, we tested the impact of our instrumental variables on CSR, while controlling for all control variables. The estimation results in column 1 show that the innovation and employee motives are both highly significant (T-values of 7.84 and 6.30 for the innovation motive and employee satisfaction motive, respectively) and therefore qualify as strong instruments. Furthermore, the estimation results show that CSR is positively related to company size, market leadership and position in the supply chain (B2C) and is relatively low for SMEs from Continental and Mediterranean Europe.

Based on these results, we proceeded with the second-stage regression analysis of the intensity of CSR monitoring. The Hausman–Wu test confirms that CSR is endogenous ($p < 0.00$). The Sargan test shows that the instrumental variables pass the exogeneity requirement ($p > 0.05$). The estimation results show that a

TABLE 5.2 Results of multivariate regression analysis[a]

	CSR	*CSR monitoring*	*CSR criticism*	
	1	*2*	*3*	*4*
Innovation motive	0.20***			
Employee motive	0.16***			
CSR		0.30***	0.00	
CSR * ln size (centered)		0.07**		
CSR monitoring * (CSR_{max}-CSR)			0.16*	0.18***
CSR monitoring			0.03	
Estimation method	OLS	2SLS	2SLS	2SLS
R^2	0.20	0.09	0.15	0.15
Hausman–Wu test (*p*-value)		0.00***	0.25	0.23
Sargan test (*p*-value)		0.29	0.30	0.18

a Standardized coefficients; * $p < 0.05$; ** $p < 0.01$; and *** $p < 0.001$. The estimation results are controlled for company size, market position, position in the chain, intensity of price competition, region, sector, and Inverse Mill's ratio.

firm with a higher CSR in 2011 faces a higher intensity of CSR monitoring by NGOs and media in 2014. Hence, our results support Hypothesis 5.1. In addition, the interaction term of CSR and (the natural logarithm of) firm size has a significant positive effect, which supports Hypothesis 5.2 that the strength of the reputation liability effect increases with firm size.

Third, we estimated the equation for CSR criticism. We define the interaction term as the intensity of CSR monitoring multiplied by the difference between the maximum CSR score in the sample and the actual CSR score of the company. In column 3, we find a significant positive influence of the interaction term, whereas the linear specifications of CSR and intensity of monitoring are both insignificant. These results imply that low CSR only elicits criticism insofar a company's CSR is monitored. In the last column, we drop the linear specifications of CSR and CSR monitoring, which further enhances the significance of the moderating effect.

5.5 Conclusion

For firms, reputation is very important in attracting and keeping customers. One of the ways a firm can build up its reputation is by engaging in CSR activities. Most academic literature regarding CSR looked at ways in which CSR could benefit a firm by improving its reputation (Gardberg and Fombrun, 2006; Heikkurinen, 2010; Babiak and Trendafilova, 2011). Lin et al. (2016) found that the reputation damage of information on environmental irresponsibility is lower for companies with CSR activities than for companies without CSR activities. Schons and Steinmeier (2016) found that symbolic actions directed at low-proximity stakeholders increase profitability as long as the gap with substantive CSR is not too large, which suggests that symbolic actions improve reputation, even if substantial CSR lags behind.

This chapter explores a potential negative effect of engaging in CSR, namely that it invites more CSR monitoring by NGOs and media and therefore puts reputation at risk by increasing complaints. Earlier research based on experiments with students showed that a company's communication of investments in environmental measures may increase the perception of corporate greenwashing if people suspect strategic behaviour (Vries et al., 2015). But, as far as we know, there are only two studies that tested the so-called reputational liability effect among activist movements (King and McDonnell, 2012; McDonnell et al., 2015). These studies have been done by analysing boycotts against large, public firms. There has been no research yet that looked at the relevance of this reputational liability effect for SMEs and how it affects their reputation by inviting criticism. Furthermore, whereas previous literature focused on the US, our analysis pertains to a sample of SMEs from 12 European countries.

Our results confirm that the reputational liability effects identified for large companies by King and McDonnell (2012) and McDonnell et al. (2015), also hold for SMEs. We find that there is a significant positive effect of CSR on the intensity of CSR monitoring in later periods. This effect is moderated by company size, meaning that medium-sized companies are more influenced by the reputational liability effect than micro or small companies. Furthermore, we find that the intensity of monitoring moderates the effect of low CSR on complaints about the company's CSR.

Whereas earlier findings of Gardberg and Fombrun (2006), Melo and Garrido-Morgado (2012), and Lin et al. (2016) showed that CSR improves reputation and that this reputational advantage motivates managers to pursue CSR (Brønn and Vidaver-Cohen, 2009; Babiak and Trendafilova, 2011), our results imply that if an SME starts CSR activities, it creates more exposure to external criticism on its CSR. The message of Godfrey et al. (2009) that CSR has insurance-like properties is therefore, at least partly, misleading. This is significant because many SMEs may not realize that by engaging in CSR activities, they are setting themselves up to be monitored more intensely. The higher intensity of CSR monitoring increases the probability that NGOs find reasons to criticize an SME's CSR. Moreover, these negative publications by NGOs and media will have more severe consequences for an SME if it has fuelled the expectations of society.

This creates what we could like to call a 'social licence trap' for SMEs. Once a firm starts engaging itself with CSR, it may be forced to subsequently dedicate even more resources to CSR because of the higher public attention. A vicious circle follows, wherein more CSR practices are necessary to prevent reputational damage, which again causes the firm being a target of CSR monitoring. Firms that do not pay attention to CSR can sit back as they receive considerably less attention from NGOs or media. As long as they are ignored, they have a negative incentive to engage in CSR to prevent entering the 'social licence trap' and are probably able to get away with their low CSR. The strategic implication is that SMEs that want to move away from this poor CSR profile must be prepared to go all the way and transform themselves into companies that command respect because of their high CSR.

These effects are illustrated by a fictitious case in Table 5.3 that we can derive from the estimation results in Table 5.2. Suppose that in an initial situation, an SME does not pay attention to CSR at all and is not monitored by external parties (period 1 in Table 5.3). Because the company's CSR is not externally observed, it receives no criticism in the media. Suppose now that in period 2 this company initiates some CSR initiatives causing its CSR to increase to 25% of the maximum CSR score. This raises the external visibility of the company and hence the likelihood that the attention to its CSR from external parties is growing. Based on the estimation results in Table 5.2, we can calculate that the intensity of CSR monitoring and criticism increases. The criticism makes the SME aware that its CSR is being monitored by external parties and this creates a further incentive to improve its CSR to 50% (period 3). Then the reputational consequences are again negative, because the increased CSR invites an even more

TABLE 5.3 Effects of CSR on monitoring and criticism[a]

Period	*CSR*[b]	*CSR monitoring*	*CSR criticism*
1	0	0	0
2	25	0.75	0.22
3	50	1.50	0.29
4	75	2.25	0.21
5	100	3.00	0

a based on a fictitious SME with no CSR that is not monitored and criticized in period 1. The increase in CSR monitoring and CSR criticism in periods 2–5 due to the increase in CSR are calculated by use of the estimation results reported in Table 5.2.

b as % of maximum CSR in the sample.

intensive CSR monitoring. And since the CSR of the company is still lacking behind that of SMEs at the frontier of CSR, there is still room for criticism. Suppose the company responds again by improving its CSR. In this way, it gradually closes the gap between the company's CSR and that of the frontrunners with a 100% score, which diminishes criticism. In period 5, when the company belongs to the top CSR performers, there is no reason for external parties to criticize the SME's CSR. But in terms of CSR criticism, the company is not better off in period 5 in comparison to period 1 where the SME did not engage at all in CSR.

Notes

* An extended text of this chapter has been published as an open access article under the terms of the Creative Commons Attribution License in: Graafland, J. (2018). Does corporate social responsibility put reputation at risk by inviting activist targeting? An empirical test among European SMEs. *Corporate Social Responsibility and Environmental Management*, 25: 1–13.

1 Schons and Steinmeier (2016) found that a gap between symbolic and substantial CSR has a positive effect (although decreasing with the size of the gap) on financial performance if CSR is directed to low-proximity stakeholders. Cho et al. (2012) even found that reputation is negatively related to environmental performance, because reputation is largely driven by the disclosure level of companies and it is particularly low-performing companies that pay attention to disclosure.

PART II

Internal Drivers of Corporate Social Responsibility

6

INTRINSIC VERSUS EXTRINSIC MOTIVATIONS AND COMPANY SIZE

6.1 Introduction

Motivation (i.e. the reason upon which one acts) is an important antecedent to behaviour (Treviño et al., 2006).[1] Companies may have different motives for actively pursuing CSR. Literature often distinguishes extrinsic motives that encourages CSR because of its strategic benefits (market demand and reputation) from intrinsic motives that perceive CSR as an end in itself (Scopelliti et al., 2018; Coppa and Sriramesh, 2013; Muller and Kolk, 2010; Paulra, 2009; Aguilera et al., 2007; Child and Tsai, 2005; Lindenberg, 2001; Weaver et al., 1999; Swanson, 1999). Often, it is assumed that executives are motivated by extrinsic motives because CSR has been shown to improve a corporation's profitability (Orlitzky et al., 2003). However, non-strategic (intrinsic) motives may also drive CSR. Executives may derive personal satisfaction from CSR or may perceive CSR as a moral duty to be observed.

Previous research on the motives around CSR has produced mixed results. Several researchers have found that extrinsic motives, such as company reputation or financial performance, are more important than intrinsic motives. For example, Lougee and Wallace (2008) found that companies use CSR mainly as a form of 'risk management'. Brønn and Vidaver-Cohen (2009) found that a company's long-term interest and image feature among the most frequently mentioned reasons for CSR. In contrast, Graafland and Van de Ven (2006) found a significant relationship between CSR and intrinsic motives but no significant relationship between CSR and the strategic motive of financial benefit. Graafland and Mazereeuw-Van der Duijn Schouten (2012) found evidence of a parallel existence of strategic, ethical, and altruistic motives, but estimate that overall

DOI: 10.4324/9781003216483-8

CSR is more driven by intrinsic motives (ethical and altruistic) than by extrinsic motives (strategic).

One of the reasons for the variance in these results is a difference in the sample used. Whereas Graafland and Van de Ven (2006) and Graafland and Mazereeuw-Van der Duijn Schouten (2012) used a sample of both SMEs and large companies from the Netherlands, Brønn and Vidaver-Cohen (2009) researched 1,644 Norwegian companies with more than 50 employees and Lougee and Wallace (2008) researched only large companies rated by the S&P 500 and Domini 400. The size of the company may affect the type of motivation for CSR. SMEs are more often privately owned and managed by their owners than large companies (Lepoutre and Heene, 2006). The policies of these family businesses tend to reflect the values of the managers. Because these businesses are closer to home and to the personal lives of their managers, the CSR of SMEs is more likely to reflect the ethical concerns of the individuals involved than strategic motivations.

This chapter therefore aims to investigate two sets of research questions: 1. To what extent do intrinsic and extrinsic motives stimulate CSR? 2. How are both types of motives related to company size? In the following sections, we first introduce the hypotheses. Then we describe the methodology of the research. In section 6.4, we present the outcomes of the empirical analysis. In section 6.5, we summarize the main findings.

6.2 Conceptual Framework

In this section, we first describe the extrinsic and intrinsic motives of CSR. Next, we consider how company size may influence intrinsic and extrinsic CSR motives. The overall conceptual framework is depicted in Figure 6.1.

Extrinsic Motives

The extrinsic motive encourages CSR because it has an instrumental value for strategic benefits. It refers to the 'business case' argument (Berger et al., 2007). For companies driven by the business case for CSR, the challenge is to find the nexus of business opportunity and social responsibility and then to develop CSR initiatives that provide financial return.

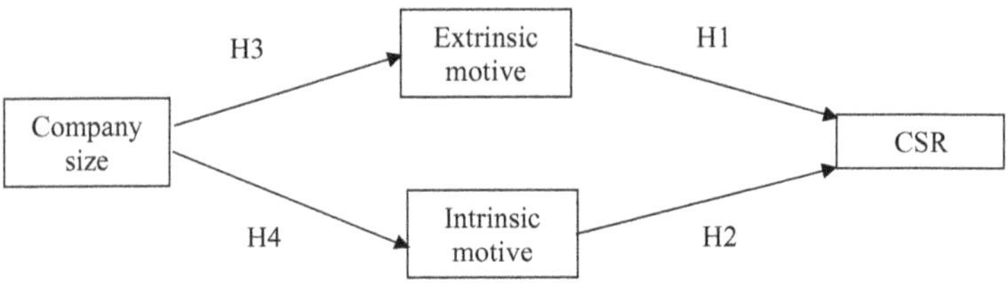

FIGURE 6.1 Conceptual framework

The strategic benefits that firms may attain from CSR derive from various sources. As theorized by the resource-based view (Branco and Rodrigues, 2006) and by stakeholder theory (Surroca et al., 2010), one of the most important strategic benefits is that CSR may enhance the company's reputation (Kurucz et al., 2008). In their study of corporate motives for CSR, Brønn and Vidaver-Cohen (2009) found that improving the company's image ranks first among 16 motives. Orlitzky (2008) noted that from theoretical and practical perspectives, organizational reputation ranks as one of the most important mediating variables linking CSR to CFP. Firms that are most vulnerable to unfavourable publicity are those with high brand recognition (Laudal, 2011) and a strong CSR programme can help limit reputational damage if accidents happen (Lougee and Wallace, 2008). For this reason, the financial market may put pressure on companies to pursue an active CSR policy.

As discussed in Chapter 4, CSR also has strategic value because it may contribute to innovation (Porter and Kramer, 2006; Clausen and Loew, 2009; Wagner, 2009, 2010; Halme and Laurila, 2009). Introducing new EMSs involves the development of strategic resources and this can have a positive impact on innovation capabilities in general (Wagner, 2007b; Frondel et al., 2007). A high level of CSR may enable firms to recruit more innovative employees, which may positively affect firm-level innovation (Turban and Greening, 1997). With environmental innovations in place and competition among firms more focused on environmental benefit, there will be greater urgency for firms to respond to social demand and try environmentally friendly alternatives (Lee et al., 2006). Managers may therefore now express interest in those approaches to CSR that are linked to innovation as a way of delivering competitive advantage.

Third, companies may be motivated to CSR because it can reduce costs and improve the (long-term) financial performance of the company. Several empirical studies found a positive relationship between CSR and profitability (Orlitzky et al., 2003; Waddock and Graves, 1997) or shareholder value (Tudway and Pascal, 2006). There are several ways in which CSR can affect profitability. First, firms investing in pollution prevention for reasons of CSR, may reduce the costs of energy, waste management, packaging and transportation, as well as the risk of accidents. Second, CSR can improve the company's output market (Brown and Dacin, 1997) and help companies to differentiate themselves from their competitors with the aim of increasing sales and market share. Goods with a high social value that serve the interest of society at large may both generate a quantity premium as well as an additional price premium (Auger et al., 2003). Consumer boycotts in reaction to a poor social reputation can operate as a social control mechanism. In the case of SMEs operating in B2B relationships, large customers may demand CSR. Third, CSR may also be rewarding by making it easier to attract qualified employees (Albinger and Freeman, 2000). This especially holds for companies that target highly educated workers. Besides the reputation effect on potential employees, good CSR will also have a direct favourable influence on the performance of the company by stimulating the commitment of the workers to the company. A good work climate may lead to more trust in the company, stronger commitment from employees, lower absenteeism and turnover rates, higher profitability and productivity, and a more positive attitude to work and good conduct (Sims and Keon, 1997; Turban and Greening, 1997). More satisfaction of the workforce, in turn, will increase the readiness of employees to invest in relation-specific assets.

A final strategic motive for CSR is that organizations that have high CSR may be more successful in avoiding regulatory intervention and in meeting existing regulations (Berman et al., 1999). If a company is environmentally proactive, it can lower the costs of complying with present and future environmental regulations as well as improve company efficiencies and drive down operating costs, resulting from net cost savings through enhanced resource use (Shrivastava, 1995; Porter and Kramer, 2011). For example, when attempting to enter new markets, companies with good CSR reputations rarely face the same level of resistance as companies with poor CSR reputations (Lougee and Wallace, 2008).

Intrinsic Motives

Besides strategic reasons, companies may also have intrinsic, non-strategic motives to pursue CSR (Kuckertz and Wagner, 2010; Muller and Kolk, 2010; Aguilera et al., 2007; Child and Tsai, 2005; Lindenberg, 2001; Weaver et al., 1999; Swanson, 1999). These can relate to the individual values and beliefs of managers. Managers' personal values can be an important motivating factor for CSR, particularly for owners of SMEs, but also for larger companies. While empirical evidence supports the view that it is CEOs that tend to establish the ethical norms for corporations, middle managers can also play an important role in acting as socially responsible agents for change and are able to display their personal values, whilst exercising managerial discretion (Hemingway and Maclagan, 2004).

Intrinsic motives perceive CSR as an end in itself, independent from financial benefits. We distinguish two types of intrinsic motives (Meijer, 2007): CSR as a responsibility towards society (i.e. a sense of felt obligation to act) and CSR as a source of personal satisfaction. The moral duty to be socially responsible can be justified by several ethical theories, for example, Kantian ethics (Evan and Freeman, 1988) and virtue ethics (Solomon, 1992). Evan and Freeman (1988) argued that according to the second formulation of Kant's categorical imperative, each stakeholder group has a moral right not to be just treated as a means to some end (maximization of the shareholder value) but as an end in itself. Management is accountable not only to shareholders but also to other stakeholders. Its task is therefore to balance the conflicting claims of a multitude of stakeholders. For our purposes, it is immaterial which moral philosophy one chooses to defend this claim. A positive moral view on CSR implies that CSR-related efforts are regarded as a moral duty towards society. That means that one is obliged to do something because it is right, not because it is enjoyable (Etzioni, 1988).

The other intrinsic motive is personal satisfaction. Executives and employees may contribute to CSR because they enjoy helping others and contributing to the common good. This is also called impure altruism (Ribar and Wilhelm, 2002) and is contrasted with so-called pure altruism where an executive values CSR solely because of its positive societal consequences (Rabin, 1998). Pure altruism therefore belongs to the former class of intrinsic motives where one supports CSR because it is right. In the case of impure altruism, executives also derive personal enjoyment from the act of performing CSR.

The Influence of Company Size on Extrinsic and Intrinsic Motivation

The type of CSR motivations a company has is not given, but will depend on the company size.

First, it is likely that extrinsic CSR motivation is positively related to company size. Institutional theory stresses that the monitoring of corporate performance by stakeholders is an important factor that increases the likelihood that companies will pursue CSR (Campbell, 2007). The strength of the reputation mechanism depends on the availability of the information about the past performance of the company. The more information is available, the more transparent is the company's performance and the easier it is for its stakeholders to punish and reward the company. An important informal institution that enforces the transparency on CSR is the presence of NGOs or media that actively monitor the CSR of a company and keep the public and government officials informed. It is likely that this reputation mechanism is stronger for large companies than for small companies because it is more rewarding for NGOs and the media to focus attention on large companies as this will attract more public attention. In particular, multinationals are targets of the NGOs; in particular, those that are brand-based and most vulnerable to consumer boycotts. NGOs will have few incentives to scrutinize small companies because it is not possible for them to examine each small company. Large firms are more visible than small firms and therefore such influences are likely to affect large firms more than small firms (Udayasankar, 2008). For this reason, Lynch-Wood and Williamson (2007) argue that the social licence motive will not be sufficient to induce SMEs to go beyond compliance with the law.

A second reason that extrinsic motives are positively related to company size is that in the short-term CSR often requires expending significant resources on such things as installing equipment (Hart, 1995). Because of their small scale, SMEs find the introduction of CSR relatively costly. The systems of large firms with well-defined management structures and decision processes to deal with external issues may be better developed and better positioned to efficiently organize CSR. Some forms of CSR may require implementation on a large scale to be effective. This will deter small firms from participating in these initiatives (Udayasankar, 2008). Many studies suppose that formal measures are generalizations which do not fit the nature of SMEs (Perrini, 2006; Russo and Tencati, 2009; Spence et al., 2003; Tilley, 2000; Welford and Frost, 2006; Welsh and White, 1981). Because of their small size, SMEs are more often organized on an informal basis and therefore less in need of formal CSR instruments than large companies. Graafland et al. (2003) indeed found that large Dutch companies make more use of instruments that foster the transparency of companies, like a code of conduct, ISO certification, and social reporting. Due to a lack of sources and experience, SMEs are less able to explicitly recognize CSR issues and are less familiar with important CSR standards (Lepoutre and Heene, 2006). Time, finances, and a lack of skills and knowledge are commonly identified as constraints to CSR by SMEs (European Commission, 2002; Studer et al., 2006). Due to their small size, it is very difficult to recruit CSR specialists. In contrast, a large firm can spread the costs of CSR over a substantial larger turnover. Because of this lack of CSR competences, SMEs seem to favour external forms of regulation rather than self-regulation, because this generates a 'level playing field' that allows them to concentrate on the economic aspects and leave social and environmental aspects to the government (Williamson et al., 2006). In line with this, Studer et al. (2006) found that legislation remains the key driver for SMEs to engage in environmental change. According to Williamson et al. (2006), this implies that the use and development of existing regulatory structures, providing minimum standards for many activities covered by CSR, remains the most effective means to influence behaviour of SMEs. On the other hand, a study by Petts et al. (1999) showed that managers of SMEs believe that regulation on its own will not be sufficient because of the inadequacies of the regulatory regimes. They estimated the pressure of the reputation mechanism to be at least as effective as the threat of prosecution.

Whereas it is likely that extrinsic motives are positively related to company size, we expect a negative relationship for intrinsic motives. Intrinsic motives may be relatively more important for SMEs because most of them are privately owned and managed by their owners (Spence, 1999; Jenkins, 2009). Family businesses have been characterized by long-term commitment, superior employee care and loyalty, long tenure of leadership, and exhibiting a strong religious/philanthropic approach to CSR (Laudal, 2011). The policies of family business tend to reflect the values of the managers (Lepoutre and Heene, 2006). One would therefore expect that family companies will be more directly concerned about CSR because of a closer relationship between the business and the personal life of the managers. Besides, director-owners will also have more freedom to weigh up financial and non-financial goals than managers in a larger company because they are free to decide how to spend their own money, whereas the manager is accountable to the owners (or shareholders) of the company. Furthermore, because of their small size, SMEs are often more oriented towards the local market and have a more intimate relationship with the community in which they operate. The personal contacts between the director-owner and various stakeholders help to build trustful partnerships in a natural way. Therefore, many scholars use the social capital approach as a tool for understanding CSR for SMEs, as informal relationships, trust, and solidarity are important aspects for SMEs (Granovetter, 2000; Murillo and Lozano, 2006; Avram and Kühne, 2008). As a result, SMEs are more sensitive to signals from local customers and suppliers and this will foster an attitude of responsibility towards the community and enforce the intrinsic motivation to CSR.

Set of Hypotheses

Based on these arguments, we hypothesize that:

Hypothesis 6.1 Extrinsic motives stimulate CSR.
Hypothesis 6.2 Intrinsic motives stimulate CSR.
Hypothesis 6.3 Extrinsic motivation is positively related to company size.
Hypothesis 6.4 Intrinsic motivation is negatively related to company size.

6.3 Methodology

In this section, we present the methodology we use to empirically test the hypotheses. The data were taken from the survey conducted in 2011. The distribution of the size of the companies is reported in Table 6.1. It shows that a relatively small share of the sample concerns large companies with more than 250 employees.

CSR was measured by 76 indicators, which can be grouped into three subindicators on instruments, the social dimension of CSR and an environmental dimension of CSR (see Table 6.2). The first scale refers to the general organizational management instruments to integrate CSR into the company's organization (Ulrich et al., 1998). Examples are training managers and other employees in CSR, CSR-related remuneration, or management and reporting systems. Management systems can be divided into those that concern environmental issues (e.g. ISO 14001, EMAS, or Greenhouse Gas Protocol) or social issues (e.g. SA8000). The ISO 14001 standard deals with EMSs. The Greenhouse Gas Protocol (GHG Protocol) is an international accounting tool to understand, quantify, and manage greenhouse gas emissions. Besides the use of management systems, companies can create relationships with external stakeholders. Examples are an active dialogue

TABLE 6.1 Company size and sample distribution

Size (in FTE)	*0–10*	*11–50*	*50–100*	*100–250*	*>250*
%	27	37	18	8	9

TABLE 6.2 Measurement of CSR indices[a]

Index	*Sub indices*	*mean*	*SD*
Instruments	Average score on: internal code, external code, dialogue with NGOs, cooperation in supply chain, partnerships, participation in local initiatives, director is answerable to CSR, CSR-related remuneration, confidential person, ethics committee, CSR training of employees, reference guide, membership global initiatives, ISO 9001, ISO 14001, SA8000, and other certifications (42–59)	27	20
Social aspects	Average score for measurement, targeting, reporting, efforts to improve CSR, and change in outcomes in CSR during 2007–2010 on the following aspects: women in the board, recruitment of disadvantaged workers, work–life balance, employee training, work accidents, and working conditions suppliers (60–66, 74–87)	43	11
Environmental aspects	Average score for measurement, targeting, reporting, efforts to improve CSR, and change in outcomes in CSR during 2007–2010 on the following aspects: CO2 emission, energy consumption, water consumption, waste disposal, and environmental conditions suppliers (90–106)	12	15
Overall	Average of sub indicators	27	12

a All sub-indices are scaled to the range from 0 (lowest value) to 100 (highest value). The numbers in brackets refer to the numbers of the survey questions reported in Appendix 1.

with NGOs, cooperation with other companies in the supply chain, partnerships with professional training institutes, and participation in the local initiatives of governments or social organizations in order to achieve CSR objectives.

The second and third scales measure six social and five environmental aspects of CSR, respectively. While environmental aspects are considered as prevailing in the CSR debate, the social dimension is perceived to be comparatively underexposed. In our research, we therefore also include various quality-of-job dimensions, namely gender equality, diversity and non-discrimination, work organization and work–life balance, skills and life-long learning, health and working conditions, and respect for human rights in the supply chain. For each environmental and social aspect, we included questions on three procedural instruments that facilitate the organization of CSR accountability in the company (which is an important aspect of AA 1000), a question on efforts to improve performance on the specific issue and a question on improvements in the outcomes of each social and environmental aspect during the period 2007–2010. The three procedural measures that we examined are a measurement of the actual outcomes, the use of targets for improving outcomes in the future, and whether the company reports the achievement of these targets (RARE, 2006). The question on efforts does not refer to formal procedures or instruments but rather measures the informal efforts that companies put into CSR. We included this measure in our survey because our pilot interviews indicated that SMEs may actually proactively foster their CSR without using the formal procedures or programmes that are more often used by large companies. Merely measuring the use of formal instruments to implement CSR may therefore bias the measurement of the actual implementation of CSR by SMEs.

The respondent's view on the CSR motivation of the company was measured by eight questions. Six of them refer to extrinsic motivations and two refer to intrinsic motivations. Table 6.3 shows that, on average, the two intrinsic motivations (responsibility and personal satisfaction) are the most important motives. The expected long-term effect on profitability turns out to be the least important motive. We performed an exploratory factor analysis using principal component analysis with an Oblimin rotation to test whether the various types of motivations can be clustered.

The outcomes of Table 6.3 show that the eight motives can be grouped into two factors. The first factor comprises the six extrinsic motives; the second factor

TABLE 6.3 Motives of CSR[a]

Your company engages in CSR activities because:	*Mean*	*SD*	*Factor loadings*	
It serves the long-term financial interests of shareholders and/or director owner (20)	3.78	1.84	0.65	
It helps to meet (future) government regulations (21)	4.14	1.68	0.57	
It leads to innovation (22)	4.69	1.60	0.79	
It reduces operational costs (23)	4.30	1.70	0.66	
It limits reputational risks (24)	4.57	1.59	0.81	
Large customers ask for it (27)	3.95	1.88	0.61	
Your enterprise feels responsible for the planet and society (25)	5.23	1.48		0.88
It creates personal satisfaction for the people in your enterprise (26)	5.10	1.42		0.85
Initial Eigen value			3.60	1.14
Proportion of total variance			45.1	14.2
Cronbach's alpha reliability			0.80	0.73

a Mean response to the seven-point scale ranging from 'not at all' (1) to 'very much' (7). The numbers in brackets refer to the numbers of the survey questions reported in Appendix 1. Factor analysis: Extraction Method: Principal Component Analysis; Rotation Method: Oblimin with Kaiser Normalization; Pattern Matrix.

the two intrinsic motives. The loadings of the items are all significant (Hair et al., 1998). Bartlett's test of sphericity (Chi-square = 21675; $df = 28$; $p = 0.000$) and the Kaiser–Meyer–Olkin (KMO) measure of sampling adequacy (0.843) show that there are sufficient numbers of significant correlations among the items that justify to undertake a factor analysis (Pett et al., 2003). Based on these results, we construct two motive variables, extrinsic motive as an average of the reputation, innovation, profit, cost reduction, regulation, and customer motives and intrinsic motives as an average of the responsibility and personal satisfaction motive.

6.4 Results

Table 6.4 reports the estimation results of the multivariate regression analysis.

The results in the first column show that extrinsic motivation is positively related to company size, which supports Hypothesis 6.3. The estimation results in the second column of Table 6.4 rejects Hypothesis 6.4 that intrinsic motivation is negatively related to company size. The third column reports the estimation results for CSR. The estimation results show that both the extrinsic motive and intrinsic motive have a significant influence on CSR. Intrinsic motivation has a significant higher influence on CSR than extrinsic motivation. We also find significant direct effects for company size. Large companies show significantly higher CSR than very small companies (which is used as the reference dummy).

6.5 Conclusion

In this chapter, we researched the relationships between intrinsic and extrinsic motivations, company size, and CSR. We found that both intrinsic and extrinsic motivations significantly increase CSR and that intrinsic motivations have a (significantly) larger influence than extrinsic motivations.

TABLE 6.4 Results of regression analysis[a]

	Extrinsic motivation	*Intrinsic motivation*	*CSR*
	1	2	3
Extrinsic motive			0.18***
Intrinsic motive			0.29***
Size: 11–50	0.05**	0.01	0.12***
Size: 50–100	0.08***	0.03*	0.18***
Size: 100–250	0.06***	0.02	0.17***
Size >250	0.11***	0.05**	0.29***
R^2	0.040	0.015	0.302

a standardized coefficients; * $p < 0.05$; ** $p < 0.01$; and *** $p < 0.001$. Very small companies are used as reference. Controlled for sectors and countries.

Extrinsic CSR motivation is positively related to company size. Opposite to our expectations, intrinsic motivation also tends to increase with company size. This is in line with Jamali et al. (2008) who found that SMEs and large companies rate their stakeholders in a similar way. One of the explanations may be that regulation is relatively more important for SMEs and that extensive government regulations may crowd out intrinsic motivations. Managers of a company who intrinsically care for the health and welfare of their employees will take precautionary measures to protect them. But external health regulations imposed by the law may well discourage that proactive attitude and reduce intrinsic motivation (Frey, 1998).

Note

1 In the four component analysis of Rest et al. (1999), moral motivation is the element that immediately informs behaviour and mediates the influence of moral awareness and moral judgment on ethical behaviour.

7

FAMILY BUSINESS OWNERSHIP, FAMILY MANAGEMENT, AND COMPANY SIZE*

7.1 Introduction

Family business ownership (FBO) has been proposed to stimulate cleaner production (Berrone et al., 2010). In the literature, the motives that encourage family businesses to adopt CSR practices have often been linked to the concept of socioemotional wealth (SEW). Socioemotional wealth refers to the nonfinancial aspects of the firm that meet the family's affective needs (Zellweger et al., 2011) such as the family's image, binding social ties, and emotional attachment to the firm (Berrone et al., 2012). Socioemotional wealth may provide an extra motive for family businesses to improve their CSR. For example, if better EP increases the family's image, this creates an incentive for family companies to engage in environmental practices. However, recent theoretical research has argued that SEW is ambiguous in nature and that, because of concern about SEW, family owners might adopt a selective and instrumental approach to CSR as a means of obtaining various self-interested gains (Le Breton-Miller and Miller, 2016).

In this study, we focus on the environmental dimension of CSR. Empirical studies on the link between FBO and EP are still scarce and have produced contradictory findings. Among the 27 studies discussed in an overview article on social issues in family enterprise by Van Gils et al. (2014), only a few researched the relationship between FBO and EP. Dyer and Whetten (2006) and Berrone et al. (2010) found that family firms have significantly better EP than non-family firms, whereas Cruz et al. (2014) did not find a significant relationship between FBO and EP. Craig and Dibrell (2006) found, on one hand, that non-family companies have a more positive attitude towards the natural environment than family companies, but, on the other hand, that family firms are better able to leverage capabilities associated with the natural environment into greater innovation

DOI: 10.4324/9781003216483-9

or financial performance. This lack of consistent empirical findings may be due to the different samples and different measures of key constructs. But, given the ambiguity in the predictions of SEW theory, these disparate findings may also suggest several contextual factors that create contingencies in the FBO–EP relationship (López-González et al., 2019).

In order to increase the insight into these factors, we set out to research two conditions that moderate the FBO–EP relationship. First, it is likely that it is contingent on the representation of family members in the management of the company. In contrast to López-González et al. (2019), who researched the moderating effect of family involvement in management (FIM) on the relationship between FBO and CSR (which includes, among others, EP), we expect that this moderation effect is non-linear. Although the SEW theory suggests that FIM strengthens the FBO–EP relationship, firms that are fully managed by family members may also pursue narrow-minded policies that benefit the family rather than other stakeholders' interests. Non-family members in the management team who participate in a wider variety of stakeholder-oriented activities may then stimulate EP (Yong Oh et al., 2011). Secondly, this chapter contributes to previous scientific literature by studying company size as a moderating variable. If family firms grow larger, the relationships between family members and the various types of stakeholders become more distant (Le Breton-Miller and Miller, 2016). This weakens the relationship between FBO and EP.

This chapter contributes to the literature by researching the previously untested hypotheses that the relationship between FBO and EP is moderated by company size and (non-linearly) by the FIM. The core research question is therefore: How does FBO affect EP and how do family involvement in management and firm size moderate this relationship? The hypotheses are tested on a sample of 3,816 companies that includes both family and non-family companies and companies of different sizes, as well as companies displaying different degrees of managerial involvement by family members. The next sections present the conceptual framework, methodology, results, followed by the conclusion.

7.2 Conceptual Framework

In this section, a conceptual model is developed that specifies how FBO affects EP (see Figure 7.1). FBO is defined as the share of equity owned by the family (Anderson and Reeb, 2003). FIM is the share of family members in the management of the company. Both FBO and FIM are dimensions of family involvement in the definition offered by O'Boyle et al. (2010: 311): 'family involvement in a company represents a substantial family presence in ownership, governance, management, succession, and/or employment'.

In the following section, first the SEW theory and its predictions regarding the relationship between FBO and EP are described. Next, the moderation by FIM (Hypothesis 7.1) and company size (Hypothesis 7.2) are discussed.

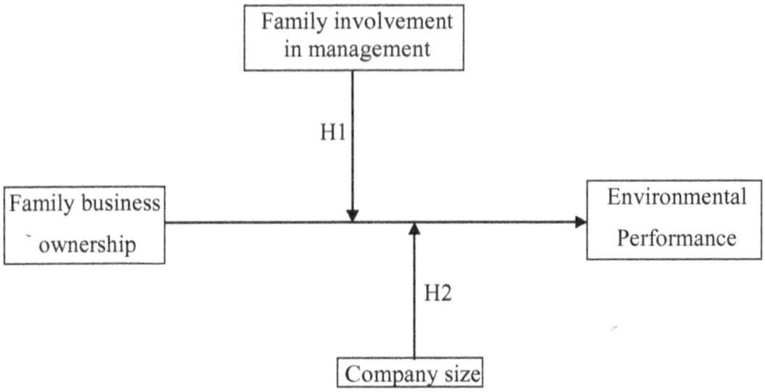

FIGURE 7.1 Conceptual framework

SEW Theory on Family Business Ownership and Environmental Performance

One of the lenses used to explain the FBO-EP relationship is SEW theory. Maintaining SEW has an intrinsic value to family members whose identity is inextricably tied to the organization (Sharma and Sharma, 2011; Brigham et al., 2014). Berrone et al. (2012) proposed five dimensions (labelled as FIBER): family control and influence; identification of family members with the firm; binding social ties; emotional attachment to the firm; and renewal of family bonds to the firm through dynastic succession.

As SEW is unique to family companies, family-owned companies will be more inclined to pursue environmental policies than non-family companies if it can be shown that SEW stimulates corporate environmental responsibility. The literature has given several arguments for this proposition (Berrone et al., 2010). First, the identification with the firm of family members makes them sensitive about the image of the firm (Campopiano et al., 2019). This creates incentives to improve EP because EP might contribute to the corporate reputation, and hence, as family and the business are conceptualized by the stakeholders as one and the same, to the family's image (Sánchez-Medina and Díaz-Pichardo, 2017). Secondly, binding social ties promote collective social capital, relational trust, and feelings of closeness and interpersonal solidarity (Marques et al., 2014). These reciprocal bonds are not limited to family members but are likely to extend to a wider range of stakeholders (Berrone et al., 2012). Given these reciprocal bonds in family businesses, these firms are more inclined to pursue the welfare of those who surround them. Thirdly, because of the emotional attachments of family managers to their business, family managers might exhibit marked levels of stewardship over the continuity of the family business (Miller et al., 2008). Together with the ability and willingness to pass the business on to the next generation (transgenerational succession), this will give family businesses an incentive to pursue environmental strategies, as they will contribute to the stability of the firm's prospects (Le Breton-Miller and Miller, 2006; Delmas and Gergaud, 2014). Since the family business supports multiple family members belonging to the present and perhaps future generations and wants to ensure them a better future, SEW considerations will instil a long time-horizon vis-à-vis the business. As attending to the environmental demands of society requires long-term vision, family companies are more likely to engage in environmental policies than non-family-owned companies (Berrone et al., 2010).

However, recent literature has argued that family companies may also have a dark side and that particular SEW elements can be positively as well as negatively valenced (Zientara, 2017). For example, Miller and Le Breton-Miller (2014) argued that the family members' desire for control over a business and guaranteed security for later generations may induce dysfunctional conservatism. This conservatism may give rise to resistance over revitalising the firm (Le Breton-Miller and Miller, 2016) and weaken the incentive to undertake risky investments in environmental improvements.

Based on these arguments, we conclude that the predictions of the SEW theory regarding the relationship between FBO and EP are ambiguous.

The (Non-linear) Moderating Role of Family Involvement in Management

The ambiguity in the relationship between FBO and EP might suggest that this relationship is contingent. Following López-González et al. (2019), we propose that family involvement in management (FIM) might moderate this relationship. But in contrast to López-González et al. (2019), we argue that the moderating influence of FIM is non-linear instead of linear. On one hand, and as argued by López-González et al. (2019), family involvement in management might strengthen the positive relationship between FBO and EP. If family owners are involved in the management of the company, their identification with the firm and the importance of the firm's reputation will be stronger than if they are not involved in the management. This will enforce the incentives to improve EP, as EP is likely to enhance the firm's image in the communities and networks in which it participates (Zellweger et al., 2011; Marques et al., 2014). Second, if family owners are more involved in the management of the company, they more frequently personally interact with stakeholders, and this strengthens social binding ties between a family and its stakeholders and community. This will make them more inclined to contribute to the wider societal interests by improving EP. Bingham et al. (2011) found that firms with higher FIM have greater concern for the broader collective's welfare and therefore adopt a more collectivist than individualistic stakeholder orientation. Thirdly, FIM will increase the emotional commitment to the firm. Lamb and Butler (2018) argued that owners who are also managers of the company are more likely to behave like stewards. In combination with the long tenure of family managers, this stewardship mentality will make them more inclined to improve EP than non-family managers.

On the other hand, beyond a certain level, more FIM may signal a family's preference for excessive family control over the firm. Some scholars have argued that family control over the firm (one of the five SEW dimensions proposed by Berrone et al. (2012)) has a negative influence on EP (Miller and Le Breton-Miller, 2014). If the family is heavily involved in management, these members might experience greater pressure to perform well financially, in order to justify their position to other family members (Block and Wagner, 2014) or to adopt policies that benefit the family rather than other stakeholders (Chang, 2003; Yong Oh et al., 2011). If managers own a significant share of equity, they are more likely to make decisions maximizing shareholders' value (Denis et al., 1997). Small business literature has shown that business performance is the overarching driver of environmental actions by SMEs (Williamson et al., 2006). The level-playing field on which most SMEs (the majority of which consists of family-owned companies) operate means that they face severe competition and this puts attention to EP under pressure (Ates and Bititci, 2011; Graafland, 2016). As Stoian and Gilman (2017) showed that environmental responsibility reduces economic growth of SMEs, a strong profit orientation of fully family-owned companies will discourage EP. Worries about family security may give rise to risk aversion, conservative policies, and a myopia that precludes moving beyond narrow market boundaries (Miller and Le Breton-Miller, 2014). Research has shown that if family power goes unchecked and is not balanced by independent directors, opportunistic behaviour by the family may increase (Anderson and Reeb, 2004). Furthermore, Le Breton-Miller and Miller (2016) argued that if management is fully in the hands of family members, there is a danger of narrow-mindedness, because there are no influential outsiders to introduce new and broader perspectives. This may blind the family members to emerging environmental trends and make them less likely to invest in EP. Non-family members in the management team, having more varied experience and views, may then help prevent narrow-minded family concerns dominating the company strategy. They can assist an organization in dealing with its business environment by participation in a wider variety of stakeholder-oriented activities (Yong Oh et al., 2011). Creating more diversity by employing outside managers will then foster EP.

Consequently, we surmise a non-linear moderation effect, the relationship between FBO and EP becoming more positive when FIM is increasing, but only up to some level of FIM. Beyond this level, the relationship between FBO and EP becomes more negative. This leads to the first hypothesis:

Hypothesis 7.1 The influence of FBO on EP is non-linearly moderated by the FIM.

The Moderating Role of Company Size

Le Breton-Miller and Miller (2016) argued that family firms will engage less in sustainable behaviour when they become larger, because, as firms grow large, they become more impersonal. SEW dimensions, which distinguish family from non-family companies, may therefore be less important for large companies than for small companies. Hence, the difference in EP between family and non-family companies is likely to decline with company size.

First, it is expected that the personal identification of family members with the firm will decline with company size. Le Breton-Miller and Miller (2016) acknowledged, however, that this may not always occur. If, for example, the family name is on the firm, the identity of family members is still strongly related to the business. As argued by Deephouse and Jaskiewicz (2013), the presence of the family's name in the firm's name raises the family members' awareness of the membership of the family business and make them more conscious of their position in the community. However, the correspondence between the name of the family company and the name of an individual family member is also likely to diminish over time if, for example, daughters of family members take their husbands' names after marriage. Company size is likely to be related to company age and hence to family size. The overlap in the identity of the family member and that of the firm will thus become smaller if the company grows larger. Less identification with the family firm diminishes the importance of pursuing a favourable corporate reputation that enables family members to 'feel good about who they are and what they do' (Deephouse and Jaskiewicz, 2013).

Other SEW concerns, such as binding social ties, emotional commitment, and renewal of family bonds to the firm through dynastic succession, will also be weaker in large family companies than in small family companies (Berrone et al., 2012). Less-frequent personal interaction between family members and stakeholders makes the emotional connection between a family and its stakeholders and community more remote. Since SEW dimensions distinguish family companies from non-family companies and encourage EP, the weakening of SEW dimensions due to a rise in company size will decrease the positive difference in EP between family and non-family firms. Hence, it is expected that the relationship between FBO and EP is negatively moderated by company size.

Based on these arguments, we propose:

Hypothesis 7.2 Company size negatively moderates the influence of family business ownership on EP.

7.3 Methodology

Family business involvement was measured using two survey questions on FBO and FIM in the 2014 survey. Respondents were asked whether the company is fully, partly, or not owned by a family and whether the business was fully, partly, or not managed by family members. Fifty four per cent of the companies were fully and 13% were partly family-owned companies and 33% was not family owned. 45% were fully managed by family members, 18% by a combination of family and non-family members, and 36 % were not managed by family members (see Table 7.1). Based on the responses, measures for FBO and FIM were constructed, ranging from 1 for fully family owned, 0.5 for partly family owned, and 0.0 for non-family-owned companies, respectively, 1 for fully family managed, 0.5 for partly family managed, and 0.0 for non-family managed. For small enterprises, the number of owners or managers in the company is not very large and this three-part division seems sufficient. In the literature, authors have often used binary measurements for larger companies (Martínez-Ferrero et al., 2016) and found no difference if more continuous measurements were used (Chrisman and Patel, 2012).

Company size was measured by the (natural logarithm of the) number of employees (in full time equivalent (FTE)). Many small firms participated in the survey: 35% were micro companies (FTE ≤ 10), 36% were small companies (10 < FTE ≤ 50), 22% were medium-sized companies (50 < FTE ≤ 250), and 7% large companies (>250 FTE).

Environmental performance (EP) was measured by the use of two environmental procedures – setting targets to improve environmental outcomes and reporting the realization of these targets – for energy consumption, water consumption, waste disposal, and environmental conditions of suppliers. Target setting is a proven management tool to reduce energy consumption, waste disposal, and water consumption (see Chapter 2). Wakabayashi and Arimura (2016) also employ self-reported data on the use of targets to measure EP. Reporting provides an instrument for analysing to what extent the outcomes, once realized, meet the targets (Mitchell and Hill, 2009). Reporting requires the collection of data and an analysis of these data. Based on these reports, companies can plan for improvement and redefine targets (Hummels and Karssing, 2007). The advantage of these data on EP is that the questions are simple, concise, and inquire into

TABLE 7.1 Sample characteristics (in %)[a]

Family Business ownership (3)	*Family involvement in management (4–5)*				*Company size (114)*	
	Full	*Partial*	*Not*	*Total*		
Full	41	11	2	54	Micro:≤10 FTE	35
Partial	4	7	1	13	Small:10–50 FTE	36
Not	0	0	33	33	Medium:51–250 FTE	22
Total	45	18	37	100	Large (>250 FTE)	7

a The numbers in brackets refer to the number of the survey question reported in Appendix 1.

very specific activities. By asking simple yes/no questions to measure the implementation of very concrete practices, one reduces ambiguity in the response to the survey question (Podsakoff et al., 2003). Moreover, social desirability bias is reduced because false answers would boil down to conscious lying. This is supported by the low scores for the share of companies adopting these procedural measures, ranging from 19% for waste to 16% for energy, 14% for water, and 9% for environmental conditions of suppliers (confirming that involving suppliers is a more ambiguous form of EP). These low scores indicate that the responses to these survey questions are not biased by social desirability bias and thus provide reasonable reliable indicators. Based on the responses, four measures for energy consumption, water consumption, waste disposal, and environmental conditions of suppliers were constructed with three options per measure: 0 if the company did not report or use targets; 0.5 if only one of these procedures was used; and 1 if both were employed. We performed confirmatory factor analysis to research the validity of the constructs of EP. The measurement model was estimated by SEM in STATA (for the estimation results, see Table 7.2). The composite reliability equals 0.84 and the average variance extracted 0.57, which both meet the condition for convergent validity.

When testing for moderation, one should control for the linear influence of the moderating variables. Therefore, we controlled for FIM and company size.

TABLE 7.2 Estimation results of environmental performance[a]

	1	*2*	*3*
FBO	0.20*	0.08	0.22*
FIM	0.05	−0.03	0.04
FBO * FIM	−0.02		−0.04
FBO * FIM²	−0.23*		−0.24*
Ln company size	0.20***	0.19***	0.19***
FBO * ln company size		−0.07*	−0.08**
Measurement model of environmental performance			
Energy consumption	0.80***	0.80***	0.77***
Water consumption	0.80***	0.80***	0.80***
Waste disposal	0.81***	0.81***	0.81***
Environmental conditions of suppliers	0.61***	0.61***	0.61***
Global fit indices			
RMSEA	0.022	0.923	0.021
CFI	0.977	0.976	0.977
TLI	0.968	0.966	0.967

a Standardized coefficients. * $p < 0.05$, ** $p < 0.01$, and *** $p < 0.001$. Robust standard errors. Controlled for the age of the firm, presence of the family's name in the firm's name, skill level, age structure, type of respondent, organizational culture, sector, region, position in the chain, and intensity of price competition. Details of the measurement and statistics of the control variables are reported in Appendices 1 and 2.

7.4 Results

Table 7.2 reports the estimation results. Structural equation modelling (SEM) in STATA with maximum likelihood with missing values was used. Non-linearity is tested by using the interaction between FBO and FIM as well as between FBO and squared FIM.

The estimation results in the first column show that FBO has a positive effect on EP and that the influence of FBO is negatively moderated by squared (standardized) FIM. These findings support Hypothesis 7.1 and imply that the influence of FBO on EP is maximal if FIM is equal to the sample average, which indicates a hump-shaped relationship.

The estimation results in the second column of Table 7.2 show that the interaction term of FBO and company size has a significant negative effect on EP, which provides support for Hypothesis 7.2.

These results are robust if we test the interaction effects simultaneously (see column 3). In this integrated model, both hypotheses are confirmed.

Besides the interaction terms, we find a significant positive direct effect of firm size on EP. This is in line with other research that found a positive relationship between company size and CSR and can be explained by the increase in visibility (Lynch-Wood and Williamson, 2007). Large companies attract more attention of NGOs and media (Graafland and Smid, 2017) than small firms and face more pressure from customers and other stakeholders. These stakeholders are inclined to ascribe more environmental responsibility to large firms than small firms because a large firm has more means and is more powerful than a small firm. This size effect is not only unique for family-owned businesses but also applies to non-family-owned companies and therefore does not moderate the effect of FBO on EP. Interestingly, this positive stakeholder-driven effect of company size on EP is opposite to its (negative) moderation effect. The latter effect reflects that an increase in company size weakens the emotional connection of family members with the stakeholders of the firm (e.g. employees, customers, suppliers, and representatives of local NGOs or local community). Overall, the estimation results in Table 7.2 show that the positive direct effect of company size on EP dominates the negative moderation effect for the whole range of companies.[1]

7.5 Conclusion

Recent theoretical and empirical research has found that the influence of FBO on CSR is ambivalent (Cruz et al., 2014; Zientara, 2017). This has stimulated research into moderating factors in the relationship between FBO and CSR, both theoretically (Le Breton-Miller and Miller, 2016) and empirically (López-González et al., 2019).

This chapter contributes to the scientific literature by analysing the moderating effects of company size and family involvement in management on the relationship between FBO and EP. This study is the first to show empirically that company size negatively moderates the influence of FBO on EP. The positive relationship between FBO and EP for small companies is reversed into a negative relationship for large companies. Previous empirical studies into the relationship between FBO and EP by Dyer and Whetten (2006), Berrone et al. (2010), and Craig and Dibrell (2006) did not investigate the moderating role of company size. Since family businesses are, on average, relatively small in comparison with non-family companies, family ownership and company size are highly related. Identifying the moderating effect of company size on the FBO-EP relationship thus requires a large sample of companies that vary in size and ownership. A major strength of this research is the use of a unique database that comprises data of EP, family ownership, and management for 3,816 enterprises including family and non-family companies of micro, small, medium and large size, which enables an accurate analysis of differences in the relationship between FBO and EP that are due to variation in company size.

Second, whereas previous literature theorized that family involvement in management might explain contingencies in the FBO-EP relationship (López-González et al., 2019), it did not conceive possible non-linearities in this moderating relationship. In this study we delve into the 'how' of the interaction between FBO and family management involvement by theorizing that the moderation effect is non-linear. More specifically, we argue that the relationship between FBO and EP is more positive for family owned businesses that are jointly managed by family and non-family members than for family companies that are either fully family managed or not managed by family members at all. We also provide empirical evidence of non-linearity in the moderating influence of FIM. We show that these results can explain the ambiguity in the relationship between FBO and EP. By theorizing and empirically testing this contingency, this study clarifies the boundaries in the generalizability of a positive FBO-EP relationship and alters scientific understanding of the role of family involvement in management in this relationship. These findings divert from most other studies that have found that EP or CSR rises with FIM (Niehm et al., 2008; O'Boyle et al., 2010; Bingham et al., 2011; Marques et al., 2014), but did not test for moderation of the FBO-EP relationship. The findings of this study also differ from López-González et al. (2019) who did test for moderation and found that FIM positively moderates the relationship between FBO and CSR. However, in their study López-González et al. (2019) analysed dimensions of CSR relating to internal stakeholders (mostly aspects of employee relations) and external stakeholders (including human rights, customer and supplier relations, general stakeholder issues, and charity) rather than EP. Furthermore, they did not test for a non-linear moderating influence of FIM on the relationship between FBO and CSR. The non-linear moderating influence of FIM illustrates a dark side of family companies and suggests that SEW considerations may not always foster EP. When the firm is fully managed by family members, narrow minded policies that benefit the family may receive more priority than policies that contribute to other stakeholders' interests, preventing investments in environmental improvements.

Another contribution is that this study explains contingencies in the FBO–EP relationship by SEW theory. We do not only reaffirm the relevance of SEW theory but also improve it by showing the ambiguity of its predictions under different conditions. The study suggests a more nuanced look at how SEW shapes the decision-making within family firms and offers an explanation of the variance in the relationship between FBO and EP by considering two contextual factors that arbitrate under which conditions family firms are more apt to perform environmentally well than non-family firms.

Notes

* An extended text of this chapter has been published in: Graafland, J.J. (2020). Family business ownership and cleaner production: Moderation by company size and family management. *Journal of Cleaner Production*, 255: article 120120.

1 Summing up both effects gives: 0.19 * ln company size * (1 – (0.08 / 0.19) * FBO^n). FBO^n denotes normalized FBO. The effect of company size on EP is positive if FBO^n < 0.19/0.08, which holds for the whole sample of companies.

8

WOMEN IN MANAGEMENT AND RELATIONAL ENVIRONMENTAL MANAGEMENT INSTRUMENTS*

8.1 Introduction

Research into the relationship between gender diversity – defined in this study as the share of women in management positions – and EP has produced mixed findings (Rao and Tilt, 2016). Whereas some studies found no relationship between gender diversity in management and EP (Schaper, 2002; Galbreath, 2011; Deschênes et al., 2015; Cucari et al., 2018), other studies found that the two are positively associated (Post et al., 2011; Ciocirlan and Pettersson, 2012; Kassinis et al., 2016; Birindelli et al., 2019). Earlier research used samples of large publicly traded companies but there are to date no studies available that have analysed the gender–EP link for SMEs. SMEs are central to the efforts to achieve sustainable development because they cause approximately 64% of the industrial pollution in Europe (Prieto-Sandoval et al., 2019). Moreover, carrying out tests on a sample of SMEs might help to better identify the relationship between gender diversity and EP, as our findings are unfiltered by the bureaucratic processes of larger corporations and avoid environmental findings driven more by legislation (from which small business are often excused) than by voluntary practice.

Another gap in the literature is that previous studies did not analyse mediating mechanisms that explain the positive relationship between gender diversity in management and EP. SMEs have profiles that are notably distinct from those of their larger counterparts (Wickert et al., 2016). These are of theoretical interest when researching why women managers have an effect on the EP of businesses. The close community connections familiar in small firms allow for higher levels of social capital, reciprocity, and trust from stakeholders (Lähdesmäki et al., 2019). Rather than emphasizing hierarchical and bureaucratic control, relational management approaches are more productive and effective (Spence, 2016). As women are thought to pay more attention to informal relationships (Williams and Polman,

DOI: 10.4324/9781003216483-10

2015), it is expected that a higher representation of women in management will stimulate the firm to use relational management instruments that produce more substantial environmental impacts in SMEs than standardized instruments.

To fill both gaps, this chapter addresses the following research question: How does the gender composition of management affect the EP of SMEs and what is the role of relational management instruments in this relationship? The chapter contributes in two ways to the literature. First, this study is the first that researches the influence of gender structures of management on the EP of SMEs rather than large businesses. Second, this study not only analyses the relationship between gender diversity in management and EP but also generates insight into the 'how' of this relationship by researching the mediating role of relational management instruments.

8.2 Conceptual Framework

Gender and Relational Environmental Management Instruments

A widespread, though not uncontested, belief is that men differ in relational orientation from women (Held, 2006). According to gender socialization theory (Gilligan, 1982; Setó-Pamies, 2015), men and women may respond differently to the same set of conditions due to differences in their early social development, and these differences will persist even if they take on similar positions in the workspace environment. Playing activities teach girls collaboration and connection from a young age and it is a natural progression that the scope of relationships widens when growing older. Women are therefore more concerned about the commitments that arise out of relationships (Williams and Polman, 2015). For men, moral interactions are more likely to take place primarily at the political and legal level, in the realm of abstract laws and social contracts (Held, 2006).

Furthermore, the social role theory predicts that the social context puts pressure on men and women to fulfil certain societal expectations. Violating these expectations can result in social disapproval (Heilman et al., 2004). Men are usually socialized into agentic values involving self-expansion, self-assertion, and mastery and are positively evaluated if they show self-reliance, competitiveness, aggressiveness, and success. They are task-oriented and their self-schema (i.e. the way individuals think about themselves in their social interactions) has been characterized as instrumental and self-confident (Belansky and Boggiano, 1994). In contrast, women are more socialized into communal values reflecting a concern for others (Williams and Polman, 2015). They are positively valued if they express attributes that are relationship-oriented and socially sensitive (Eagly, 1987). Their self-schema can be characterized as reflective or interpersonal oriented (Spence and Helmreich, 1980) and their leadership styles have been shown to be more participative, democratic, and communal (Setó-Pamies, 2015). The ability to connect to others and to operate in a social context stimulates women managers to take into account a broader range of stakeholders. Women have wide networks of contacts from previous work experiences (Galbreath, 2011).

Women managers are therefore more likely than their male counterparts to bring in diverse stakeholder perspectives and pursue long-term strategies that can be helpful in addressing EP (Birindelli et al., 2019). Building and maintaining relationships with stakeholders is an acknowledged core element of CSR (Hawn and Ioannou, 2016). Stakeholder relations are, according to Dahlsrud (2008), one of the five qualifying dimensions of CSR (besides the economic, social, environmental, and voluntariness dimensions). CSR requires that while economic shareholders need to be understood and attended to, the interests of a much larger group of stakeholders (including employees, suppliers, communities, and governments) should also be taken into account. It is important to connect productively to these other stakeholders if the company wants to find common ground between the business and stakeholder interests. CSR therefore fits well with a relational orientation in the ethics of women managers.

Based on the gender socialization theory and social role theory, we conjecture that, because of their relational orientation, women managers are more inclined to make more use of relational environmental management instruments (abbreviated by REMIs) than male managers. SMEs can use various types of management instruments to improve their EP. REMIs are non-standardized, company specific, and tailor-made tools by which businesses strive to improve their EP in cooperation with various stakeholders. These relationships, collaborations, and networks provide SMEs with valuable input that can be used to improve EP. It therefore follows that the higher the share of women in management, the more the organization will employ REMIs to improve its EP.

However, as described by the critical mass theory (Kanter, 1977), women managers may only have a marginal influence on corporate decision-making if their share in management is very small. The number of women in management must reach a certain threshold to enabling them to influence major strategic decisions (Fernández-Feijoo et al., 2014). This suggests that the influence of women managers on a firm's environmental policies is non-linear and progressively increases with the share of women in management. Based on these arguments and findings, we postulate that the effect of more women in management on the use of REMIs is positive and non-linear:

Hypothesis 8.1 Having more women in management has a positive, non-linear, effect on an SME's use of relational environmental management instruments.

Relational Management Instruments and Environmental Performance of SMEs

Relational management instruments are closely related to the concept of environmental collaborations introduced by Wassmer et al. (2014) (e.g. arrangements between a firm and one or more other organizations with the goal of reducing negative or generating positive environmental impact in domains such as energy, resource efficiency, and natural resource depletion). A growing literature and awareness has emerged on the importance of relational approaches to environmental responsibility (Perz et al., 2010).

REMIs are particularly appropriate for small businesses in improving environmental impacts because they are often part of a larger enterprise's network of suppliers or of a local network of SMEs (Battaglia et al., 2010). As small firms have limited expertise and financial resources to invest in environmentally responsible practices (Prieto-Sandoval et al., 2019), REMIs are helpful in bringing EP expertise to the small business. Collaboration with suppliers and customers in the supply chain, or with knowledge institutions or networks for co-development of new products or processes, compensates for a lack of technical capacity and business skills in small businesses (Wohlfarth et al., 2017). Supply chain management and practices implemented along the supply chain are an important driver of EP in SMEs (Bos-Brouwers, 2010). This leads to our second hypothesis:

Hypothesis 8.2 The use of relational environmental management instruments improves the EP of SMEs.

Mediation

The overall conceptual model is depicted in Figure 8.1.

Based on the combination of hypotheses 8.1 and 8.2, it is expected that the effect from gender on a firm's EP is mediated by the type of management instruments. Mediation models give insight into how an independent variable affects the dependent variable by influencing an intermediate variable, the so-called mediator (Preacher et al., 2007). As women are more relationally oriented in their management of EP, companies with a higher share of women in management will be inclined to make more use of REMIs. Given that REMIs are relatively effective in improving EP of SMEs, it is expected that gender diversity affects their EP positively.

Hypothesis 8.3 The use of relational environmental management instruments mediates the relationship between women in management and an SME's EP.

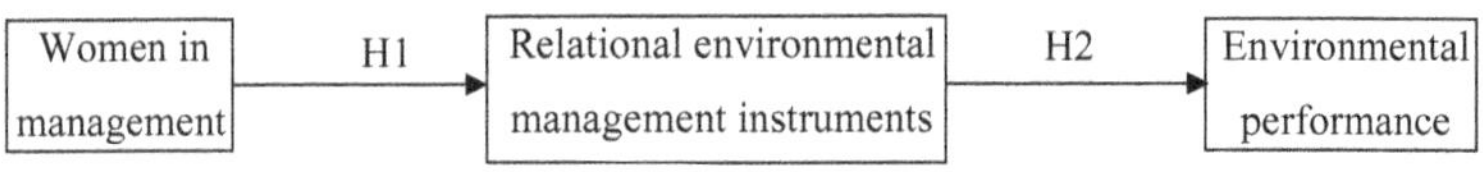

FIGURE 8.1 Conceptual framework

8.3 Methodology

The data were taken from the survey in 2011. The use of REMIs is measured by four indicators. First, companies can participate in networks in the supply chain that identify best practice on how to integrate EP into the small business and provide guidance as to the most salient issue to focus on (Wohlfarth et al., 2017). Second, small businesses can participate in the local initiatives of governments, NGOs, or benefit corporations as an expression of the company's commitment to the community in which it operates (Graafland, 2018a). Third, we include partnerships with professional training institutes in order to anticipate the technological evolution of products or services (Bos-Brouwers, 2010). Finally, in order to obtain legitimacy, companies often respond to social licence pressure by involving societal organizations and local communities through stakeholder dialogue (Hall et al., 2015). Three options per instrument are distinguished: 'no' (0), 'yes' (1), and 'unfamiliar with this measure'. The third option is recoded into 'no'.

Environmental performance is measured by the use of two relatively simple tools: setting targets to reduce energy consumption, water consumption, and waste disposal and reporting the realization of these targets (see also Chapters 2 and 7).

Prior studies have measured the representation of women in management by means of a variety of different constructs, such as the number of women (Torchia et al., 2011), a dummy variable indicating a critical mass of women (three or more women, Fernández-Feijoo et al., 2014), and the ratio of women on the board (Birindelli et al., 2019). In this study, respondents were asked through an open-ended question to indicate the share of women in the management of their respective enterprises (survey question 67). The mean share of women in management was 23%.

In order to research the validity of the constructs of the use of REMIs and EP, we performed factor analysis. Table 8.1 supports the construction of two factors. The factor loadings for all individual variables exceed 0.50, and this can be considered very significant (Hair et al., 1998). The Cronbach's alphas confirm that both factors are internally reliable.

A potential bias in the regression analysis is reverse causality. This may result if firms using REMIs attract relatively more women managers (sorting effect). In order to prevent simultaneity bias, we included the sector in which the firm operates as a control variable to control for the possibility that women managers are more attracted to sectors with more sustainable companies. Moreover, we used an instrumental variable approach to test for reverse causation. For REMIs, the intensity with which the firm's EP was monitored by NGOs and the media was used. Regression analysis showed that this instrumental variable has a positive and very significant effect on REMIs (the T-value was 13.12). Next, IV regression analysis showed that the effect of instrumented REMIs on women in management was

TABLE 8.1 Exploratory factor analysis[a]

Variables	*Mean*	*SD*	*Factor loadings*	
			Relational environmental management instruments	*Environmental performance*
Cooperation supply chain (46)	0.37	0.48	0.67	
Partnerships with training institutes (47)	0.36	0.48	0.65	
Participation in local initiatives (48)	0.42	0.49	0.72	
Active dialogue with NGOs (45)	0.17	0.38	0.64	
Targets and reporting energy consumption (96)	0.11	0.23		0.88
Targets and reporting water consumption (97)	0.12	0.24		0.88
Targets and reporting waste disposal (98)	0.09	0.21		0.88
Eigenvalue			1.66	2.70
% of variance explained			20.7	33.8
Cronbach alpha			0.63	0.88

a Extraction method: Principal component analysis. Structure matrix. Rotation method: Oblimin. KMO measure = 0.762; P value Bartlett's Test of Sphericity = 0.000. The numbers in brackets refer to the number of the survey question reported in Appendix 1.

insignificant (unstandardized coefficients of 0.013 with p-value = 0.50). Based on these results, we conclude that the estimated effects from women in management on REMIs are not biased by reverse causality.

8.4 Results

The model was estimated by structural equation modelling (SEM) in STATA (Version 14) with maximum likelihood as the estimation technique. The structural paths were estimated simultaneously with the measurement model. The model is confirmed by the global fit indices. The Comparative Fit Index (CFI), the Tucker–Lewis Index (TLI) and RMSEA measure are all acceptable (Byrne, 2010). The test results are reported in Table 8.2.

The share of women in management has a significant positive effect on the use of REMIs. The negative coefficient of the quadratic term means, however, that the relationship is degressive rather than progressive as predicted by the critical mass theory. This result only partly supports Hypothesis 8.1. It can be calculated that the optimal share of women managers that maximizes the use of REMIs equals 54%.[1] Beyond a share of 54%, having more women in management decreases EP. A possible explanation for the degressive relationship

TABLE 8.2 Estimation results of the structural equation model[a]

	1	*2*
	Relational environmental management instruments	*Environmental performance*
Structural paths		
Share of women in management	0.35***	0.07
Idem, quadratic	−0.27***	−0.05
Relational instruments		0.24***
R^2	0.23	0.14
Measurement model		
Relational instruments	CSR cooperation supply chain	0.50***
	Partnerships with training institutes	0.49***
	Participation in local CSR initiatives	0.61***
	Active dialogue with NGOs	0.45***
Sustainability	Energy consumption	0.80***
	Water consumption	0.80***
	Waste disposal	0.76***

a Standardized coefficients. * $p < 0.05$; ** $p < 0.01$; and *** $p < 0.001$. Controlled for company size, time horizon, skill level, age structure, type of respondent, organizational culture, ISO 14001 certification, sector, region, position in the chain, and intensity of price competition. Santorra–Bentler global fit indices: RMSEA = 0.024; CFI = 0.933; TLI = 0.906; SRMS = 0.012; and R^2 = 0.291, N = 3663.

is given by Birindelli et al. (2019) who also found no support for the critical mass theory, and instead identified an inverted U-shaped relationship between women in management and a firm's EP. Birindelli et al. (2019) explain this finding by a 'dual critical mass perspective', which theorizes that it is the combination of male and female managers that leads to greater attention to EP and more effective implementation of environmental policies. Furthermore, the estimation results show that REMIs have a significant positive effect on EP which supports Hypothesis 8.2.[2]

To test Hypothesis 8.3, the SEM estimates for indirect effects can be used. The indirect effect of women in management on EP equals a * b, where *a* is the unstandardized coefficient of the share of women management in the equation of REMIs and *b* is the unstandardized coefficient of REMIs in the equation of EP. The test results in Table 8.3 show that the use of REMIs significantly mediates the relationship between the (linear and quadratic) share of women in management and EP, supporting Hypothesis 8.3. The total effects of gender diversity on EP are equal to the sums of the direct effects of gender diversity on EP and the indirect effects mediated through REMIs.

TABLE 8.3 Indirect effects of the share of women in management on environmental performance[a]

	Direct effect	*Indirect effect*	*Total effect*
Linear	0.061	0.071***	0.132***
Quadratic	−0.054	−0.069***	−0.123**

a Unstandardized coefficients. * $p < 0.05$; ** $p < 0.01$; *** $p < 0.001$.

8.5 Conclusion

This chapter shows that women in management positions improves the CSR of SMEs by encouraging the use of relational management instruments. The effect is non-linear and CSR reaches its maximum when the proportion of women managers is 54%.

The study makes two major contributions to the scientific literature. Scientific literature on the relationship between gender diversity in management and EP of large companies has reflected mixed results. As women's presence in management is higher in small businesses than in large companies (Bertrand and Hallock, 2001), a focus on small business might help to better identify the effect of gender on environmental responsibility. This study is the first to analyse the relationship between women managers and EP for SMEs. By using data on managers in small businesses, we were able to observe findings which are unfiltered by the inevitable structures, processes, and bureaucracies of larger corporations (Grinyer and Yasai-Ardekani, 1981). A small business focus also allows us to avoid environmental findings which are driven more by legislation than voluntary practice, as small businesses are often excused the full regulatory requirements of environmental legislation. Instead, this research takes advantage of the short reporting lines, low hierarchies, and voluntariness in small business to study the effects of women managers.

Second, in the gender–EP literature, almost no attention has been given to mediating mechanisms. Although some studies do consider relational perspectives in arguing women's ability to maintain positive stakeholder relations (Galbreath, 2011), these mechanisms were not tested. Only research by Post et al. (2015) on publicly traded oil and gas companies headquartered in the US had shown that EP-themed alliances mediate the relationship between the representation of women in a firm's board or in executive positions and corporate EP. Our study postulated the type of management instrument as a mediation mechanism. This chain of relationships implies that EP improves with the share of women in management. The findings support a renewed focus on both gender and relational theories of environmental responsibility.

Notes

* An extended text of this chapter has been published as an open access article under the terms of the Creative Commons Attribution-NonCommercial-NoDerivs License

(permission granted by Wiley) in: Graafland, J. (2020). Women in management and sustainable development of SMEs: Do relational environmental management instruments matter? *Corporate Social Responsibility and Environmental Management*, 27: 2320–2328.

1 The last column of Table 4 implies that the maximum effect is obtained if 0.132–2 * 0.123 * X = 0 ◊ X=0.54, where X is the share of women in management.

2 In addition to REMIs, ISO 14001 certification, which was used as a control variable, also significantly improves environmental performance, but the effect is not as large as that of REMIs. If we include ISO 14001 certification as a dependent variable in the SEM model, we find that the share of women in management has a small negative effect of −0.03 (p value = 0.04). This further confirms that women managers encourage the use of relational management instruments, rather than bureaucratic, standardized instruments.

9

BUSINESS CULTURE AND CORPORATE SOCIAL RESPONSIBILITY

9.1 Introduction

Companies are increasingly scrutinized by governments as well as the general public and interest and advocacy groups (Helmig et al., 2016) and firms encounter coercive, mimetic, and normative pressures to conduct policies that are socially responsible (Matten and Moon, 2008). However, CSR is a requirement that needs to be balanced with other corporate exigencies, like profitability, growth, or more generally building and maintaining competitiveness. The literature on CSR suggests that if CSR is made an integral part of a firm's strategy, CSR can increase the competitiveness of the firm (Porter and Kramer, 2006).

CSR activities are often fragmented and disconnected from the firm's strategy (Porter and Kramer, 2006). Research has shown that the way in which an issue is interpreted (e.g. as a threat or as an opportunity) leads to divergent strategies (Sharma, 2000). Likewise, we may assume that pressures to behave socially responsible may be interpreted by firms in divergent ways, making some firms more inclined to integrate CSR in their strategy in order to meet CSR expectations, and other firms less or not at all.

This begs the question of what factors make some firms interpret pressures for CSR as a strategic issue, and others not. Interpretation of strategic issues within firms is influenced by the characteristics of individuals, such as schemas to categorize information (Dutton and Jackson, 1987), as well as factors in the macro environment of an organization, like the culture of the country in which the organization is located (Peng et al., 2014). A third relevant level where influences on the way in which strategic issues are interpreted, is that of the firm itself. Firms differ in their structures, processes, and strategies, and these are likely to impact on their strategic responses (e.g. Thomas and McDaniel, 1990).

DOI: 10.4324/9781003216483-11

In a review of the factors influencing organizational innovation, Crossan and Apaydin (2010) distinguished various 'managerial levers' at the organizational level. Some of these are explicit and can deliberately be manipulated by top management, for example, the firm's mission and goals, structure and systems, and resource allocation. Other factors, and most strongly the organizational culture of the firm, are less open to deliberate manipulation. This makes organizational culture a relatively stable factor distinguishing between firms, and presumably a factor that will influence how a firm deals with CSR. Organizational culture, strongly linked to the identity of a firm (Hatch and Schultz, 2002), is a key characteristic that influences multiple aspects of how organizations behave (see, e.g., Ashkanasy et al., 2000), including how they perceive and respond to strategic issues (Julian and Ofori-Dankwa, 2008; Thomas and McDaniel, 1990; White et al., 2003). For a firm to be effective in CSR, it is imperative that the relevant policies are framed in such a way that they fit the firm's organizational culture (Howard-Grenville and Hoffman, 2003). Studies employing the so-called competing values framework of organizational culture have indicated that a flexibility orientation and an external focus are positively related to CSR (Berger et al., 2007; Linnenluecke and Griffiths, 2010). However, robust empirical evidence is still lacking. Whereas Berger et al. (2007) tested their theory on a limited number of interviews, Linnenluecke and Griffiths (2010) did not test their hypotheses by empirical research.

The central research question in this chapter therefore is: How does business culture, as conceptualized in the competing value framework, affect CSR? In line with Berger et al. (2007) and Linnenluecke and Griffiths (2010), our findings confirm that an open systems business culture combining external focus and a flexibility orientation stimulates various dimensions of CSR. Our study contributes to the literature on business culture and CSR by demonstrating that theoretical notions and explorative research are confirmed by a more representative study. A second contribution is that, because our sample contains many SMEs, we redress the dominant focus on large, often multinational firms in studies of both CSR and organizational culture (Baumann-Pauly et al., 2013).

In the next section, we will discuss our conceptual framework linking organizational culture to CSR and formulate hypotheses pertaining to the relationships between these concepts. After that, we discuss the operationalization of variables. Next, we present our empirical findings, followed by a conclusion.

9.2 Conceptual Framework

Although the concept of CSR has been around for a long time (Carroll, 2008), there is little doubt that the pressure on firms to comply with CSR demands has increased dramatically in the past few decades (Babiak and Trendafilova, 2011) and that CSR has become 'mainstream' (Helmig et al., 2016). In linking CSR to strategy, companies need to take stock of where in their value chain of activities there are opportunities to minimize societal damage or create shared social value in such a way that it enhances their competitiveness (Porter and Kramer, 2006).

Open Systems Business Culture

Strategic issue interpretation is influenced in general by factors at the level of the individual manager (e.g. Julian and Ofori-Dankwa, 2008), the organization (Delmas and Toffel, 2008), and the environment (Barr and Glynn, 2004). In this chapter, we are particularly interested in factors at the organizational level that can explain why one firm in a particular industry and country interprets CSR issues different from another firm in the same industry and country. We propose that the cultural orientation of a firm influences the likelihood it will engage in CSR. Organizational culture is strongly linked to the identity of a firm (Hatch and Schultz, 2002) and is a key characteristic that influences multiple aspects of how organizations behave (see, e.g. Ashkanasy et al., 2000), including how they perceive and respond to strategic issues (White et al., 2003).

Linnenluecke et al. (2009) specifically focus on external focus and flexibility orientation as dimensions of organizational (sub)culture that influence perceptions of strategic CSR issues. Internal versus external focus and control versus flexibility orientations are the two basic dimensions distinguished in the Competing Values Framework (CVF) (Cameron and Quinn, 1999).[1] The CVF aligns with well-known and widely accepted categorical schemes that outline how people think, how they organize their values and ideologies, and how they process information. The first dimension pertains to the degree to which the organization is oriented toward its own internal environment versus the external environment and relationships with outside entities, such as regulators, suppliers, competitors, and customers. The second dimension juxtaposes emphasis on centralization and control over organizational processes with decentralization and flexibility (Denison and Spreitzer, 1991). Companies that manage by control use all kinds of formal mechanisms, such as rules, directives, and direct supervision, to direct the organization towards the organizational goals. In contrast, companies that have a management style characterized by flexibility rely on participation, intrinsic commitment, and autonomy to realize the company goals.

Combining these two dimensions leads to four ideal types of organizational cultures: the internal process model (internal focus plus control orientation), the rational goal model (external focus plus control orientation), the human relations model (internal focus plus flexibility orientation), and the open systems model (external focus and flexibility orientation). These four ideal types differ not only in the ends that are typically pursued but also in the means employed to reach those ends. For instance, for the internal process model ends are related to the stability of the organization and control, and typical means are formal rules and procedures. The open systems model, in contrast, strives for growth and external support and employs more informal coordination. The CVF because of its general nature can be seen as a metatheory of organizational culture (Denison and Spreitzer, 1991), or 'an elegant way to summarize the wide range of issues that have been studied under the cultural rubric' (Schneider et al., 2012: 377). The framework has been used and validated extensively in empirical research (Cameron et al., 2006; Howard, 1998; Zammuto et al., 2000).

Open Systems Business Culture and CSR

In literature, CVF dimensions have been typically related to innovation. Various studies found that a flexibility orientation and an external focus positively affect innovation outcomes (Fey and Denison, 2003; Naranjo-Valencia et al., 2011; Büschgens et al., 2013). There is much less literature linking CVP dimensions to CSR but some conjectures can be made. Following the categorization of CSR by Dahlsrud (2008), who distinguished five qualifying dimensions of CSR (economic performance, stakeholder relations, EP, social performance, and voluntariness dimensions), we focus on three different domains of CSR. Leaving economic performance out, we distinguish (voluntary) instruments that help building stakeholder relations, informal efforts to improve EP, and informal efforts that foster social performance.

First, we postulate that an open systems business culture fosters the use of instruments that help building good relationships with stakeholders. An external focus implies that a firm is more open to external audiences and stakeholders (Russo and Perrini, 2010), whereas a flexibility orientation improves the participation of employees in decision-making. This has been argued to be an important condition for CSR. Basu and Palazzo (2008: 129) maintain that 'an open posture is oriented toward learning that is based on the organization's willingness to listen and respond to alternative perspectives offered by others. An open posture allows the organization to be ready to share not simply solutions but also its perception of the issue with others and to debate and discuss the nature of the transformation, both internal and external, that might be necessary to bring about real change'. This argumentation undergirds the assumption that an open systems business culture is conducive to the use of instruments that strengthen stakeholder relations.

Hypothesis 9.1 Firms with an open systems business culture are more likely to engage in stakeholder relations.

Second, we postulate that an open systems business culture increases efforts to improve EP. Linnenluecke and Griffiths (2010) argued that organizations with an internally focused culture will place greater emphasis on economic performance, growth, and long-term profitability in their pursuit of corporate sustainability. Because of the strong focus on achieving economic outcomes, they easily miss out on sustainability innovations, as such innovations require flexibility, learning, and change. An external focus enables a firm to better anticipate changing market conditions (Naranjo-Valencia et al., 2011) and stimulates a firm to engage in a process of knowledge exploration (Zhang et al., 2006). An externally oriented firm will therefore be more able to respond to society's demand for more sustainable production patterns. In addition, the flexibility orientation of the open systems business culture may be assumed to contribute to engagement in environmental CSR. Kitazawa and Sarkis (2000), on the basis of three case studies claimed that employee empowerment, willingness to make suggestions, and participation in decision-making are critical elements in the capability of a firm to pursue continuous reduction of impacts on the natural environment. Škerlavaj et al. (2007) argued that flexibility orientation is conducive to organizational learning because employees of firms with such a culture will be more open to cognitive change. Companies with a flexible management style will therefore more proactively apply corporate sustainability practices and are most likely to innovate for achieving ecological sustainability. This is in line with explorative work by Berger et al. (2007), who, based on 100 interviews, concluded that companies with comparatively flat hierarchies more often pursue CSR policies in a broad range of areas. Companies that display a high degree of uncertainty avoidance by using norms, rules, or procedures (characteristic for a control orientation) are less involved with CSR than companies that do not adhere to established routines and extensive planning procedures. As both external focus and flexibility orientation are conducive to EP, we propose:

Hypothesis 9.2 Firms with an open systems business culture are more likely to put effort into improving EP.

Third, we propose that an open systems business culture will also foster social dimensions of CSR, like the quality of labour within the firm and respect of human rights in the chain. As argued by Linnenluecke and Griffiths (2010), companies with a flexibility orientation will more likely adopt a clear position on social aspects of CSR, such as the creation of a humane working environment. This suggests that a flexibility orientation will foster responsibility for providing training and education to employees, securing health and safety and promoting workplace diversity and work–life balance. In companies with high power distance, there is greater acceptance, both by the leaders of the organization and the followers, that the leaders are entitled to privileges. In companies where power distance is low, participation by internal stakeholders is important (Berger et al., 2007). Whereas the flexibility orientation particularly stimulates the social dimension of CSR within the firm, the external focus will enforce social aspects of CSR outside the firm, like respect of human rights in relationships with suppliers. Companies with an external focus will recognize the relevance of CSR in the wider social and economic environment as well as social pressures from activists to respect human rights. Society expects that companies take wider responsibility towards various stakeholder groups and that includes labour conditions in the chain. We therefore surmise that a company with an open systems business culture that combines flexibility orientation with external focus will be more conducive to social aspects of CSR than other companies.

Hypothesis 9.3 Firms with an open systems business culture are more likely to put effort into improving social performance.

9.3 Methodology

The data are taken from the surveys in 2011 (independent variables) and 2014 (dependent variables). An overview of the dependent and independent variables in our study is given in Table 9.1. Given the strong validation that measures of

TABLE 9.1 Descriptive and exploratory factor analysis[a]

			Factor loadings		
	Mean	*SD*	*Stakeholder relations*	*Environmental effort*	*Social effort*
External focus (15)	4.57	1.43			
Flexibility orientation (16)	5.06	1.39			
Internal code (43)	0.39	0.49	0.50		
CSR training (53)	0.23	0.42	0.55		
ISO 14001 (57)	0.13	0.32			
Dialogue with NGOs (45)	0.14	0.34	0.63		
CSR cooperation supply chain (46)	0.31	0.46	0.65		
Partnerships with training institutes (47)	0.28	0.45	0.63		
Participation in local CSR initiatives (48)	0.33	0.47	0.70		
Effort energy consumption (91)	0.69	0.36		0.79	
Effort water consumption (92)	0.61	0.39		0.80	
Effort waste disposal (93)	0.79	0.33		0.78	
Effort environmental performance suppliers (94)	0.63	0.40		0.65	
Effort employee training (63)	0.75	0.30			0.72
Effort employee health (65)	0.80	0.32			0.80
Effort labour conditions suppliers (66)	0.59	0.41			0.65
Eigenvalue			3.97	1.61	1.14
Cronbach alpha			0.71	0.76	0.61

[a] Extraction method: Principal component analysis. Structure matrix. Rotation method: Oblimin. Factor loadings <0.50 are not reported. The numbers in brackets refer to the numbers of the survey questions reported in Appendix 1.

the CVF have received in earlier studies (Howard, 1998; Kwan and Walker, 2004; Lavine, 2014; Quinn and Spreitzer, 1991) and the length of our questionnaire, we have operationalized the two dimensions with two questions. We measured external focus by the response to the statements 'In your enterprise you focus on optimizing the internal organizational efficiency' and 'In your enterprise you focus on adapting to the demands of the external environment'. The respondent could fill in seven options ranging from (1) (sole focus on optimizing the internal organizational efficiency) to (7) (sole focus on adapting to the demands of the external environment). We asked the respondents to select the answers on the seven-point scale and informed them that (4) indicates an intermediate position. The flexibility orientation was measured by the response to the statements: 'In your enterprise you focus on managing employees by supervision and strict compliance mechanisms' and 'In your enterprise you focus on employees autonomy and participative decision making'. The respondent could chose among seven options to identify if the company can be characterized by a flexibility orientation.

For measuring stakeholder relations we used seven indicators (Graafland et al., 2003; Ulrich et al., 1998), including two instruments that foster relations with internal stakeholders (internal code and employee training) and four instruments that help building relations with external stakeholders (stakeholder dialogue, cooperation in the chain, partnerships with professional training institutes, and participation in local initiatives of governments and social organizations) (Bos-Brouwers, 2010; Pirsch et al., 2006; European Commission, 2007; Barth and Wolff, 2009). We also included ISO 14001 certification, which may affect both internal stakeholder relations (by increasing employees' focus on environmental improvements) as well as external stakeholder relations (by providing evidence of the company's efforts to improve EP through certification).

For EP, we used four indicators inquiring whether the company has taken concrete actions to reduce energy consumption, water consumption and waste production, and improve EP of suppliers, respectively. For social performance, we measured the efforts of the company to improve the training of employees, prevent accidents at the work floor, and foster the respect of human rights in the production chain. Environmental and social efforts were measured by three options, distinguishing between 'no effort' (0), 'incidental effort' (0.5) and 'continuous effort' (1).

To assess the construct validity of CSR, we performed an exploratory factor analysis and used the results to evaluate the reliability of the composite variables based on various statistical criteria (Hair et al., 1998). Table 9.1 shows three factors expressing eigenvalues larger than 1.00. In the regression analysis, we used the estimated factors from the exploratory factor analysis.

9.4 Results

Table 9.2 presents the estimation results of the multiple regression analysis for CSR.

TABLE 9.2 Results of multivariate regression analysis of CSR[a,b]

	Stakeholder relations	*Environmental efforts*	*Social efforts*
External focus	0.05*	0.07*	0.00
Flexibility orientation	0.06*	0.10***	0.11***
R^2	0.25	0.12	0.13

[a] OLS. $N = 1{,}485$. Standardized coefficients; * $p < 0.05$; ** $p < 0.01$; and *** $p < 0.001$. Controlled for time horizon, skill level of employees, age structure, company size, sector, region, position in the chain, intensity of price competition, and inverse Mill's ratio (see Appendices 1 and 2 for details).

The results show that an external focus and flexibility orientation foster the use of instruments that strengthen stakeholder relations and environmental efforts, providing support for hypotheses 9.1 and 9.2. Social efforts are only positively related to flexibility orientation, providing partly support for Hypothesis 9.3.

9.5 Conclusion

In this study we theorized that the cultural orientation of a company influences CSR. Specifically, we hypothesized that an open systems business culture stimulates the use of voluntary instruments that help build stakeholder relations and efforts to improve environmental and social performance. Our findings point in the direction of strong interconnections between the aspects of organizational culture and engagement of companies in CSR.

Whereas our findings generally confirmed our hypotheses, we also see that the two dimensions characterizing the open systems organizational culture differentially impact the various dimensions of CSR. External focus has a positive effect on organizational measures, which makes sense as four of them are externally oriented, and on environmental efforts. Flexibility orientation affects all CSR dimensions and particularly social efforts. Based on these effects, we find that a flexibility orientation provides a more general and overall stronger impulse to CSR than an external focus orientation.

Note

1 Different versions of the CVF have been developed, and the terms used to describe the dimensions and types of cultures vary slightly; we use the terminology of Zammuto et al. (2000).

PART III

Impacts of Competition on Corporate Social Responsibility

10

PRICE COMPETITION, SHORT-TERMISM, AND CORPORATE SOCIAL RESPONSIBILITY*

10.1 Introduction

Globalization and economic growth have put pressure on the environment because of negative external effects of production and consumption patterns. This challenge has generated a strong interest in the CSR of companies. Indeed, CSR is often seen as 'corporate externality recognition' (Crouch, 2006). In 2011, the European Commission defined CSR as the responsibility of enterprises for their social and environmental impacts on society (European Commission, 2011: 6). An important policy question is how companies can be incentivized to adopt this responsibility and improve their corporate EP. Whereas much is known of the micro-barriers to CSR (Hemel and Cramer, 2002; Shi et al., 2008; Mathiyazhagan et al., 2013; Trianni et al., 2013), recently research has become more focused on the institutional roots of CSR (Brammer, Jackson et al., 2012; Campbell, 2007; Gjølberg, 2009). One of the hypotheses that Campbell (2007) develops is that the odds of companies acting in socially responsible ways depend on the intensity of competition they face. If price competition is very intense, profit margins will be low and companies will have a strong incentive to save costs, and this may cause them to act in socially irresponsible ways. As Van de Ven and Jeurissen (2005) and Dubbink and Van der Putten (2008) argued, in a perfect market, individual companies will have hardly any room to pursue a proactive policy on CSR because any cost disadvantage will harm their market share.

Building on institutional literature on CSR, other theoretical studies have conceptualized CSR as resulting from a combination of institutional factors and factors internal to the company (Delmas and Toffel, 2004; Aguilera et al., 2007; Brown et al., 2010). As yet underexposed in the literature, one of the internal factors through which price competition may affect CSR is the time horizon

DOI: 10.4324/9781003216483-13

that the company employs in its strategic decision-making. If companies are less profitable, they will have fewer resources; consequently, that makes it harder to make investments that are likely only to pay off in the long term, and the resulting 'short-termism' may discourage CSR.[1] As Yong Oh et al. (2011) argue, CSR investments are most likely to pay off in the long run. The longer the time horizon of the company, the more the company is concerned about corporate reputation and the quality of stakeholder management (Rehbein et al., 2013). Companies with a long-term orientation will therefore use CSR as an instrument to achieve long-term success. Based on this literature, we hypothesize that price competition reduces CSR by shortening the time horizon of the company.

One would expect that the links between competition, time horizon, and CSR described earlier are particularly relevant for SMEs. The SME manager tends to focus on survival (Burt and Van der Heijden, 2003) and is therefore less likely to carry out strategic planning (Laverty, 2004; Ates and Bititci, 2011). Because of their small size, most SMEs operate on markets with severe competition, and this puts their profitability under pressure. Time, finances, and a lack of skills and knowledge are commonly identified by SMEs as constraints to CSR (Studer et al., 2006). The long-term strategic benefits from CSR in terms of reputation, cost reduction, increased consumer demand, and reduction in risks therefore often remain beyond the strategic horizon of SMEs. This implies that, as Lynch-Wood and Williamson (2007) argued, the social licence motive will not be sufficient to induce SMEs to go beyond compliance to the law.

Currently, there is no empirical research that provides evidence of the mediation of the influence of price competition on CSR by time horizon. There are some studies that show that time horizon and CSR are related (Berger et al., 2007; Mallin et al., 2013; Neubaum and Zahra, 2006; Slawinski and Bansal, 2009; Yong Oh et al., 2011) and that competition is mildly antithetical to CSR (Cottrill, 1990). But the links between time horizon and the intensity of price competition, and how price competition affects CSR through time horizon, have not yet been researched. In this chapter, we aim to fill this gap by using a large sample of 3,152 companies from 12 European countries that largely consist of SMEs to analyse the relationship between price competition and CSR and the role of time horizon as mediator.

Given the present state of research, this chapter makes three contributions. First, we develop a conceptual framework that links price competition to CSR by postulating a mediating role of time horizon. Second, we test the model empirically, thus providing insight into the quantitative effects of price competition on time horizon and CSR, and the role of time horizon as a mediation path between price competition and CSR. The third contribution is that we test the model with a unique dataset that contains 3,152 observations, of which more than 90% concern SMEs. The focus on SMEs in the sample is motivated by the expectation that the hypothesized relationships between price competition, time horizon, and CSR might be particularly relevant for SMEs, as discussed earlier.

In what follows, we first present the hypotheses, then describe the methodology and report the results of the empirical analysis, and finally summarize the main findings in the concluding section.

10.2 Conceptual Framework

Following recent theoretical studies (Delmas and Toffel, 2004; Aguilera et al., 2007; Brown et al., 2010), we conceptualize CSR as resulting from a combination of external factors and internal factors (see Figure 10.1). More specifically, we assume that the implementation of CSR is related to the company's time horizon (internal condition) and that the company's time horizon depends on the intensity of price competition (external condition). Here, we first argue that price competition is expected to decrease the time horizon of a company. Then we explain that the implementation of CSR instruments will increase with the time horizon that the company applies in its strategic decisions. Finally, we describe the relationship between implementation of CSR instruments and CSR impacts.

Price Competition and Time Horizon

Neoclassical economic theory conceptualizes a well-organized market as a 'perfect market' (Baumol and Batey Blackman, 1991). In the neoclassical paradigm, the basis of economic growth is a well-functioning price mechanism that coordinates the decisions of economic subjects. Consequently, it is important that the government secures a high level of price competition, for example through antitrust policies. While stimulating economic growth, price competition may, however, also have negative effects on social welfare if it increases negative externalities. In this chapter we focus on one particular mechanism, namely that intense price competition may reduce initiatives to improve EP by shortening the time horizon of companies. Short-termism refers to an excessive focus on short-term results at the expense of long-term interests. There are several reasons why intense price competition may induce short-termism.

First, fierce price competition puts a negative pressure on profitability and increases the risk of bankruptcy. This will induce low-cost strategies and reduce

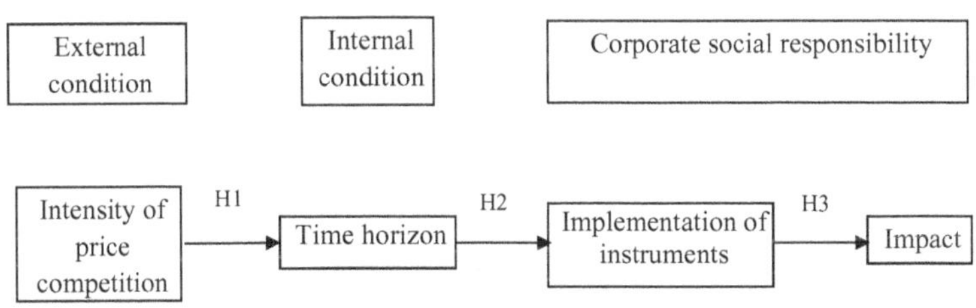

FIGURE 10.1 Conceptual framework

a long-term orientation (Mittra et al., 1995). As argued by Campbell (2007), if the continuity of the company is at risk because of low profit margins, there is a strong incentive to cut corners and save money where possible to survive in the short run and refrain from investments that pay off in the long run, even if that causes the company to compromise on product quality or employees' safety. Segelod (2000) found that the scope for long-term investments decreases when profit is low because companies need to have a sufficient cash flow to be able to develop their long-term projects and make them profitable. Companies that focus on survival exhibit short-termism and are less able to deal with strategic long-term developments (Burt and Van der Heijden, 2003; Laverty, 2004; Ates and Bititci, 2011).

Second, low profitability leads to more dependence on external financers. If companies have fewer resources available for long-term investments, they become more dependent on credit from external financers such as banks. This may lead to loan monitoring that is more bottom-line oriented and further increases the focus on short-term performance (Rappaport, 2005). External financers may undervalue investments that will pay off only in the long run (Laverty, 1996). Hence, external financial intermediaries will put pressure on the management to be pragmatic and reap benefits as soon as possible (Porter and Kramer, 2011).

Therefore, the following hypothesis is proposed:

Hypothesis 10.1 A higher intensity of price competition shortens the time horizon of the company.

Time Horizon and Implementation of CSR

Literature has argued that a long time horizon will foster the implementation of CSR of companies (Berger et al., 2007; Slawinski and Bansal, 2009; Porter and Kramer, 2006). The reason is that investments in CSR in the short-term cost money (Wang, 2013; Hart, 1995; Brammer and Millington, 2008; Shi et al., 2008), whereas the benefits from engaging in CSR mainly pay off in the long run (Mallin et al., 2013; Neubaum and Zahra, 2006; Rehbein et al., 2013; Yong Oh et al., 2011). A company with an excessive focus on short-term results will reckon with a lower net discounted value from investments in CSR than a company that takes account of long-term results and therefore will be less inclined to implement CSR.

CSR can produce several types of benefits. As theorized by the resource-based view (Branco and Rodrigues, 2006) and by the stakeholder theory (Surroca et al., 2010), one of the most important strategic benefits is that CSR may enhance the company's reputation. These reputational advantages typically pay off in the long run because it takes time to build up a good reputation. Moreover, as CSR often effectively carry with them a kind of insurance-type protection – in the sense of reducing business and corporate risks (Godfrey et al., 2009) – and since such unexpected events generally occur only now and then, the benefits of these investments appear only in the long run. The longer the time horizon of the enterprise, the more it will take account of the long-term benefits and the more priority CSR will have.

Furthermore, companies with a good CSR reputation are able to attract better employees and improve commitment of existing workers (Reinhardt, 1999). It may lead to stronger commitment from employees, lower absenteeism and turnover rates, higher productivity, and a more positive attitude to work and good conduct (Turban and Greening, 1997). These effects of CSR generate a permanent reduction in labour costs, and so the pay-off typically increases over time.

CSR also has long-term strategic value because it may contribute to process or product innovation (Hemel and Cramer, 2002; Demirel and Kesidou, 2011). But developing business opportunities to meet consumers' increasing demand for environmentally friendly products often takes a long time (Dijk et al., 2013). Hence, the benefits from such investments in lowering production costs and augmenting the environmental quality of products also mainly exist in the long run.

A final strategic motive for CSR is that organizations that integrate CSR in their policies may be more successful in avoiding excessive regulatory intervention and meeting existing regulations (Shrivastava, 1995; Hart, 1995). But, again, the pay-off of such insurance-type benefits is only significant if the company has a long-term orientation.

Whereas the various types of benefits of CSR often take substantial time to materialize, the costs associated with CSR are mostly immediate (Wang, 2013). The implementation of CSR often requires putting in significant financial and other resources in the short run, for example for installing equipment (Hart, 1995; Brammer and Millington, 2008) or for developing management skills to apply EMSs and obtaining certifications, which may undermine the competitive position in the market place (Shi et al., 2008). If funds for environmental projects are lacking, the consideration that the return on investment period after implementing green management is very long hampers investment (Mathiyazhagan et al., 2013). A cost-benefit analysis of such investments will only yield a positive result if the company focuses on the benefits *after* the short run.

For implementation of CSR, we distinguish two types of measures: formal organizational procedures to integrate CSR in the company's operations and (informal) efforts (concrete actions) to improve environmental impacts. Since both types of measures are costly in the short run, whereas their benefits accrue in the long run, we posit that a company's implementation of both types of instruments will increase as the time horizon of the company increases:

Hypothesis 10.2a CSR efforts are positively related to the time horizon of a company.

Hypothesis 10.2b CSR procedures are positively related to the time horizon of a company.

CSR Implementation and CSR Impacts

The final piece of the conceptual framework is that the implementation of CSR will improve CSR impacts, such as a reduction in energy consumption or waste (see also Chapter 2). Although there is evidence that firms' motive to implement CSR instruments is to improve CSR impacts (Johnstone and Labonne, 2009), literature on decoupling has shown that implementation does not always lead to better outcomes (Bromley and Powell, 2012). Nash and Ehrenfeld (2001) showed, for example, that two organizations that implement identical environmental management systems (EMSs) can realize very different results. Furthermore, due to the informal and diversified nature of SMEs, many studies argued that formal environmental management tools do not fit them (Spence et al., 2003; Studer et al., 2006; Welford and Frost, 2006; Battaglia et al., 2010). The general opinion in literature, therefore, is that SMEs should not implement CSR by using procedural tools but stick to practical measures to improve CSR. However, as discussed in Chapter 2, using formal instruments may also benefit SMEs, for example by raising the quality of internal management and stimulating organizational learning and innovativeness. Furthermore, owner-directors can be erratic in their environmental management and therefore not realize its full potential. It is also frequently claimed that a gap exists between what SME owner-managers say about the importance of environmental issues and their actual efforts to improve environmental impacts. Using formal management instruments can help diminish this so-called value-action gap and make EP less dependent upon the erratic actions of the SME's director. Also empirical research showed that formal procedures may improve environmental outcomes. For example, Friedman and Miles (2001) and Ammenberg and Hjelm (2003) found that the establishment of an EMS by SMEs in Britain and Sweden, respectively, resulted in environmental improvements.

Our framework thus posits the following two final hypotheses:

Hypothesis 10.3a The more effort a company undertakes to take concrete actions to improve CSR, the better its CSR impacts.

Hypothesis 10.3b The use of formal procedures to integrate CSR in the company's operations reinforces the impacts of CSR.

10.3 Methodology

For formal procedures we used two, relatively simple, tools: setting targets to improve environmental outcomes and reporting on the realization of these outcomes (see also Chapters 2, 7, and 8).[2] Formal procedures were measured on a three-point scale ranging from 1 (no target, no reporting), 2 (targets or reporting), to 3 (targets and reporting). Efforts refer to concrete actions to improve performance in the future and were measured on a three-point scale ranging

TABLE 10.1 Descriptive statistics[a]

Variable	*Mean*	*SD*
Effort to reduce energy consumption (91)	2.51	0.68
Effort to reduce water consumption (92)	2.34	0.76
Effort to reduce waste (93)	2.67	0.59
Procedural steps to reduce energy consumption (96)	1.56	0.64
Procedural steps to reduce water consumption (97)	1.45	0.58
Procedural steps to reduce waste (98)	1.60	0.60
Reduction in energy consumption during 2007–2010 (102)	0.57	1.50
Reduction in water consumption during 2007–2010 (104)	0.41	1.18
Reduction in waste during 2007–2010 (105)	0.45	1.31
Time horizon for financial targets (17)	2.73	1.32
Time horizon for CSR investments (29)	2.74	1.38
Intensity of price competition (121)	5.02	1.89

a $N = 3{,}152$. The numbers in brackets refer to the numbers of the survey questions reported in Appendix 1.

from 1 (no), 2 (on an ad hoc basis), to 3 (continuously). The reason we added this measure to the survey is that our pilot interviews indicated that SMEs may actually be proactively fostering EP without using formal procedures. Merely measuring the use of formal procedures may therefore bias the measurement of the actual implementation of environmental practices. The survey outcomes reported in Table 10.1 show that the average effort to reduce energy consumption, waste, and water consumption is substantially higher than the use of process steps, which confirms that the implementation of environmental measures is mostly informal. For environmental impacts, we use three questions about energy consumption, water consumption, and waste, measured by a seven-point scale for the change in the respective variable between 2007 and 2010 (see Chapter 3). The internal reliability of the environmental measures has been assessed by Cronbach alpha, and all meet the accepted threshold of 0.60 (Hair et al., 1998).

For time horizon, we used two questions measuring the time horizon employed in the strategic financial decisions of the company and the time horizon for investments in CSR. On average, the time horizon is about 2.5 years.

We measured the intensity of price competition by the company's perception of the intensity of price competition in the market for its main product or service. The question was administered on a Likert scale ranging from not at all (1) to very much (7).[3]

10.4 Results

We estimate the model with structural equation modelling using maximum likelihood as the estimation technique. The measurement model and the structural model are estimated simultaneously. The estimation results are reported in Table 10.2.

The estimation results show that the intensity of price competition significantly reduces time horizon, which confirms Hypothesis 10.1. Hypotheses 10.2a and 10.2b that time horizon will increase informal efforts to improve CSR impacts and foster the use of formal CSR procedures are also supported. Finally, the estimation results confirm Hypotheses 10.3a and 10.3b: both efforts and procedural measures improve environmental impacts.

The SEM technique can also be used to calculate the extent and significance of the indirect effects of the intensity of price competition on environmental outcomes, as mediated by the time horizon, efforts, and procedures. Table 10.3 shows that the indirect effects of the intensity of price competition on environmental outcomes are significant but very small in absolute terms.

TABLE 10.2 Estimation results[a]

	Time horizon	*Environmental efforts*	*Environmental procedures*	*Environmental impacts*
Structural paths				
Intensity of price competition	−0.10***			
Time horizon		0.13***	0.07***	
Environmental efforts				0.24***
Environmental procedures				0.07***
Measurement model				
Time horizon	Financial	0.65***		
	CSR	0.74***		
Environmental efforts	Energy	0.62***		
	Water	0.71***		
	Waste	0.62***		
Environmental procedures	Energy	0.80***		
	Water	0.74***		
	Waste	0.75***		
Environmental impacts	Energy	0.79***		
	Water	0.85***		
	Waste	0.75***		

a Standardized coefficients. * $p < 0.05$; ** $p < 0.01$; *** $p < 0.001$. Controlled for size of the company, sector, country, company's age structure, and average tenure of employees. For details of the control variables, see Appendices 1 and 2. Global fit indices: RMSEA = 0.028; CFI = 0.965; TLI = 0.954; SRMR = 0.026; $R^2 = 0.195$; $N = 3{,}152$.

TABLE 10.3 Indirect effects of price competition on environmental impacts[a]

	Reduction in:		
	Energy consumption	*Waste*	*Water consumption*
Intensity of price competition	−0.003**	−0.002**	−0.003**

a Standardized coefficients; * $p < 0.05$; ** $p < 0.01$; *** $p < 0.001$.

10.5 Conclusion

In this chapter we studied the relationships between the intensity of price competition, time horizon, and environmental impacts. Based on a sample of 3,152 companies from 12 European countries, we find that (1) price competition has a significant negative influence on the time horizon that a company applies in its financial and CSR decisions; (2) time horizon exerts a significant positive effect on the company's implementation of environmental actions and procedures to improve EP; (3) the implementation of concrete actions and formal procedures significantly improves environmental outcomes as measured by a reduction in energy consumption, waste, and water consumption. This chapter therefore, for the first time, shows that the theoretical argument, that price competition significantly worsens EP by stimulating short-termism, is valid. However, the estimation results also show that the magnitude of this effect (although significant) is very small.

Interestingly, if we extend the final model of Table 10.2 by adding direct relationships between price competition and environmental efforts, procedures, or outcomes, we find no significant effects (p-values vary between 0.35 and 0.67). In our model the only reason that more intense price competition reduces EP is that it shortens the time horizon of strategic decisions by the company. This has theoretical implications for slack resource theory, which states that the availability of slack (financial and other) resources provides a company with more opportunity to invest in CSR (Waddock and Graves, 1997). Firms that are in financial trouble may lack the resources to invest in CSR-related activities. A better financial performance increases the availability of slack and would therefore lead to better CSR. Several empirical studies confirmed the relevance of this mechanism (Orlitzky et al., 2003). Taking CSR as the dependent variable and using lagged financial performance as the independent variable (controlling for debt, size, and industry), Waddock and Graves found strong support for the slack resource hypothesis. Since improved CSR performance in turn results in better financial performance, this creates an interesting virtuous circle whereby responsibility and economic success go hand in hand. As slack resources are obtained through profitability and profitability depends negatively on the intensity of price competition, our empirical results indicate that the reason that lack of slack resources might negatively affect CSR is because it induces short-termism. This result can be used to develop a new hypothesis in slack resource theory, namely that time horizon mediates the influence of profitability on CSR.

Notes

* An extended text of this chapter has been published in: Graafland, J.J. (2016). Price competition, short-termism and environmental performance. *Journal of Cleaner Production*, 116: 125–134.

1 CSR may, however, also be low in a monopolistic market with weak competition, because stakeholders have then fewer possibilities to punish the company. Hence, companies will be less likely to pursue a CSR strategy if there is either too much or too little competition (Campbell, 2007).

2 Also major ESG rating agencies, like Sustainalytics and ASSET4, include parameters for the use of programs and targets to reduce water consumption and for outcomes in terms of water intensity/efficiency/use as part of their measurement of the E(nvironmental) performance of companies. This illustrates that water consumption is commonly considered an environmental impact measure. Lambooy (2011) argued that sustainable water use can be considered part of CSR, because water stress is increasingly viewed as a potential constraint to economic growth, and as a threat to preserving healthy ecosystems and to promoting social justice, particular in regions where governance of water is weak and water supply is limited.

3 In order to check the reliability of this measure, we performed regression analysis relating the intensity of price competition to the market structure of the company, controlling for company size, region, sector, age structure and tenure. In the structure-conduct-performance paradigm used in industrial economics, market structure is one of the key factors driving competition intensity (Greer, 1992). In literature, four typical market structures are distinguished: monopoly, oligopoly, monopolistic competition and perfect competition (Samuelson, 1980; Greer, 1992). We measure market structure by questions for each of these types of market structure (see survey question 119 in Appendix 1). Using monopolies as reference, the estimation results showed that price competition is strongest for companies operating in perfect markets (0.44, $p<0.001$), whereas companies operating in monopolistic markets face significantly more intense price competition (0.31, $p<0.001$) than oligopolies (0.23, $p<0.001$), and oligopolies significantly more than monopolies. These results are in line with the structure-conduct-performance paradigm that price competition decreases with concentration. This provides confidence in the reliability of our measurement of the intensity of price competition.

11

TECHNOLOGICAL COMPETITION, INNOVATION MOTIVE, AND CORPORATE SOCIAL RESPONSIBILITY*

11.1 Introduction

In light of the salience of social and environmental challenges in society, over the last quarter century several studies have explored motives for CSR (Muller and Kolk, 2010; Aguilera et al., 2007; Bansal and Roth, 2000). Whereas most studies explored engagement among large companies, other studies focused specifically on CSR motives of SMEs. For example, using a sample of 102 SMEs from a variety of industrial sectors in the UK, Brammer, Hoejmose, and Marchant (2012) distinguished six strategic motives: long-term financial benefits, short-term financial benefits, legislative compliance, customer pressure, supplier initiative, and market position and market share. These authors found that managers of both small and medium-sized enterprises rate legislative compliance highest, but also agree that long-term financial benefits and customer pressures drive their CSR.

However, previous research into the motives of CSR has paid no attention to another likely motive to act in socially responsible ways: innovation. There is evidence that CSR may be of strategic value for companies because it can stimulate innovation (Wagner, 2007b; Hull and Rothenberg, 2008; MacGregor and Fontrodana, 2008; Padgett and Galan, 2009; Ziegler and Nogareda, 2009; Bocquet et al., 2011; Jamali et al., 2011; Lioui and Sharma, 2012; Luo and Du, 2015; Flammer and Kacperczyk, 2016). However, while the aforementioned studies establish a statistical link between CSR and innovation, this does not mean that managers of firms engage in CSR because of the expected positive impact on the innovativeness of their company.

In this study we explore whether managers invest in CSR because they expect this to have a positive impact on innovation. We base our reasoning on expectancy theory (Vroom, 1964), which posits that the motivation for an action is

DOI: 10.4324/9781003216483-14

the product of the belief that the action will lead to a certain outcome and the value of that outcome to the decision-maker. Building on this, we theorize that managers (next to other motives) choose to invest in CSR because they believe that this leads to innovation, and they see innovation as important to their firm.

We focus on top managers of SMEs because while top managers generally have an important influence on strategic decisions (Hambrick and Mason, 1984), this is particularly the case in SMEs (Laufs et al., 2016). SMEs are more flexible and adaptable and can therefore more rapidly take advantage of new niche markets that incorporate social and environmental benefits. SMEs may also be more creative and innovative, and innovation is therefore a viable source of competitiveness for SMEs (Jenkins, 2009). Of the studies cited earlier, only MacGregor and Fontrodana (2008) looked at the link between CSR and innovation for SMEs, but their explorative research is limited to 60 firms and does not allow them to test hypotheses.

Business strategies and top managers' motivations, however, do not develop in a vacuum but are influenced by the external environment of companies. The role of technological competition in driving CSR has remained underexposed in the literature. Building on institutional literature (Aguilera et al., 2007; Campbell, 2007; Brown et al., 2010), we conjecture that top managers' motivation to engage in CSR depends on the market environment in which the company operates. Top managers of companies operating in a market with strong technological competition will attach a higher value to innovation. As the value of the outcome of an action increases the motivation for this action, expectancy theory predicts that technological competition increases the innovation motive of CSR. If the innovation motive drives CSR, the strength of the innovation motive for CSR of top managers will mediate the positive effect of technological competition on CSR.

Our study makes three major contributions to the literature. First, this chapter theorizes the importance of innovation as a motive for CSR of SMEs. Second, we develop a conceptual framework linking the innovation motive to the competitive environment of the company and postulate a mediating role of the innovation motivation of top managers in the relationship between technological competition and CSR. By focusing on top managers, we tap into the knowledge of the group of managers that are most well informed about the CSR motives of the SME. Top managers are constantly shaping the strategic direction of the company (Weaver et al., 1999) and are often directly involved in decisions on CSR (Waldman et al., 2006). Therefore, they have first-hand knowledge of the motives that drive the company's CSR policies. Third, we empirically test predictions based on this model using a unique dataset containing more than 2,000 observations of top managers of large companies and SMEs. In this way, we can test whether the links between competitive environment, top managers' innovation motive, and CSR hold for large as well as for small companies.

In what follows, we first discuss our conceptual framework and hypotheses. Next, we describe data and methods. Subsequently, we present our empirical findings. We conclude with a summary of our results.

11.2 Conceptual Framework

Following other studies (Weaver et al., 1999; Aguilera et al., 2007; Brown et al., 2010), we assume that engagement in CSR depends on a combination of external pressures and factors internal to the company. More specifically, we postulate that motivations of top managers towards CSR mediate the influence of pressure from technological competition on the implementation of CSR at the company level (see Figure 11.1). Here we will first argue that innovation motivation of top managers stimulates a company's engagement in CSR (Hypothesis 11.1). Next, we postulate that innovation motivation is more likely to arise if a company faces intensive technological competition on its output market (Hypothesis 11.2). Third, we present the mediation hypothesis (Hypothesis 11.3).

Innovation Motivation of Top Managers and CSR

In the CSR literature different motives for CSR have been distinguished. One of the most important strategic benefits of CSR is that it may enhance the company's reputation (Surroca et al., 2010) and help to receive or maintain a licence to operate from society. In their study of corporate motives for CSR, Brønn and Vidaver-Cohen (2009) found that improving the company's image ranks first among 16 motives. Managers may also be motivated for CSR because they see it as being able to help them differentiate their company from competitors and in this way to strengthen their competitive position. Furthermore, CSR can be seen as increasing the commitment of employees and helping firms to attract talented new employees (Jones et al., 2014; Albinger and Freeman, 2000). Finally, a strategic motive for CSR can be that it helps firms in avoiding regulatory intervention, meeting existing regulations, and preventing costly lawsuits started against firms, which apply inadequate standards for their suppliers and vendors (Carroll and Shabana, 2010).

However, so far no research has focused on innovation as a motive for CSR. This is surprising, as CSR has been claimed to stimulate innovation, for several reasons, as has been argued in Chapter 4. Given these positive effects of CSR on innovation, we expect that top managers might be aware that CSR stimulates innovation. In the view of the theory of reasoned actions (Ajzen,

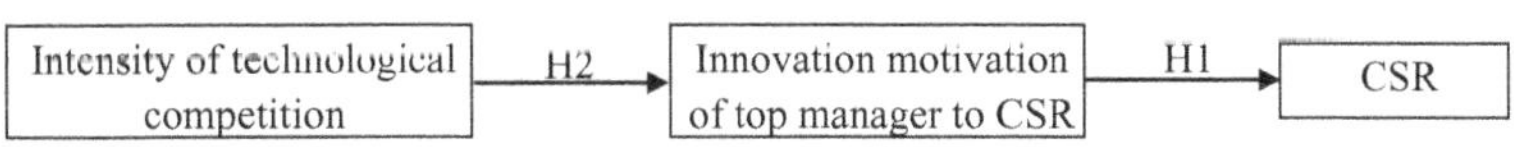

FIGURE 11.1 Conceptual framework

1991), this belief provides the cognitive foundation of their CSR motivation. Moreover, according to expectancy theory the motivation to engage in a particular action is the product of the belief that the action will lead to a certain outcome and the value of that outcome to the decision-maker (Vroom, 1964). Predictions of this theory have generally received support in management research (Yang et al., 2018). As the motivation of the top manager is an antecedent to his/her behaviour (Treviño et al., 2006), it is reasonable to expect that the top manager's innovation motive towards CSR will translate into a stronger engagement of the company in CSR. Hence, we propose the following hypothesis:

> *Hypothesis 11.1 The stronger the top manager's innovation motivation towards CSR, the more the firm will engage in CSR.*

Technological Competition and the Innovation Motive

Business strategies and motivations are not developed in a vacuum but are influenced by the environment of companies. Building on institutional literature, several studies have conceptualized CSR as resulting from a combination of external factors and factors internal to the company (Aguilera et al., 2007; Brown et al., 2010). Recent literature has started to explore the relationship between the level of competition and CSR. Fernández-Kranz and Santaló (2010) found that more competition in the marketplace leads to better CSR outcomes, and they conclude that CSR is used strategically by profit-maximizing firms. Empirical findings by Flammer (2015) also point into the direction of a positive relationship between the level of competition and CSR.

Firms can compete in many different dimensions, like price, distribution channels, supplier inputs, and technology (Vickers, 1995; Shapiro, 1989). We focus here on technological competition as previous research by Graafland and Smid (2015) showed that this type of competition stimulates CSR. In this chapter, we argue that the intensity of technological competition has a positive but indirect influence on CSR through the innovation motivation of top managers to engage in CSR. In markets where technological competition plays an important role, achieving sustainable competitive advantage depends on the innovativeness of a company (Humphreys et al., 2005). Consequently, senior managers will particularly pay attention to business strategies that encourage the innovativeness of their company (Cottam et al., 2001).

The influence of the competitive environment on business strategies works through the perceptions of top managers, in general (Tang, 2006) and also for SMEs (De Jong, 2011). Top managers of companies that operate in a highly innovative business environment will particularly value strategies that strengthen the innovative capability of their firm because these are crucial for the firm's profitability and continuity. In terms of expectancy theory this means that, at a given level of the perception or belief that CSR leads to innovation, operating in an environment with more intense technological competition will increase the value attributed to innovation, and hence the motivation to engage in CSR will be stronger. We therefore propose the following hypothesis:

Hypothesis 11.2 The intensity of technological competition increases a top manager's motivation to engage in CSR because of its innovation enhancing effects.

Mediation

The argumentation and hypotheses developed here imply that we theorize the relationship between technological competition and firms' engagement in CSR to be mediated by the innovation motivation of top managers. Mediation analysis permits examination of processes and gives insight into how an independent variable exerts an effect on the dependent variable. Most explanations of behaviour rely, whether implicitly or explicitly, on some attribution of motive to actors (Jones et al., 2014). In our framework, we have argued that technological competition increases the innovation motive of top managers towards CSR. Since the innovation motive of top managers is an important driver of CSR, this motivation is likely to mediate the relationship between technological competition and CSR of firms. This leads to our third hypothesis:

Hypothesis 11.3 A top manager's innovation motive to engage in CSR mediates the effect of the intensity of technological competition on CSR.

11.3 Methodology

The data were taken from the survey in 2011. Following Graafland and Smid (2015), we measured technological competition by a question on the intensity of technological competition in the market for the company's main product or service. The response was administered on a Likert scale ranging from 'not at all' (1) to 'very much' (7). The average mean is 5.24 (SD = 1.64). In order to check the reliability of the measurement of technological competition, we used data for innovation in 19 sectors, measured by aggregating the outcomes of two survey questions on process and product innovation for all companies per sector (survey question 123 and 124 in Appendix 1). At the sectoral level, the bivariate correlation coefficient between the average of process and product innovation and the intensity of technological competition is 0.78 ($p < 0.001$), which is in line with our expectation and provides confidence in our measurement. Multiple regression analysis (controlling for control variables) showed that the intensity of technological competition at the firm level is also significantly related to the average innovation in the sector in which the company operates (estimated coefficient is 0.081; $p < 0.001$).

Motivation refers to the internal state of the manager, and self-reporting is an appropriate way to tap into this internal state (O'Mahoney, 2012). We measured the top manager's innovation motivation by two survey questions. The first question gauges the respondents' beliefs regarding the effect of CSR on innovation by their agreement with the statement 'CSR improves innovative capacity', as beliefs are an important antecedent of motivation. The second survey question measured innovation motivation more directly by asking the respondent's agreement with the statement 'CSR leads to innovation' in response to the question 'How important are the following motives for your enterprise to engage in CSR?' The response was administered on a Likert scale ranging from 'not at all' (1) to 'very much' (7).

CSR was operationalized by eight process measures indicating the efforts of companies to improve social performance and EP (see Table 11.1). Environmental efforts were measured by four survey questions measuring concrete actions to reduce energy consumption, water consumption, and waste disposal, and to improve EP of suppliers. Social efforts were measured by four survey questions measuring efforts to improve the work–life balance of employees, employee training, labour conditions of suppliers and respect of human rights, and employee health by reducing workplace accidents and worker's absence rate. For each issue, we used a three-point scale ranging from 0 (no effort), 0.5 (incidental effort), to 1 (continuous effort). In order to ascertain the validity of the construct of CSR, we used Principal Component Analysis (with Oblimin rotation). We found two different factors reflecting environmental and social CSR. In the regression analysis, we will use these two factors as measures of CSR.

TABLE 11.1 Factor analysis of CSR[a]

Variables	*Mean*	*SD*	*Loadings*	
			Environmental CSR	*Social CSR*
Effort energy consumption (91)	0.66	0.37	0.77	
Effort water consumption (92)	0.59	0.40	0.80	
Effort waste disposal (93)	0.77	0.34	0.79	
Effort environmental performance suppliers (94)	0.49	0.42	0.68	
Effort work–life balance (62)	0.60	0.37		0.65
Effort employee training (63)	0.74	0.30		0.74
Effort health employees (65)	0.79	0.32		0.73
Effort social performance suppliers (66)	0.58	0.42		0.61
Eigenvalue			2.96	1.32
Cronbach alpha (α)			0.76	0.62

a Extraction Method: Principal Component Analysis; Rotation Method: Oblimin with Kaiser Normalization. The Kaiser–Meyer–Olkin (KMO) indicator equals 0.788 and the *p*-value of Bartlett's Test of Sphericity is 0.000. The numbers in brackets refer to the numbers of the survey questions reported in Appendix 1.

In the regression analysis, we included four other types of motivations for CSR: to increase personal satisfaction of employees, to meet customers' demands, to limit reputational risks, and to meet (future) government regulation (Surroca et al., 2010; Brammer, Hoejmose, and Marchant, 2012). These motivations were measured in the same way as the innovation motive for CSR.

Table 11.2 reports Cronbach alphas for the five CSR motivations (innovation, reputation, customer, employee satisfaction, regulation). All except that for customer motivation meet the accepted threshold of 0.60 (Hair et al., 1998). The inter-item correlation for customer motivation is, however, equal to 0.395 ($p < 0.001$), which fits the optimal range for internal reliability of 0.20–0.40 (Briggs and Cheek, 1986), indicating that the customer motivation measure is also internally reliable. In the regression analysis, we measure motivations by averaging the response to the two survey questions per type of motive.

11.4 Results

Before estimating the model, we standardized technological competition, the five CSR motivations, and the two CSR factors.

The estimation results reported in Table 11.3 show that the innovation motive of the top manager stimulates the company's engagement in both environmental and social CSR. These results provide support for Hypothesis 11.1. For environmental CSR, the innovation motive appears to be the strongest driver of CSR, compared to other motives. For social CSR, the innovation motive is the second most important motive, after the employee satisfaction motive.

Furthermore, we find that technological competition strengthens the top manager's motivation to engage in CSR because CSR improves the firm's innovative

TABLE 11.2 Internal reliability of CSR motives[a]

Motives	*Measures*	*Mean*	*SD*
Innovation	CSR improves innovative capacity (37)	4.19	1.71
($\alpha = 0.79$)	CSR leads to innovation (22)	4.68	1.60
Reputation	CSR limits reputational risks (39)	4.34	1.70
($\alpha = 0.78$)	CSR limits reputational risks (24)	4.50	1.63
Customer	CSR increases turnover (35)	3.13	1.66
($\alpha = 0.56$)	Large customers ask for it (27)	3.77	1.89
Employees	CSR motivates the employees (33)	4.31	1.68
($\alpha = 0.74$)	CSR creates personal satisfaction for the people in our enterprise (26)	5.15	1.41
Regulation	CSR helps meeting (future) government regulation (36)	3.94	1.69
($\alpha = 0.78$)	CSR helps to meet (future) government regulation (21)	4.01	1.70

a The numbers in brackets refer to the number of the survey question reported in Appendix 1.

TABLE 11.3 Estimation results[a]

	Environmental CSR	*Social CSR*
Effects from motivations on CSR		
Innovation motive	0.148***	0.091***
Reputation motive	0.010	0.020
Customer motive	0.044	–0.019
Employee motive	0.101***	0.206***
Regulation motive	0.047*	0.030
Effects from technological competition on motivations		
Innovation motive	0.086***	
Reputation motive	0.028	
Customer motive	0.041*	
Employee motive	0.059**	
Regulation motive	0.038	

a $N = 2{,}579$. * $p < 0.05$; ** $p < 0.01$; *** $p < 0.001$. Controlled for sector, country, position in the production chain, market position, intensity of price competition, company size (measured by number of employees in FTEs), skill structure, age structure, and age respondent.

capacity, which supports Hypothesis 11.2. Besides innovation motivation, technological competition is also found to affect the customer and employee satisfaction motivations, but not as strong as the innovation motivation.

Table 11.4 reports the outcomes for the indirect and total effects of technological competition on environmental and social CSR through motivations. The indirect effect is equivalent to the multiplication of path a and path b in Figure 11.1. Table 11.4 shows that the indirect effects of technological competition on environmental and social CSR mediated through innovation motivation and employee motivation are all significant, as well as the total indirect effects of all five CSR motivations together on environmental and social CSR. These results support Hypothesis 11.3 that innovation motivation mediates the influence of technological competition on CSR. Also the total effects (i.e. the sum of direct and indirect effects) are significant for both environmental and social CSR.

11.5 Conclusion

Our study makes several contributions. First, using a large sample of 2,579 top managers of companies from 12 European countries, of which the majority are SMEs, we find that the innovation motivation of the top manager is an important determinant of firms' CSR. For environmental CSR the innovation motive is more important than any other CSR motive; for social CSR it is the second most important driver of CSR, after the employee satisfaction motive. In previous research into the motives of CSR of SMEs (Brammer, Hoejmose, and Marchant, 2012), no attention has been paid to the innovation motive as a driver of CSR of SMEs.

TABLE 11.4 Estimation results of indirect and total effects[a]

	Environmental CSR	*Social CSR*
Indirect effect from technological competition on CSR through motivations		
Innovation motivation	0.013**	0.008**
Reputation motivation	0.000	0.001
Customer motivation	0.002	−0.001
Employee motivation	0.006*	0.012**
Regulation motivation	0.002	0.001
Total effects from technological competition on CSR		
Direct effect on CSR	0.025	0.036
Total indirect effect, mediated through motives	0.023***	0.021***
Total effect on CSR	0.047*	0.057**

a * $p < 0.05$; ** $p < 0.01$; *** $p < 0.001$. Regression using macro for SPSS of Preacher and Hayes (2008) with 1,000 bootstrap samples.

A second major contribution of our study is that we show that the innovation motivation to engage in CSR is influenced by the intensity of technological competition. Earlier studies have shown that technological competition stimulates CSR (Graafland and Smid, 2015). In this study we deepen these studies by considering mediation mechanisms that can explain the positive relationship between technological competition and CSR. We find that technological competition enhances top managers' innovation motivation to engage in CSR, which in turn increases CSR. Besides, we found that technological competition instils CSR motivation of top managers because CSR raises the satisfaction of the firm's employees. This mechanism can be explained by the argument that creating a good working environment for employees is an important condition for realizing the innovative potential of the company (Mandl and Dorr, 2007).

Note

* An extended text of this chapter has been published as an open access article under the terms of the Creative Commons Attribution 4.0 International License (http://creativecommons.org/licenses/by/4.0/) in: Graafland, J.J., and Noorderhaven, N. (2020). Technological competition, innovation motive and corporate social responsibility: Evidence from top managers of European SMEs. *De Economist*, 168: 1–22. Niels Noorderhaven is affiliated to the department of Management at Tilburg University in the Netherlands.

12

COMPETITION IN INNOVATION, INTRINSIC MOTIVATION, AND ENVIRONMENTAL POLICY*

12.1 Introduction

As discussed in Chapter 6, managers may have different motives for actively pursuing CSR. Literature often distinguishes extrinsic motives driven by market incentives from intrinsic motives driven by morality or personal satisfaction (Weaver et al., 1999; Lindenberg, 2001; Aguilera et al., 2007; Muller and Kolk, 2010). When managers are extrinsically motivated, they are driven not by the activity itself but by the consequences associated with performing the activity, such as financial benefits. Intrinsically motivated actions are actions for which there is no reward but the behaviour itself.

Previous research did, however, not consider the possibility that intrinsic CSR motives may also depend on market incentives. Motivation crowding theory has recognized that financial rewarding of a desired behaviour may crowd *in* intrinsic motivation towards this type of behaviour if the financial reward is perceived as supporting the agent in performing the action (Eisenberger et al., 1999). Since CSR has been shown to stimulate innovation (Wagner, 2007b; Surroca et al., 2010; Luo and Du, 2015; Flammer and Kacperczyk, 2016; Briones Peñalver et al., 2018; Marin et al., 2017; Jiménez-Parra et al., 2018; Guerrero-Villegas et al., 2018; see also Chapter 4), a market environment that competes on technology and rewards CSR because of its innovation-enhancing effects will support managers to shape the company's strategic direction towards a higher CSR profile. This support will enlarge the moral motivation to improve EP by environmental policy practices. However, market incentives may also crowd *out* intrinsic motivation if the manager feels that these incentives are coercive, reducing the freedom to act otherwise (Lindenberg, 2001; Frey and Jegen, 2001; Treviño et al., 2006; Patzelt and Shepherd, 2011; Bowles and Polania-Reyes, 2012). In order to

DOI: 10.4324/9781003216483-15

understand how market incentives stimulate environmental policy practices, we therefore need more empirical insight into how intrinsic motives are related to market incentives. The core research question that this chapter addresses is therefore: How do market incentives affect intrinsic motivation of managers, and how do these crowding effects impact environmental policy practices?

We test the model on a sample of 650 owner-managers of SMEs from 12 European countries. Compared with their larger counterparts, the behaviour of small firms is disproportionately driven by the values and motives of the managers (Revell et al., 2010). Therefore, crowding effects are more likely to occur for SMEs than for large companies. By concentrating on owner-managers, we focus on the motives of the individuals who exert a crucial influence on their company's environmental policies (Kim et al., 2017).

This chapter makes three major contributions to literature. First, it theorizes how competitive pressures affect moral CSR motivation of owner-directors. In previous literature on CSR motives (Graafland and Van de Ven, 2006; Paulrai, 2009; Muller and Kolk, 2010; Ditlev-Simonsen and Midttun, 2011), external pressures and intrinsic motivations have always been conceptualized as independent from each other. But if intrinsic motivations are dependent on external pressures, this would lead to an underestimation of the relevance of these pressures for CSR. Second, whereas recent literature explored the relationship between competition and CSR (Fernández-Kranz and Santaló, 2010; Flammer, 2015; Graafland and Smid, 2015), no research has yet investigated the type of motivational forces that explain this relationship or contingencies in this relationship. This study will do both by researching the impact of technological competition on environmental policy practices by considering its effect on intrinsic CSR motivation and the moderating role of perceptions of owner-managers regarding the impact of CSR on the innovative capability of their firm. A third contribution of this chapter is that it applies motivation crowding theory to CSR motives of owner-managers. Literature on motivation crowding theory has, until now, focused on behaviour of households (Frey and Jegen, 2001), employees (Hossain and Li, 2014; Gubler et al., 2016), and executives (Pepper and Gore, 2015). But how intrinsic motivations of owner-managers are affected by market incentives has not been theorized or empirically researched.

In what follows, we first present the theoretical framework and the hypotheses, then describe the methodology and report the estimation results, and finally summarize the findings in the conclusion.

12.2 Conceptual Framework

Motivation Crowding Theory

Motivation (i.e. the reason upon which one acts) is an important antecedent to behaviour (Treviño et al., 2006). The literature distinguishes extrinsic from intrinsic motives. An extrinsic motive encourages behaviour because it has instrumental value for other goals, such as financial benefits. Intrinsically motivated actions are actions for which there is no reward but the behaviour itself (Muller and Kolk, 2010).

As argued by Lindenberg (2001), one type of intrinsic motivation concerns feelings of moral obligations (Frey and Jegen, 2001). If one is morally motivated, one acts out of a sense of obligation, responsibility, or concern with the social good rather than out of self-interest. The goal is to act appropriately. This type of intrinsic motivation is particularly relevant for CSR because responsibility belongs to the core of the Corporate Social *Responsibility* concept. Owner-managers may care about CSR intrinsically because they feel that they are responsible for the prevention of negative impacts of their companies on society and the natural environment.

Motivation crowding theory has recognized that financial rewards of a desired behaviour may crowd *in* or crowd *out* intrinsic motivations to perform the behaviour (Lindenberg, 2001; Bowles and Polania-Reyes, 2012). The effect of a given reward in terms of intrinsic motivation is contingent on how it affects an individual's perceived autonomy because freedom of choice is a precondition for the possibility of taking responsibility (Velasquez, 2011). According to motivation crowding theory, intrinsic motivation is activated when conditions are conducive to its expression (Eisenberger et al., 1999). Hence, crowding in of intrinsic motivation is observed if external rewards are enlarging the freedom to act (Frey and Jegen, 2001; Lindenberg, 2001; Bowles and Polania-Reyes, 2012). In contrast, crowding out is observed if external incentives are perceived as an external, controlling intervention that removes the locus of control from the person affected (Deci et al., 1999).

Technological Competition, Innovation, and Intrinsic CSR Motivation

In this section we consider the relationship between intrinsic motivation of owner-managers towards CSR and competitive environment. Firms can compete in many different dimensions, such as price, distribution channels, supplier inputs, and technology (Vickers, 1995; Shapiro, 1989). In this chapter, we focus on technological competition because earlier research by Graafland and Smid (2015) showed that technological competition rather than price competition drives CSR. Literature has given several arguments and empirical support for a positive effect of CSR on innovation (Wagner, 2007b; Surroca et al., 2010; Luo and Du, 2015; Flammer and Kacperczyk, 2016; Briones Peñalver et al., 2018; Marin et al., 2017; Jiménez-Parra et al., 2018; Guerrero-Villegas et al., 2018). For example, CSR attracts more intelligent, motivated, experienced, visionary, creative, and committed employees who foster the innovative capability of the firm (Guerrero-Villegas et al.,

2018). Furthermore, CSR is likely to relieve customers and employees from short-termism, stimulate customers to be more loyal to the firm and tolerate failures from new products, and encourage employees to invest more effort in risky innovation (Flammer and Kacperczyk, 2016). Given these innovation-enhancing effects of CSR, an environment where companies compete on innovation will make CSR a more valuable strategic option. On the basis of the tenets of motivation crowding theory, we therefore conjecture that the intensity of technological competition may increase the moral motivation of owner-managers towards CSR.

However, this crowding-in effect is conditional on the owner-managers' perception that CSR increases the innovative capability of their company because only then the owner-manager will perceive that such a market context will be supportive for CSR and convey freedom to the owner-manager to shape the company's strategic direction towards a higher CSR profile, increasing intrinsic motivation. If the owner-manager does not believe that CSR enforces the firm's innovation, it is expected that a market environment with more intense competition on technology decreases the owner-manager's intrinsic motivation towards making costly investments into CSR. Experiencing autonomy requires that owner-managers have a set of options available (Patzelt and Shepherd, 2011). The more intense technological competition, the more the owner-manager will feel pressure to spend the available company's resources on investments that he/she believes will improve the firm's innovation and the less options there are to invest in CSR-related actions if they do not foster the firm's innovation. In a market context in which CSR would harm the company's competitiveness and put the continuity of the company at risk, the owner-manager has less freedom to pursue a CSR policy and will be more inclined to deny a moral duty to CSR because taking responsibility assumes freedom (Velasquez, 2011). If it is impossible to pursue CSR without endangering the future of the company, this will lessen the owner-manager's responsibility to CSR because owner-managers also have a moral duty towards their own company, such as providing job security for the employees.

In other words, we surmise that the relationship between intensity of technological competition and intrinsically motivation of CSR is likely to be positively moderated by the perceived effect of CSR on the innovative capability of their company. Moderation means that the influence of an independent variable on a dependent variable is conditional on a third variable (the moderator) (Preacher et al., 2007). The reward of CSR that results from the interaction between technological competition and perceived effect of CSR on innovation creates the freedom to engage in CSR that crowds in intrinsic motivation. But if CSR is not conducive to the innovative capability of the firm, owner-managers of companies that are operating in a highly technological competitive environment feel pressure to invest the financial resources in other ways that are believed to be more innovation enhancing. This pressure reduces the freedom to pursue an active

CSR policy and decreases intrinsic CSR motivation. This leads to the following hypothesis:

Hypothesis 12.1 The owner-manager's perception that CSR enforces the innovative capability of the firm positively moderates the relationship between technological competition and intrinsic CSR motivation.

Intrinsic Motivation and Environmental Policy Practices

We complement Hypothesis 12.1 by a second hypothesis on the effects of intrinsic motivation on environmental practices. Research has shown that the greater intrinsic motivations towards CSR, the more likely it is that a firm will engage in CSR. Muller and Kolk (2010) found that moral commitment has a strong and significant effect on CSR. Ditlev-Simonsen and Midttun (2011) researched the perceptions of three stakeholder groups regarding the motivations of managers towards CSR and found that these groups estimate that intrinsic motivations, such as morality and sustainability, affect managers' CSR engagement, but less than financial motives. Masurel (2007) analysed a sample of 57 SMEs and found that moral duty is mentioned by 51 companies as a reason to invest voluntarily in environmental measures, which is the third most important motive out of 12 motives. Paulrai (2009) found that environmental practices are more often morally motivated than motivated by legislative requirements or market competitiveness. Coppa and Sriramesh (2013) found that, for a sample of 105 SMEs, moral motivation proved to be the most important reason to engage in CSR, followed by long-term sustainability. On a sample that mainly consisted of SMEs, Graafland and Van de Ven (2006) found that the use of CSR instruments, including ISO certification, is more related to moral motivation than to financial motivation. On the basis of these researches, we expect that the intrinsic motivation of the owner-manager of an SME will encourage the use of environmental policy practices by the firm:

Hypothesis 12.2 Environmental policy practices are positively related to the intrinsic CSR motivation of the owner-manager.

The full model is depicted in Figure 12.1.

12.3 Methodology

The data have been taken from the survey in 2014. Environmental practices are operationalized by ISO 14001 certification. Following Oliveira et al. (2016), ISO 14001 certification was measured by a three-point scale, with 0 if the enterprise is not certified for ISO 14001 at all, 0.5 if it is certified for part of the enterprise's operational sites, and 1 if it is certified for all operational sites of the enterprise.

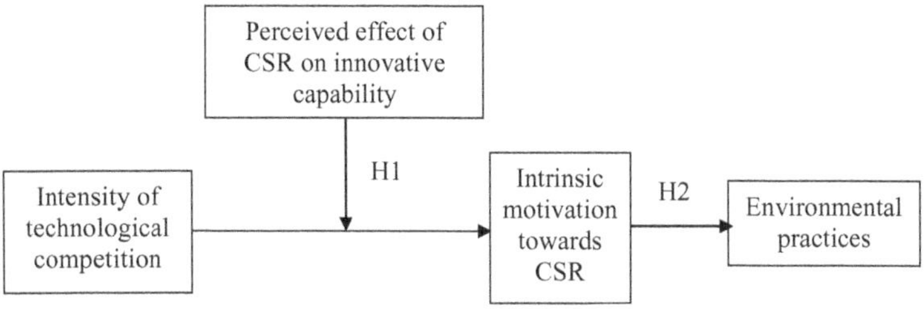

FIGURE 12.1 Conceptual framework

Following Graafland and Van de Ven (2006), the intrinsic (moral) motivation of the owner-manager was measured by the response to the statement 'It is a moral duty of a company to engage in CSR' in response to the survey question: 'How important are the following motives to engage in CSR?' The perception of the owner-manager that CSR enforces the innovative capability of the firm was measured by the response to the statement 'CSR improves the innovative capability' in response to the survey question 'To what extent does engagement in CSR influence the following aspects for your enterprise?' Following Graafland and Smid (2015), we measured technological competition with a survey question asking the respondent to reflect on the extent to which his or her enterprise 'is prone to competition on product innovation in the market for your main product or service'. The responses to the three survey questions for moral motivation, perceived CSR effect on innovation and intensity of technological competition were all administered on a seven-point Likert scale ranging from 'not at all' (1) to 'very much' (7).

12.4 Results

Because of the discrete measurements of intrinsic CSR motivation and ISO 14001 certification, we used ordered logit regression analysis, which is often used in analyses of human preferences. The (country-weighted) estimation results are reported in Table 12.2. The interaction term between the intensity of

TABLE 12.1 Descriptives[a]

Variables	*Mean*	*SD*
ISO 14001 certification (57)	0.10	0.28
Intrinsic CSR motivation (25)	5.1	1.5
Perceived CSR effect on innovative capability (37)	4.2	1.7
Intensity of technological competition (122)	5.1	1.7

a The numbers in brackets refer to the number of the survey question reported in Appendix 1.

technological competition and the perceived effect of CSR on innovative capability of the firm has a significant positive effect on intrinsic motivation towards CSR, supporting Hypothesis 12.1 that the perceived innovation effect of CSR moderates the influence of technological competition on intrinsic CSR motivation. Intrinsic CSR motivation is found to encourage ISO 14001 certification, which supports Hypothesis 12.2. Also the interaction term is seen to increase ISO 14001 certification. Since the interaction term reflects external rewards of CSR due to the innovation-enhancing effect of CSR, this effect can be interpreted as a direct influence of extrinsic motivation on the implementation of ISO 14001 certification.

Based on the estimation results of Table 12.2, it can be calculated that technological competition increases intrinsic motivation and ISO 14001 certification if the perceived effect of CSR on innovative capability exceeds 3, which holds for 64% of the owner-managers in our sample (see Table 12.3). For 20% of the owner-managers (with perceived effect of CSR on innovative capability lower than 3), the intensity of technological competition has a negative effect on moral motivation and ISO 14001 certification.

TABLE 12.2 Estimation results[a]

	Intrinsic CSR motivation	*ISO 14001 certification*
Technological competition (TC)	−0.27*	−0.39*
Perceived CSR effect on innovative capability (PCI)	−0.18	−0.44
Interaction term (TC * PCI)	0.11***	0.10*
Intrinsic CSR motivation		0.20*
R^2 (Nagelkerke)	0.28	0.28

a Ordered logit regression analysis. * $p < 0.05$, ** $p < 0.01$, *** $p < 0.001$. Controlled for country, sector, position in the chain, company size (measured by the number of employees in FTEs), age structure and skill structure of the labour force of the company, and the age of the respondent.

TABLE 12.3 Effects of technological competition on intrinsic CSR motivation and ISO 14001 certification

Perceived CSR effect on innovative capability	*1*	*2*	*3*	*4*	*5*	*6*	*7*
% of sample	*10*	*10*	*14*	*22*	*21*	*17*	*7*
Effect of intensity of technological competition on:							
Intrinsic CSR motivation[a]	−0.16	−0.05	0.06	0.17	0.28	0.39	0.50
ISO 14001 certification[b]	−0.06	−0.03	0.00	0.03	0.06	0.10	0.13

a Calculated as -0.27 + 0.11 * perceived CSR effect on innovative capability. The coefficients are taken from Table 12.2.

b Calculated as 0.20 * (-0.27 + 0.11 * perceived CSR effect on innovative capability) + 0.10 * (-0.39 + 0.10 * perceived CSR effect on innovative capability). The coefficients are taken from Table 12.2.

12.5 Conclusion

In this chapter, we have tested the relevance of motivation crowding theory to the moral motivations of owner-managers towards CSR on a sample of 650 owner-managers from 12 European countries. Our research indicates that financial rewards of CSR crowd in the intrinsic moral motivation of owner-managers towards CSR. Previous studies by Weaver et al. (1999), Graafland and Van de Ven (2006), Aguilera et al. (2007), Paulrai (2009), and Muller and Kolk (2010) did not take account of the interrelationship between external pressures and intrinsic motivation towards CSR through motivation crowding. By providing scientific insight into motivation crowding effects, our study develops a more nuanced understanding of the motivating power of market conditions for CSR. As market competition that rewards CSR stimulates moral drivers, the disregard of this relationship in literature leads to an underestimation of the relevance of market incentives for CSR.

Our analysis also contributes to institutional theory and its application to CSR. Previous research has shown that free market institutions (Baughn et al., 2007; Hartmann and Uhlenbruck, 2015) and intensity of competition in the marketplace lead to better CSR outcomes (Fernández-Kranz and Santaló, 2010; Flammer, 2015; Graafland and Smid, 2015). Both are connected because free market institutions stimulate a market environment where companies compete on technology (Nyström, 2008; Herrera-Echeverri et al., 2014). But no research has yet investigated the type of motivational forces that explain the positive effects of market institutions and competition on CSR. Our analysis indicates that, under certain conditions, crowding in of intrinsic motivation is one of the channels that explain these positive influences from free market institutions and intensity of competition on CSR. Our study also makes a start with research in contingencies in the relationship between competitive pressures and CSR. More specifically, we find that whether technological competition enforces moral motivation and the implementation of EMSs depends on the perception of owner-managers regarding CSR impacts on innovative capability of their firm.

Third, previous literature on motivation crowding theory has analysed various types of consumer and household behaviour (Frey and Jegen, 2001; Bowles and Polania-Reyes, 2012) as well as responses of employees and executives to internal reward systems (Pepper and Gore, 2015; Hossain and Li, 2014; Gubler et al., 2016). Our study contributes to this literature on motivation crowding theory by applying it to strategic decision-making on CSR by owner-managers. Whereas the majority of studies into crowding effects on behaviour of consumers, households, and employees support the crowding out hypothesis, our study indicates that crowding-in effects are relevant in the CSR behaviour of owner-managers. A possible explanation for this difference in findings is that rewarding socially desirable behaviour is more likely to be perceived as supportive and increasing self-determination in a business context than in the context of a private household. Companies that face severe competition may not be able to survive if costly investments in CSR are not rewarded by market parties, whereas financial rewarding of household contributions to the common good, such as blood donation, will only have a negligible effect on the continuity of their way of life.

Note

* An extended text of this chapter has been published as an open access article under the terms of the Creative Commons Attribution-NonCommercial-NoDerivs License (permission granted by Wiley) in: Graafland, J. (2020). Competition in technology and innovation, motivation crowding, and environmental policy. *Corporate Social Responsibility and Environmental Management*, 27: 137–145.

PART IV

Institutional Drivers of Corporate Social Responsibility

13

RECONSIDERING THE RELEVANCE OF SOCIAL LICENCE PRESSURE AND GOVERNMENT REGULATION FOR ENVIRONMENTAL IMPACTS OF SMEs*

13.1 Introduction

Recently, research into CSR has become more focused on its institutional roots (Doh and Guay, 2006; Aguilera et al., 2007; Matten and Moon, 2008). An important institutional constituent that affects CSR is the monitoring of CSR by NGOs and media (Campbell, 2007; Bartley, 2007). Campbell (2007: 958) hypothesized that

> corporations will be more likely to act in socially responsible ways if there are private, independent organizations, including NGOs, social movement organizations, institutional investors, and the press, in their environment who monitor their behavior and, when necessary, mobilize to change it.

This institutional factor is often held to be particularly relevant for large multinational enterprises that have increasingly become global operators. Indeed, because of the weak enforcement capacities of national governments to regulate multinational enterprises, a growing number of non-state actors have appeared, pressuring enterprises to take on greater responsibility for the social and environmental consequences of their operations by naming and shaming irresponsible enterprises (Locke et al., 2006). This has led to enterprises having a greater interest in obtaining a social licence to operate from civil society and to involve communities from a very early stage in their environmental decision-making.

Social licence has been described as an informal social contract existing between an industry and the community in which it operates (Lacey and Lamont, 2014). It refers to the broad and ongoing acceptance or approval of a company's operations by local communities and other stakeholders, who can affect the profitability of

DOI: 10.4324/9781003216483-17

those operations (Zhang et al., 2015). Whereas social licence pressures give large multinational enterprises a strong incentive to actively engage with CSR, its relevance for SMEs has been disputed (Jeppesen, 2006). Hendry (2006) found that the smaller the effect an enterprise has on a certain issue, such as GHG emissions, the less likely it is to be targeted by NGOs. Indeed, the concept of social licence to operate originated from CSR in the mining and minerals industry (Hall et al., 2015). Actions against mining projects at a local level because of visible effects on the environment and social impacts on the lives of the neighbouring communities, induced mining industries to increase the focus on stakeholders, and social obligations to ensure social licence and prevent high financial costs created by such conflicts. Lynch-Wood and Williamson (2007) argued that a small enterprise that has little potential to cause significant environmental harm will be less visible and of less concern to a greater range of stakeholders than a larger enterprise with more capacity for harm. Furthermore, small enterprises mostly operate as market followers, whereas for NGOs it is more efficient to target influential enterprises such as market leaders in their organizational field, as this could also induce other enterprises to change their behaviour (Hendry, 2006).

SMEs comprise the vast majority of all European firms (98%) and collectively are the largest employer in the EU (67%) (European Commission, 2002). Although small enterprises individually have a negligible influence on the macro level, collectively they cause significant environmental damage because of the large number of small enterprises. Hillary (2000) estimated that SMEs together account for up to 70% of industrial pollution worldwide. Hence, it is evidently important to stimulate CSR of SMEs. The view that, when it comes to SMEs, social licence pressures for improving environmental impacts are weak might imply that traditional forms of government regulation providing minimum standards for the environmental impacts of SMEs remain the most effective means to influence the behaviour of SMEs. In their overview of the literature, Williamson et al. (2006) showed that a number of studies have identified legislation as the key driver of environmental initiatives of SMEs, and this result is confirmed in their own empirical research (based on 31 interviews with manufacturing SME owners/managers). However, other studies have been more critical. For example, Petts et al. (1999) demonstrated that managers of SMEs believe that regulation on its own will not be sufficient because of the inadequacies of the regulatory regimes (Petts et al., 1999). Regulation can be excessive, unnecessary, or poorly implemented, which may be particularly a problem for small businesses by creating costs in terms of time or money that bear more heavily on smaller than larger business.

Also the view of Williamson et al. (2006), Lynch-Wood and Williamson (2007), and others that social licence pressures are too weak to motivate SMEs to improve environmental impacts (beyond compliance behaviour) can be questioned. Whereas large enterprises can more easily transfer activities to other regions in which they operate, SMEs are much more embedded in, and therefore restricted to, their local community (Doshi et al., 2013; Fuller and Tian, 2006; Jenkins, 2009). Therefore, small enterprises may be seriously challenged if their environment becomes hostile to the enterprise, if it becomes known that they cause harm to their local communities by their environmental impacts, and if they fail to adequately respond to the community's grievances (Aragón-Correa et al., 2008). Furthermore, as previous research has shown that SMEs are heterogeneous in nature (Brammer, Jackson et al., 2012; Jenkins, 2004), propositions about the significance of the social licence concept to SMEs cannot be assumed to apply to all sizes of SMEs.

The research questions of this chapter are therefore: (1) Do social licence pressures affect environmental impacts of different types of SMEs; how robust are these effects for micro, small, and medium-sized enterprises? (2) How do social licence pressures influence environmental impacts of SMEs? Do they have a direct effect or can we also detect indirect effects in the sense that social licence pressures mobilize market parties thereby inducing strategic market benefits that stimulate SMEs to improve their environmental impacts? (3) How do the direct and indirect effects of social licence compare to the effects of government regulation on environmental impacts?

Currently, there are no large-scale empirical studies into the relevance of the social licence pressures for the environmental impacts of SMEs that incorporate the heterogeneous nature of SMEs. In this chapter, we focus on perceived social licence pressure instead of real social licence pressure, not only because gathering data of real social licence pressure would be very costly, but also because it is the perceived rather than the real social licence pressure that shapes the motivation of the SME to improve environmental impacts and hence its behaviour. The company's perception refers to the way in which issues that arise in the company's environment are understood by the company, including their salience and centrality to the business. If companies do not recognize increasing environmental concerns in the local media, public opinion, or societal organizations, they will not respond and act upon them. Reversely, if the real social licence pressure is weak but companies perceive them as strong, they will respond stronger than can be expected on basis of the real social licence pressure. The model is tested on a large sample of 1,349 micro, 2,096 small, and 1,484 medium-sized enterprises in 12 European countries.

The content of this chapter is as follows. Section 13.2 presents the conceptual framework. Section 13.3 describes the methods. Section 13.4 presents the empirical analysis, and Section 13.5 summarizes the main findings.

13.2 Conceptual Framework

Following Lynch-Wood and Williamson (2007), social licence pressure is defined as a form of control mechanism that requires enterprises to meet demands and expectations that emerge from neighbourhoods, environmental groups, community members, and other elements of the surrounding civil society (Lynch-Wood and Williamson, 2007: 321–322). This concept is applicable to both large and small enterprises, as it includes (among others) the demands and expectations of international NGOs (which are more relevant for large companies) as well as the demands and expectations of local communities or neighbourhoods (which may particularly challenge SMEs). Since stakeholders often represent a broad range of interests across a range of societal levels, Dare et al. (2014) conceptualize social licence as a continuum of multiple licences. This conceptualization recognizes the existence of multiple and often overlapping social licences across various communities, such as neighbours, local residents, local governments at the local level; NGOs and governments at the regional level; and national government and international NGOs at the societal level.

The conceptual framework is depicted in Figure 13.1. Next, the framework is discussed in more detail.

Social Licence and Company Size

We take our starting point in institutional theory, which considers the constraints on organizations to conform to external expectations (DiMaggio and Powell, 1983). Companies operate in an external context regulated by institutions that define what constitutes legitimate behaviour (Shah, 2011). Companies that do not meet society's expectations regarding CSR risk losing their licence to operate from civil society and hence their institutional legitimacy. Societal organizations often put indirect pressure on the enterprise by increasing the demand for transparency on corporate practices and attracting public attention to misbehaviour (King, 2008; Bartley and Child, 2011). In this way they can substantially affect the institutional legitimacy of a company and mobilize various types of stakeholders on the capital market, product market, and labour market if the companies abuse the power society grants them.

In literature, several authors have claimed that the importance of social licence as control mechanism is likely to depend on the size of the enterprise. Because of their smaller size, Brammer, Hoejmose, and Marchant. (2012) argued that

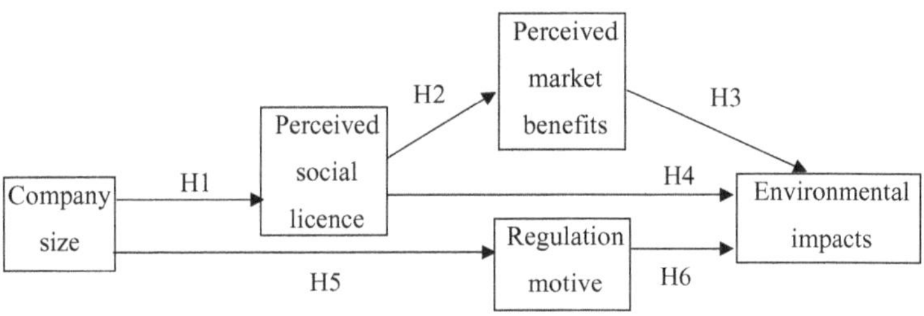

FIGURE 13.1 Conceptual framework

SMEs are less visible to NGOs and media and cannot take advantage of the same publicity as large enterprises. Naming and shaming strategies are therefore less relevant for SMEs (Gunningham et al., 2004). Furthermore, large enterprises, more often than small enterprises, tend to be market leaders that set an example for other enterprises. Hence, it is more efficient for environmental groups and media to target large enterprises, as in this way they can also indirectly induce other enterprises to change their behaviour (Hendry, 2006). Hendry (2006) also found that the larger the effect an enterprise has on a certain issue, the more likely it is to be targeted by societal organizations. An enterprise that has the potential to cause significant environmental harm will be more visible, and of more concern to a greater range of stakeholders, than an enterprise with less capacity for harm (Lynch-Wood and Williamson, 2007). The power of customers manifests itself through collective market pressure, and this pressure is normally targeted at large enterprises because it requires the mobilization of many individual customers. Furthermore, the density of the NGOs itself – that is, the number of ties that actually exist among NGOs as compared with the number that could exist (Hendry, 2006: 55) – is also important. If multiple organizations are monitoring an enterprise and share information, an enterprise is more likely to be targeted (Hendry, 2006). Finally, NGOs usually target larger enterprises because these enterprises are more likely to respond in order to protect their reputations (Baron and Diermeier, 2007; McDonnell and King, 2013). The enterprises most vulnerable to negative publicity are those with high brand recognition that are targeting young consumers (Elliot and Freeman, 2001). The overwhelming proportion of these enterprises is large enterprises. According to Unido (2006), enterprises producing for non-branded or extremely price-sensitive consumer markets and with no connections to foreign markets experience low pressure to implement CSR. As Williamson and Lynch-Wood (2001) discussed, key stakeholders of such SMEs would have limited interest in their CSR. This leads to our first hypothesis:

> *Hypothesis 13.1 The social licence pressure perceived by a company depends positively on its size.*

Social Licence and CSR: Mediation by Market Benefits

The importance of institutional legitimacy for the company can be argued by resource dependency theory, which states that the success of a company crucially depends on the availability of certain resources. Underlying the resource-based view of the firm is the premise that differences in enterprise performance occur directly as a result of the resources that enterprises acquire (Branco and Rodrigues, 2006). One of the most valuable resources for enterprises is a good reputation (Galbreath, 2005; Orlitzky, 2008; Roberts and Dowling, 2002). Intangibles like reputation may be mediators through which CSR improves the (long-term) financial performance of the enterprise (Surroca et al., 2010). If it becomes known in the marketplace that an enterprise is involved in an environmental scandal, its reputation will be harmed. This will provoke negative reactions from various types of stakeholders on the financial markets (Hamilton, 1995), output markets (Fombrun and Shanley, 1990; Brown and Dacin, 1997; Logsdon and Wood, 2002; Gardberg and Fombrun, 2006), and labour markets (Turban and Greening, 1997; Reinhardt, 1999). Enterprises that are viewed negatively by the public may also lose the loyalty of their internal stakeholders (Barney and Hansen, 1994).

Although social licence pressure is particularly relevant for large companies, it may be expected that small, and even micro, companies will also be sensitive to potential harmful reputational effects if their CSR is monitored by local NGOs or local media. Small enterprises rely to a much greater extent than large enterprises on the local communities in which they operate (Marquis and Battilana, 2009). Due to their financial power and size, larger enterprises can more easily escape the pressures from the local community to which small enterprises are restricted (Doshi et al., 2013). As there are locational sunk costs that restrict their geographical mobility, a good reputation has an important strategic value for small enterprises too (Crouch, 2006). According to Fuller and Tian (2006), the legitimacy with immediate stakeholders, employees, customers, suppliers, and their local community is at stake in a far more direct way for small enterprises than it is with large enterprises. Because of their intimate relationship with the community in which they operate, SMEs also need to pursue a community-friendly policy (Jenkins, 2009). If a local NGO or newspaper spreads negative news about a small company, it might directly harm its reputation at its location, and the company would run the risk of economic loss (Kusyk and Lozano, 2007; Russo and Tencati, 2009). Hence, also an SME will realize that negative environmental impacts may have serious consequences for the enterprise's reputation and economic performance if it has indications that local NGOs or media observe its CSR. This leads to the second hypothesis:

Hypothesis 13.2 The market benefits that a company perceives from its CSR depend positively on the perceived social licence pressure.

The perception that CSR creates substantial market benefits provides an important motivation to improve environmental impacts (Aguilera et al., 2007; Bansal and Roth, 2000). Expectancy (or instrumentality-valence) theory argues that motivation depends on a combination of perceived instrumentality, the probability that a certain effort will lead to a certain benefit, and valence, the anticipated value or the perceived motivational strength of that benefit (Porter and Lawler, 1968; Campbell et al., 1970). In the case of CSR, this theory implies that if the managers of a company perceive that CSR has substantial instrumental value for reputation and economic success, both of which have a high valence to the company, the company will be more motivated towards CSR. Since motivation (i.e. the reason upon which one acts) is an important antecedent to behaviour (Treviño et al., 2006; Kuckertz and Wagner, 2010), we posit a third hypothesis:

Hypothesis 13.3 The environmental impacts of a company depend positively on the perceived market benefits from CSR.

If both Hypothesis 13.2 and Hypothesis 13.3 are supported, the perceived market benefits from CSR mediate the influence of social licence pressures on environmental impacts.

Direct Effect of Social Licence on CSR

Besides influencing enterprises indirectly through the market response of various types of stakeholders of the enterprise on the capital market, product market, and labour market, societal organizations can also appeal directly to the enterprise itself (Hendry, 2006; King, 2008). In order to obtain legitimacy, companies often respond to social licence pressure by forming alliances with NGOs (Shah, 2011) and involving societal organizations and local communities in their complex environmental decision-making through stakeholder dialogue (Hall et al., 2015). These direct contacts between the enterprise and societal organizations may make managers more aware of the moral dimensions of being socially responsible and thus stimulate their environmental impacts for other reasons than market benefits. NGOs and media are important institutional players that have the ability to influence social norms, values, and societal expectations on corporate behaviour (Weaver et al., 1999). The standards that societal institutions refer to when pressuring companies to pursue CSR are often framed in terms of ethical values (Suchman, 1995). In this way, NGOs and media can stimulate the awareness of moral reasons for CSR and foster the internalization of societal values related to CSR. Revell et al. (2010) found that awareness about environmental impacts stimulates SMEs to get involved in it. Based on this, we hypothesize that SMEs that perceive that they are confronted with social licence pressure of environmental groups, members from the local community, or other elements of the surrounding civil society are more likely to implement measures to improve their environmental impacts:

Hypothesis 13.4 The environmental impacts of a company are positively associated with the perceived social licence pressure.

Environmental Impacts and Government Regulation

Besides social licence pressure and the market benefits of CSR, enterprises may also want to improve environmental impacts in order to comply with (future) government regulation – the regulation motive. There is a spectrum of policies which governments may use to encourage CSR, and these vary by their 'regulatory density' in that they impose different levels of requirements and space for discretion upon business. According to Rivera et al. (2009), compliance with environmental public policies and their regulations is the prevalent response of firms in the United States. Environmental legislation can affect the continued growth of an enterprise. Stricter environmental regulation can therefore be a major reason why an enterprise is concerned about its impact on the natural environment (Brammer, Hoejmose, and Marchant, 2012). Literature frequently mentions that government regulation is a major driver for companies' environmental management, as non-compliance may increase the threats of penalties and fines (Agan et al., 2013). The regulation motive may not only induce companies to comply to current environmental legislation but also stimulate them to invest proactively in improving their environmental impacts beyond compliance in order to lower the costs of adapting to future regulations (Masurel, 2007; Berman et al., 1999). Darnall (2009) showed that proactive companies are more likely to improve their environmental impacts when environmental regulation becomes more stringent, while diminishing the profits of other firms.

As societal pressures particularly induce beyond compliance environmental behaviour among large companies, Lynch-Wood and Williamson (2007) and Williamson et al. (2006) argued that government regulation is more relevant in the case of small companies. Also, small companies themselves might favour external forms of regulation because this generates a 'level playing field' that allows them to concentrate on the economic aspects and leave social and environmental aspects to the government (Studer et al., 2006). Similarly, Revell and Blackburn (2007) found in a study among 40 SMEs in the UK that they prefer regulation for environmental problems instead of solving them voluntarily. Based on these arguments and findings, we posit the following hypotheses:

Hypothesis 13.5 The regulation motive is more important for small companies than for large companies.

Hypothesis 13.6 The environmental impacts of an SME depend positively on the regulation motive.

13.3 Methodology

The data are taken from the survey in 2011. The analysis focuses on the environmental dimension of CSR.

Environmental impacts are operationalized by several indicators for environmental management practices and for impacts on energy consumption, waste, and water consumption. For each issue, we use two measures for environmental management (efforts and formal procedures) and one measure for impact. For formal procedures we use targets for environmental impacts and (internal) reporting on the realization of these impacts, measured on a three-point scale ranging from

TABLE 13.1 Descriptive statistics of variables[a]

Variable	*Measurement*	*Mean*	*SD*
Environmental impacts (α = 0.70)[e]	Effort to reduce energy consumption (91)	0.66	0.37
	Effort to reduce waste (93)	0.77	0.34
	Effort to reduce water consumption (92)	0.61	0.40
	Procedural steps to reduce energy consumption (96)	0.27	0.24
	Procedural steps to reduce waste (98)	0.29	0.23
	Procedural steps to reduce water consumption (97)	0.09	0.21
	Decrease in energy consumption during 2007–2010 (102)	0.44	1.38
	Decrease in waste disposal during 2007–2010 (105)	0.37	1.21
	Decrease in water consumption during 2007–2010 (104)	0.34	1.09
Perceived market benefits (α = 0.74)	Reputation (39)	4.54	1.59
	Financial market (30)	2.72	1.59
	Product market (35)	3.26	1.66
	Labour market (32)	4.36	1.64
Regulation motive (α = 0.78)	Motive (21)	4.10	1.67
	Perceived effect (36)	4.04	1.68
Perceived social licence pressure (α = 0.70)	Local community (13)	4.29	1.92
	Societal organizations (14)	3.70	1.94
	Intensity of CSR monitoring by NGOs and/or media (42)	2.30	1.67
Company size	Natural log of number of FTEs	3.17	1.32

a The numbers in brackets refer to the number of the survey question reported in Appendix 1.

0 (no targets and reporting), 0.5 (targets or reporting), to 1 (targets and reporting) (see Chapters 7 and 8). Besides formal procedures, we use a measure for the (informal) efforts (e.g. concrete actions) to improve environmental impacts in the future (see Chapters 2, 9, and 11), measured on a three-point scale ranging from 0 (no effort), 0.5 (incidental effort), to 1 (continuous effort). For example, construction enterprises can take various practical measures to substitute energy-intensive building materials by less energy-intensive materials, such as the use of environmentally friendly cooling systems.

For environmental impacts, we use questions measuring the actual use of energy consumption, waste, and water consumption during the period 2007–2010. We measure enterprise size by the (natural logarithm of the) number of employees (in FTEs).

The perceived market benefits from CSR are measured by four questions on reputation as a motivation for CSR and the perceived effects of CSR on the financial, product, and labour market. The regulation motive is measured by two questions on the motivation and the perceived effects of CSR on the ability to meet (future) government regulation.

The perceived social licence pressure is measured by three questions measuring the perceived importance of the company's relationship with the local community and with societal organizations, and the perceived intensity of the monitoring of the company's CSR by NGOs and media.

The internal reliability of the dependent and independent variables has been assessed by Cronbach's alpha (α). Table 13.1 shows that the Cronbach's alpha of the estimated models varies between 0.70 and 0.78, indicating good internal consistency (Hair et al., 1998).

13.4 Results

We used structural equation modelling to test the structure of our conceptual model using maximum likelihood as estimation technique. The structural model included the measurement model. The main estimation results are reported in the first four columns of Table 13.2.

The estimation results show that the perceived social licence pressure increases with company size, which confirms Hypothesis 13.1. Perceived social licence pressure has a significant positive effect on perceived market benefits from CSR, supporting Hypothesis 13.2. Environmental impacts significantly, positively, depend on perceived market benefits from CSR, which supports Hypothesis 13.3. The perceived social licence pressure has also a significant direct effect on environmental impacts, providing support for Hypothesis 13.4. Also, the regulation motive improves environmental impacts, which supports Hypothesis 13.6, but Hypothesis 13.5 – that the strength of the regulation motive decreases with company size – is rejected.

Table 13.3 presents estimation results of three structural equation models that test the four hypotheses regarding the effects of social licence pressures on market

TABLE 13.2 Estimation results of structural equation models[a]

	1	*2*	*3*	*4*
	Perceived social licence pressure	*Regulation motive*	*Perceived market benefits*	*Environmental impacts*
Perceived social licence pressure			0.38***	0.12***
Perceived market benefits				0.20***
Regulation motive				0.10***
Company size	0.14***	0.12***	0.07***	0.11***
R^2	0.04	0.05	0.18	0.20

a Standardized coefficients; * $p < 0.05$, ** $p < 0.01$, ***, $p < 0.001$. Controlled for sector, region, and inverse Mill's ratio. CFI = 0.96; TLI = 0.94; RMSEA = 0.03; SRMR = 0.02; N = 4,929

TABLE 13.3 Estimation results for subsamples[a]

Enterprise size	*Micro*		*Small*		*Medium-sized*	
	5	*6*	*7*	*8*	*9*	*10*
	Perceived market benefits	*Environmental impacts*	*Perceived market benefits*	*Environmental impacts*	*Perceived market benefits*	*Environmental impacts*
Perceived social licence pressure	0.35***	0.12**	0.35***	0.13***	0.44***	0.10*
Perceived market benefits		0.15***		0.19***		0.26***
Regulation motive		0.10**		0.10**		0.07
Company size	0.04	−0.01	0.06*	0.04	0.07*	0.02
R^2	0.16	0.16	0.15	0.17	0.22	0.21
Global fit indices for structural model						
CFI	0.96		0.95		0.95	
TLI	0.94		0.93		0.94	
RMSEA	0.03		0.03		0.03	
SRMR	0.03		0.03		0.03	
N	1,349		2,096		1,484	

a Standardized coefficients; * $p < 0.05$; ** $p < 0.01$; *** $p < 0.001$. Controlled for sector, region, and inverse Mill's ratio.

benefits and the effects of social licence pressures, market benefits, and regulation motive for three subsamples of micro, small, and medium-sized enterprises.

The results show that all four hypotheses are also supported on these subsamples. Hence, the finding that perceived social licence pressures affect environmental impacts, directly as well as indirectly through perceived market benefits, is robust for different class sizes of enterprises.

On the basis of the estimation results of the structural equation models in Table 13.3, we can calculate the total effects of social licence pressure on environmental impacts as the sum of the direct effect of perceived social licence pressure on environmental impacts and the indirect effect through mediation by perceived market benefits for the three subsamples (see Table 13.4). The first row in Table 13.4 presents the direct effects of perceived social licence pressure on environmental impacts as reported in Table 13.3. The second row presents the indirect effects, which are equal to the multiplication of the coefficient of perceived social licence pressure in the regression analysis of market benefits and the coefficient of perceived market benefits in the regression analysis of environmental impacts (Preacher et al., 2007). For all size classes of companies, both the direct and indirect effects through mediation by perceived market benefits are significant. The indirect effect of perceived social licence pressure mediated through

TABLE 13.4 Effects of social licence pressure and regulation motive on environmental impacts[a]

	Micro	*Small*	*Medium-sized*
Perceived social licence pressure			
-Direct effect	0.12**	0.13**	0.10*
-Indirect effect	0.05**	0.07***	0.12***
-Total effect	0.18***	0.20***	0.22***
Regulation motive	0.10**	0.10**	0.07

a Standardized effects; * $p < 0.05$; ** $p < 0.01$; *** $p < 0.001$.

market benefits tends to increase with company size and so does the total effect of perceived social licence pressure on environmental impacts. For all three size classes, the total influence of perceived social licence pressure on environmental impacts is higher than that of the regulation motive.

13.5 Conclusion

In this chapter, we tested a model that traces the influence of (perceived) social licence pressure on the environmental impacts of 4,929 micro, small, and medium-sized enterprises from 12 European countries. The study contributes in three ways to the scientific literature. First, in contrast to previous literature that focused on large companies, we studied the influence of perceived social licence pressures on micro, small and medium-sized enterprises. There are no large-scale empirical studies into the effects of social licence pressures on the environmental impacts of SMEs that incorporate the heterogeneous nature of SMEs. Although there are studies that use surveys to take stock of perceptions and motivations of SMEs regarding environmental impacts (Brammer Hoejmose, and Marchant, 2012), they did not test if these attributions explain cross-company differences in environmental impacts. A second contribution to literature is that this study analyses the pattern of the influence of perceived social licence pressures on environmental impacts of SMEs by distinguishing direct effects from indirect effects mediated by perceived market benefits of CSR. Third, the estimation results give insight into how the sum of the direct and indirect effects of perceived social licence pressures on environmental impacts compare to the effects of the perceived benefit of better compliance with government regulation.

We find empirical support that (1) perceived social licence pressure increases environmental impacts of SMEs directly; (2) perceived social licence pressure increases environmental impacts of SMEs indirectly through mediation by market benefits of CSR; (3) environmental impacts are more stimulated by the perceived social licence pressure than by the motive to meet government regulations, even in the case of micro companies; and that (4) perceived social licence pressure increases with company size.

Note

* An extended text of this chapter has been published in: Graafland, J., and Smid, H. (2017). Reconsidering the relevance of social license pressure and government regulation for environmental performance of European SMEs. *Journal of Cleaner Production*, 141: 967–977. Hugo Smid co-authored this article when he was PhD at Tilburg University. Hugo Smid published his dissertation (titled 'Rhetoric and realities of corporate social responsibility') in 2014. He is currently working at De Nederlandsche Bank.

14

HOW NGO AND MEDIA PRESSURE INFLUENCE INTRINSIC MOTIVATION OF CORPORATE SOCIAL RESPONSIBILITY*

14.1 Introduction

Over the last decades, much research has been conducted to identify what motivates firms and their managers to engage with CSR (cf. Croson and Treich, 2014; De Jong and Van der Meer, 2017; Muller and Kolk, 2010), in both developed and developing countries (Ali et al., 2017; Zhang et al., 2019). Executives are shown to have various intrinsic and extrinsic motives for actively pursuing CSR (Hafenbrädl and Waeger, 2017; Kuckertz and Wagner, 2010). Intrinsically motivated actions are those for which there is no direct reward but the behaviour itself; extrinsically motivated actions are driven by the consequences associated with performing the activity (Allison et al., 2015).

Previous research has shown that intrinsic motivation plays a decisive role in fostering EP (Graafland and Bovenberg, 2020; Paulrai, 2009), raising the question whether intrinsic motivation has its own underlying drivers. A substantial theoretical literature suggests that financial incentives tend to crowd out, or undermine, intrinsic motivation (Bowles, 2016). Experimental studies confirm this; if individuals derive intrinsic benefits from behaving altruistically or from honouring civic duties, financial incentives can discourage this type of conduct (for extensive literature reviews, see Bowles and Polania-Reyes (2012) or Rode et al. (2015)). The mechanism received ample attention in environmental economics and focused on households' and consumers' motivations and behaviours (cf. Agrawal et al., 2015; Chervier et al., 2019; Grillos et al., 2019; Han et al., 2018; Marsiglio and Tolotti, 2020; Pellerano et al., 2017; Steinhorst and Klöckner, 2018; Tabernero and Hernández, 2011). Yet motivation crowding is studied way less in the context of enterprises. We argue that the same mechanisms can, and should, be examined in the setting of enterprises, but that firms may

DOI: 10.4324/9781003216483-18

respond differently to financial incentives because of the competitive environment in which they operate. Because profitability is a necessary condition for a firm to survive in a competitive environment, financial incentives are more likely to enforce (crowd in) rather than curb (crowd out) intrinsic motivations in the business context.

Several types of stakeholders (e.g. suppliers, clients) can stimulate or press enterprises to engage in CSR, but these stakeholders often depend on information on the CSR performance of enterprises provided mainly by non-governmental organizations (NGOs) and media (Doh and Guay, 2006; Graafland and Smid, 2017). We therefore analyse motivation crowding effects of external pressures from NGOs and media, either from direct interaction with enterprises or from indirect influences if NGOs and media target consumers and other external stakeholders put market pressure on enterprises. The mediation mechanism is the role played by financial incentives to engage in CSR. The research question in this chapter is thus: How do external pressures from NGOs and media affect intrinsic motivations of (managers of) enterprises, and how do the financial CSR benefits that these pressures generate, mediate this relationship?

This chapter contributes to the literature in three ways. First, it develops a framework that theorizes how pressures from NGOs and media affect intrinsic motivation of (managers of) enterprises towards CSR. Second, it investigates the role of perceived market benefits of CSR as a mediator in the relationship between NGO and media pressure and intrinsic CSR motivation. Third, whereas motivation crowding theory has been tested on several types of behaviour of households and consumers, there is scant empirical research on crowding-in or crowding-out effects of financial incentives on the intrinsic motivation for CSR in enterprises. We thus contribute to practice by examining the motivation crowding effects of financial incentives on the intrinsic motivation for CSR in these enterprises, highlighting how NGOs and media play an important role here and hence could be involved more in advancing CSR initiatives.

In the remainder of this chapter, first, the theoretical framework and hypotheses are outlined. Then we present the methodology, followed by the results of our empirical analysis. The chapter concludes with a summary of the findings.

14.2 Conceptual Framework

Motivation, the reason upon which one acts, is an important antecedent to behaviour (Kuckertz and Wagner, 2010). Behaviour can be driven by intrinsic and extrinsic motives (Lindenberg, 2001; Scopelliti et al., 2018). Within psychology, intrinsic motivation is related to the joy and satisfaction derived from an activity (Deci and Ryan, 1985). Intrinsic motivation does not only cover behaviour based on enjoyment but also a motivation to act appropriately (Lindenberg, 2001). This type of intrinsic motivation stems from the inner desire to follow a particular norm or principle.

Motivation crowding theory has argued that intrinsic motivations are not independent from external pressures that drive extrinsic motives (Frey, 1992). More specifically, crowding theory has recognized that external pressures may crowd *in* or reinforce intrinsic motivation if the individual concerned perceives these external pressures as supportive (Eisenberger et al., 1999). However, external pressures may also crowd *out* intrinsic motivations (Han et al., 2018). This idea stems from literature on cognitive social psychology and implies that external rewards or pressures may reduce intrinsic motivation (Bowles, 2016).

In this chapter, we focus on the influence of external pressures generated by NGOs and media on intrinsic CSR motivation of managers in enterprises. Figure 14.1 presents our conceptual framework which distinguishes between a direct (Hypothesis 14.1) and an indirect influence. The indirect effect reflects that NGOs and media can increase market benefits of CSR by activating external stakeholders (Hypothesis 14.2) and that these market benefits subsequently can affect intrinsic motivation through crowding mechanisms (Hypothesis 14.3). The framework focuses on *perceived* external and market pressures instead of on real pressures because it is the perceived rather than the real pressures that shape enterprises' motivation to engage in CSR. After all, managers generally shape their environment through 'enactment' – by constructing interpretations and then acting as if such interpretations are reality (Fassin et al., 2011).

We complement the hypotheses by two other relationships of the effects of intrinsic motivation and market benefits on EP (A and B in Figure 14.1), assuming that both intrinsic motivation and market benefits motivate a company to improve its EP.

Hypothesis 14.1, Hypothesis 14.2, and Hypothesis 14.3 are discussed in detail later.

NGOs and Media: Direct Effects on Intrinsic Motivation

Social movements, from grassroots organizations at the local level to more formalized NGOs at the regional, national, or international level, can shape CSR activities (Den Hond and de Bakker, 2007). NGOs play a fundamental role, monitoring enterprises and generating attention in the media about situations

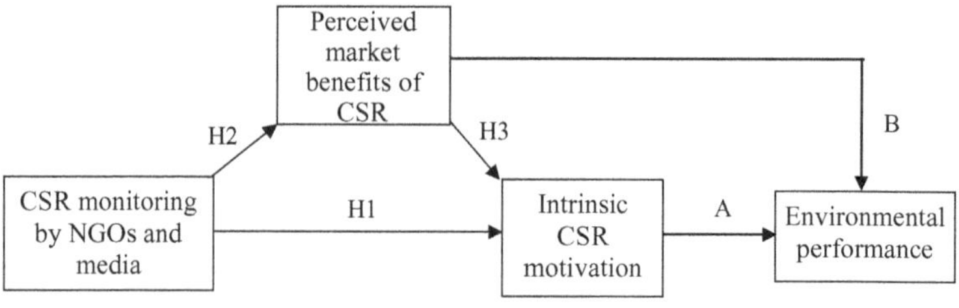

FIGURE 14.1 Conceptual framework

they deem undesirable, which reflect negatively on the public's perception of the firm (Deegan and Islam, 2014). Therefore, enterprises may be seriously challenged if they perceive that their environment becomes hostile to their business when NGOs or media find out that they cause some harm to their community (Aragón-Correa et al., 2008).

When local NGOs or media monitor an enterprise's CSR, they can use their knowledge to directly appeal to the enterprise, trying to influence the CSR activities (Den Hond and de Bakker, 2007). NGOs have specialist knowledge and can be specific in how environmental issues should be resolved by the enterprise. This reduces the managers' room for manoeuvre and discretion. When NGOs and media gain more influence, motivation crowding theory predicts that this will reduce managers' own intrinsic motivations because the meaning of a CSR activity changes from one that expresses autonomy and taking responsibility into one that expresses compliance to directives (Graafland and Bovenberg, 2020), in this case those coming from NGOs or media.

Another mechanism predicted by motivation crowding theory is that the effect of external pressure on intrinsic motivation depends on the display of trust (Bowles and Polania-Reyes, 2012). When NGOs and media signal distrust in the business leader's motivation to perform well, they deny the enterprise's internal motivation and by doing so erode existing intrinsic motivation. Based on these arguments, we expect that intrinsic CSR motivation of an enterprise is negatively related to perceived NGO and media pressure.

However, there are also effects that predict a crowding-in effect. First, NGOs and media have the ability to influence social norms, values, and societal expectations on corporate behaviour (Den Hond and de Bakker, 2007; Doh and Guay, 2006). NGOs and media alter the context in which preferences are acquired and change the process of preference-updating by which managers internalize new social norms. When new rules or norms are broadly diffused and supported, meaning that their social validity is largely unquestioned, enterprises will acquiesce to these (Oliver, 1991). Second, the attention of NGOs or media to the enterprise's CSR may lead to more contacts between the enterprise's managers and NGO representatives or journalists. If these intensify, these personal relationships can become an inspiration for managers of the enterprise. Research shows that the frequency of interaction with peers in social networks influences how people respond to moral issues (Weaver et al., 2005). That is, the intrinsic motivation that drives representatives of NGOs spills over to the managers of the enterprise who then gradually develop intrinsic motivation towards CSR. Third, the contacts with NGOs or media may also induce managers to frame the decision on CSR in a moral context (Bowles and Polania-Reyes, 2012). The moral frame related to the goal 'to do the right thing' will affect the processes of information gathering and the choice of the options that are relevant for considering moral issues of the operations of the enterprise. NGOs then are willing to provide enterprises with relevant environmental, scientific and legal information on CSR issues (Den Hond et al., 2015).

Therefore, we posit two competing hypotheses stating that NGO and media pressure crowd in or crowd out intrinsic motivation:

Hypothesis 14.1a/b Intrinsic CSR motivation of an enterprise is negatively/positively related to perceived NGO and media pressure.

Effects of NGOs and Media on Intrinsic Motivation Through Market Benefits

The direct effects of NGO and media pressure on intrinsic motivation can be positive, negative, or insignificant. But there is also an indirect effect. NGOs and media attract public attention to corporate practices and mobilize stakeholders to exert market pressure on an enterprise, improving profits conditional on CSR (Den Hond and de Bakker, 2007). Neo-institutional theorists have argued that transparency of CSR performance through monitoring by societal organizations is essential for effective market pressure (Doh and Guay, 2006). Not only so for large enterprises, small enterprises are also subject to reputational effects from CSR pressure by (local) NGOs or media (Fraj-Andrés et al., 2012). Moreover, given locational sunk costs that restrict geographical mobility, a good reputation has an important strategic value for small enterprises too (Graafland and Smid, 2017). Hence, managers will be more aware of the market benefits of CSR if they perceive that local NGOs or media monitor their enterprise's CSR. This leads to the second hypothesis:

Hypothesis 14.2 The market benefits of CSR, as perceived by the enterprise's managers, are positively related to perceived CSR pressure from NGOs and media.

In turn, there are several reasons for (perceived) market benefits of CSR to affect intrinsic motivation of managers. Freedom to act is a precondition for value expression and taking responsibility. Experiencing autonomy requires that managers have a set of options available (Patzelt and Shepherd, 2011). When CSR generates market benefits because market parties reward CSR, then this provides managers with more opportunities to take CSR initiatives. For example, the development of environmentally aware consumers who are prepared to pay a mark-up for environmentally responsible products provides managers with the opportunity for a strategy to enter that market. The market benefits created by CSR signal freedom of action rather than social control. This enlarges managers' perceived autonomy, fostering their intrinsic motivation to engage in CSR.

A related argument stems from the notion that CSR may be perceived by managers as a conditional or so-called *prima facie* moral duty rather than as an all-things-considered moral duty (Ross, 1930). If managers expect that pursuing

CSR will harm their enterprise's financial performance, they hesitate to implement CSR as they also consider other moral duties towards their enterprise, such as providing job security for employees. The survival of the enterprise is essential and job creation and continuation are often seen as the first responsibility of businesses (Fassin et al., 2011). Lack of anticipated market benefits will then weaken intrinsic motivation because CSR can only be considered a moral duty if there are no other, more important, moral reasons against it (Kuckertz and Wagner, 2010). That is, perceiving that CSR has financial value leads to greater acceptance of CSR as a moral obligation on which managers should act.

However, perceived market pressures on CSR may also crowd out intrinsic motivation. First, it is possible that managers perceive market pressure as a threat that compels them to improve the enterprise's CSR, leaving them less room for manoeuvre. CSR that does not leave room for free choice intrudes directly into the manager's realm of self-determination, decreasing their locus of control (Frey, 1992; Graafland and Bovenberg, 2020). Second, and more subtle, if managers perceive that they are rewarded for their CSR by stakeholders, they may attribute their CSR policies to the reward rather than to their own intentions and thus discount their intrinsic interest in the activity as the cause of their decisions (Lindenberg, 2001). The mechanism is known as over-justification and leads to lower post-behaviour intrinsic motivation (Deci et al., 1999). Third, a change in perceived market effects of CSR changes the frame of managers' decision context. Goals influence the frame within which cognitive processes take place (Linder and Foss, 2018). The frame influences the information attended to, the processing of this information, and the alternatives considered (Lindenberg, 2001). Market benefits of CSR create a so-called 'gain frame', for example a frame linked to the goal of improving one's resources while curtailing attention to moral obligation. CSR aspects generating positive market benefits then become more salient, stimulating managers' attitudes towards extrinsic motivation for CSR (Lindenberg, 2003). This means that an increase in perceived market benefits crowds out intrinsic CSR motivation. These arguments together lead to two competing crowding out hypotheses:

Hypothesis 14.3a/b Intrinsic CSR motivation of enterprises is positively/negatively related to perceived market benefits of CSR.

Mediation

Mediation analysis permits examination of processes and gives insight into how an independent variable exerts an effect on a dependent variable via the inclusion of a third variable, known as the mediator variable (Fiedler et al., 2011). Next to the three main hypotheses outlined earlier, we need to examine whether the perceived market benefits of CSR act as a mediator between NGO and media pressure on the one hand and intrinsic CSR motivation on the other hand. Such mediation effects in motivation crowding have been rarely examined before (Resh et al., 2019). As NGOs and media can attract public attention to misbehaviour, they can mobilize various types of stakeholders on the capital market, product market, and labour market and thus potentially increase perceived market benefits from CSR. As these market benefits from CSR may, in turn, crowd in or crowd our intrinsic motivations to CSR, we expect that NGO and media pressures indirectly affect intrinsic motivations through the perceived market benefits of CSR to some extent. Hence, it is hypothesized that:

Hypothesis 14.4 The perceived market benefits of CSR mediates the effect of NGO and media pressure on intrinsic CSR motivation of enterprises.

14.3 Methodology

The data are taken from the survey in 2011. The perceived CSR pressure by NGOs and media on the enterprise's CSR was measured by a survey question asking 'To what extent do NGOs and/or (social) media monitor the enterprise's CSR?' The answers were measured by a seven-point Likert scale, ranging from 'not at all' (1) to 'very much' (7).

Perceived market benefits were measured by four questions, surveying managers' perceptions of the reputational effects of CSR, the effects of CSR on profit margins and sales of the enterprise, and the effect on profitability in the long term. In response to the question 'To what extent does engagement in CSR influence the following aspects for your enterprise?', managers again could fill out a seven-point Likert scale, again ranging from 'not at all' (1) to 'very much' (7) for each item.

Following Graafland and Bovenberg (2020) the intrinsic CSR motivation was measured by the survey question 'How important are the following motives for your enterprise to engage in CSR?' Two measures were used. First, respondents could respond by a seven-point Likert scale ranging from 'not at all' (1) to 'very much' (7) to the statement 'We engage in CSR because we feel responsible for the planet and the society'. Furthermore, we asked respondents to respond to the statement 'We engage in CSR because it creates personal satisfaction for the people in our enterprise' using the same seven-point Likert scale.

Environmental performance was operationalized by four measures indicating the efforts of companies to improve EP. We used four survey questions measuring concrete actions to reduce energy consumption, water consumption, and waste disposal, and to improve EP of suppliers. For each issue, we used a three-point scale ranging from 0 (no effort), 0.5 (incidental effort), to 1 (continuous effort).

We used both explorative and confirmatory factor analysis to test the clustering of the survey variables in the three factors identified by our labels 'Perceived market benefits', 'Intrinsic CSR motivation', and 'Environmental performance'. The results are reported in Table 14.1. The factor loadings for all individual

TABLE 14.1 Descriptive statistics and factor analysis of survey items[a]

Variables	*Mean*	*SD*	*Factor loadings*		
			Perceived market benefits	*Intrinsic motivation*	*Environ. performance*
CSR increases turnover (35)	3.26	1.66	0.88		
CSR increases profit margins on products (34)	3.24	1.63	0.89		
CSR limits reputation risks (39)	4.42	1.67	0.67		
CSR improves long term profitability (38)	4.11	1.70	0.86		
We engage in CSR because we feel responsible for the planet and the society (25)	5.21	1.48		0.88	
We engage in CSR because it creates personal satisfaction for the people in our enterprise (26)	5.09	1.42		0.86	
Energy consumption (91)	0.67	0.37			0.78
Water consumption (92)	0.61	0.40			0.80
Waste disposal (93)	0.77	0.34			0.78
Environmental performance suppliers (94)	0.52	0.41			0.67
Eigenvalue			3.57	1.19	1.98
Cronbach alpha			0.87	0.70	0.77
Construct reliability			0.90	0.86	0.84
Average variance extracted			0.69	0.76	0.58

a Extraction Method: Principal Component Analysis; Rotation Method: Oblimin with Kaiser Normalization. KMO = 0.795, *p*-value Bartlett's Test of Sphericity = 0.000. The numbers in brackets refer to the numbers of the survey questions reported in Appendix 1.

variables exceed 0.50. The Cronbach's alphas indicate the internal consistency of both factors. The construct reliability and convergent validity (measured by the average variance extracted) for both factors satisfied the accepted thresholds of 0.70 and 0.50, respectively (Hair et al., 2010). In the regression analysis, the three factors for market benefits, intrinsic motivation, and EP are used. The factors are standardized and normalized to zero mean and unit standard deviation.

A potential bias in the regression analysis is reverse causality bias. Enterprises with intrinsically motivated owner-managers might show more consistency in their CSR strategy. They may therefore be more able to convince stakeholders of the quality of their CSR efforts, increasing the market rewards for CSR (Wang and Choi, 2013). Moreover, intrinsically motivated managers who want CSR for its own sake will show more perseverance in developing market opportunities, even if market effects are not visible in the short term (Kuckertz and Wagner,

2010). Theoretically, it is therefore possible that intrinsic motivation has a positive reverse causal effect on perceived market benefits of CSR. We test for reverse causality through instrumental variables (IV), but with a subtle extension to the standard procedure, because good instrumental variables for the perceived market benefits, the independent variable in the second equation, were lacking, while a good instrument for intrinsic motivation, the dependent variable, was available. This enabled us to examine if there is causality from the dependent to the independent variable. To be specific, we test the reverse effect from intrinsic motivation on perceived market benefits of CSR directly, using the share of female executives in the board of the enterprise as instrumental variable for intrinsic motivation. Regression analysis (controlling for all control variables) showed that this instrumental variable indeed has a positive and very significant effect on intrinsic motivation (*t*-value 4.52). Next, we used IV regression analysis to estimate the effects of (instrumentalized) intrinsic motivation on perceived market benefits, and the results showed that the effect is negligible (*p*-value is 0.943). Based on these findings it can be concluded that there is no reverse causality from intrinsic motivation on perceived market effects.

14.4 Results

The results of the structural equation modelling are reported in Table 14.2. The estimation results in column 1 show that perceived market effects of CSR depend positively on perceived CSR monitoring by NGOs and media, which provides support for Hypothesis 14.2. In column 2 intrinsic motivation is found to be significantly positively related to perceived market benefits but not to CSR monitoring by NGOs and media. These results support Hypothesis 14.3a and reject Hypothesis 14.3b, while providing no support for Hypothesis 14.1a or 14.1b.[1] From column 3 it can be concluded that both perceived market benefits of CSR (which is an indicator of extrinsic motivation) and intrinsic motivation stimulate companies to improve their EP. Particularly, intrinsic motivation is a strong driver; its impact is twice that of perceived market benefits.

An advantage of SEM is that it provides a convenient method to test the significance of indirect effects (Shrout and Bolger, 2002). The indirect effect of CSR monitoring by NGOs and media on intrinsic motivation through perceived market benefits is highly significant (see Table 14.3). Hence, although CSR monitoring by NGOs and media has no direct effect on intrinsic motivation, it indirectly crowds in intrinsic motivation by increasing perceived market benefits. This provides support for Hypothesis 14.4. More specifically, the findings show that the perceived market benefits of CSR positively mediate the effect of NGO and media pressure on intrinsic CSR motivation of enterprises.

Table 14.3 also compares the direct effect of perceived market benefits on EP and the indirect effect mediated by intrinsic motivation. These effects have a

TABLE 14.2 Estimation results[a]

		1	*2*	*3*
		Perceived market benefits	*Intrinsic motivation*	*Env. performance*
Structural model				
CSR monitoring NGOs and media		0.31***	0.02	
Perceived market benefits			0.57***	0.16***
Intrinsic motivation				0.31***
Measurement model				
Perceived market benefits	CSR increases sales			0.59***
	CSR increases profit margins on products			0.55***
	CSR reduces reputation risks			0.76***
	CSR improves profitability in the long term			0.73***
Intrinsic motivation	We feel responsible for the planet and the society			0.73***
	CSR creates personal satisfaction for the people in our enterprise			0.78***
Environmental performance	Energy consumption			0.53***
	Water consumption			0.59***
	Waste disposal			0.57***
	Environmental performance suppliers			0.60***

a Standardized coefficients. * $p < 0.05$; ** $p < 0.01$; *** $p < 0.001$. Controlled for region, sector, market position in the chain, intensity of price competition, business culture, company size, the skill and age structure of the enterprise, the function and the age of the respondent. Details on the measurement of control variables are reported in Appendices 1 and 2. Global fit indices: RMSEA = 0.033; CFI = 0.942; TLI = 0.917; SRMR = 0.017; R^2 = 0.462.

similar magnitude. Thus, the influence of external pressure from CSR monitoring by NGOs and media on EP is equally motivated by intrinsic and extrinsic motives.

14.5 Conclusion

This chapter develops a framework that theorizes how external pressures from NGOs and media affect intrinsic motivation of (managers of) enterprises towards CSR. Whereas in earlier literature on CSR (cf. Muller and Kolk, 2010; Weaver et al., 2005), intrinsic and extrinsic motives have often been conceptualized as independent from each other, we theorize several types of mechanisms that can cause motivation crowding effects of external pressures on intrinsic CSR

TABLE 14.3 Direct and indirect effects[a]

From:	*On:*	*Mediated by*	*Estimate*
Indirect effects			
CSR monitoring NGOs and media	Intrinsic motivation	Perceived market benefits	0.197***
Perceived market benefits	Environmental performance	Intrinsic motivation	0.039***
Direct effects			
Perceived market benefits	Environmental performance		0.035***

a Unstandardized coefficients; *** $p < 0.001$.

motivation of enterprises, such as freedom to act, framing, self-attribution, signalling of (dis)trust, and preference update. Through this study we thus suggest that motivation crowding theory offers an alternative focus on understanding a variety of motivations of SMEs to engage in CSR, giving rise to further research on how these motivations may interact.

Whereas motivation crowding theory has been tested on several types of behaviour of households and consumers, there is scant empirical research on crowding effects of financial incentives on the intrinsic motivation for CSR in enterprises. By testing the mechanisms on a sample of 4,364 enterprises in 12 European countries, the study complements the empirical literature in a setting that is highly relevant for working towards sustainability, given that most CSR impacts appear at the production stage, that is, through enterprises.

Developing further insight into motivation crowding effects is important for a nuanced understanding of the motivating power of external pressures on an enterprise's CSR efforts, not only in theory but also in practice. If external pressures that drive extrinsic motives positively affect intrinsic motivations, the disregard of this relationship may lead to an underestimation of their relevance for CSR. After all, next to their motivating effect on CSR through extrinsic motivations, external pressures will then also foster CSR indirectly by stimulating intrinsic motivations. But if, conversely, managers are motivated to CSR by intrinsic motives, and external pressures are liable to crowd out these motives, such pressures may even weaken the enterprise's engagement in CSR, working counter-productively. A better understanding of all these motivations and their interactions will contribute to more effective ways to stimulate CSR initiatives in enterprises.

This chapter specifically investigated the role of perceived market benefits of CSR as a mediator in the relationship between NGO and media pressure and intrinsic CSR motivation. Within the ongoing debates on drivers for CSR within SMEs (cf. Baumann-Pauly et al., 2013; Hamann et al., 2017), this is a relevant contribution to interpret such drivers. The study indicates that crowding in rather than crowding-out effects are relevant in the CSR behaviour of enterprises that are pressured by NGOs and media. This finding is opposite to many studies of motivation crowding in environmental behaviour of households or consumers that support the crowding out hypothesis (Pellerano et al., 2017; Rode et al., 2015). These results beg the question why crowding in is more relevant for CSR behaviour of business organizations than for social behaviours of private households or individual consumers. A possible reason for these deviating responses can be found in the arguments underpinning Hypothesis 14.3a on crowding in. For example, rewarding environmentally desirable behaviour *can* increase perceived self-determination in a business context, more so than in the context of a private household. Enterprises that face severe competition may not be able to survive if their (often costly) investments in CSR are not rewarded by market parties. This is particularly relevant for SMEs. Because of their small scale, CSR measures can be relatively costly for SMEs. In this context, an increase in market demand for environmentally responsible products will be perceived as a business opportunity that substantially increases the freedom of the enterprise to pursue a CSR strategy, which triggers a higher intrinsic motivation. This argument applies less to financial rewarding of household contributions to environmental goods, for which findings are mixed at best and where crowding-out effects have regularly been observed (Schwartz et al., 2019). In these cases, it is more likely that, as Frey and Oberholzer (1997) argued, individuals often perceive price incentives as an external intervention controlling their behaviour, which decreases their self-determination and hence their intrinsic motivation.

Notes

* An extended text of this chapter has been published as an open access article under the terms of the Creative Commons Attribution-NonCommercial-NoDerivatives License in: Graafland, J.J., and de De Bakker, F.G.A. (2021). Crowding in or crowding out? How non-governmental organizations and media influence intrinsic motivation towards corporate social and environmental responsibility. *Journal of Environmental Planning and Management*, https://doi.org/10.1080/09640568.2021.1873110. Copyright © University of Newcastle Upon Tyne, reprinted by permission of Taylor & Francis Ltd, www.tandfonline.com on behalf of University of Newcastle Upon Tyne. Frank de Bakker is affiliated to IESEG School of Management, Division Management & Society to LEM-CNRS UMR 9221 in Lille in France.

1 We also tested for non-linearities, as previous research has shown that financial benefits impact intrinsic motivations only beyond a certain level (Ezzine-de-Blas et al., 2019). Hence, the probability of crowding out may increase when NGO and media pressures and perceived market effects become so pressing that they leave little room for manoeuvre by the owner-manager. The test results partly support this intuition, as squared perceived market benefits have a significant negative effect on intrinsic motivation. However, the effect is rather small in comparison to the positive linear effect. Hence, even for enterprises that perceive large market benefits from CSR, an increase in perceived market benefits does not crowd out intrinsic motivation. Furthermore, squared NGO and media pressure was found to have a small, but significant negative effect on perceived market benefits, but no significant effect on intrinsic motivation was detected.

15

GOVERNMENT REGULATION, BUSINESS LEADERS' MOTIVATION, AND ENVIRONMENTAL IMPACTS*

15.1 Introduction

The literature on motivation crowding has theorized that incentives-based policies designed to recruit self-interest might harm the intrinsic motivation to supply public goods (Boyer et al., 2016). Also in the environmental domain, studies have shown that price incentives can crowd out intrinsic motivations (Pellerano et al., 2017). These effects pertain also to other types of external interventions, such as government regulation. In an influential paper, Cardenas et al. (2000) showed that the introduction of modestly enforced government-imposed regulations in three rural villages in Colombia increased resource extraction. They suggested that one of the interpretations of this finding is that regulation crowds out other-regarding behaviour. Also, Vollan (2008) found that imposing external penalties through outside regulations tends to worsen the situation, whereas employing enabling rewards does not. Recent research by Abatayo and Lynham (2016), however, did not confirm this finding. They found no differences between externally imposed regulations and self-governing regulations and between weak externally imposed regulation and no regulation. They concluded that externally imposed regulations do not crowd out intrinsic motivation. In contrast, Choi (2015) found that a mandatory carbon price reduces the willingness to pay for voluntary carbon offsets, whereas Han et al. (2018) found that an increase in garbage fees crowds out households' pre-existing motivations for sorting waste, again supporting the crowding-out mechanism.[1]

The literature on motivation crowding in the environmental domain has focused on the behaviour of only individuals or households. How government intervention impacts intrinsic motives of firms has neither been theorized nor empirically tested, even though business organizations are a major source of

DOI: 10.4324/9781003216483-19

environmental damage. This chapter takes a first step to fill this research gap by focusing on motivations of top managers of SMEs to adopt CSR. Compared to their larger counterparts, the behaviour of small firms is disproportionately driven by the values and motives of the managers (Wickert et al., 2016). Therefore, crowding-out effects are more likely to occur for SMEs than for large companies.

A second shortcoming of previous studies on crowding effects of government regulation of environmental behaviour is that they researched the relationship between various types of regulations and environmental outcomes without measuring intrinsic motivation and testing how intrinsic motivation affects this relationship between regulation and EP. In a literature overview of 18 studies on the impact of economic incentives on conservation policy, Rode et al. (2015) found that only four studies measure intrinsic motivation (of which, none investigated the effects of government regulation). They argued that explicit information about intrinsic motivation is essential to develop an understanding of the specific conditions under which crowding effects occur, as 'observing behaviour does not make it possible to isolate economic from intrinsic motivations' (Rode et al., 2015: 280). If government regulation is found to improve EP, the literature interprets this finding as evidence that crowding out of intrinsic motivation does not occur. However, it cannot be ruled out that other factors affect this relationship. Empirical evidence on whether government regulation crowds out intrinsic motivation is therefore still lacking. Our research fills this second research gap by measuring intrinsic motivation and testing how government regulation impacts this motivation. Our results show that a positive relationship between government regulation and EP actually goes together with crowding out of intrinsic motivation. We thus correct the standard interpretation in the literature that a positive relationship between government regulation and EP implies that crowding out of intrinsic motivation is absent.

The research question in this chapter is therefore twofold. First, to what extent does government regulation crowd out intrinsic motivation towards improving EP in SMEs? Second, how do indirect effects caused by crowding out of intrinsic motivation compare with the direct effects of government regulation on EP? The chapter contributes to the previous literature on motivation crowding in CSR in two important ways. First, instead of analysing individual or household behaviour, we research to what extent government regulation crowds out intrinsic motivation towards EP of SMEs. Second, by separating the effect of government regulation on intrinsic motivation from its direct effect on EP, our study is the first that empirically identifies crowding out of intrinsic motivation by government regulation. Our approach allows us to disentangle the effects of government regulation on EP caused by crowding out of intrinsic motivation from other effects of government regulation on EP.

Here, we first develop a conceptual framework for exploring how government regulation influences voluntary initiatives to protect the environment through the intermediation of motivations of top managers of SMEs. Next, we discuss the methodology of our research. Section 15.4 presents the estimation results and various types of robustness analyses. The last section summarizes the findings.

15.2 Conceptual Framework

This section first discusses how the motivation of business leaders affects voluntary initiatives of SMEs to improve their EP. Next, we describe the tenets of motivation crowding theory and provide reasons for why government regulation may crowd out intrinsic and extrinsic motivations of business leaders. Finally, we present the overall conceptual framework.

Motivation and Environmental Performance of Small Businesses

Motivation refers to the reason upon which one acts. The literature distinguishes between intrinsic motives and extrinsic motives (Frey, 1998; Weaver et al., 1999; Lindenberg, 2001; Scopelliti et al., 2018) (see Chapter 6). Business leaders who feature intrinsic motives for improving EP perceive good EP as an end in itself, independent of other (mostly financial) benefits (Muller and Kolk, 2010). An extrinsic motive encourages EP because it has instrumental value for other goals than good EP, such as reputation and long-term financial performance of the company.

Various types of intrinsic motivation exist (Lindenberg, 2001). First, in Deci et al. (1999), enjoyment or fun derived from the activity is at the heart of the conceptualization of intrinsic motivation. For example, business people may enjoy a 'warm glow' from contributing to a public good. However, as argued by Frey (1998) and Lindenberg (2001), intrinsic motivation may also involve moral obligations. This motivation stems from the feeling that one must follow a particular rule, norm or principle. The goal is to act appropriately. Business leaders feel that they are responsible to prevent negative impacts of their companies on the natural environment.

Although it seems obvious that motives drive behaviour, in the context of business organizations the role of motives is more complex because motivation is basically an individual-level construct rather than a company level construct (Katz and Kahn, 1978). We bypass this theoretical concern by focusing our research on director-owners of SMEs. As regards behaviour of businesses, the upper echelon theory argues that organizational strategies reflect the values and beliefs of powerful actors in the organization (Hambrick and Mason, 1984). Business leaders are shaping the strategic direction of their company. Their motives therefore affect the strategic initiatives of the firm, such as engaging in CSR to enhance EP. The dominant influence of leaders in defining the interests of the company will be particularly strong for business leaders of SMEs. They are often directly involved in decisions on CSR and can change the CSR strategy of the firm substantially

(Waldman et al., 2006). Their value-laden decisions are observed and interpreted by subordinates and will also influence the subordinates' values, beliefs, and behaviour (Kim et al., 2017). As the leader with high status and power, the business leader will in fact serve as a role model for the employees in the organization and foster their cooperation in the implementation of environmental policies. Lynch-Wood and Williamson (2014) found that in smaller firms the responsibility for environmental issues tends to reside with owners or directors, whereas in larger firms it is often delegated. The motives of business leaders of SMEs therefore have a decisive influence on the company's policies. These arguments yield the following hypothesis:

Hypothesis 15.1 The stronger the intrinsic CSR motivation of its business leader is, the more voluntary initiatives an SME will take to improve its EP.

Hypothesis 15.2 The stronger the extrinsic CSR motivation of its business leader is, the more voluntary initiatives an SME will take to improve its EP.

Government Regulation and Motivations

Motivation crowding theory has recognized that external pressures may crowd out intrinsic motivation (Frey and Jegen, 2001). However, whether government regulation crowds out intrinsic motivation of business leaders of SMEs to improve EP has not yet been researched. Motivation crowding theory provides various reasons for the crowding-out phenomena (Deci et al., 1999; Frey and Jegen, 2001; Bowles and Polania-Reyes, 2012; Han et al., 2018). First, crowding out is observed if the external pressure is perceived to be coercive, thereby decreasing self-determination and the freedom to act (Frey, 1998). Compared to market incentives, government regulations are typically perceived as more restrictive to self-determination. The government interventions interfere directly with the business leader's realm of self-determination. This particularly applies to hard regulations with convincing threats of punishments of non-compliance. In that case, business leaders have no discretion regarding how they respond to this pressure, and this will reduce their enjoyment from engaging in environmental actions.

As the second reason for impacting intrinsic motivation, government regulation may affect the salience of moral preferences by framing effects. In particular, the regulation may frame choice behaviour of business leaders in terms of the self-interest of avoiding government intervention rather than the responsibility for the common good of protecting a public good. Ostman (1998) suggests that external control of common pool resources increases an orientation on self-interest, as it shifts responsibility to the regulatory agency and thereby absolves individuals from other-regarding moral obligations. However, the framing argument can also explain crowding in (meaning that regulations enforce motivations), as government regulation may provide certain cues for appropriate moral behaviour and trigger moral engagement (Bowles and Polania-Reyes, 2012). Governments are in fact important institutional players with the ability to influence social norms, values, and societal expectations on appropriate corporate behaviour (Weaver et al., 1999). Government regulations may thus signal to the business leader that moral values are at stake in EP, thereby enhancing his or her intrinsic motivation.

A third channel through which government regulation crowds out intrinsic motivation is that it conveys information about the motives of the regulator (Sliwka, 2007). The implicit bad news of regulations is that they signal distrust in the business leader's motivation and willingness to protect the public good of the environment. Moreover, these regulations convey the desire of the regulator to control the behaviour of the company. This makes the business leader feel that his or her competence and involvement are neither recognized nor appreciated by the regulator, which leads the business leader to reduce intrinsic motivation.[2] The conclusion is that impairing self-determination and signalling lack of trust and respect provide reasons for government regulations to crowd out the intrinsic motivation of business leaders of SMEs to improve EP. Only the framing arguments are ambiguous.

Government regulations may not only harm intrinsic motivation but also crowd out extrinsic motivation. The market failures that cause environmental degradation provide companies with market opportunities to realize strategic benefits (Dean and McMullen, 2007). For example, companies that address environmental degradation may improve their reputation and their profitability (Surroca et al., 2010). Regulatory policies addressing negative externalities of environmental degradation reduce these pay-offs (Hunt and Fund, 2016). By forcing all companies to improve their EP by meeting common standards that apply to all, government regulations reduce the opportunities of companies to distinguish themselves from other companies.

Based on these considerations, we formulate the following hypotheses:

Hypothesis 15.3 Government regulation crowds out the intrinsic motivation of a business leader towards improving EP of the SME.

Hypothesis 15.4 Government regulation crowds out the extrinsic motivation of a business leader towards improving EP of the SME.

Conceptual Framework

We complement hypotheses 15.1–15.4 by two other relationships of the direct effects of voluntary initiatives by individual companies and government regulation on EP (A and B in Figure 15.1), assuming that both channels are likely to improve a firm's EP.

Figure 15.1 shows that our analysis extends the literature on motivation crowding effects in environmental economics by separating out the effects of government regulation on intrinsic and extrinsic motivations. In this way, we

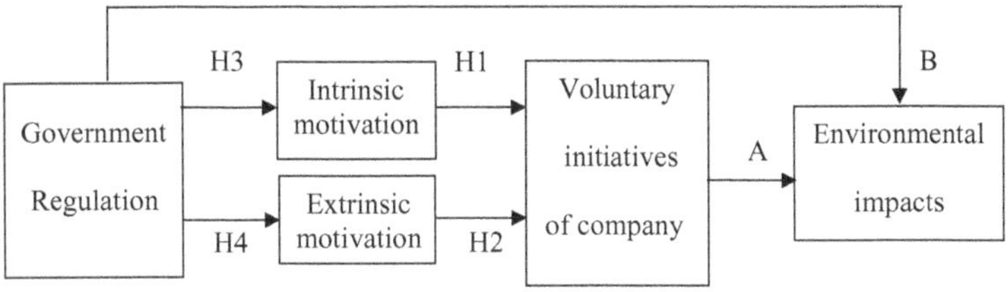

FIGURE 15.1 Conceptual framework

disentangle the regulatory impact on EP caused by indirect effects due to crowding effects on intrinsic and extrinsic motivation from the direct effects of government regulation on EP.

15.3 Methodology

We measured motivation by eliciting the reason for the company's engagement in CSR using the following survey question: 'How important are the following motives for your enterprise to engage in CSR?' The intrinsic motivation of the business leader was measured by the response to two statements reflecting on this survey question. The first statement inquired into the extent to which personal satisfaction is a motive to engage in environmental responsibility. The second statement measured the extent to which the company engages in CSR because the company feels responsible for the environment and society. Extrinsic motivation was measured by the responses to three statements on financial and reputational benefits of EP. The responses to all statements were measured by a seven-point Likert scale.

In order to measure legal enforcement of EP, and voluntary initiatives by the enterprise itself, we asked respondents to indicate which cause contributed most to reductions in the company's energy consumption, waste disposal and water consumption during the period 2007–2010. Two dummies for each of the causes measure the two alternative options. For example, for legal enforcement the dummy equals 1 if the respondent agreed that EP was improved mainly because of legal requirements. A substantial share of business leaders did not select either of these options and, instead, selected the option 'non-applicable.' Since the question inquired into the causes of the reduction in energy consumption, waste disposal and water consumption, the most likely reason for selecting the option 'non-applicable' is that the company did not reduce energy consumption, waste disposal and/or water consumption during the period 2007–2010.

We measured EP by the use of two procedural measures: setting targets to improve environmental outcomes and reporting the realization of these targets (see Chapters 2, 7, and 8). Environmental performance is measured on a three-point scale: no use of targets and reporting (0), use of targets or reporting (0.5), and use of targets and reporting (1). The advantage of simple, specific and concise questions on the use of procedural measures to measure EP is that they diminish social desirability bias (Podsakoff et al., 2003). Also Wakabayashi and Arimura (2016) employed these self-reported data to measure EP. As reported in Table 15.1, only 10–13% of the companies responded that they adopt these procedural measures. These low scores indicate that the responses to these survey questions are not biased by social desirability bias and thus provide reasonable reliable indicators.

In order to research the validity of the constructs of government regulation, voluntary own initiatives, intrinsic motivation, extrinsic motivation and EP, we performed Principal Component Analysis (with Oblimin rotation). Table 15.1 reports the results. The Cronbach's alphas indicate the internal consistency of six factors. We tested the reliability of the factors further by confirmatory factor analysis using structural equation modelling. The global fit indices (CFA = 0.939; TLI = 0.923; SRMR = 0.025) indicate a good model fit. The construct reliability and convergent validity (measured by the average variance extracted) for all factors satisfied the accepted thresholds of 0.70 and 0.50, respectively. The predicted factor values identified by the measurement model are standardized to zero mean and unit standard deviation. We included these factors in our regression analysis.

A possible complication for our empirical research is that companies with strongly motivated business leaders are more likely to go beyond external requirements and thus are less likely to report that government regulations were the most important cause for improved EP during the period 2007–2010. In order to test for reverse causality, we employed the share of women managers as instrumental variable for intrinsic motivation. According to the gender socialization theory, women demonstrate more concern for others, are more emphatic, and show more altruistic attitudes (Williams and Polman, 2015). Hence, we expect a positive influence of the share of women managers on intrinsic motivation. Multiple regression analysis (controlling for all other control variables) indeed showed a significantly positive effect (t-value = 4.93). For extrinsic motivation, we adopt as an instrument the intensity of monitoring of the company's social and EP by NGOs and media; in a transparent environment, EP yields more strategic market value (Campbell, 2007). Multiple regression analysis showed a significantly positive effect (t-value = 12.79). When using IV analysis, we found that neither intrinsic nor extrinsic motivation reversely affect the government regulation (p-values vary from 0.299 to 0.827). Hence, motivation does not reversely impact government regulation.

15.4 Results

In the regression analysis, we employed the conditional mixed process estimator in order to control for correlation between the residuals for intrinsic and extrinsic motivation, voluntary initiatives and EP. We distinguished two samples. In the

TABLE 15.1 Factor analysis of survey items[a]

Variables	*Mean*	*SD*	*Factor loadings*				
			Gov. regulation	*Vol. initiative*	*Intrinsic motivation*	*Extrinsic motivation*	*Env. Perf.*
Lower energy consumption due to (108):							
- legal requirements	0.07	0.25	0.91				
- own voluntary initiatives	0.50	0.50		0.88			
Lower waste due to (111):							
- legal requirements	0.08	0.26	0.89				
- own voluntary initiatives	0.40	0.49		0.85			
Lower water consumption due to (110):							
- legal requirements	0.06	0.24	0.93				
- own voluntary initiatives	0.45	0.50		0.90			
We engage in CSR because:							
- my enterprise feels responsible for the planet and the society (25)	5.28	1.47			0.88		
- it creates personal satisfaction for the people in my enterprise (26)	5.15	1.41			0.89		
- it serves long-term financial interests of shareholders and/or owner (20)	3.72	1.89				0.76	
- it limits reputational risks (24)	4.50	1.63				0.75	
- large customers ask for it (27)	3.77	1.89				0.73	
Environmental performance:							
- energy consumption (96)	0.11	0.23					0.87
- waste disposal (98)	0.13	0.24					0.86
- water consumption (97)	0.10	0.21					0.86
Eigenvalue			2.56	3.53	1.75	1.00	1.08
Cronbach's alpha			0.89	0.85	0.70	0.62	0.87
Construct reliability			0.94	0.91	0.83	0.79	0.90
Average variance extracted			0.83	0.77	0.72	0.56	0.75

a The numbers in brackets refer to the numbers of the survey questions reported in Appendix 1. Extraction Method: Principal Component Analysis; Rotation Method: Oblimin with Kaiser Normalization.

first sample, the reference option to which we compare government regulation are those companies for which business leaders had selected 'voluntary own initiatives' in the survey question as the main cause of environmental improvements by the company. In this sample, companies for which the business leader had selected 'not applicable' for this survey question are not included. In the second sample, we employed companies for which the business leader had selected 'not applicable' as reference option for government regulation. In this sample, companies for which the business leader had selected 'voluntary initiatives' are excluded. Correlation analysis showed that intrinsic and extrinsic motivation of business leaders who had selected 'not applicable' is significantly lower than for business leaders who had selected 'voluntary own initiatives'. Accordingly, crowding-out effects from government regulation are less likely. Hungerman (2009) showed that crowding-out effects are stronger if intrinsic motivation is high. Indeed, only if companies are intrinsically motivated to start with, can government regulation crowd out intrinsic motivation. For the other equations for voluntary initiatives and EP, we used a sample consisting of all respondents. In these equations, companies whose business leader had selected the 'non-applicable' option are the reference category.

The estimation results in column (1) of Table 15.2 support Hypotheses 15.1 and 15.2 that intrinsic and extrinsic motivations stimulate voluntary initiatives to enhance EP. Columns (2a) and (3a) report the estimation results explaining

TABLE 15.2 Estimation results[a]

	1	*2[ab]*	*2b[c]*	*3a[b]*	*3b[c]*	*4*
	Vol. initiatives	*Intrinsic motivation*		*Extrinsic motivation*		*Env. performance*
Gov. regulation		−0.28***	−0.05**	−0.15***	0.07**	0.10***
Voluntary initiatives						0.43***
Intrinsic motivation	0.75***					
Extrinsic motivation	0.41**					
R^2	0.07	0.12	0.11	0.10	0.09	0.13
N	2,373	1,648	1,046	1,648	1,046	2,373

a * $p < 0.05$; ** $p < 0.01$; *** $p < 0.001$. Controlled for company size, time horizon, skill level, age structure, organizational culture, region, industry, position in the chain, and intensity of competition.

b Reference: companies that filled in 'voluntary initiatives' in the survey question on the main cause of the improvement in EP

c Reference: companies that filled in 'non-applicable' in the survey question on the main cause of the improvement of EP motivations for the first sample in which companies that selected 'voluntary own initiatives' are the reference option. The results show that government regulation crowds out intrinsic and extrinsic motivation of business leaders. These results support hypotheses 15.3 and 15.4. Columns (2b) and (3b) report the estimation results explaining motivations for the second sample in which companies for which business leaders had selected 'non applicable' are the reference option. Once again the results indicate crowding out of intrinsic motivation by government regulation, but the magnitude of the crowding effect appears to be much smaller. For extrinsic motivation, the crowding-out effects turn into crowding-in effects.

Column (4) shows that government regulation and voluntary initiatives significantly enhance EP. Voluntary initiatives are substantially more effective in stimulating EP than government regulation is.

Table 15.3 reports the indirect and total effects of government regulation on EP. The first column of Table 15.3 shows the (positive) direct effects of government regulation on EP from column (4) of Table 15.2. The second column reports the indirect effects of government regulation on EP through crowding effects on intrinsic and extrinsic motivations. The total effects are equal to the sum of the direct and the indirect effects of government regulation. For the first sample, Table 15.3 shows that the negative indirect effect of government regulation through crowding out intrinsic and extrinsic motivations offsets the direct positive effect of government regulation. Bowles (2016) calls this 'strong crowding out'. These empirical results confirm the crowding-out mechanism: government regulation significantly harms intrinsic and extrinsic motivations of business leaders, thereby reducing voluntary initiatives of SMEs to protect the environment. Crowding-out effects are almost absent in the second sample. Accordingly, the total effect of government regulation is substantially positive. This implies that only if intrinsic motivation is already low to begin with, does government regulation contribute to EP of SMEs.

TABLE 15.3 Direct, indirect, and total effects of regulation on environmental performance[a]

Direct effect	*Indirect effect*			*Total effect*
	Through intrinsic motivation	*Through extrinsic motivation*	*Total*	
Reference: voluntary initiatives				
0.10***	−0.09***	−0.03**	−0.12***	−0.02
Reference: no voluntary initiatives				
0.10***	−0.01**	0.01**	−0.01	0.09***

a * $p < 0.05$; ** $p < 0.01$; *** $p < 0.001$.

15.5 Conclusion

This chapter sets out to research to what extent government regulation crowds out intrinsic motivation towards EP in SMEs and how the indirect effects caused by crowding out of intrinsic motivation compare with the direct effects of government regulation on EP.

Over the last quarter century, much research has been performed on motives of CSR, distinguishing between extrinsic and intrinsic motives (Muller and Kolk, 2010). Previous research did not, however, consider that intrinsic motives can depend on external pressures that drive extrinsic motivations. This study develops a more nuanced understanding of how external pressures and intrinsic motives relate by advancing the hypothesis that government regulation impacts intrinsic motivation. Insight into motivation crowding effects is important, because disregarding motivation crowding out leads to overestimation of the influence of government regulations on EP. This study therefore adds to the literature that studied the effects of government regulation on environmental innovation of companies (Hunt and Fund, 2016) but did not explore the impact of public policy on intrinsic and extrinsic motivations. Our study shows that the effectiveness of government regulation in stimulating EP of SMEs is contingent on the intrinsic motivation of its business leaders.

Our results are in line with previous research concluding that government regulation generates motivation crowding effects on environmental behaviour of rural households (Cardenas et al., 2000; Choi, 2015; Han et al., 2018) and farmers (Vollan, 2008), but diverge from the results of Abatayo and Lynham (2016). They found that government regulation improves EP and interpreted this finding as evidence that crowding out of intrinsic motivation does not occur, although they did not test this explicitly. Our results show that a positive relationship between government regulation and EP actually can go together with crowding out of intrinsic motivation. These findings suggest that Abatayo and Lynham (2016) may have misinterpreted their results as evidence against crowding out of intrinsic motivation.

An unexpected outcome of our research is that for companies in the second sample, government regulation increases rather than decreases extrinsic motivation, which is opposite to Hypothesis 15.4. The reason may be that government regulations teach business leaders of companies with low EP that improvements required by government regulations yield financial and other benefits, thereby boosting extrinsic motivation to enhance EP. Another explanation is that environmental improvements mandated by government regulations are relatively costly and that the regulations make business leaders realize that voluntary proactive measures might be more cost-efficient.

An important implication of our research is that motivation crowding out may occur, even if government regulation improves EP. Previous studies' assumption that a positive correlation between government regulation and EP indicates no crowding out of intrinsic motivation is unwarranted. Our study provides a more refined analysis of the crowding mechanism by separating it from the direct effects of government regulation on EP. It provides empirical evidence that a positive relationship between government regulation and EP does not exclude crowding out of intrinsic motivation. The reason is that the negative effects of motivation crowding out on EP can be offset by the positive direct effects of government regulation on environmental quality.

Notes

* An extended text of this chapter has been published by Informa UK Limited, trading as Taylor & Francis Group on behalf of University of Newcastle upon Tyne, as an open access article under the terms of the Creative Commons AttributionNon Commercial-NoDerivatives License (http://creativecommons.org/licenses/by-nc-nd/4.0/) in: Graafland, J., and Bovenberg, L. (2020). Government regulation, business leaders' motivations and environmental performance of SMEs. *Journal of Environmental Planning and Management*, 63(8): 1335–1355. Lans Bovenberg is affiliated to the department of Economics of Tilburg University in The Netherlands.

1 Demirel et al. (2018) found that effective environmental protection entails collaboration between government regulation and voluntary environmental measures. Coercive legislation does not leave much room for flexibility and voluntary choices by managers and frequently pushes the manager to adopt environmental measures without considering effectiveness (Daddi et al., 2016). Both Daddi et al. (2016) and Demirel et al. (2018) did, however, not analyze effects of government regulation on intrinsic motivations.

2 However, Rode et al. (2015) provide several arguments that government regulation can also crowd-in intrinsic motivation. One of the arguments is that it is easier for intrinsically motivated companies to act upon their motivation if the government regulation creates a level playing field by compelling companies that are not intrinsically motivated to invest in environmental improvements.

16

ECONOMIC FREEDOM AND CSR

Moderation by Intrinsic Motivations*

16.1 Introduction

CSR is conditioned on the role and responsibilities of business in society with regard to social and environmental issues. Whether free market capitalism is compatible with or harmful to CSR is strongly debated. Various authors argue that capitalism may inhibit CSR, because private industry will invest in the most profitable technologies, which leads to a focus on the cheapest rather than socially responsible processes (Williamson et al., 2006; Bell, 2015). Other authors argue that economic freedom in markets and competition stimulate CSR (Baughn et al., 2007; Jackson and Apostolakou, 2010; Kinderman, 2012; Hartmann and Uhlenbruck, 2015), and that businesses has expressed its interest in adopting a more extensive CSR approach conditional upon receiving greater freedom from the state (Kinderman, 2008). In an extensive welfare state, this role has been traditionally marginal in relation to the democratic political decision-making process regarding social issues. Social policies were the domains of the public sector, whereas issues directly related to conditions of work should be negotiated with unions, often backed by a legal rule that extended the outcome of these negotiations to other employees. Issues like unemployment insurance and health care are therefore not the result of voluntary initiatives of companies, but are either determined at the political level by the state or by negotiations with unions. Similarly, intensive government regulation of environmental aspects of business operations leaves little room for CSR. Assuming diminishing returns from CSR, the more intensive and elaborate government regulation, the less profitable any additional voluntary CSR policy will be. The main task left for companies is to run their corporations in a rational and efficient way, while respecting both the outcomes of the negotiations with trade unions as well as the extensive government

DOI: 10.4324/9781003216483-20

regulation with regard to safety and health standards, equal opportunities, waste disposal, pollution and all other social and environmental issues regulated by law (De Geer et al., 2010). This is particular relevant for SMEs in relation to environmental issues, because they base their environmental practices almost exclusively on achieving compliance with regulations.

While others have considered the benefits and costs of regulation (cf. Brammer, Hoejmose, and Marchant, 2012; Agan et al., 2013), in this chapter we look at the broad measure of economic freedom. Economic freedom means that property rights are secure and that individuals are free to use, exchange, or give their property to another as long as their actions do not violate the identical rights of others (Gwartney and Lawson, 2003). Economic freedom declines if the government intervenes through taxation, trade tariffs or other trade barriers, or regulations of credit, output and labour markets. A stronger protection of property rights has been found to lead to CSR improvements (Ioannou and Serafeim, 2012). Free trade, another exponent of economic freedom, has however, ambiguous effects. Whereas the so-called gains-from-trade hypothesis presumes that trade has a positive effect on the environment, the so-called race-to-the-bottom hypothesis states that open countries adopt lax environmental standards and become pollution havens in order to attract multinational corporations or export pollution-intensive goods (Frankel and Rose, 2005). A literature study of Carson (2010) shows that the supporting empirical evidence of either hypothesis remains scant and fragile. Also for state regulation, evidence is mixed. Camisón (2010) found that the effectiveness of coercive regulation in promoting environmental innovation is lower than voluntary policies. Demirel et al. (2018) found that effective environmental protection entails collaboration between government regulation and voluntary environmental measures. Coercive legislation does not leave much room for flexibility and voluntary choices by managers and frequently pushes the manager to adopt environmental measures without considering effectiveness (Daddi et al., 2016). For economic freedom more generally, Jackson and Apostolakou (2010) argued and found that firms in liberal market economies outstrip firms in coordinated market economies, because their voluntary CSR initiatives substitute for the lack of government interventions. Kinderman (2012) stated that during the period of rapid deregulation and liberalization in the UK (a typical liberal market economy) CSR not only developed and thrived, but even managed to outperform the previous economic model in terms of corporate accountability and corporate standards.

We contribute to this literature, presenting evidence for an important modification of the argument of Jackson and Apostolakou (2010) and Kinderman (2012) that companies voluntarily adopt a more extensive CSR approach if the state reduces its interventions: the positive effect of economic freedom on CSR is conditional on internal motivations to CSR. The literature on motives for CSR distinguishes between extrinsic and intrinsic motives (Muller and Kolk, 2010). An extrinsic motive encourages CSR if it is instrumental for other goals, such as financial performance or the company's reputation. Intrinsic motives perceive CSR as an end in itself, independent from other benefits. Intrinsic (environmental) motivation may stem from personal satisfaction of engaging in CSR when executives enjoy helping others or from a sense of responsibility to contribute to society and the welfare of future generations (Lindenberg, 2001). Previous studies have focused on drivers external and internal to the firm (Weaver et al., 1999; Aguilera et al., 2007; Bracke et al., 2008; Haller and Murphy, 2012), but did not consider that the influence of internal drivers interact with the external drivers. We fill a gap in this literature studying this interaction, exploiting the variation between companies in their environmental motivation and between countries in their level of economic freedom. We hypothesize and test that economic freedom increases CSR for firms with internally motivated managers, for example through voluntary actions (Alberini and Segerson, 2002), while absence of economic freedom increases CSR for firms without. This chapter thereby fits in a growing literature that considers more 'behavioural' drivers for environmental impacts (Croson and Treich, 2014).

This chapter thus makes two major contributions to existing literature. First, we extend and deepen existing literature on institutional drivers of CSR by arguing that the impacts of market institutions on CSR depend on their virtuous interaction with internal motivations towards CSR. Second, we test empirically if and what kind of motivation interacts with economic freedom in their influences on CSR. In our empirical research, we focus on SMEs.

16.2 Conceptual Framework

Following other studies (Weaver et al., 1999; Aguilera et al., 2007), we assume that CSR depends on a combination of external pressures (economic freedom in our context) and factors internal to the company. We extend previous studies as we postulate that the CSR is influenced by the interaction between internal motivations and economic freedom. More specifically, we assume that the interaction between economic freedom and internal motivations stimulates the participation in environmental networks that improves environmental impacts at company level (see Figure 16.1). Here, we will first discuss Hypothesis 16.1. Next, we elaborate on Hypothesis 16.2, which concerns the main contribution of this chapter.

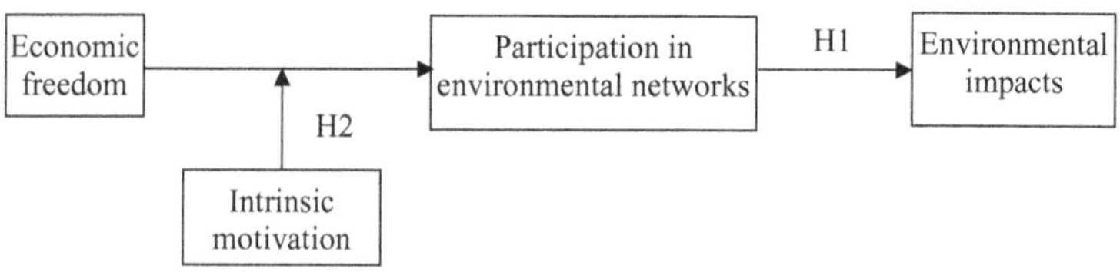

FIGURE 16.1 Conceptual framework

Participation in Environmental Networks and Environmental Impacts

In the small business context, a growing literature and awareness has emerged on the effectiveness of implicit and embedded approaches to environmental responsibility (Wickert et al., 2016). Effective implementation for SMEs requires cooperation, in which firms draw on their social capital and connections to stakeholders with high proximity. External knowledge compensates the constrained in-house expertise and provides appropriate solutions to ecological challenges (Bos-Brouwers, 2010). Participation in external networks to share best practices is particularly appropriate for this purpose (Valentine, 2016). Indeed, small businesses that invest in tools and solutions with significant pro-environmental impact identify these solutions through other participants in their networks (Wohlfarth et al., 2017).

Based on this argument, we expect that participation in external environmental networks helps SMEs improving their environmental impacts:

Hypothesis 16.1 Participation in environmental networks improves environmental impacts.

Economic Freedom, Internal Motivations, and Participation in Environmental Networks

Institutional theory describes how corporations' decisions depend on the institutional context (North, 1990), and this framework is central to most studies considering differences in firms' social and environmental impacts across countries (Matten and Moon, 2008; Ioannou and Serafeim, 2012). But how the free market system affects the CSR of companies is still an underdeveloped research theme. The degree of freedom of a market system can be measured by the economic freedom of a country, which refers to the personal liberty to voluntary exchange and compete in the market while enjoying security and property protection (Gwartney and Lawson, 2003). Economic freedom comprises several dimensions such as low share of government in GDP and low tax rates, protection of property rights, freedom to exchange goods and services internationally, and no regulatory restraints that limit the freedom of exchange in credit, labour, and product markets. Earlier studies by Baughn et al. (2007) and Hartmann and Uhlenbruck (2015) found that economic freedom stimulates CSR.

However, when researchers only focus on institutional factors, there is insufficient consideration for differences in CSR at the individual company level. Although some companies have incorporated CSR in their business model, it is not standard business practice. There is a flavour of social desirability in the belief that alleviating regulatory constrains from firms increases their contribution to society and the environment in terms of resources and efforts. But corporations have more options. Various authors argued that capitalism may inhibit rather than encourage improving environmental impacts, since private industry will mostly invest in technologies that it expects to be profitable (Bell, 2015).

In this chapter, we postulate that internal motivations of managers are fundamental for the company's engagement in CSR in a free market system. The literature on motives for CSR distinguishes between extrinsic and intrinsic motives (Muller and Kolk, 2010; Rode et al., 2015; Abatayo and Lynham, 2016). An extrinsic motive encourages CSR because of its instrumental value for other goals, such as financial performance or the company's reputation. Intrinsically motivated CSR requires no separate reward but the behaviour itself (Vollan, 2008). Intrinsic motivation may stem from personal satisfaction of engaging in CSR when executives enjoy helping others (Rabin, 1998) or enjoy a 'warm glow' from contributing to a public good. But intrinsic motivation may also stem from a genuine concern for the environment and a sense of obligation to contribute to society and the welfare of future generations (Lindenberg, 2001; Bansal and Roth, 2000).

We expect that economic freedom will hardly encourage companies to increase their engagement in CSR if they are not intrinsically motivated to take responsibility for the environment. That is, we expect that the positive relationship between economic freedom and CSR is conditional on intrinsic motivation. Since environmental policies may require costly investments, companies will be less motivated by the extrinsic profit motive to make investments in CSR. This particularly holds for SMEs. The level playing field on which most SMEs operate means that they face severe competition and this puts profitability under pressure. Low profitability induces low cost strategies and reduces a long-term orientation so that long-term strategic benefits from CSR in terms of improved reputation, cost reduction, increased consumer demand and reduction in risks often remain beyond the strategic horizon. Moreover, because of their smaller size, Brammer, Hoejmose, and Marchant (2012) argued that SMEs are less visible to NGOs and media, compared to large companies, and cannot take advantage of CSR as instrumental for extrinsic profit motives. This implies that, as Lynch-Wood and Williamson (2007) argue, the profit motive is potentially weak to induce SMEs to go beyond compliance to the law, though we do not want to fully exclude reputational effects, for example if their CSR is monitored by local NGOs or local media. If a local NGO or newspaper spreads negative news about a small company, it might directly harm its reputation at its location (Jamali and Mirshak, 2007) and the company would run the risk of economic loss (Russo and Tencati, 2009). Because of their intimate relationship with the community in which they operate, SMEs also need to pursue a community-friendly policy (Jenkins, 2009). Hence, also some SMEs will realize that low CSR may have serious consequences for the enterprise's reputation and economic performance and be extrinsically motivated to implement environmental policies in order to improve their environmental impacts. However, if companies are motivated by the business case, they will adopt CSR only insofar it can be aligned to narrow strategic interests (Marens,

2008). These companies will be tempted to use ceremonial instead of substantive CSR policies in order to gain social legitimacy without incurring the costs of substantive CSR policies. CSR is ceremonial if companies decouple policies from implementation and/or impacts (Jamali, 2010; Okhmatovskiy and David, 2012).

But if the management of a company is intrinsically motivated to improve CSR performance, economic freedom enables the managers to implement environmental policies that improve environmental impacts, such as participation in environmental networks, even if these are costly and not profitable. Indeed, firms whose managers are highly intrinsically motivated to CSR are likely to apply broad and effective programmes if external conditions allow them to (Muller and Kolk, 2010). If companies have little freedom to determine their own policies, internal motivations will have a lesser effect on environmental impacts. Under these conditions internally motivated companies would perhaps have a stronger inclination to do so, but in practice focus on complying with the interventions and standards prescribed by the government (Jackson and Apostolakou, 2010).

The discussion here illustrates that in free market economies companies without intrinsic motivation are unlikely to participate in environmental networks that improve environmental impacts, whereas intrinsic motivation is unlikely to stimulate participation in environmental networks if the economic freedom to undertake private initiatives is limited. In this interactive view, there must be a 'fit' between the institutional environment and firm-internal characteristics, including managers' intentions. Based on these arguments, we propose the following hypothesis.

Hypothesis 16.2 The participation in environmental networks is positively related to the interaction between the intrinsic motivation and economic freedom.

16.3 Methodology

The data are taken from the survey in 2011. Following literature (Treviño et al., 2006; Lindenberg, 2001; Muller and Kolk, 2010) motivation is defined as the reason upon which one acts. One way to empirically measure motives is by asking people for the reason for a certain action (Elster, 2007). The principle of *nemo gratis mendax* (no one lies freely) suggests that expressions of motive should not be doubted per se, but only if there is reason because of particular circumstances (O'Mahoney, 2012). We measure intrinsic motivation by two survey questions. The first question measures moral motivation by asking the respondent to state his or her view on the extent to which the company's engagement in CSR is motivated by the company's responsibility for the environment and society. The second survey question measures personal satisfaction by inquiring to what extent personal satisfaction of the people in the enterprise is a motive to engage in environmental responsibility. Extrinsic motivation was measured by three survey questions on long-term financial benefits, reduction in reputational risks and customer demand as motives for engaging in CSR. All survey questions are measured by a seven-point Likert scale.

The questions for participation in environmental networks were based on literature and in collaboration with the SME consultant. In response to the question 'Which measures are realized in your enterprise?', several measures were given, including participation in CSR networks in the supply chain (Pirsch et al., 2006; Bos-Brouwers, 2010), partnerships with professional training institutes in order to anticipate the technological evolution of products or services (Bos-Brouwers, 2010), participation in local CSR initiatives of governments or social organizations (Barth and Wolff, 2009), and dialogue with societal organizations and local communities (Hall et al., 2015). For each measure, the respondent could choose between three options: 'no' (0), 'yes' (1) and 'unfamiliar with this measure.' The third option is recoded as 'no'.

Environmental impacts were measured by the decrease in energy use, water use, and waste disposal (see Chapters 2, 3, and 10). We used both explorative and confirmatory factor analysis to test the clustering of the survey variables in the four factors identified by our labels 'Intrinsic motivation', 'Extrinsic motivation', 'Environmental networks', and 'Environmental impacts' (see Table 16.1).

We use the average score of the 'Economic Freedom of the World' index of Fraser Institute during 2008–2010, downloaded from the websites of Fraser Institute. Most statistical and other information underlying this index are received from government sources and are verified with independent, credible third-party sources.

16.4 Results

We used structural equation modelling with maximum likelihood estimation as estimation method. The structural paths and the confirmatory factor analysis are simultaneously estimated. As the economic freedom variables are country-level variables and CSR variables are firm-level variables, we cluster errors over countries to account for the unobservable factors that are correlated with firm's motivation and performance within each country and are not correlated with those from other countries (Peterson et al., 2012). Table 16.2 reports the estimation results for the structural paths and measurement model (confirmatory factor analysis).

The estimation results in columns 1 and 2 show that the interaction term of economic freedom (EF) and intrinsic motivation increases participation in environmental networks, in support of Hypothesis 16.2. The results in Columns 3 and 4 show no significant positive effect of the interaction term of economic freedom and extrinsic motivation. The last two columns show the effects to be robust, despite the correlation between the two internal motivation variables. The importance of intrinsic motivation vis-à-vis extrinsic motivation is further stressed by comparing the direct effects of intrinsic and extrinsic motivation on

TABLE 16.1 Descriptives and factor analysis[a]

Variables	*Mean*	*SD*	*Factor loadings*			
			Intrinsic motivation	*Extrinsic motivation*	*Env. networks*	*Env. impacts*
Your enterprise feels responsible for the planet and society (25)	5.21	1.48	0.88			
It creates personal satisfaction for the people in your enterprise (26)	5.09	1.42	0.87			
It serves long-term financial interests of shareholders/ director owner (20)	3.78	1.85		0.73		
It limits reputational risks (24)	4.56	1.58		0.74		
Large customers ask for it (27)	3.97	1.88		0.75		
CSR cooperation supply chain (46)	0.37	0.48			0.66	
Partnerships with training institutes (47)	0.36	0.48			0.65	
Participation in local initiatives (48)	0.42	0.49			0.73	
Active dialogue with NGOs (45)	0.17	0.38			0.66	
Decrease in energy consumption (102)	0.46	1.38				0.86
Decrease in water consumption (104)	0.34	1.09				0.88
Decrease in waste (105)	0.38	1.21				0.86
Eigenvalue			1.05	2.74	1.41	2.17
Cronbach alpha			0.73	0.62	0.62	0.83

a The numbers in brackets refer to the numbers of the survey questions reported in Appendix 1. Extraction Method: Principal Component Analysis; Rotation Method: Oblimin with Kaiser Normalization. Kaiser–Meyer–Olkin (KMO) = 0.735; *p*-value of Bartlett's Test of Sphericity = 0.000.

environmental networks. These seem highly significant when considered in isolation (columns 1–4), but the coefficient for extrinsic motivation suffers from omitted variable bias, shown in the last two columns. The joint model shows significant direct effects for intrinsic motivation and insignificant for extrinsic motivation. The last row shows that firms' participation in environmental networks have a significant positive effect on environmental outcomes, supporting Hypothesis 16.1. From these estimation results we conclude that only the interaction between intrinsic motivation and economic freedom influences CSR.

Another noteworthy aspect is that the interaction term between economic freedom and intrinsic motivation is also seen to have a direct, significant effect

TABLE 16.2 Estimation results[a]

Dependent variable	*1*	*2*	*3*	*4*	*5*	*6*
	Env. networks	*Env. outcomes*	*Env. networks*	*Env. Outcomes*	*Env. networks*	*Env. outcomes*
Structural paths interaction terms						
EF × Intrinsic motivation	0.036*	0.028*			0.037*	0.018
	(0.016)	(0.011)			(0.016)	(0.016)
EF × Extrinsic motivation			0.012	0.021	0.013	0.015
			(0.028)	(0.011)	(0.029)	(0.014)
Structural paths direct linear terms						
Intrinsic motivation	0.379***	0.023			0.333***	0.039
	(0.016)	(0.019)			(0.028)	(0.022)
Extrinsic motivation			0.280***	−0.007	0.076	−0.021
			(0.040)	(0.022)	(0.048)	(0.024)
Economic freedom (EF)	−0.022	0.075***	−0.067	0.068**	−0.031	0.073**
	(0.027)	(0.024)	(0.040)	(0.024)	(0.028)	(0.024)
Environmental networks		0.152***		0.168***		0.151***
		(0.036)		(0.035)		(0.034)
Global fit indices (for 1 and 2, 3 and 4, 5 and 6)						
RMSEA	0.02		0.03		0.03	
CFI	0.95		0.91		0.91	
TLI	0.93		0.88		0.88	
SMRM	0.02		0.02		0.02	
Measurement model (confirmatory factor analysis)						
Intrinsic motivation						
- responsibility	0.79***				0.79***	
- personal satisfaction	0.73***				0.73***	
Extrinsic motivation						
- financial benefits			0.52***		0.49***	
- reputational risks			0.71***		0.76***	
- customer demand			0.54***		0.51***	
Environmental networks						
- cooperation supply chain	0.47***		0.49***		0.48***	
- partnerships	0.47***		0.48***		0.47***	
- local initiatives	0.60***		0.58***		0.59***	
- dialogue	0.47***		0.47***		0.47***	

Dependent variable	*1*	*2*	*3*	*4*	*5*	*6*
	Env. networks	*Env. outcomes*	*Env. networks*	*Env. Outcomes*	*Env. networks*	*Env. outcomes*
Environmental outcomes						
- energy	0.76***		0.77***		0.77***	
- waste	0.77***		0.77***		0.77***	
- water	0.82***		0.82***		0.82***	

a Standardized coefficients. * $p < 0.05$; ** $p < 0.01$; *** $p < 0.001$. Controlled for GDP per capita (PPP, constant international USD in 2011), power distance, individualism, sector, the company's position in the chain, intensity of price competition, the size and growth of the company (measured by the logarithm of the number of FTEs), the skill and the age structure of the company, function and the age of the respondent. $N = 4{,}338$. Global fit indices: RMSEA = 0.03; CFI = 0.91; TLI = 0.88; SRMR = 0.02.

TABLE 16.3 Direct, indirect, and total effects on environmental impacts[a]

	Direct effect	*Indirect effect*	*Total effect*
Economic freedom (EF)	0.082 (0.000)	0.004 (0.488)	0.079 (0.000)
Intrinsic motivation	0.022 (0.226)	0.054 (0.000)	0.075 (0.000)
EF x Intrinsic motivation	0.030 (0.012)	0.006 (0.002)	0.036 (0.005)

a Unstandardized coefficients; *p*-values in brackets.

on environmental outcomes in column 2. This finding indicates that the interacting influence of intrinsic motivation and economic freedom on economic outcomes is not only mediated by cooperation in the supply chain, partnerships with training institutes, participation in local initiatives and dialogue with NGOs, but also by other measures that improve environmental impacts, that are not included in our measurement of environmental networks.

Based on the estimation results in column 1 and 2 of Table 16.2, we calculated the total effects of the interaction term of economic freedom and intrinsic motivation on environmental impacts, that is, the sum of the direct effect and the indirect effects through participation in environmental networks. The results in Table 16.3 show that the direct, indirect as well as the total effect of the interaction term of economic freedom and intrinsic motivation on environmental impacts are significant.

Next, we calculated the differential effects between Italy (lowest economic freedom) and the UK (highest economic freedom) for a firm with average, low and high intrinsic motivation. Table 16.4 shows that a rise in economic freedom induces companies with low intrinsic motivation to worsen environmental impacts, whereas companies with high intrinsic motivation use the extra economic freedom for bettering their contribution to the environment. The table

TABLE 16.4 Estimated total effect of difference in economic freedom on environmental impacts[a]

Intrinsic motivation of companies (X)		
X = Lowest in Sample	*X = Sample Average*	*X = Highest in sample*
–0.15	0.27	0.69

a a_1 $(EF_{UK} - EF_{It}) + a_2$ $(EF_{UK} - EF_{It})$ * X. a_1 and a_2 denote the total effects of economic freedom (EF) and the interaction term of economic freedom and intrinsic motivation, EF_{UK} (standardized) economic freedom of UK, EF_{It} (standardized) economic freedom in Italy, and X (standardized) intrinsic motive.

unambiguously shows the importance of the interaction between intrinsic motivation and economic freedom for environmental impacts. The average effect of economic freedom is positive, though.

16.5 Conclusion

Though awareness of the need for a transition to a more sustainable economy is widely spread, not every firm is equally supportive for (voluntarily) measures that improve environmental impacts. Particularly SMEs may be hesitant to invest resources in sustainable production processes, because of intensive competition. Governments may enforce improved environmental impacts by government interventions, but these come with the disadvantage of losing out on voluntary initiatives. The question whether more or less economic freedom results in more environmental responsible management, has remained open. Previous research has shown that (certain aspects of) economic freedom might increase CSR (Baughn et al., 2007; Jackson and Apostolakou, 2010, Ioannou and Serafeim, 2012; Kinderman, 2012; Hartmann and Uhlenbruck, 2015). But these previous studies did not consider how the free market system affects the corporate environmental impacts of companies. Although economic freedom may stimulate some companies to incorporate CSR in their business model, it is not a standard business practice.

We approached the question how economic freedom affects CSR by studying its interaction with internal motivations. For as far as we know, we are the first in the literature to consider this interaction mechanism. The main contribution of our analysis lies in the finding that the influence of economic freedom on environmental impacts appears to be contingent on the intrinsic motivation of companies. This mechanism is reminiscent to interaction effects between external pressures and internal motivation proposed by Muller and Kolk (2010). They found that firm-internal characteristics, including managers' intentions, determine CSR benefits from external pressures. Also Weaver et al. (1999) found that firms whose managers are highly committed to ethics have broader and more deeply rooted ethics programmes compared to firms engaged in response to external pressures. This indicates that intrinsic motivation increases the influence of external stimuli to perform certain types of behaviour. We postulate that such interaction also regulates the influence of institutions on company's CSR, and our empirical results confirm the hypothesis: economic freedom stimulates firms whose managers are intrinsically motivated, to integrate environmental sustainability into their operations, while firms whose managers lack intrinsic motivation reduce their environmental impacts.

Besides the interaction effect with intrinsic motivation, we also find a direct effect of economic freedom on environmental impacts. With fewer government interventions, greater pressure may come from stakeholders towards the developing CSR practices (Jackson and Apostolakou, 2010). Furthermore, economic freedom stimulates free trade, which increases the exchange of information and spurs managerial innovation and diffusion of new technologies that provide companies with more cost-efficient solutions to improve their environmental impacts (Frankel and Rose, 2005).

Note

* An extended text of this chapter has been published as an open access article under the terms of the Creative Commons Attribution 4.0 International License (http://creativecommons.org/licenses/by/4.0/) in: Graafland, J.J., and Gerlagh, R. (2019). Economic freedom, internal motivation, and corporate environmental responsibility of SMEs. *Environmental and Resource Economics*, 74: 1101–1123. Reyer Gerlagh is affiliated to the department of Economics at Tilburg University in The Netherlands.

17

ECONOMIC FREEDOM AND CORPORATE SOCIAL RESPONSIBILITY

The Role of Long-Term Orientation*

17.1 Introduction

Engagement of firms in CSR differs between countries (Gallego-Álvarez and Ortas, 2017) and understanding these differences is an important issue in international business research (Ioannou and Serafeim, 2012). In explaining these differences two perspectives stand out: the approach from national culture (e.g. Peng et al., 2014) and the approach from institutions (e.g. Young and Makhija, 2014). These two perspectives have remained largely disconnected, and in the few cases that culture and institutions are combined, they tend to be presented as separate explanatory factors without exploring possible interactive effects of cultural and institutional differences (e.g. Ioannou and Serafeim, 2012).

In this chapter, we show that integrating the cultural and institutional perspectives, by studying the combined effects of institutions and culture on CSR practices is a promising direction of research. We explore possible interdependencies between the two sets of factors by analysing how the cultural characteristic of long-term orientation (LTO) and the set of institutions associated with economic freedom, in combination, help understand international differences in CSR practices of firms. This analysis is interesting in its own right, given the increasing importance of CSR, but we also present it as an example of how looking at interdependencies between culture and institutions can be useful in international comparative management research (Peterson and Barreto, 2018).

We selected economic freedom as an indicator of institutional differences between societies because this concept captures a constellation of institutional factors that has been demonstrated to influence important economic behaviours and outcomes. However, whether economic freedom should be expected to be good or bad for CSR is not self-evident. Economic freedom could enable firms

DOI: 10.4324/9781003216483-21

to voluntarily engage in CSR (Kinderman, 2012), but freedom could also be used to economize on CSR, since private companies will only invest in activities believed to be profitable (Bell, 2015). Only if firms are long-term oriented, will CSR benefits (that mostly materialize in the long term) be seen to outweigh CSR costs (that mostly occur in the short term).

Societal-level long-term orientation distinguishes between societies in which the emphasis is on the past or present, and those that pay much attention to the future (Hofstede and Minkov, 2010). The consequences of this cultural dimension have so far remained relatively unexplored, but from a theoretical perspective time orientation has a potentially important influence on CSR (Kitzmueller and Shimshack, 2012; Durach and Wiengarten, 2017). LTO can be expected to positively influence assessments of the value of CSR initiatives, for example in terms of corporate reputation and quality of stakeholder relations (Rehbein et al., 2013). However, whether such investments are indeed undertaken also depends on economic freedom. Only if firms have the freedom to decide about their level of CSR (i.e. this is not strictly regulated by the government) an increase in LTO will result in more engagement in CSR.

In this study we extend the work of Graafland and Noorderhaven (2018), who concluded that previous studies of the relationship between national culture and one aspect of CSR, environmental responsibility, has not led to robust cumulative results. One reason for this, pursued in this chapter, could be that it is the combination of institutional and cultural factors that influences CSR. We develop hypotheses for the interactive effect of economic freedom and long-term orientation on CSR. We test these hypotheses on a sample of 4,651 SMEs from 12 European countries, and find supporting evidence that the influences of culture and institutions on CSR interact.

Next, we first present the conceptual framework and methodology. Then we describe the results and summarize the findings.

17.2 Conceptual Framework

Institutions create incentives for and constraints on firm strategies (e.g. Ingram and Clay, 2000), and they may be expected to also influence firms' decisions regarding CSR. Institutions in a country form 'the set of fundamental political, social, and legal ground rules that establishes the basis for production, exchange, and distribution' (Davis and North, 1971: 6). It is reasonable to argue that firms embedded in different national institutional environments will 'experience divergent degrees of internal and external pressures to engage in social responsibility initiatives' (Aguilera et al., 2007: 836). Ioannou and Serafeim (2012) indeed found that a number of institutional factors related to the political system, the education and labour system, and the financial system influence CSR.

While the study of Ioannou and Serafeim (2012) showed that the national institutional context matters for CSR, we are still left with some important questions. Ioannou and Serafeim (2012) analysed the influence of institutions in the form of isolated factors, like 'union density' or 'absence of corruption', but did not explore how interrelated sets of institutional factors affect CSR. Consequently, insights into the influence of institutions on CSR remain fragmented. Rather than only looking at separate variables, it is important to consider the institutional environment as an interdependent configuration of structures (Jackson and Deeg, 2008).

Economic Freedom

We propose that economic freedom forms such a configuration of institutional factors, reflecting the extent to which economic activity is promoted to be coordinated by 'personal choice, voluntary exchange, open markets, and clearly defined and enforced property rights' (Gwartney, 2009: 939). Of course, many other aspects of institutional environments could be taken into account (see, e.g., Fainshmidt et al., 2018). However, we believe that economic freedom has *prima facie* plausibility as an institutional complex influencing CSR.

Economic freedom has been demonstrated to influence important economic behaviours and outcomes (e.g. Banalieva et al., 2018), and various studies have argued that free markets and competition also stimulate CSR (El Ghoul et al., 2017; Hartmann and Uhlenbruck, 2015; Jackson and Apostolakou, 2010). However, the idea that economic freedom should be expected to be good for CSR is not self-evident. It could also lead to economizing on CSR-related expenses in order to increase immediate returns.

National Culture

We contend that the question whether economic freedom leads to more or to less CSR depends on a third factor: culture. Culture has been shown to influence many aspects of firm behaviour (Hofstede, 2001). Different dimensions of national cultures can be distinguished, and previous studies have explored possible effects of these dimensions on aspects of CSR (Graafland and Noorderhaven, 2018). The original study of Hofstede identified four dimensions: individualism-collectivism, power distance, uncertainty avoidance, and masculinity-femininity (Hofstede, 2001). Power Distance (PDI) refers to the extent to which the members of a society believe that power in the society should be concentrated in the hands of the leaders, and that these people should be obeyed without question. Individualism-collectivism (IDV) distinguishes between societies in which ties between individuals are loose and people are mainly concerned about themselves and immediate family, and societies in which people are integrated into strong groups that they will protect in exchange for unquestioning loyalty. Uncertainty avoidance (UAI) indicates a country's intolerance for uncertainty and ambiguity. It gives an indication to what extent people feel uncomfortable in unstructured situations. Masculinity-femininity (MAS) refers to the distribution of emotional roles between the genders. Masculinity stands for a society in which men are supposed to be assertive, competitive, ambitious and materialistic. Femininity involves societies in which both men and women are supposed to have a preference for caring, cooperation, modesty and quality of life.

In the literature on international differences in CSR authors have used Hofstede's framework to develop hypotheses regarding the relationship between the four dimensions of national culture and CSR. PDI has been theorized by authors to have a negative effect (Park et al., 2007; Ioannou and Serafeim, 2012; Peng et al., 2014; Thanetsunthorn, 2015; Tsoy and Yongqiang, 2016; Cox et al., 2011; Gallego-Álvarez and Ortas, 2017), because PDI decreases consumer pressure on businesses with regard to CSR-related issues and environmental accountability is more likely to be ignored for the interests of the power holders. Also masculinity reduces CSR, because materialistic, masculine values like the pursuit of economic growth may lead to slower adoption of costly technology necessary for environmental sustainability. The effect of individualism is more ambiguous. Hampden-Turner and Trompenaars (2000) argued that individualist countries tend to be more focused on shareholders' interests and therefore more concerned on tasks that create shareholder value rather than stakeholder value. In a collectivistic society people are more likely to have stronger relationships with others (Michailnova and Hutchings, 2006), succumb more to group pressure and it is therefore more common to cater to the need of all stakeholders (Williams and Zinkin, 2008; Ringov and Zollo, 2007). On the other hand, Ioannou and Serafeim (2012) argued that firms in individualist countries are more likely to undertake explicit CER activities in response to perceived expectations of their shareholders. Also on uncertainty avoidance, divergent views are voiced in the literature. On one hand, it is argued that societies with high uncertainty avoidance are less open to change and less innovative (De Mooij and Hofstede, 2010; Ringov and Zollo, 2007) and therefore less likely to adapt to changing needs of stakeholders. However, businesses can use CSR to reduce uncertainties (Williams and Zinkin, 2008; Ho et al., 2012) and then uncertainty avoidance may stimulate CSR.

Long-Term Orientation

Whereas the four dimensions of national culture discussed earlier have been identified in Hofstede's original study of IBM (Hofstede, 1980), in later work Hofstede has also included long-term orientation (Hofstede and Minkov, 2010). Given our interest in how economic freedom may influence CSR in combination with cultural characteristics, we focus on cultural influences related to time orientation, because this factor influences how firms respond to economic freedom (Kitzmueller and Shimshack, 2012; Miska et al., 2018). Time orientation plays an important role in CSR (Slawinski and Bansal, 2009). Time orientation, and specifically the extent to which people take the future into consideration in making decisions, is reflected in the long-term versus short-term orientation dimension of national cultures (Hofstede, 2001). This dimension of national cultures has a number of connotations, the most important of which in the present context is the emphasis on immediate need gratification in short-term oriented cultures, and on postponement of need gratification in long-term oriented cultures (Hofstede and Minkov, 2010).

Previous research exploring the relationship between LTO and CSR has shown ambiguous results (Graafland and Noorderhaven, 2018). We propose that these conflicting and inconsistent findings may be due to the interaction with other factors. More specifically, we contend that looking at the combined effect of economic freedom and LTO helps to develop a more robust understanding of international differences in CSR.

With more economic freedom, CSR will depend stronger on market incentives, instead of government intervention. Whether market incentives stimulate CSR crucially depends on the perception of time (Kitzmueller and Shimshack, 2012). The time horizon applied in the calculation of costs and benefits of CSR is influenced by a firm's environment. The longer the time horizon of the society, the more stakeholders of companies will value long-term benefits of voluntary CSR initiatives, for example in terms of quality of stakeholder relations (Rehbein et al., 2013). And if consumers and other stakeholders care about the quality of life of future generations, they are more likely to protest against unsustainable business practices and are more willing to punish irresponsible behaviour (King, 2008).

LTO in the national environment can press managers to engage in CSR practices that will pay out only in the future (Bénabou and Tirole, 2010). This suggests that a high level of economic freedom is associated with a high level of CSR, provided that the firm operates in a society that takes a long-term perspective. We can also argue that LTO stimulates CSR, but especially if firms have the freedom to decide about their level of CSR. Based on these arguments, we hypothesize an interactive effect of economic freedom and society-level LTO on CSR:

Hypothesis 17.1 Economic freedom and society-level long-term orientation interactively stimulate CSR.

17.3 Methodology

The data are taken from the survey in 2011. We operationalized CSR by nine concrete measures that SMEs can take to improve their CSR performance (Graafland et al., 2003) (see Table 17.1). All are measured on a binary scale ranging (0: no; 1: yes). To assess construct validity, we performed principal component analysis (with Oblimin rotation). The CSR measures load on two factors, representing the external and internal dimensions of CSR. Cronbach alpha values support

TABLE 17.1 Descriptives and factor analysis[a]

Variables	*Mean*	*SD*	*Factor loadings*	
			External CSR	*Internal CSR*
CSR cooperation supply chain (46)	0.37	0.48	0.65	
Partnerships with professional training institutes (47)	0.36	0.48	0.68	
Participation in local CSR initiatives (48)	0.42	0.49	0.75	
Active dialogue with NGOs concerning CSR issues (45)	0.17	0.38	0.60	
CSR related remuneration (50)	0.08	0.27		0.60
Whistle-blower procedure (51)	0.19	0.39		0.62
Ethics committee (52)	0.11	0.32		0.71
CSR training (53)	0.29	0.45		0.63
The use of a reference guide or external CSR tool to measure CSR performance (54)	0.23	0.42		0.64
Eigenvalue			2.95	1.09
% Variance explained			33	12
Cronbach alpha			0.62	0.65

a The numbers in brackets refer to the numbers of the survey questions reported in Appendix 1. Extraction Method: Principal Component Analysis; Rotation Method: Oblimin with Kaiser Normalization. KMO = 0.824, *p*-value Bartlett's Test of Sphericity = 0.000.

internal reliability of both factors. In the regression analysis we use the factors estimated by the factor analysis.

For economic freedom we used average scores of the 'Economic Freedom of the World' (EFW) index of the Fraser Institute as well as of those of the Heritage Foundation, over the years 2008–2010. The indices for national culture were taken from Hofstede's databank (http://geert-hofstede.com/countries.html).

17.4 Results

We estimated the model with structural equation modelling, using maximum likelihood as estimation technique. In order to control for the confounding effects that result from the use of variables at different levels of aggregation (country versus company), we used (country) clustered and robust standard errors.

The estimation results in Table 17.3 show that the centered interaction term of economic freedom and long-term orientation is significant for both internal and external CSR, and across the two indicators of economic freedom (Fraser Institute and Heritage Foundation), whereas no stable pattern is found for the two factors in isolation. This provides supports for Hypothesis 17.1.

TABLE 17.2 Descriptives macro variables

	Mean	*SD*
Economic freedom Fraser	7.33	0.23
Economic freedom Heritage	68.04	5.96
Long-term orientation	57.27	12.79

TABLE 17.3 Structural equation model[a]

	Fraser Institute		*Heritage Foundation*	
	1	*2*	*3*	*4*
	External CSR	*Internal CSR*	*External CSR*	*Internal CSR*
Economic freedom (EF)	0.02	0.01	−0.04	0.08*
Long-term orientation (LTO)	−0.08***	0.01	−0.03	0.03
Centered interaction term (EF * LTO)	0.17**	0.12*	0.10*	0.11**
R^2	0.14	0.09	0.14	0.09

a Standardized coefficients; clustered and robust standard errors; * $p < 0.05$; ** $p < 0.01$; *** $p < 0.001$; $N = 4{,}651$. Controlled for sector, position in the chain, the market position of the company, the degree of unionization of the company's employees, the size of the company (measured by the logarithm of the number of employees in FTEs), the age and skill structure of the company, the age of the respondent, and the function of the respondent. Furthermore, we controlled for the other dimensions of national culture. However, as correlation analysis showed that power distance and masculinity were highly related in our set of countries ($r = 0.88$), we dropped masculinity.

17.5 Conclusion

Institutional factors and cultural factors have been argued to explain international differences in firm behaviour, but these two sets of factors have most often be studied in isolation from each other. Both institutions and cultures function as external constraints and enablers in the strategic decision processes of firms, hence it makes sense to look at these sets of factors in conjunction. Our study shows that when looking at CSR practices, an explanation based on the combined, interactive effects of culture (represented by LTO) and institutions (reflected by economic freedom) has a stronger explanatory power than the two factors in isolation. In line with this, the contribution of this chapter is to provide more clarity on the institutional and cultural factors that contribute to international differences in levels of CSR.

Our findings suggest that research into international differences should not only look at both institutions and culture, but also specifically at the interaction between both types of factors. This point was made earlier on the level of the firm (Schultz, 2012), and we extend this to the societal level. This ties in with recent work on other topics in international management, like IPOs (Lewellyn and Bao, 2014) or venture capital (Li and Zahra, 2012). For comparative international management research to make progress it is not only important to better distinguish institutions from culture, and analyse how these two sets of factors are mutually influencing (Redding, 2008), but also to explore more broadly how culture and institutions together, rather than separately, affect important firm behaviours.

Note

* A different version of this chapter that used CSR data of large companies from ASSET4 has been published in: Graafland, J.J., and Noorderhaven, N. (2020). Culture and institutions: How economic freedom and long-term orientation interactively influence corporate social responsibility. *Journal of International Business Studies*, 51(6): 1034–1043. Niels Noorderhaven is affiliated to the department of Management at Tilburg University in The Netherlands.

18

COLLECTIVE AGREEMENTS AND EQUAL OPPORTUNITIES FOR WOMEN AND MINORITIES*

18.1 Introduction

Because of international differences in CSR policies of companies, research into CSR has become more focused on its institutional roots (Aguilera and Jackson, 2003; Campbell, 2007; Matten and Moon, 2008; Jackson and Apostolakou, 2010; Brammer, Jackson and Matten, 2012). One of the institutions that has been relatively unexplored in CSR research is collective agreements. Only Ioannou and Serafeim (2012) researched how labour unions affect CSR. Using ratings from ASSET4[1] for public companies in 42 countries, they found that union density stimulates both environmental and social CSR. The research of Ioannou and Serafeim (2012) does not, however, address which of the many social aspects, that are included in the social dimension of CSR as constructed by ASSET4, are more or less encouraged by union coverage.

The social dimension of CSR comprises very heterogeneous aspects in the rating system of ASSET4, including customer and product responsibility, community interests, respect of human rights, diversity and opportunities, quality of employer-workforce relation,[2] employment health and safety, and training and development. It is not surprising that union coverage improves aspects of the social dimension of CSR that concern core interests of incumbent employees that unions aim to protect, such as fair wages, the use of fixed-term contracts, training and development, and health and safety. Previous research has shown, for example, that, relative to uncovered workers, union-covered workers are more likely to receive more days of training (Booth et al., 2003). In addition, union-covered workers experience greater returns to training, and face a higher wage growth. In establishments where unions are recognized, labour turnover is also reduced (Blau and Kahn, 1983). Furthermore, labour unions use their

DOI: 10.4324/9781003216483-22

collective bargaining and participation in health and safety committees to influence workplace health and safety standards (for an overview, see Pouliakas and Theodossiou, 2013).

However, these findings do not give insight into how coverage by collective agreement affects labour issues that have a wider societal interest. In our research we focus on two important, yet unexplored, social aspects of CSR that go beyond the immediate interests of incumbent workers, namely gender diversity in the management of the company and equal opportunities for groups that have a relative disadvantaged position on the labour market. To date, there has been no large-scale, multi-country research in the relationship between collective agreements and these two dimensions of labour market equality. The core research question of this chapter is therefore: do collective agreements encourage gender diversity in the management of the company and equal opportunities for groups that have a relative disadvantaged position on the labour market, including migrants or their descendants?

We test our hypotheses on a sample of 4053 enterprises in 12 European countries for which detailed information of the share of employees represented by collective agreement per firm is available. This data provides information about differences in union coverage between companies within countries, and therefore provides a more accurate picture of the influence of collective agreements than macro indicators of union density. In the next section, we present the conceptual framework. In section 18.3, we describe our methodology. Next, we present our empirical findings, followed by a conclusion.

18.2 Conceptual Framework

Collective Agreements and Labour-Related CSR

One of the neglected forces in institutional CSR theory is the role of collective agreements. A collective agreement is written between a representation of workers and an entrepreneur, or business representation, and regulates the working and employment conditions as well as the labour relations management (Biedma-Ferrer et al., 2015). It is established between the elected representatives of the workers and those who act on behalf of the company, but can be extended to employees and employers of other companies. Such cases of extension mechanisms exist in varying degree in EU Member States.[3]

According to Aguilera and Jackson (2003), the lack of attention to the role of collective agreements in CSR reflects weak employee participation in the United States, where the concept of CSR originated. Also in the practice of CSR, labour unions have been largely excluded from participating as equal partners. Consequently, organized labour greeted CSR with ambivalence (Brammer, Jackson et al., 2012). To unions, the concept of CSR lacks a distinct connection to the central role that corporations have as employers (De Geer et al., 2010).

Still, unions may play an important role in the realization of CSR related goals, because they are instrumental to voicing workers' collective needs and desires to the management (Freeman and Medoff, 1984). Campbell (2007) argued that companies are more likely to behave in socially responsible ways when they are engaged in institutionalized dialogue with unions. Their influence may not be visible in voluntary, explicit CSR measures, but is more implicit through sector and national negotiations on labour-related issues (Matten and Moon, 2008).[4] In countries that showed weakening of labour unions, firms started to score higher on explicit CSR as a substitute for institutional regulation and social coordination (Jackson and Apostolakou, 2010). Still, to the extent that unions empower employees, corporations may also face pressure to adopt explicit CSR measures. For example, powerful labour unions may use their influence to pressure companies to adopt better labour standards throughout their supply chain and push for extended benefits for employees, focusing on health and safety provisions, labour relations policies, and more workplace amenities (Ioannou and Serafeim, 2012). For instance, they can pressure suppliers, who are known for the abuse of migrant workers, into paying them properly.

Collective Agreements and Equal Opportunities of Women and Disadvantaged Groups

Based on union representation theory (Lurie, 2015), we expect, however, that collective agreements might have negative effects on social issues of wider societal interest, such as equal opportunities for women and disadvantaged outsiders on the labour market. Union representation theory predicts that unions tend to advocate the interests of the median worker who often works full time for a single employer. A union's duty to protect and advance the collective interests of all of its members might conflict with the particular interests of specific groups. Although a minority of union members may significantly value equal opportunities for specific groups, the majority of union members may have little interest in these issues, which induces the union to disregard the interests of specific groups that are victims of discrimination (Widiss, 2012). Consequently, union representation may encourage packages that do not reflect the preferences of marginal worker groups (Budd, 2007).

Women and employees from disadvantaged groups are disproportionately represented in non-standard atypical work, which may include part-time work, temporary agency work, flex-work, self-employed homecare work, and contractor work (Lurie, 2013). Previous studies have found that unions tend to under-represent women's interests systematically and to promote discriminatory policies, notwithstanding high rates of unionized women (McBride, 2001). One of the reasons might be that women are under-represented in union decision-making structures (Lurie, 2015). Most of the union representatives are men and this may have a negative outcome for gender equality in the bargaining process. Previous research has also shown that unions tend to under-represent the interests of foreign workers too (Albin, 2013). Unions face the tension that the more immigrants that become active in the domestic labour market, the more competition there is for traditional groups of employees that they represent, and the worse working conditions might become for these groups. Particularly in times of ample national supply of labour, trade unions are likely to oppose recruitment of immigrant workers. Due to widespread unemployment, labour market competition might increase and inclusive union policies towards immigrants may thus clash with the interests of native workers (Penninx and Roosblad, 2000). Unions may therefore be inclined to defend the interests of national members and resist migrants or hesitate to defend them, for example against exploitation.

Based on union representation theory and previous empirical research, we therefore posit the following hypotheses:

Hypothesis 18.1 Collective agreements reduce female representation in board and executive positions.

Hypothesis 18.2 Collective agreements reduce the inflow of employees from disadvantaged groups.

Interrelationship Between Women Management and Hiring of Disadvantaged Groups

Besides a direct negative influence from collective agreements on the inflow of employees from disadvantaged groups, we also expect a negative indirect effect mediated by the share of women in the top management of the company. We base this argument on social role theory that predicts that women are more socialized into communal values reflecting a concern for others than men, (Mason and Mudrack, 1996) and therefore more likely to be motivated by altruistic concerns (Williams and Polman, 2015). This has been confirmed by research that showed that female managers are more involved in corporate philanthropy (Williams, 2003; Ibrahim and Angelidis, 2011; Marquis and Lee, 2013). Because of their altruistic concerns, it is therefore likely that female board members or executives will take more responsibility for providing job opportunities to people from disadvantaged groups than male top managers. Therefore, we hypothesize that:

Hypothesis 18.3 Female representation in board and executive positions increases the inflow of employees from disadvantaged groups.

18.3 Methodology

Table 18.1 presents an overview of the general characteristics of the companies in the sample.

The use of collective agreements differs significantly among the twelve countries in our sample, ranging from 15% in the UK to 95% in France due to the

TABLE 18.1 Sample characteristics (in %)

Country	*% in sample*	*Union density (2013)*[a]	*Extension collective agreements*[b]	*Coverage collective agreements*[c]	*Share of employees covered by collective agreement in sample*
UK	3	26	not	29	15
Denmark	7	67	not	80	65
Finland	4	69	very frequent	91	87
Sweden	5	68	not	88	84
Austria	2	28	seldom	95	72
France	7	8	very frequent	98	95
Germany	9	18	moderate	59	54
Netherlands	11	18	frequent	81	75
Hungary	4	11	seldom	33	29
Poland	7	13	seldom	25	47
Italy	31	37	not	80	94
Spain	11	17	very frequent	70	92

a Source: OECD https://stats.oecd.org/Index.aspx?DataSetCode=UN_DEN

b Source: Eurofound http://adapt.it/adapt-indice-a-z/wp-content/uploads/2013/08/efficacia_ccnl_eu.pdf

c Source: www.worker-participation.eu/National-Industrial-Relations/Across-Europe/Collective-Bargaining2

TABLE 18.2 Descriptive statistics[a]

Variable	*Mean*	*SD*
Collective agreement (70)	70.06	43.45
Women in board (67)	23.38	25.82
Inflow disadvantaged (68)	7.18	14.61

a The numbers in brackets refer to the numbers of the survey questions reported in Appendix 1.

large-scale extension of collective agreements in that country. The different shares of employees in our sample that is covered by collective agreements per country reflect the differences in macro shares reported by the European Union.

Survey data were taken from the survey in 2011. The independent variable, collective agreements, was measured by a survey question measuring the 'Share of employees covered by collective bargaining agreement as a % of the total number of employees in 2010.' The representation of females in board or executive positions was measured by a survey question asking for the 'Share of women in the board and/or executive positions in 2010.' The inflow of employees from disadvantaged groups was measured by a survey question on the 'Share of employees recruited from disadvantaged groups (e.g. migrant workers, people with disabilities, long term unemployed) as a % of the total inflow in 2010.'

TABLE 18.3 Estimation results[a]

	Women in board	*Inflow of disadvantaged*
Collective agreements	0.04***	0.06**
Women in board		0.17***
R^2	0.08	0.08

a $N = 4053$. Standardized coefficients * $p < 0.05$, ** $p < 0.01$, *** $p < 0.001$. The (Santorra-Bentler) global fit indices are: Chi2 = 0.068; RMSEA= 0.012; CFI = 0.987; TLI = 0.966; SMRS = 0.004; $R^2 = 0.133$. We controlled for sector, position in the supply chain, intensity of price competition, country, company size (number of FTEs), skill structure and age structure, and inverse Mill's ratio.

18.4 Results

We used structural equation modelling in STATA with maximum likelihood as estimation technique and Satorra-Bentler correction for non-normality. The results are reported in Table 18.3.

The estimation results show that the representation of women in the board and executive positions and the inflow of employees from disadvantaged groups are significantly positively related to collective agreements. Hence, we reject Hypotheses 18.1 and 18.2. Hypothesis 18.3 that the share of female managers increases the inflow of employees from disadvantaged groups is supported. If we test the indirect effect of collective agreements on the inflow of employees from disadvantaged groups as mediated by the share of female managers, we find a small but significant positive effect (p-value < 0.001). Hence, by fostering the share of female managers, collective agreements indirectly increase the inflow of disadvantaged employees as well.

18.5 Conclusion

In this chapter, we set out to research the effect of collective agreements on social dimensions of CSR that concern wider societal interests beyond the immediate interests of incumbent workers that unions typically represent, namely gender diversity in the management of the company and equal opportunities for groups that have a relative disadvantaged position in the labour market. Whereas previous cross-country research by Ioannou and Serafeim (2012) showed that union coverage stimulates social and EP of large companies, we expected to find opposite results for gender equality and job opportunities for applicants that have a disadvantaged position in the labour market. This expectation was based on the union representation theory that predicts that unions advocate the interests of the median worker and that advancement of these interests conflict with the particular interests of specific groups that are disproportionately represented in non-standard, atypical work.

Based on a sample of 4053 enterprises in Europe and using micro data of the share of employees covered by collective bargaining agreement per company, we found, however, that collective bargaining stimulates both the presence of women managers in the top management of the enterprise as well as the inflow of employees from disadvantaged groups. Moreover, we also detected a positive indirect effect from collective agreements on the inflow of disadvantaged employees, as women managers are more inclined to hire labour from these groups, than male managers.

These results provide additional evidence for the positive effects of union coverage on CSR identified by Ioannou and Serafeim (2012). They argued that labour unions may increase overall awareness within society by acting as the firm's ambassador for environmental and social policies. But the question remains why this is the case. A possible explanation is that unions take account of the negative societal effects that result from unemployment of employees from disadvantaged groups, because they often coordinate their actions at the macro level. For individual companies, these negative effects are largely a given and the benefits from fighting them are negligible to the individual company. At the macro level, however, the unemployment of employees from disadvantaged groups is not given and is rather dependent on the policies of unions at this level. They cause substantial societal costs that harm the interests of all union members. This motivates unions operating at the national level to bargain for policies at the meso and micro level in sectoral or firm level agreements that provide more equal opportunities for disadvantaged groups. An example of such a policy is an agreement of the Dutch national unions FNV, CNV and RMU with the company CêlaVíta that agreed to offer partly disabled employees a job.[5]

Another explanation is that the weakening of the position of trade unions during the last decennia has triggered attempts to revitalize unions, with inclusion of underrepresented groups being a foremost strategy. In Europe, such organizing has been implemented in the United Kingdom and, more recently, in the Netherlands (Marino et al., 2015). For example, in 2005 the FNV published a report '*De vakbeweging van de toekomst: Lessen uit het buitenland*' that intended to redefine itself. One of the issues addressed in this report was the importance of 'organizing' new groups of people, including migrant workers (Connolly et al., 2014).[6] Marino et al. conclude that these revalidation efforts of unions, by a more inclusive strategy that takes serious the interests of previously marginalized groups, suggest that inclusive attitudes toward migrant workers are inversely related to the degree of institutional embeddedness of unions. If the institutional power of unions reduces, they become more dependent on union membership, which stimulates them to attract new, underrepresented, groups of workers to increase union membership. However, this conclusion is not supported by our research, as our findings indicate that union coverage stimulates a wider societal orientation.[7] Consequently, collective agreements improve companies' implementation of policies that foster equal opportunities for women and employees from disadvantaged groups in the labour market.

Notes

* An extended text of this chapter has been published in an open access chapter under the terms of the Creative Commons License CC BY NC ND in Graafland, J.J. (2018). Collective agreements and equal opportunities for women and disadvantaged groups. In Rijken, C., and De Lange, T. (Eds.), *Towards a decent labour market for low-waged migrant workers* (pp. 267–282). Amsterdam: Amsterdam University Press.

1 ASSET 4 is one of the major sustainability ratings agencies, often called ESG raters, as they rate companies on the three dimensions Environment, Social and Governance. Other well-known ESG rating agencies are KLD, Sustainalytics, Vigeo and FTSE4Good.

2 It seems that Ioannou and Serafeim (2012) failed to notice that the workforce and employment category in ASSET4 includes trade union representation, which makes their analysis partly tautological.

3 Matten and Moon (2008) distinguished explicit from implicit CSR. Explicit CSR means that corporations adopt voluntary CSR programs. Implicit CSR is often not voluntary, but rather a reaction to the regulations by the state or by social partners, like vocational training, pensions or health care in collective agreements. Matten and Moon argued that the CSR in Europe is best described as implicit CSR. In liberal economies with immature welfare states and little social regulations, companies more often pursue explicit CSR.

4 As a result, collective agreements can apply to (temporary) migrant workers, whether EU or non-EU nationals, ethnic minorities and (or as) nationals alike.

5 www.rmu.nu/weblog/akkoord+over+cao+clavta_1312.

6 In 2004, former FNV chairwomen Jongerius proposed to introduce legally binding minimum quotas for the inflow of employees from migrant groups, but employers refused to support this idea. In a phone call with FNV in August 2017, it appeared that there are no examples yet of collective agreements that provide provisions to increase employment among migrant employees.

7 If we also include the degree that collective agreements are extended (based on the third column in Table 18.1) as indicator of institutional embeddedness of unions (besides the influence of coverage of collective agreements per firm), we find no significant effects on the share of women in the board or the inflow of employees from disadvantaged groups, Hence, institutional embeddedness through extension of collective agreement does not negatively affect the share of women in the board or the inflow of employees from disadvantaged groups.

PART V

Integration and Management Lessons

19

OVERVIEW OF RESULTS AND INTEGRATION

19.1 Overview of Hypotheses and Empirical Results

Impacts of CSR

In Part I we researched impacts of CSR on environment, innovation and reputation. Table 19.1 presents an overview of the hypotheses and test results.

The estimation results showed that both informal and formal instruments, such as the use of targets and ISO 14001 certification, improve EP of SMEs by reducing energy and water consumption and waste disposal. ISO 14001 certification has also an indirect positive impact in EP by stimulating the participation in external networks that provide SMEs practical knowledge and information about specific measures and technologies that reduce energy cost. Hence, we found no evidence of decoupling between the use of environmental management instruments and environmental impacts. This indicates that CSR instruments are not merely used in a ceremonial way. This finding is similar to findings of Graafland and Smid (2019) who tested the environmental impacts of CSR management instruments on a sample of 1,000 large companies in 24 countries. They found that for most CSR issues examined, CSR programmes of high quality (as measured by scope, the use of targets, and the use of strict deadlines) have relatively strong positive CSR impacts.

These studies pertain to the effectiveness of CSR at the micro business level. This leaves open the impacts of CSR on the macro level. The society is, ultimately, interested in the impacts of CSR for the economy as a whole, not only for the micro business level. Even if CSR generates positive impacts at the micro business level, its macro effect remains uncertain. One cannot simply assume that isolated successful CSR measures on the microeconomic level necessarily have

DOI: 10.4324/9781003216483-24

TABLE 19.1 Impacts of CSR: Overview of hypotheses and test results

Hypothesis		*support*
2.1	*The use of targets improves environmental impacts of SMEs*[a]	+
3.1	*ISO 14001 certification positively affects environmental impacts of SMEs*	+
3.2	*Participation in external networks positively affects the environmental impacts of SMEs*[b]	+
3.3	*ISO 14001 certification stimulates participation in external networks*	+
4.1	*The use of CSR instruments contributes to innovation*	+
4.2	*The positive impact of CSR instruments on innovation is greater in consumer-focused industries*	−
4.3	*The positive impact of CSR instruments on innovation is greater in less eco-friendly industries*	−
5.1	*High CSR intensifies CSR monitoring by NGOs and media*	+
5.2	*Firm size positively moderates the positive influence of CSR on CSR monitoring*	+
5.3	*The intensity of CSR monitoring moderates the influence of CSR on the exposure to criticism on the company's CSR*	+

a This hypothesis is similar to Hypothesis 10.3.
b This hypothesis is similar to Hypothesis 16.1.

a positive influence on related macroeconomic indicators (Korhonen, 2003). As an example, assume several companies in an industry strategically focus on CSR, thereby increasing social efficiency. It could then be the case that the other companies in the industry try to remain competitive via price cuts and cost reductions by maximized offloading on third parties. Empirical research by Graafland et al. (2016) on a sample of 22 countries and 1,576 companies showed, however, that CSR reduced greenhouse gas emissions at the country level during 2004–2011. But their estimation results also indicated that the long-term effect of CSR is rather modest. A rise in the average CSR score by 10 points (on a scale from 0 to 100) would reduce GHG emissions by approximately 2% on average. This modest impact is in line with the estimation results in Chapter 2 in this book that showed that if SMEs maximize the use of informal and formal environmental management instruments, the annual growth rate in energy, water, and waste would only fall with 0.3–0.4%.

Besides the positive effects on EP, CSR strengthens the long-term economic performance of company by encouraging innovation. Whereas previous research by Flammer and Kacperczyk (2016) had shown that CSR (measured by stakeholder orientation) has a positive causal effect on innovation, this link has not been tested for SMEs. In Chapter 4 we found confirmative evidence of the finding of Flammer and Kacperczyk (2016) that CSR sparks innovation. However, our analysis did not support two other findings of Flammer and Kacperczyk's that the CSR-innovation link is moderated by consumer-focused and high-pollution industries.

Chapter 5 analysed the effects of CSR on reputation. Literature has often argued and found that one of the advantages of engaging in CSR is that it can improve the firm's reputation. CSR helps to differentiate the firm from competitors and often carries with it a kind of insurance-type protection of reputation by reducing business and corporate risks. Reputation is a valuable resource that will lead to improved financial performance. However, most literature has overlooked that CSR may also endanger reputation, if CSR policy statements do not go together with favourable impacts. By communicating its CSR, a firm sets itself up to be targeted by activists. Then reputational benefits of CSR may easily turn into reputational liabilities if the company falls short of the CSR expectations of stakeholders. Chapter 5 showed that this so-called reputational liability is also relevant for SMEs.

Internal Drivers of CSR

In Part II we studied several internal drivers of CSR. Table 19.2 presents an overview of the hypotheses and the empirical findings.

TABLE 19.2 Internal drivers of CSR: Overview of hypotheses and test results

Hypothesis		*support*
6.1	*Extrinsic motives stimulate CSR*[a]	+
6.2	*Intrinsic motives stimulate CSR*[b]	+
6.3	*Extrinsic motivation is positively related to company size*	+
6.4	*Intrinsic motivation is negatively related to company size*	−
7.1	*The influence of family business ownership on EP is non-linearly moderated by the involvement of family members in management*	+
7.2	*Company size negatively moderates the influence of family business ownership on EP*	+
8.1	*Having more women in management has a positive, non-linear, effect on an SME's use of relational environmental management instruments*	+
8.2	*The use of relational environmental management instruments improves the EP of SMEs*	+
9.1	*Firms with an open systems business culture are more likely to engage in stakeholder relations*	+
9.2	*Firms with an open systems business culture are more likely to put effort into improving EP*	+
9.3	*Firms with an open systems business culture are more likely to put effort into improving social performance*	+

a A similar hypothesis is Hypothesis 15.2.

b Similar hypotheses are Hypotheses 12.2 and 15.1.

In Chapter 6, we found that CSR is positively affected by intrinsic and extrinsic motives. The effect of intrinsic motives appears to be stronger than the effect of extrinsic motives. As expected, large companies have a stronger extrinsic motivation towards CSR than small companies. But Hypothesis 6.4 that intrinsic motives are stronger for small companies is not supported. The implication is that company size has a positive effect on CSR through both extrinsic and intrinsic CSR motives.

Motives are grounded in the value system of the company, which can be classified as an information institution (see Chapter 1). Besides motives, we researched several other internal institutional factors: ownership structure, gender structure of management, and business culture. Chapters 7 and 8 showed that ownership and gender structure affect CSR, but the effects are non-linear and context dependent. Family ownership stimulates CSR most in small companies and if the company is jointly managed by family and non-family members. Furthermore, more women in management increases CSR because women managers make more use of relational environmental instruments than men managers. However, this positive effect only holds to some level. More specifically, if the share of women in management exceeds 54%, negative effects set in. Chapter 9 showed that business culture is an important internal driver of CSR. Companies combining an external focus with a flexible management style (the so-called open systems business culture) are more actively engaging in CSR than companies with an internal focus and an emphasis on centralization and control over organizational processes.

Competition and CSR

Part III analysed the effects of competition on CSR. The competitive environment of the company is not an institutional factor (Campbell, 2007) but closely related to institutions such as antitrust laws of governments. Table 19.3 presents an overview of the hypotheses and the empirical findings of Part III.

Chapter 10 showed that the intensity of price competition worsens EP by stimulating short-termism. Besides the mediation effect through time horizon, no direct effect from price competition on CSR was found. The total effect of price competition on EP is therefore rather small. Besides price competition, companies can also compete on innovation. Chapter 11 found that this type of competition encourages the innovation motive of CSR, meaning that companies are motivated to engage in CSR because it stimulates the innovation of the company. In a competitive environment with intense technological competition, innovation is conceded to be essential for survival. Chapter 12 showed, furthermore, that technological competition does not only trigger an innovation motive, which can be classified as an extrinsic CSR motive, but also intrinsic CSR motivation.

These results are in line with research by Graafland and Smid (2015) on a sample of large companies rated by Sustainalytics. They found that the intensity

TABLE 19.3 Competition and CSR: Overview of hypotheses and test results

Hypothesis		*support*
10.1	*A higher intensity of price competition shortens the time horizon of the company*	+
10.2	*CSR efforts and procedures are positively related to the time horizon of a company*	+
11.1	*The stronger the top manager's innovation motivation towards CSR, the more the firm will engage in CSR*	+
11.2	*The intensity of technological competition increases a top manager's innovation motive to engage in CSR*	+
11.3	*A top manager's innovation motive to engage in CSR mediates the effect of the intensity of technological competition on CSR*	+
12.1	*The owner-manager's perception that CSR enforces the innovative capability of the firm positively moderates the relationship between technological competition and intrinsic CSR motivation*	+

of technological competition significantly increases CSR, whereas the effect of the intensity of price competition is insignificant.

Institutional Drivers of CSR

Part IV analysed the relationship between CSR and several external institutions, including social licence pressure by NGOs and media, government regulation, economic freedom, and collective bargaining. In some of the estimated models, we found that the effects of external institutions on CSR are mediated by internal factors. For example, the impact of social licence on CSR is mediated by the perceived strategic benefits of CSR. Another example is the impact of government regulation on CSR, which is mediated by intrinsic CSR motivation through crowding-out effects. In some other chapters, we found evidence of internal factors moderating the impact of external institutions on CSR. For example, the impact of economic freedom on CSR was found to depend on intrinsic CSR motivation. External institutions may also interactively influence CSR, such as economic freedom and the cultural characteristic of long-term orientation. The moderation of the relationship between economic freedom and CSR by long-term orientation has also been found by other recent research by Graafland and Noorderhaven (2020b) on a sample of large companies rated by ASSET4. Besides societal long-term orientation, we found a negative effect of power distance and positive effects of individualization and uncertainty avoidance. The results for individualization are supported by research by Graafland and Noorderhaven (2020b), who found similar effects. Finally, opposite to our expectations, we found that collective bargaining agreements stimulate gender equality and opportunities for disadvantaged groups. These findings show that labour unions act as the firm's ambassador for the social dimensions of CSR.

19.2 An Integrative Analysis of the Effects of Company Size on CSR

As discussed in Chapter 1, one of the gaps that this book aims to fill is large-scale empirical research of the impacts and drivers of CSR by SMEs. Literature

TABLE 19.4 Institutions and CSR: Overview of hypotheses and test results

Hypothesis		*support*
13.1	*The social licence pressure perceived by a company depends positively on its size*	+
13.2	*The market benefits that a company perceives from its CSR depend positively on the perceived social licence pressure*[a]	+
13.3	*The environmental impacts of a company depends positively on the perceived market benefits from CSR*	+
13.4	*The environmental impacts of a company is positively associated with the perceived social licence pressure*	+
13.5	*The regulation motive is more important for small companies than for large companies*	–
13.6	*The environmental impacts of an SME depends positively on the regulation motive*	+
14.1	*Intrinsic CSR motivation of an enterprise is positively related to perceived NGO and media pressure*	–
14.3	*Intrinsic CSR motivation of enterprises is positively related to perceived market benefits of CSR*	+
14.4	*The perceived market benefits of CSR mediates the effect of NGO and media pressure on intrinsic CSR motivation of enterprises*	+
15.3	*Government regulation crowds out the intrinsic motivation of a business leader towards improving EP of the SME*	+
15.4	*Government regulation crowds out the extrinsic motivation of a business leader towards improving EP of the SME*	+/–
16.2	*The participation in environmental networks is positively related to the interaction between the intrinsic motivation and economic freedom*	+
17.1	*Economic freedom and society-level long-term orientation interactively stimulate CSR*	+
18.1	*Collective agreements reduce female representation in board and executive positions*	–
18.2	*Collective agreements reduce the inflow of employees from disadvantaged groups*	–
18.3	*Female representation in board and executive positions increases the inflow of employees from disadvantaged groups*	+

a A similar hypothesis is Hypothesis 14.2.

has argued that SMEs differ in many respects from large companies. First, they are often privately owned and managed by their owners (Spence, 1999; Jenkins, 2009). As discussed in Chapter 8, family businesses differ in various respects from non-family-owned firms. They have different stakeholder orientation, with a greater focus on internal aspects like work–family issues (Jamali et al., 2008). They forge strong caring relationships with employees and are important players within their local community. Another difference is that SMEs are often organized on an informal basis – and so are their CSR policies. Many scholars suggest that SMEs are even often unknowingly socially responsible. As far as existing legislation and regulations are concerned, the majority of SMEs are 'vulnerable compliant'. That means that they do not know enough about environmental legislation to ensure that they are always compliant (European Commission, 2002). Furthermore, as it is practically impossible for NGOs and media to monitor each small company, they attract less public attention than large companies. For this reason, Lynch-Wood and Williamson (2007) argued that the social licence motive will not be sufficient to induce SMEs to go beyond compliance to the law. They are just too small to be visible. Finally, as small companies often lack strategic assets that reduce the competition, they can less afford themselves to apply a long-time horizon on the return on investments (Segelod, 2000).

On the other hand, because of their intimate relationship with the community in which they operate, SMEs have a stronger need to pursue a community-friendly policy. SMEs rely to a much greater extent than large enterprises do on the prosperity of the local communities in which they operate. The reputation of a company at its locations, as employer, producer or actor, strongly influences its competitiveness. Managers of SMEs often interact with stakeholders in network relations, where stakeholders communicate their expectations informally. The personal contacts between the owner-manager and various stakeholders help to build trustful partnerships in a natural way. As a result, SMEs are more sensitive to signals from local customers and suppliers. Furthermore, as cited by Williamson et al. (2006: 318): 'SMEs, being flatter and potentially quicker on their feet and without analysts and shareholders fixated by price/earnings ratios, are better placed than major corporates to take advantage of the fact that society and the media revere qualities such as honesty, integrity and the ability to say sorry.' Also, the employee loyalty and the long tenure of leadership may encourage a positive attitude towards CSR.

In the previous chapters, we tested and found confirmation of several of these notions on the effect of company size on CSR in literature. However, we did not provide a full, integrative analysis of how company size affects CSR through the various internal and external factors that drive CSR. The goal of this section is to do just that. For this goal, Tables 19.5 and 19.6 present the results of a structural equation model that integrates most of the research in the preceding chapters. As the model is very large (including 18 dependent variables and 36 explanatory

TABLE 19.5 Results of structural equation model[a]

	External factors				*Internal factors*								*CSR implementation (direct effects)*					
	Pcom	*Tcom*	*NGO*	*CA*	*TH*	*ExtMot*	*InnMot*	*IntMot*	*FBO*	*WM*	*EO*	*FO*	*EFS*	*EFE*	*TRE*	*RelIn*	*ISO14*	*IntIn*
Company size	−0.04	**0.09**	**0.15**	**0.23**	**0.07**	**0.08**	**0.06**	*0.04*	**−0.29**	−0.03	**−0.06**	**−0.08**	**0.16**	**0.14**	**0.10**	**0.20**	**0.23**	**0.18**
External factors																		
Price competition (PCom)					**−0.07**					−0.03		*−0.04*				−0.03	*0.04*	
Technological competition (Tcom)					**0.07**	**0.24**	**0.26**	**0.26**	0.04	*0.05*	**0.12**	**0.20**		*0.04*				
Monitoring NGO & media (NGO)					**0.08**	**0.24**	**0.24**	**0.19**	*−0.06*		**0.08**	**0.04**	**0.04**	**0.08**	*0.03*	**0.23**	**0.09**	**0.15**
Government regulation								*−0.04*				**−0.07**			0.03	**−0.05**		
Collective agreements (CA)										**0.10**			**0.10**	**0.07**	*0.04*	0.03		
Internal factors																		
Time horizon (TH)													**0.06**	*0.05*	0.03	**0.06**	*0.03*	*0.04*
Extrinsic motive (ExtMot)													*0.04*	**0.10**	0.02	−0.03	*0.04*	**0.07**
Innovation motive (InnMot)													**0.07**	*0.06*	*0.03*	**0.14**	0.03	**0.10**
Intrinsic motive (IntMot)													**0.21**	**0.16**	**0.04**	**0.13**	0.03	**0.08**

Family business ownership (FBO)														0.04				
Women management (WM)													**0.12**	**0.05**	*0.04*	**0.04**	*−0.04*	0.03
External orientation (EO)																		
Flexibility orientation (FO)													**0.09**	*0.04*				
R^2	0.10	0.02	0.07	0.28	0.06	0.11	0.11	0.08	0.09	0.24	0.05	0.10	0.22	0.19	0.05	0.26	0.14	0.18

a Based on data from 2011 survey (except for family business ownership). Estimated with missing variables. $N = 13{,}637$. Controlled for region, sector, skill level, age, tenure, B2C, function of the respondent, company age, respondent age, and inverse Mill's ratio. For the estimation results of the control variables, see Tables A2.5 and A2.6 in Appendix 2. Standardized coefficients. Normal: $p < 0.05$; Italics: $p < 0.01$; Bold: $p < 0.001$. Global fit statistics: RMSEA = 0.009; CFI = 0.989; TLI = 0.975; $R^2 = 0.70$. ESF and EFE represent social and environmental efforts and are based on questions 62/63/65/66 and 91–94 in Appendix 1, respectively; TRE is the use of environmental targets and reporting and is based on questions 96–98; RelIn, ISO14 and IntIn are relational instruments, ISO 14001 certification and internal instruments. RelIn is based on questions 45–48 and IntIn on questions 50–54 in Appendix 1. ExtMot, InnMot, and IntMot are based on questions 20/21/23/24/27, 22/37, and 25/26, respectively; TH on questions 17/29.

variables), we excluded moderation effects and the impacts part of Part II to keep the model manageable. Furthermore, in successive rounds of estimation we dropped all relationships that appeared to be insignificant ($p > 0.05$).

Table 19.5 shows that company size is negatively related to the intensity of price competition and positively related to the intensity of technological competition. This means that SMEs face more intense price competition than large firms and less technological competition. Price competition negatively affects CSR by shortening time horizon (see Chapter 10). Technological competition has a positive impact on CSR through the innovation motive, other extrinsic motives, and through intrinsic motives (Chapters 11 and 12). Besides, Table 19.5 shows that technological competition is positively related to time horizon, external orientation, and flexibility orientation, all of which stimulate CSR. Therefore, we conclude that small companies engage less in CSR than large companies through the channels of price and technological competition.

Regarding external institutions, company size is found to be positively related to CSR monitoring by NGOs and media (see also Chapter 13). Because of more intense CSR monitoring, large companies perceive larger strategic benefits from CSR, which in turn encourages their extrinsic and intrinsic CSR motivation (Chapter 14). Furthermore, Table 19.5 shows that CSR monitoring by NGOs and media is positively related to time horizon, external and flexibility orientation and has a direct positive impact on the implementation of CSR. All together, CSR monitoring is one of the main channels through which company size has a positive impact on CSR and a main explanation why small companies engage less in CSR than large companies.

Company size is not related to government regulation, indicating that small and large companies perceive equal pressure from government regulations to improve their EP. Furthermore, large companies more often participate in collective agreements, which has a positive effect on the share of women in management and inflow of employees from disadvantaged groups (Chapter 18). The share of women in management, in turn, positively affects various types of CSR implementation (see Table 19.5). Table 19.5 shows that collective agreements also directly stimulate the implementation of CSR.

For internal factors, we find that company size is positively related to time horizon, meaning that large companies are more long-term oriented than small companies. As time horizon encourages the implementation of CSR (see Chapter 10), company size has a positive influence on the implementation of CSR through this internal factor. Furthermore, we find a small positive effect of company size on intrinsic CSR motivation and a relative large effect on extrinsic motivations (in line with the results in Chapter 6). The second effect reflects the positive relationship between company size and strategic benefits from CSR that inform the extrinsic motivation. A similar channel is the innovation motive, which can also be perceived as an extrinsic motive to engage in CSR (Chapter 11). As all three motives stimulate the implementation of CSR, these findings imply that the three motivational factors induce large companies to engage more in CSR than small companies.

As discussed earlier, family owner structures are more common for small firms than for large firms. This observation is supported by the negative relationship between company size and family ownership in Table 19.5. As the impact of FBO on environmental CSR is positive for small companies (see Chapter 8), small companies will engage more in CSR than large companies through ownership structures.

Table 19.5 shows, furthermore, that the share of women is slightly higher in small companies than in large companies. Although the effect of company size through the share of women on CSR is context dependent (see Chapter 7), given that the average share of women in management is well below the turning point of 54%, the negative correlation between company size and women management implies that small companies engage more in implementing CSR than large companies through a higher share of women management. Only for ISO 14001 certification, the effect of share of women is slightly negative.

A similar effect is found for business culture. As both the external focus and flexibility orientation are stronger for small companies than for large companies, and as the open systems business culture stimulates CSR (see Chapter 9), company size negatively affects CSR through business culture.

Besides the indirect effects through external and internal drivers of CSR, we find substantial direct effects of company size that are not mediated by the external and/or internal drivers. Due to a lack of sources and experience, SMEs are less able to explicitly recognize CSR issues and are less familiar with CSR standards (Lepoutre and Heene, 2006). Time, finances, and a lack of skills and knowledge are commonly identified as constraints to CSR by SMEs (Studer et al., 2006). Due to their small size, it is often too costly to recruit CSR specialists. Taking responsibility for the complex supply chain in which they operate would be simply too costly. Overall, the direct effect explains about ¾ of the total positive effect on CSR implementation, about ¼ is explained by indirect effects through external and internal factors (see Table 19.6).

19.3 Limitations and Directions for Future Research

This study is characterized by several limitations and leaves open several other relevant research questions, all of which provide avenues for future research.

Data and Measurement Limitations

A potential weakness of this study is the use of self-reported data of CSR. A great advantage of using survey data is that surveys provide an efficient way to gather lots of information from many companies. Particular for SMEs, basing data on observations of real behaviour would be very costly, as SMEs provide substantial

TABLE 19.6 Indirect and total effects[a]

	Indirect effects						*Total effects*					
	EFS	*EFE*	*TRE*	*RelIn*	*ISO14*	*IntIn*	*EFS*	*EFE*	*TRE*	*RelIn*	*ISO14*	*IntIn*
Company size	**0.06**	**0.05**	**0.03**	**0.07**	**0.03**	**0.05**	**0.23**	**0.19**	**0.13**	**0.27**	**0.27**	**0.23**
External factors												
Price competition	**−0.01**	**−0.01**	*−0.01*	**−0.01**		*−0.00*	**−0.01**	**−0.01**	*−0.01*	*−0.04*	*0.04*	*−0.00*
Techn. competition	**0.10**	**0.04**	**0.03**	**0.03**	**0.01**	**0.06**	**0.10**	**0.09**	**0.03**	**0.03**	**0.01**	**0.06**
NGO & media	**0.07**	**0.07**	**0.03**	**0.06**	**0.03**	**0.06**	**0.12**	**0.16**	**0.06**	**0.28**	**0.11**	**0.20**
Gov. regulation	**−0.02**	**−0.01**	−0.00	*−0.01*		−0.00	**−0.02**	**−0.01**	0.03	**−0.05**		−0.00
Collective agreements	**0.01**	*0.01*	*0.01*	0.00	−0.00	0.00	**0.12**	**0.07**	**0.04**	*0.04*	−0.00	0.00

a Standardized coefficients. Normal: $p < 0.05$; Italics: $p < 0.01$; Bold: $p < 0.001$. The total effects are equal to the direct effects on CSR implementation reported in Table 19.5 and the indirect effects reported in the left part of Table 19.6. ESF and EFE represent social and environmental efforts; TRE is the use of environmental targets and reporting; RelIn, ISO14 and IntIn are relational instruments, ISO 14001 certification and internal instruments.

less information to external parties than large companies. But a possible disadvantage is that the survey data do not accurately reflect the real performance because of social desirability bias. The results should thus be interpreted with some caution even though self-reported data are common in the literature (Arimura et al., 2008; Wakabayashi and Arimura, 2016). To address social desirability, common method, and non-response bias, we adopted several precautionary remedies and ex-post tests.[1] Second, as we have collected all our data by means of a single questionnaire, our research design obligated us to practice economy in our research, as a too lengthy questionnaire would likely lead to lower response rates. Given the relatively less mature state of the field of CSR research, we dedicated a large part of our survey to the measurement of CSR. Other variables were, however, measured by a limited number of survey questions. For example, in Chapter 4, wherein we explored the relationship between CSR and innovation, we employed only two survey questions to measure innovation. Future studies could elaborate on the measurement of innovation and use more advanced indicators. A similar limitation applies to Chapter 9 that analysed the influence of business culture on CSR. In our analysis, we employed only two survey questions to measure organizational culture. Although the Competing Values Framework is widely accepted and strongly validated, it is still possible that we have missed important aspects of organizational culture that may influence CSR. Future studies could explore the role other dimensions of organizational culture play, for example the dimensions distinguished by Hofstede et al. (1990). Furthermore, in various chapters we measured intrinsic motivation by only two or three survey questions. Future studies could explore the role of other dimensions of intrinsic motivations, such as professional interest in internal goods of practices. However, we do not expect that this will fundamentally change our conclusions. The arguments we developed for intrinsic motivation will probably also hold for competence-related types of intrinsic motivation, as rewards have symbolic properties related to perceived competence or self-efficacy, causing individuals to care more about doing the task well (Eisenberger et al., 1999). For example, Harackiewicz and Manderlink (1984) found that performance-contingent rewards stimulate intrinsic motivation more than favourable performance feedback without reward.

Third, we examined a varied set of SMEs all over Europe. This is helpful to obtain a first view on CSR in these organizations, but a more in-depth analysis of SMEs from a particular industry and from other parts of the world would be a useful next step. Future research should therefore broaden the scope of the research to other regions in order to further test the generalizability of the findings. For instance, are SMEs operating in a business-to-business context in, say, Asia driven by different motivations in their CSR initiatives? Nevertheless, we believe that this extensive European study of SMEs offers a useful starting point for such further work.

Finally, it should be noted that the analyses in this book are based on data collected in 2011 and 2014. It is likely that CSR has evolved since then. However, it should be noted that in Europe the focus on CSR started in the 1990s and gradually increased. By 2011, the relevance of CSR was broadly recognized by business in Europe. Although it has still increased since then, it is not expected to have changed that much. This is confirmed if one compares the results of the more recent survey held in 2014 with the results in 2011. As can be seen from Tables A2.4 and A2.5 in Appendix 2, CSR only slightly changed from 2011 to 2014. Also the internal and external drivers of CSR hardly changed during this period. From these results, it can be assumed that the results of the study are likely to be still largely valid in more recent years than 2014.

New Hypotheses

As each chapter investigated a limited number of hypotheses, there is ample room for extending the research in new directions.

A first type of limitation that calls for model extensions is that the theories that underlie the hypotheses are not tested. For example, in Chapter 7 we show that family ownership stimulates CSR under certain conditions. However, the underlying SEW-related theory is not investigated. For example, is it because family companies attach a higher value to the company having a good reputation that they use more often CSR instruments, or are other variables causing this relationship, such as care for future generations of the family? Future research could target these underlying causes to provide more detailed tests of the predictive value of the theory.

A related limitation is that in most chapters we only researched a limited number of independent, mediation, and dependent variables. For example, in Chapter 3 we analysed the environmental impact of ISO 14001 certification through external networks. Besides stimulating participation in external networks, ISO 14001 may also yield other benefits. For example, Poksinska et al. (2003) and Arimura et al. (2008) have argued that ISO 14001 does not only serve ecological improvements but also contributes to regulatory compliance, ecological transparency, and/or enterprise image. Future research could investigate other impacts of ISO 14001 in the context of small business, to determine how valuable the standard is for SMEs.

Third, in Chapter 6 we showed that a company will be driven by a mixture of intrinsic and extrinsic motivations. In Chapter 14 it was argued, however, that CSR may be perceived by managers as a conditional or so-called prima facie moral duty. If managers expect that pursuing CSR will harm their enterprise's financial performance, they hesitate to implement CSR, as the survival of the enterprise is essential and job creation and continuation are often seen as the first responsibility of businesses. This suggests that the influences of intrinsic and extrinsic motivations may be moderated by the financial situation of the company. When the external economic factors become too strenuous, the influence of intrinsic motivation on CSR may go down and extrinsic motivation will become more important.

Another example is Chapter 8 that studied relational management instruments as mediator between the share of women managers and CSR. Future research could focus on other mediators. For example, it can be argued that type of motivation mediates this relationship (e.g. intrinsic versus extrinsic motivation). Second, one can reasonably ask how the impact of women managers on sustainable business practice changes if the size of the business grows or declines, as it is unclear what the tipping point is for any of the findings presented as firm size changes. Third, the finding that a higher representation of women in management contributes to CSR opens up new avenues for future research into the relationship between gender and product and process innovation. Literature has recognized that gender diversity and CSR increase innovation (Miller and del Carmen Triana, 2009). By relating CSR to the representation of women in management, our findings point at a new hypothesis, namely that CSR mediates the effect of women managers on product and process innovation.

In Chapter 11, we focused on the effect of the innovation motive and various other strategic motives on environmental and social CSR. As our research indicates that motives may have different relevance for environmental and social

CSR, future research could elaborate on theorizing the differences in the relationship between various sets of motives and different dimensions of CSR. Furthermore, in this chapter we focused on one specific aspect of the environment of companies, the intensity of technological competition, and how this affects CSR through top manager's motivations. Future research should go beyond this starting point and analyse what kind of other external factors or factors internal to the company make business leaders more aware of the link between CSR and innovation and stimulate them to be more proactive in responding to CSR trends in the market.

Note

1 See Appendix 2 for an overview of various procedures we used to increase the reliability of the responses to the survey questions.

20
POLICY AND MANAGEMENT IMPLICATIONS

20.1 Impacts of CSR

The results of Part I of this book have a number of policy implications.

First, SMEs may be encouraged to formalize their environmental management by simple measures like the use of targets. Our empirical analysis in Chapter 2 shows that there would be much to gain in terms of environmental impacts if companies were to exploit the potential of formalizing environmental management, since most companies currently still refrain from targeting their environmental impacts. This kind of process step may contribute to greater awareness and may improve the quality and durability of the environmental management because subjective elements are supplemented with objective measures.

SMEs could further improve their environmental impacts by more elaborate management systems, such as ISO 14001. If the effects of ISO 14001 on environmental impacts were to be absent or weak for SMEs, promoting the use of this relatively costly instrument among SMEs would be inadvisable. This reflects the view expressed by Fassin (2008) that standardized schemes are of no use for SMEs. The research in Chapter 3 indicates, however, that this view is too pessimistic, because the findings show that ISO 14001 provides SMEs with an incentive to cooperate with other enterprises in order to improve their environmental impacts. The policy implication of these findings is that stimulating the use of ISO 14001 among SMEs is particularly fruitful for realizing energy savings and better waste and water efficiency when combined with participation in networks with external parties. Such relational environmental management instruments are particular appropriate for small businesses in improving environmental impacts, as small firms have limited expertise and financial resources to invest in environmentally responsible practices. Even if individual SMEs were to realize only small

DOI: 10.4324/9781003216483-25

savings, the total overall environmental impact could be huge because of the very large number of enterprises involved.

Third, the willingness to engage in CSR may be stimulated by communication of the finding that CSR stimulates innovation, as it suggests that CSR policies have important strategic value to the company (Porter and Kramer, 2006). Participation in networks in the supply chain or local community to improve CSR are also useful from this point of view, as it may be conducive to formation of alliances that benefit innovation as well. Few innovations can be developed unless SMEs cooperate with other businesses and other parties. Engagement in innovation-motivated CSR may thus be a double-edged sword: improving CSR helps to strengthen the firm's reputation and to comply with legal requirements, while also helping the firm to become more competitive in the long run. For policy makers these findings are relevant because they show that stimulating CSR creates a win-win situation by simultaneously improving the social and environmental contribution to society and promoting innovation by SMEs and therefore the long-term competitiveness of the economy. The innovation motive allows policy makers to invoke a proactive, strategic argument in 'selling' CSR to companies, including SMEs.

However, SMEs should also be aware that seeking public recognition of their CSR put themselves in the spotlight of public opinion and scrutiny. Formal procedural measures to obtain legitimacy from external stakeholders, such as ISO 14001 and ISO 26000 certifications, may backfire if they are decoupled from real sustainable development (Schwarz and Tilling, 2009). If NGOs start monitoring a company in response to the larger visibility of the environmental policies of the company, they might identify this gap and criticize the company for not meeting the expectations raised by the ISO 14001 or ISO 26000 certification. The managerial lesson for SMEs is that they should be careful in positioning themselves as sustainable firms that proactively pursue CSR policies once they started to develop CSR initiatives. They should not focus too much on the reputational benefits of CSR, because these may easily turn into reputational liabilities. Symbolic adoptions of CSR policies meant to appease certain stakeholders may, in fact, have negative consequences by changing the relationship between an organization and NGOs. Firms that want to improve their image through CSR policies should anticipate that their policies empower external monitors that can criticize the company in media if its CSR is more symbolic than substantive in nature. Rather than a means of image management, the CSR strategy be therefore better content driven. It is advisable to initially limit the visibility of the CSR policies and let it substantially lag behind the actual implementation of CSR policies within the firm (Wagner et al., 2009). Certifications such as ISO 14001 should not be used primarily as a means to show off to clients or other stakeholders, but rather as an instrument to foster the integration of CSR in the organizational procedures so that the firm is on track in improving its EP before using it as a means to enhance its reputation.

A similar recommendation can be given for participation in local initiatives with local governments and activist organizations to meet social or environmental objectives or starting a dialogue with NGOs. Although this kind of cooperation may improve a company's reputation, it also makes it more vulnerable to public criticism if the company performs poorly in other aspects of CSR. By making itself more visible, chances are higher that the SME cannot hide inconsistencies in the quality of different stakeholder relations. The firm is therefore recommended to take care that its CSR policies are mutually consistent before participating in such initiatives. Dialogues may make it easier to legitimate a firm's activities and help it to progress its CSR (Agudo-Valiente et al., 2015). However, by inviting local NGOs to participate in a dialogue, the SME puts itself also in the picture of these NGOs. The dialogue may not only inform the NGOs about the strengths of the SME's CSR, but also about its weaknesses. If not genuinely adopted, the dialogue will not meet the expectations of a participating NGO, which may induce the NGO to use this inside information to raise public criticism. The policy implication is that when preparing a stakeholder dialogue, SMEs should be careful in their selection of stakeholders and take care that the expectations are not set too high to prevent disappointment. Furthermore, if the SME is predominantly interested in the dialogue because of economic reasons, it better just communicates this motivation, because research has shown that this raises less suspicion than communication of intrinsic motives (Leonidou and Skarmeas, 2017; De Vries et al., 2015).

20.2 Internal Drivers of CSR

In Part II we analysed a set of internal drivers of CSR. From Chapter 6 we learn that the best strategy to stimulate CSR would be to combine institutional measures that stimulate extrinsic as well as intrinsic motivation, as both motivate companies to engage in CSR. Intrinsic motivation requires a business culture that stimulates moral sensitivity or awareness. The ethical cultures of companies are the result of a complex interaction between societal, organizational and personal factors (Paolillo and Vitell, 2002). It is not sufficient to change the formal structures of the business (Ford and Richardson, 1994). Changes in ethical cultures require attention to symbolic management that makes use of rituals, symbols and stories that stimulate moral awareness (Treviño and Nelson, 1999). This has important implications for the recruitment policies and the socialization and training programmes at the company level. At the institutional level, moral motivation can be fostered by normative calls for social responsible behaviour in important business publications and curricula in business schools and by dialogues with unions, employees, community groups and other stakeholders, because it appears that companies then better appreciate the concerns of these other actors (Campbell, 2007).

SMEs may also benefit from the fact that many of them are family-owned businesses. For several reasons, selling your family company is not only a financial but also an ethical decision, and the consequence for the company's CSR is one of those ethical dimensions that should be carefully considered. However, selling a micro family company to a large non-family company may also have some advantages. For example, if a small family company is taken over by a large public company that already employs more instruments to improve CSR (because of its large size), the public company might also implement these procedures in the newly acquired company, benefiting its CSR. Because, as shown in Chapter 19, company size has a positive effect on CSR and if a small family company is sold to a big non-family company, this positive effect outbalances the negative effect caused by the change in type of ownership. Furthermore, the non-linear moderation of the relationship between family-business ownership and CSR by the family involvement in management suggests that appointment of non-family members in the management of a company fully managed by family members stimulates CSR. Although the increase in non-family managers may weaken the identification with the company, this disadvantage is overcome by the advantages in terms of broadening the focus on a variety of stakeholder interests.

Chapter 8 sought to develop the understanding of the role of gender in environmentally responsible small business practice by analysing how the use of management instruments mediates this relationship. The findings showed that the proportion of women managers encourages the use of relational environmental management instruments and that this type of management instrument positively mediates the relationship between women's management and SME's EP. These findings imply that increasing the representation of women in management in SMEs is not only desirable from the point of view of providing more equal opportunities between men and women, but also has a wider societal contribution by improving the EP of SMEs, which in turn increases their shared value by bettering reputation. Since we find that sustainable performance is optimal when the share of women equals 54% (which is more than twice the current share), the company should seek to create a balanced management team that mixes male and female managers. As our study does not support critical mass theory for small business, legal requirements that set minima quota for the share of women in executive management levels in small business seem to be too restrictive, as they reduce the SME's freedom to employ the managers that best fit their needs in the context in which they are operating.

Our analysis in Chapter 9 suggests that management can influence their CSR by working towards a stronger external focus and flexibility orientation in their organizational culture (Berger et al., 2007). Cameron and Quinn (1999) described the various skills and attitudes that should be encouraged in employees if an organization is to move in this direction. A cautious and incremental change process is advisable. '[A] culture change is not that management tries to impose new behaviours (or talk), but a change of ideas, values and meanings of large groups of people' (Alvesson and Sveningsson, 2008: 42). While these ideas, values and meanings cannot be changed directly, management can manipulate the organizational context, and in this way influence the 'internal market' for employee behaviours conducive to CSR (Berger et al., 2007). The changes needed include moving to a more participative decision style (Berger et al., 2007; Dunphy et al., 2003). Aligning corporate culture and CSR requires a long-term policy. This view fits with the emerging perspective that becoming a sustainable corporation requires 'sufficient persistence, over many years' (Eccles et al., 2014: 2853). Various practitioner-oriented approaches and tools can be used in culture change programmes, like vision formulation and communication, establishing a sense of urgency, creation of role models, and encouraging employee ownership of changes. Finally, organizational cultures cannot directly be influenced by governments, but abandoning rigid regulation that hinders internal or functional labour flexibility can make it easier for firms to move in this direction (Kleinknecht et al., 2006).

20.3 Impacts of Competition on CSR

Chapter 10 showed that the intensity of price competition diminishes the long-term orientation of a company, which in turn reduces CSR. The finding that long-time orientation encourages CSR has important policy implications, both at the institutional level and at the intermediate level of industrial organizations. At the institutional level, governments should seek to enforce the time horizon of companies, for example by stimulating banks that provide credit to SMEs to consider the long-term potential of companies. At the level of industrial organizations, norm-setting for corporate governance can contribute to the long-term orientation of SMEs. Sacrificing long-term prospects to meet short-term earnings expectations can be reduced by proper executive compensation schemes that make remuneration dependent on long-term, instead of short-term, financial performance (Mallin et al., 2013).

Furthermore, the finding that the intensity of price competition reduces the time horizon of companies and hence indirectly discourages CSR may have implications for competition policy. The guidelines of the European Commission for the application of article 101 TFEU (formerly article 81 of the EC Treaty) state that consumer welfare is the only goal of EU antitrust law. Limitations to competition can only be justified by improvements to efficiency, either by lowering costs, improving quality, or creating more opportunities for innovation. Practices that contribute to overall welfare by improving CSR are only allowed if consumers obtain a fair share of the resulting benefit. The aim of antitrust policy to increase consumer welfare by intensifying market competition may, however, collide with other government policies that aim at sustainability goals, since stimulating competition may simultaneously hamper CSR and the realization of the environmental goals that CSR contributes to. Our results show, however, that the net negative influence of the intensity of price competition on EP, although significant, is nevertheless very small in absolute magnitude. Hence, although the argument that price competition worsens EP through increasing short-termism is valid, it does not have much practical consequences and is therefore hardly worth considering from a practical or policy point of view. The policy implication is that there is scarcely a trade-off between the economic benefits from competition policy, on one hand, and sustainability on the other hand. Hence, competition policy will probably not lead to a net loss of social welfare caused by lower EP.

Whereas price competition has a small negative effect on CSR, we found that the intensity of technological competition has a substantial positive effect. As already noted in section 20.1, the perspective that CSR stimulates innovation allows firms to incorporate CSR policies into their competitive strategy (Porter and Kramer, 2006). Engagement in innovation-motivated CSR may thus be a double-edged sword: improving CSR helps to meet society's expectations and to comply with legal requirements, while also helping the firm to become more competitive in the longer run. By appealing to the innovation motive, top managers of SMEs can be more effectively induced to develop a proactive CSR strategy than by forced legal compliance. For policy makers, the results imply that governments can stimulate CSR by economic policies that encourage technological competition, for example by funding R&D or offering tax credits to the companies for the R&D expenditure made by those companies. Government grants to directly fund innovative activities are known to have the most impact when directed to SMEs. If such policies are targeted at CSR-related innovation, they encourage CSR not only directly, but also indirectly by fostering a competitive technological environment.

The fear that extrinsic motives arising from more intense technological competition may reduce intrinsic motivation by crowding out, is not supported by the analysis in Chapter 12. In this chapter, we show that intrinsic CSR motivation is enforced by extrinsic motivations arising from external pressures to CSR. This implies that it is also important to emphasize the business case. The expectation that incentivizing companies in this way might be counterproductive because of crowding-out effects on intrinsic motivations, as suspected by Graafland and Van de Ven (2006), is unwarranted. This provides further support for the notion that there need not be a trade-off between economic benefits from more competition (the usual policy goal of competition policy) and social or environmental benefits from CSR. Only if owner-directors are not aware of the positive effects of CSR on innovation, such policies may harm intrinsic motivation. Therefore, policy makers who aim at stimulating innovation as well as CSR in the marketplace by market incentives, should inform managers about the innovation-enhancing effects of CSR. By appealing to the innovation motive, owner-managers of SMEs can be more effectively induced to develop a proactive CSR strategy, as it will both increase extrinsic motivations towards CSR (because of its direct incentive effect) as well as intrinsic motivation (because of the crowding in of this incentive effect). This awareness can be stimulated if policy makers target their policies at CSR related innovation.

20.4 External Institutional Drivers of CSR

In Chapter 13 we analysed the influence of social licence pressure on CSR. We found that, by increasing the transparency on CSR in the marketplace, NGOs and media can increase the responsiveness of external stakeholders to enterprises' CSR initiatives. In Chapter 14 we found that social licence pressure from CSR monitoring of NGOs and media does not only raise extrinsic CSR motivation arising from higher market benefits from CSR, but also enforce intrinsic CSR motivation through this channel. A policy implication then is that the free functioning of societal organizations and free press should be respected and not hindered by political agendas. This countervailing power is vital for any society that wants to limit potential negative externalities caused by free market operations in a capitalistic economic system (Ali et al., 2017; Doh and Guay, 2006). If social licence pressures for environmental impacts were to be absent or weak for SMEs, the use and development of existing regulatory structures providing minimum standards for many activities covered by CSR would remain the most effective means to influence the environmental impacts of SMEs. This research shows, however, that this view is too pessimistic for SMEs. We find that compliance with legislation is less important than market-related strategic benefits from CSR. Therefore, governments should not rely on regulation only. To stimulate SMEs' CSR, it is better to publicly award enterprises with excellent CSR performance, and couple this with soft regulations that induce enterprises to publish some key performance indicators on CSR. This kind of information makes it easier for local NGOs or media to collect information on the CSR impacts of enterprises and enhances the perception of SMEs of the working of the social licence mechanism. The guidelines for the information that should be provided should fit the nature of SMEs and therefore be simpler than comparable publication guidelines for large enterprises.

In literature it is argued that SMEs would favour external forms of regulation rather than self-regulation, because this generates a 'level playing field' that allows them to concentrate on the economic aspects and leave social and environmental aspects to the government (Williamson et al., 2006). According to Williamson et al. (2006), this implies that the use and development of existing regulatory structures, providing minimum standards for many activities covered by CSR, remains the most effective means to influence behaviour of SMEs. However, it is important for governments to acknowledge the specific nature of SMEs. Because of their small size, imposing regulatory compliance to CSR related regulations disproportionally increases their non-productive overheads. Another problem of strict government regulation addressed in Chapter 15 is that government regulation crowds out intrinsic CSR motivation of companies with high intrinsic motivation. Therefore, it is important to estimate the importance of intrinsic motivation, before any government regulation is implemented. If only few businessmen are intrinsically motivated to begin with, government regulation cannot crowd out intrinsic motivation. But if intrinsic motivation is strong, government regulation should be handled with care. Governments should then rather aim at increasing the awareness among SMEs of (relatively easy ways of) implementing CSR management instruments. Johnson (2015) found that in SMEs, managers' awareness of CSR management instruments is the major determinant for the implementation of instruments. In addition, other studies show that awareness-raising programmes targeted at SMEs may be the best chance for higher adoption rates of CSR management instruments, for example through mandatory free audits on how to improve impacts (Bradford and Fraser, 2008). Furthermore, Campbell (2007) advocates regulations based on consensus-building among companies, government and other relevant stakeholders. This is in line with previous experimental studies that showed that crowding effects decline if regulation respects the self-determination of participants (Vollan, 2008) and facilitates communication (Abatayo and Lynham, 2016). From a motivation crowding perspective, it indeed seems crucial to seek cooperation with the stakeholders by respecting their legitimate concerns, engaging their moral preferences, and allowing businesses discretion on how to enhance the public good. Another policy implication of the research in Chapter 15 is that government regulation may want to focus on setting minimum requirements for EP. In this way, it will enhance the EP of companies that have not taken voluntary initiatives because of low intrinsic or extrinsic motivation. Our estimation results indicate that crowding-out effects from government regulation are largely absent in this group. For countries with little or no environmental regulation, our policy advice is for the government to introduce minimum requirements to compel companies that lag behind to improve their EP. This allows companies that are frontrunners in reducing environmental harm to retain the scope to distinguish themselves from other companies by expressing their commitment to social responsibility through voluntary initiatives.

Our analysis in Chapter 16 has shown that intrinsic motivation does not only play an important role in stimulating CSR in itself, but also moderates the effects of economic freedom on CSR. This finding implies that societies with free market economies can flourish in-so-far as key market actors have positive intrinsic motivation and act virtuously. In Chapter 17, we furthermore identified a culture of long-term orientation as a moderating factor in the relationship between economic freedom and CSR. The policy and management implications of this finding are, however, not so obvious, are long-term orientation at the level of the society cannot be influenced policy makers. What our analysis does show is that in countries with high long-term orientation this characteristic of national culture can only stimulate CSR if firms have sufficient economic freedom, a factor that can be influenced by policy makers at the level of the society.

Finally, Chapter 18 has shown that collective bargaining agreements positively rather than negatively affect CSR. The policy implication that can be derived from these findings is that societies should be careful in diminishing the role of unions, for example, by abolishing the legal extension of collective agreements. The results indicate that nullifying the power of unions may reduce the incentives for creating more equal opportunities for women in board positions and for hiring employees from groups with a disadvantaged position in the labour market. If the influence of unions diminishes, public spirit may decline and this will make it more challenging to integrate people with a migrant history, into the labour market, among them, the refugees that recently entered Europe.

REFERENCES

Abatayo, A.L., and Lynham, J. (2016). Endogenous vs. exogenous regulations in the commons. *Journal of Environmental Economics and Management*, 76: 51–66.

Adams, J.S., Tashchian, A., and Shore, T.H. (2001). Codes of ethics as signals for ethical behavior. *Journal of Business Ethics*, 29: 199–211.

Agan, Y., Acar, M.F., and Borodin, A. (2013). Drivers of environmental processes and their impact on performance: A study of Turkish SMEs. *Journal of Cleaner Production*, 51: 23–33.

Agrawal, A., Chhatre, A., and Gerber, E.R. (2015). Motivational crowding in sustainable development interventions. *American Political Science Review*, 109: 470–487.

Agudo-Valiente, J.M., Garcés-Ayerbe, C., and Salvador-Figueras, M. (2015). Corporate social performance and stakeholder dialogue management. *Corporate Social Responsibility and Environmental Management*, 22: 13–31.

Aguilera, R.V., and Jackson, G. (2003). The cross-national diversity of corporate governance: Dimensions and determinants. *Academy of Management Review*, 28: 447–465.

Aguilera, R.V., Rupp, D., Williams, C.A., and Ganapathi, J. (2007). Putting the S back in corporate social responsibility: A multi-level theory of social change in organizations. *Academy of Management Review*, 32: 836–863.

Ajzen, I. (1991). The theory of planned behavior. *Organizational Behavior and Human Decision Processes*, 5: 179–211.

Albareda, L., Lozano, J., and Ysa, T. (2007). Public policies on corporate social responsibility: The role of governments in Europe. *Journal of Business Ethics*, 74(4): 391–407.

Alberini, A., and Segerson, K. (2002). Assessing voluntary programs to improve environmental quality. *Environmental and Resource Economics*, 22(1–2): 157–184.

Albin, E. (2013). Union responsibility to migrant workers: A global justice approach. *Oxford Journal of Legal Studies*, 34: 133–153.

Albinger, H.S., and Freeman, S.J. (2000). Corporate social performance and attractiveness as an employer to different job seeking populations. *Journal of Business Ethics*, 28(3): 243–253.

Albino, V., Dangelico, R.M., and Pontrandolfo, P. (2012). Do inter-organizational collaborations enhance a firm's environmental performance? A study of the largest U.S. companies. *Journal of Cleaner Production*, 37: 304–315.

Ali, W., Frynas, J.G., and Mahmood, Z. (2017). Determinants of corporate social responsibility (CSR) disclosure in developed and developing countries: A literature review. *Corporate Social Responsibility and Environmental Management*, 24: 273–294.

Allison, T.H., Davis, B.C., Short, J.C., and Webb, J.W. (2015). Crowdfunding in a prosocial microlending environment: Examining the role of intrinsic versus extrinsic cues. *Entrepreneurship Theory and Practice*, 39: 53–73.

Alvesson, M., and Sveningsson, S. (2008). *Changing organizational culture; cultural change work in progress*. London: Routledge.

Ammenberg, J., and Hjelm, O. (2003). Tracing business and environmental effects of environmental management systems – a study of networking small and medium-sized enterprises using a joint environmental management system. *Business Strategy and the Environment*, 12(3): 163–174.

Anderson, R.C., and Reeb, D.M. (2003). Founding-family ownership and firm performance: Evidence from the S&P 500. *Journal of Finance*, 58: 1301–1327.

Anderson, R.C., and Reeb, D.M. (2004). Board composition: Balancing family influence in S&P 500 firms. *Administrative Science Quarterly*, 49(2): 209–237.

Antonakis, J., Bendahan, S., Jacquart, P., and Lalive, R. (2010). On making causal claims: A review and recommendations. *The Leadership Quarterly*, 21(6): 1086–1120.

Aragón-Correa, J.A., Hurtado-Torres, N., Sharma, S., and Garcia-Morales, V.J. (2008). Environmental strategy and performance in small firms: A resource-based perspective. *Journal of Environmental Management*, 86: 88–103.

Aravind, D., and Christmann, P. (2011). Decoupling of standard implementation from certification. *Business Ethics Quarterly*, 1: 73–102.

Arimura, T.H., Hibiki, A., and Katayama, H. (2008). Is a voluntary approach an effective environmental policy instrument? A case for environmental management systems. *Journal of Environmental Economics and Management*, 55: 281–295.

Armas-Cruz, Y. (2011). Determinants of environmental management and implications for firms' economic performance. *Journal of Environmental Planning and Management*, 54(8): 1077–1106.

Ashkanasy, N.M., Wilderom, C.P.M., and Peterson, M.F. (Eds.). (2000). *Handbook of organizational culture & climate*. Thousand Oaks, CA: Sage.

Ates, A., and Bititci, U. (2011). Change process: A key enabler for building resilient SMEs. *International Journal of Production Research*, 49(18): 5601–5618.

Auger, P., Burke, P., Devinney, T.M., and Louviere, J.J. (2003). What will consumers pay for social product features? *Journal of Business Ethics*, 42: 281–304.

Avram, D., and Kühne, S. (2008). Implementing responsible business behavior from a strategic management perspective: Developing a framework for Austrian SMEs. *Journal of Business Ethics*, 82(2): 463–475.

Babiak, K., and Trendafilova, S. (2011). CSR and environmental responsibility: Motives and pressures to adopt green management practices. *Corporate Social Responsibility and Environmental Management*, 18: 11–24.

Baden, D., Harwood, I., and Woodward, D. (2011). The effects of procurement policies on 'downstream' corporate social responsibility activity: Content-analytic insights into the views and actions of SME owner-managers. *International Small Business Journal*, 29(3): 259–277.

Banalieva, E.R., Cuervo-Cazurra, A., and Sarathy, R. (2018). Dynamics of pro-market institutions and firm performance. *Journal of International Business Studies*, 49(7): 858–880.

Banerjee, S. (2008). Corporate social responsibility: The good, the bad and the ugly. *Critical Sociology*, 34(1): 51–79.

Bansal, P., and Roth, K. (2000). Why companies go green: A model of ecological responsiveness. *Academy of Management Journal*, 43(4): 717–736.

Barney, J.B., and Hansen, M.H. (1994). Trustworthiness as a source of competitive advantage. *Strategic Management Journal*, 15: 175–190.

Baron, D.P., and Diermeier, D. (2007). Strategic activism and nonmarket strategy. *Journal of Economics & Management Strategy*, 16(3): 599–634.

Barr, P.S., and Glynn, M.A. (2004). Cultural variations in strategic issue interpretation: Relating cultural uncertainty avoidance to controllability in discriminating threat and opportunity. *Strategic Management Journal*, 25(1): 59–67.

Barth, R., and Wolff, F. (2009). *Corporate social responsibility in Europe: Rhetoric and realities.* Cheltenham: Edward Elgar Publishing Ltd.

Bartley, T. (2007). Institutional emergence in an era of globalization: The rise of transnational regulation of labor and environmental conditions. *American Journal of Sociology*, 113: 297–351.

Bartley, T., and Child, C. (2011). Movements, markets and fields: The effects of anti-sweatshop campaigns on U.S. firms, 1993–2000. *Social Forces*, 90: 425–451.

Basu, K., and Palazzo, G. (2008). Corporate social responsibility: A process model of sensemaking. *Academy of Management Journal*, 33(1): 122–136.

Battaglia, M., Bianchi, L., Frey, M., and Iraldo, F. (2010). An innovative model to promote CSR among SMEs operating in industrial clusters: Evidence from an EU project. *Corporate Social Responsibility and Environmental Management*, 17(3): 133–141.

Battisti, M., and Perry, M. (2011). Walking the talk? Environmental responsibility from the perspective of small-business owners. *Corporate Social Responsibility and Environmental Management*, 18(3): 172–185.

Baughn, C.C., Bodie, N.L., and McIntosh, J.C. (2007). Corporate social and environmental responsibility in Asian countries and other geographical regions. *Corporate Social Responsibility and Environmental Management*, 14: 189–205.

Baumann-Pauly, D., Wickert, C., Spence, L.J., and Scherer, A.G. (2013). Organizing corporate social responsibility in small and large firms: Size matters. *Journal of Business Ethics*, 115: 693–705.

Baumol, W.J., and Batey Blackman, S.J. (1991). *Perfect markets and easy virtue: Business ethics and the invisible hand.* Oxford: Basil Blackwell.

Beaver, G., and Prince, C. (2004). Management, strategy and policy in the UK small business sector: A critical review. *Journal of Small Business and Enterprise Development*, 11(1): 34–49.

Belansky, E.S., and Boggiano, A.K. (1994). Predicting helping behaviors: The role of gender and instrumental/expressive self schemata. *Sex Roles*, 30(9): 647–661.

Bell, K. (2015). Can the capitalist economic system deliver environmental justice? *Environmental Research Letters*, 10: 125017.

Bénabou, R., and Tirole, J. (2010). Individual and corporate social responsibility. *Economica*, 77: 1–19.

Bengtsson, M. (1998). *Climates of competition.* Amsterdam: Harwood Academic Publishers.

Berger, I.E., Cunnigham, P.H., and Drumwright, M.E. (2007). Mainstreaming corporate social performance: Developing markets for virtues. *California Management Review*, 49: 132–157.

Bergman, J., Viljainen, S., Kässi, T., Partanen, J., and Laaksonen, P. (2006). Managing the exploration of new operational and strategic activities using the scenario method – assessing future capabilities in the field of electricity distribution industry. *International Journal of Production Research*, 104(1): 46–61.

Berman, S.L., Wicks, A.C., Kotha, S., and Jones, T.M. (1999). Does stakeholder orientation matter? The relationship between stakeholder management models and firm financial performance. *Academy of Management Journal*, 42(5): 488–506.

Berrone, P., Cruz, C., and Gomez-Mejia, L.R. (2012). Socioemotional wealth in family firms: Theoretical dimensions, assessment approaches, and agenda for future research. *Family Business Review*, 25(3): 258–279.

Berrone, P., Cruz, C., Gomez-Mejia, L.R., and Larraza-Kintana, M. (2010). Socioemotional wealth and corporate responses to institutional pressures: Do family-controlled firms pollute less? *Administrative Science Quarterly*, 55(1): 82–113.

Bertrand, M., and Hallock, K.F. (2001). The gender gap in top corporate jobs. *Industrial and Labor Relations Review*, 55(1): 3–21.

Biedma-Ferrer, J.M., Lopez-Fernandez, M., and Romero-Fernandez, P.M. (2015). *The collective labour agreement as a key tool for driving corporate social responsibility: Banking sector analysis*, www.ehu.eus/cuadernosdegestion/ documentos/150525jb.pdf.

Bingham, J.B., Dyer, W.G., Smith, I., and Adams, G.L. (2011). A stakeholder identity orientation approach to corporate social performance in family firms. *Journal of Business Ethics*, 99: 565–585.

Birindelli, G., Patrizia Iannuzzi, A., and Savioli, M. (2019). The impact of women leaders on environmental performance: Evidence on gender diversity in banks. *Corporate Social Responsibility and Environmental Management*, 26(6): 1485–1499.

Blau, F.D., and Kahn, L.M. (1983). Unionism, seniority, and turnover. *Industrial Relations*, 22(3): 362–373.

Block, J., and Wagner, M. (2014). The effect of family ownership on different dimensions of corporate social responsibility: Evidence from large US firms. *Business, Strategy and Environment*, 23(7): 475–492.

Bocquet, R., Le Bas, C., Mothe, C., and Poussing, N. (2011). *CSR firm profiles and innovation: An empirical exploration with survey data.* Working Paper WP 1117. Lyon-St Étienne: Gate.

Boiral, O. (2012). ISO certificates as organizational degree? Beyond the rational myths of certification. *Organization Studies*, 6: 633–654.

Booth, A.L., Francesconi, M., and Zoega, G. (2003). Unions, work-related training, and wages: Evidence for British men. *Industrial and Labour Relations Review*, 57(1): 68–91.

Bos-Brouwers, H.E.J. (2010). Corporate sustainability and innovation in SMEs: Evidence of themes and activities in practice. *Business Strategy and the Environment*, 19(7): 417–435.

Bowles, S. (2016). *The moral economy: Why good incentives are no substitute for good citizens.* New Haven: Yale University Press.

Bowles, S., and Polania-Reyes, S. (2012). Economic incentives and social preferences: Substitutes or complements? *Journal of Economic Literature*, 50(2): 368–425.

Boyer, P.C., Dwenger, N., and Rincke, J. (2016). Do norms on contribution behavior affect intrinsic motivation? Field-experimental evidence from Germany. *Journal of Public Economics*, 144: 140–153.

Bracke, R., Verbeke, T., and Dejonckheere, V. (2008). What determines the decision to implement EMAS? A European firm level study. *Environmental and Resource Economics*, 41(4): 499–518.

Bradford, J., and Fraser, E.D.G. (2008). Local authorities, climate change and small and medium enterprises: Identifying effective policy instruments to reduce energy use and carbon emissions. *Corporate Social Responsibility and Environmental Management*, 15(3): 156–172.

Brammer, S., Hoejmose, S., and Marchant, K. (2012). Environmental management in SMEs in the UK: Practices, pressures and perceived benefits. *Business Strategy and the Environment*, 21: 423–434.

Brammer, S., Jackson, G., and Matten, D. (2012). Corporate social responsibility and institutional theory: New perspectives on private governance. *Socio-Economic Review*, 10: 3–28.

Brammer, S., and Millington, A. (2008). Does it pay to be different? An analysis of the relationship between corporate social and financial performance. *Strategic Management Journal*, 29(12): 1325–1343.

Brammer, S., and Pavelin, S. (2006). Corporate reputation and social performance: The importance of fit. *Journal of Management Studies*, 43: 435–455.

Branco, M., and Rodrigues, L. (2006). Corporate social responsibility and resource-based perspectives. *Journal of Business Ethics*, 69(2): 111–132.

Briggs, S.R., and Cheek, J.M. (1986). The role of factor analysis in the development and evaluation of personality scales. *Journal of Personality*, 54: 106–148.

Brigham, K.H., Lumpkin, G.T., Payne, G.T., and Zachary, M.A. (2014). Researching long-term orientation. *Family Business Review*, 27(1): 72–88.

Briones Peñalver, A.J., Bernal Conesa, J.A., and de Nieves Nieto, C. (2018). Analysis of corporate social responsibility in Spanish agribusiness and its influence on innovation and performance. *Corporate Social Responsibility and Environmental Management*, 25(2): 182–193.

Bromley, P., and Powell, W.W. (2012). From smoke and mirrors to walking the talk: Decoupling in the contemporary world. *The Academy of Management Annals*, 6(1): 483–530.

Brønn, P.S., and Vidaver-Cohen, D. (2009). Corporate motives for social initiative: Legitimacy, sustainability or the bottom line? *Journal of Business Ethics*, 87: 91–109.

Brown, D.L., Vetterlein, A., and Roemer-Mahler, A. (2010). Theorizing transnational corporations as social actors: An analysis of corporate motivations. *Business and Politics*, 12: 1–37.

Brown, T.J., and Dacin, P.A. (1997). The company and the product: Corporate associations and consumer product responses. *Journal of Marketing*, 61: 68–84.

Budd, J.W. (2007). The effect of unions on employee benefits and non-wage compensation: Monopoly, power, collective voice and facilitation. In Bennett, J.T., and Kaufman, B.E. (Eds.), *What do unions do? A twenty year perspective* (pp. 162–164). London: Routledge.

Bullock, H.E., Harlow, L.L., and Mulaik, S.A. (1994). Causation issues in structural equation modeling research. *Structural Equation Modeling: A Multidisciplinary Journal*, 1(3): 253–267.

Burt, G., and Van der Heijden, K. (2003). First steps: Towards purposeful activities in scenario thinking and future studies. *Futures*, 35: 1011–1026.

Büschgens, T., Bausch, A., and Balkin, D.B. (2013). Organizational culture and innovation: A meta-analytic review. *Journal of Product Innovation Management*, 30(4): 763–781.

Byrne, B.M. (2010). *Structural equation modeling with AMOS: Basic concepts, applications, and programming*. New York and London: Routledge.

Cameron, K.S., and Quinn, R.E. (1999). *Diagnosing and changing organizational culture; based on the competing values framework*. Reading, MA: Addison-Wesley.

Cameron, K.S., Quinn, R.E., DeGraff, J., and Thakor, A.V. (2006). *Competing values leadership: Creating value in organizations*. Northampton, MA: Elgar.

Camisón, C. (2010). Effects of coercive regulation versus voluntary and cooperative auto-regulation on environmental adaptation and performance: Empirical evidence in Spain. *European Management Journal*, 28(5): 346–361.

Campbell, J.L. (2007). Why would corporations behave in socially responsible ways? An institutional theory of corporate social responsibility. *Academy of Management Review*, 32: 946–967.

Campbell, J.P., Dunette, M.C., Lawler, E.E., and Weick, K.E. (1970). *Managerial behavior performance and effectiveness*. New York: McGraw-Hill.

Campopiano, G., Romana Rinaldi, F., Sciascia, S., and De Massis, A. (2019). Family and non-family women on the board of directors: Effects on corporate citizenship behavior in family-controlled fashion firms. *Journal of Cleaner Production*, 214: 41–49.

Cañón-de-Francia, J., and Garcés-Ayerbe, C. (2009). ISO 14001 environmental certification: A sign valued by the market? *Environmental and Resource Economics*, 44(2): 245–262.

Cardenas, J.C., Stranlund, J., and Willis, C. (2000). Local environmental control and institutional crowding-out. *World Development*, 28(10): 1719–1733.

Carroll, A.B. (1979). A three-dimensional conceptual model of corporate performance. *Academy of Management Review*, 4(4): 497–505.

Carroll, A.B. (2008). A history of corporate social responsibility: Concepts and practices. In Crane, A., McWilliams, A., Matten, D., Moon, J., and Siegel, D. (Eds.), *The Oxford handbook of corporate social responsibility* (pp. 19–46). Oxford: Oxford University Press.

Carroll, A.B., and Shabana, K.M. (2010). The business case for corporate social responsibility: A review of concepts, research and practice. *International Journal of Management Reviews*, 12(1): 85–105.

Carson, R. (2010). The environmental Kuznets curve: Seeking empirical regularity and theoretical structure. *Review of Environmental Economics and Policy*, 4(1): 3–23.

Cassells, S., and Lewis, K. (2011). SMEs and environmental responsibility: Do actions reflect attitudes? *Corporate Social Responsibility and Environmental Management*, 18(3): 186–199.

Castka, P., and Prajogo, D. (2013). The effect of pressure from secondary stakeholders on the internalization of ISO14001. *Journal of Cleaner Production*, 47: 245–252.

Certo, S., Busenbark, J., Woo, H., and Semadeni, M. (2016). Sample selection bias and Heckman models in strategic management research. *Strategic Management Journal*, 37: 2639–2657.

Chang, S.J. (2003). Ownership structure, expropriation and performance of group-affiliated companies in Korea. *Academy of Management Journal*, 46: 238–253.

Chervier, C., Le Velly, G., and Ezzine-de-Blas, D. (2019). When the implementation of payments for biodiversity conservation leads to motivation crowding-out: A case study from the Cardamoms forests, Cambodia. *Ecological Economics*, 156: 499–510.

Child, J., and Tsai, T. (2005). The dynamic between firms' environmental strategies and institutional constraints in emerging economies, evidence from China and Taiwan. *Journal of Management Studies*, 49: 95–125.

Cho, C.H., Guidry, R.P., Hageman, A.M., and Patten, D.M. (2012). Do actions speak louder than words? An empirical investigation of corporate environmental reputation. *Accounting, Organizations and Society*, 37(1): 14–25.

Choi, A.S. (2015). An experimental study to explore WTP for aviation carbon offsets: The impact of a carbon tax on the voluntary action. *Journal of Environmental Planning and Management*, 58(9): 1617–1634.

Chrisman, J.J., and Patel, P.C. (2012). Variations in R&D investments of family and non-family firms: Behavioral agency and myopic loss aversion perspectives. *Academy of Management Journal*, 55: 976–997.

Christmann, P. (2000). Effects of 'best practices' of environmental management on cost advantage: The role of complementary assets. *Academy of Management Journal*, 43(4): 663–680.

Ciocirlan, C., and Pettersson, C. (2012). Does workforce diversity matter in the fight against climate change? An analysis of fortune 500 companies. *Corporate Social Responsibility and Environmental Management*, 19(1): 47–62.

Clausen, J., and Loew, T. (2009). *CSR und innovation: Literaturstudie und befragung*. Berlin: Institute 4 Sustainability.

Connolly, H., Marino, S., and Lucio, M.M. (2014). Trade union renewal and the challenges of representation: Strategies towards migrant and ethnic minority workers in the Netherlands, Spain and the United Kingdom. *European Journal of Industrial Relations*, 20(1): 5–20.

Coppa, M., and Sriramesh, K. (2013). Corporate social responsibility among SMEs in Italy. *Public Relations Review*, 39(1): 30–39.

Cottam, A., Ensor, J., and Band, C. (2001). A benchmark study of strategic commitment to innovation. *European Journal of Innovation Management*, 4(2): 88–94.

Cottrill, M.T. (1990). Corporate social responsibility and the marketplace. *Journal of Business Ethics*, 9: 723–729.

Cox, P.L., Friedman, B.A., and Tribunella, T. (2011). Relationships among cultural dimensions, national gross domestic product, and environmental sustainability. *The Journal of Applied Business and Economics*, 12(6): 46.

Craig, J., and Dibrell, C. (2006). The natural environment, innovation, and firm performance: A comparative study. *Family Business Review*, XIX(4): 275–288.

Croson, R., and Treich, N. (2014). Behavioral environmental economics: Promises and challenges. *Environmental and Resource Economics*, 58(3): 335–351.

Crossan, M.M., and Apaydin, M. (2010). A multi-dimensional framework of organizational innovation: A systematic review of the literature. *Journal of Management Studies*, 47(6): 1154–1191.

Crouch, C. (2006). Modelling the firm in its market and organizational environment: Methodologies for studying corporate social responsibility. *Organization Studies*, 27(10): 1533–1551.

Cruz, C., Larraza-Kintana, M., Garcés-Galdeano, L., and Berrone, P. (2014). Are family firms really more socially responsible? *Entrepreneurship Theory and Practice*, 38(6): 1295–1316.

Cucari, N., De Falco, S.E., and Orlando, B. (2018). Diversity of board of directors and environmental social governance: Evidence from Italian listed companies. *Corporate Social Responsibility and Environmental Management*, 25(3): 250–266.

Daddi, T., Testa, F., and Frey, M. (2016). Exploring the link between institutional pressures and environmental management systems effectiveness: An empirical study. *Journal of Environmental Management*, 183: 647–656.

Dahlsrud, A. (2008). How corporate social responsibility is defined: An analysis of 37 definitions. *Corporate Social Responsibility and Environmental Management*, 15(1): 1–13.

Dare, M.L., Schirmer, J., and Vanclay, F. (2014). Community engagement and social licence to operate. *Impact Assessment & Project Appraisal*, 32(3): 188–197.

Darnall, N. (2009). Regulatory stringency, green production off sets, and organizations' financial performance. *Public Administration Review* (May–June): 418–434.

Darnall, N., and Sides, S. (2008). Assessing the performance of voluntary environmental programs: Does certification matter? *Policy Studies Journal*, 36: 95–117.

David, P., Bloom, M., and Hillman, A.J. (2007). Investor activism, managerial responsiveness, and corporate social performance. *Strategic Management Journal*, 28(1): 91–100.

Davis, G.F. (2005). Firms and environments. In Smelser, N.J., and Swedberg, R. (Eds.), *Handbook of economic sociology* (2nd ed., pp. 478–503). Princeton, NJ: Princeton University Press.

Davis, L.E., and North, D.C. (1971). *Institutional change and American economic growth*. Cambridge: Cambridge University Press.

Dean, T., and McMullen, J. (2007). Toward a theory of sustainable entrepreneurship: Reducing environmental degradation through entrepreneurial action. *Journal of Business Venturing*, 22: 50–76.

Deci, E.L., and Ryan, R.M. (1985). *Intrinsic motivation and self-determination in human behavior*. New York, NY: Plenum Press.

Deci, E.L., Koestner, R., and Ryan, R.M. (1999). A meta-analytic review of experiments examining the effects of extrinsic rewards on intrinsic motivation. *Psychological Bulletin*, 125: 627–668.

Deegan, C., and Islam, M.A. (2014). An exploration of NGO and media efforts to influence workplace practices and associated accountability within global supply chains. *British Accounting Review*, 46: 397–415.

Deephouse, D.L., and Jaskiewicz, P. (2013). Do family firms have better reputations than non-family firms? An integration of socioemotional wealth and social identity theories. *Journal of Management Studies*, 50(3): 337–360.

De Geer, H., Borglund, T., and Frostenson, M. (2010). Reconciling CSR with welfare state actor roles – the problematic Swedish case. *Journal of Business Ethics*, 89: 269–283.

De Jong, J.P. (2011). Perceived competition and innovative intentions in Dutch small and medium-sized enterprises. *International Journal of Innovation Management*, 15(4): 687–707.

De Jong, M.D.T., and Van der Meer, M. (2017). How does it fit? Exploring the congruence between organizations and their corporate social responsibility (CSR) activities. *Journal of Business Ethics*, 143: 71–83.

Delmas, M., and Burbano, V.C. (2011). The drivers of greenwashing. *California Management Review*, 54(1): 64–87.

Delmas, M., and Gergaud, O. (2014). Sustainable certification for future generations: The case of family business. *Family Business Review*, 27(3): 228–243.

Delmas, M., and Montes-Sancho, M. (2011). An institutional perspective on the diffusion of international management system standards: The case of the environmental management standard ISO14001. *Business Ethics Quarterly*, 21(1): 103–132.

Delmas, M., and Toffel, M. (2004). Stakeholders and environmental management practices: An institutional framework. *Business Strategy and the Environment*, 13(4): 209–222.

Delmas, M., and Toffel, M. (2008). Organizational responses to environmental demands: Opening the black box. *Strategic Management Journal*, 29(10): 1027–1055.

Demirel, P., Iatridis, K., and Kesidou, E. (2018). The impact of regulatory complexity upon self-regulation: Evidence from the adoption and certification of environmental management systems. *Journal of Environmental Management*, 207: 80–91.

Demirel, P., and Kesidou, E. (2011). Stimulating different types of eco-innovation in UK: Government policies and firm motivations. *Ecological Economics*, 70: 1546–1557.

De Mooij, M., and Hofstede, G. (2010). The Hofstede model: Applications to global branding and advertising strategy and research. *International Journal of Advertising*, 29(1): 85–110.

Den Hond, F., and de Bakker, F.G.A. (2007). Ideologically motivated activism: How activist groups influence corporate social change activities. *Academy of Management Review*, 32: 901–924.

Den Hond, F., de Bakker, F.G.A., and Doh, J. (2015). What prompts companies to collaboration with NGOs? Recent evidence from the Netherlands. *Business & Society*, 54: 187–228.

Denis, D.J., Denis, D.K., and Sarin, A. (1997). Agency problems, equity ownership, and corporate diversification. *The Journal of Finance*, 52: 135–160.

Denison, D.R., and Spreitzer, G.M. (1991). Organizational culture and organizational development: A competing values approach. *Research in Organizational Change and Development*, 5: 1–21.

Deschênes, S., Rojas, M., Boubacar, H., Prud'homme, B., and Ouedraogo, A. (2015). The impact of board traits on the social performance of Canadian firms. *Corporate Governance*, 15(3): 293–305.

Dewhurst, H., and Thomas, R. (2003). Encouraging sustainable business practices in a non-regulatory environment: A case study of small tourism firms in a UK national park. *Journal of Sustainable Tourism*, 11(5): 383–403.

Dijk, M., Orsato, R.J., and Kemp, R. (2013). The emergence of an electric mobility trajectory. *Energy Policy*, 52(1): 135–145.

DiMaggio, P.J., and Powell, W.W. (1983). The iron cage revisited: Institutional isomorphism and collective rationality in organizational fields. *American Sociological Review*, 48: 147–160.

Ditlev-Simonsen, C.D., and Midttun, A. (2011). What motivates managers to pursue corporate responsibility? A survey among key stakeholders. *Corporate Social Responsibility and Environmental Management*, 18: 25–38.

Djupdal, K., and Westhead, P. (2015). Environmental certification as a buffer against the liabilities of newness and smallness: Firm performance benefits. *International Small Business Journal*, 33(2): 148–168.

Doh, J.P., and Guay, T.R. (2006). Corporate social responsibility, public policy, and NGO activism in Europe and the United States: An institutional-stakeholder perspective. *Journal of Management Studies*, 43: 47–73.

Doshi, A.R., Dowell, G.W., and Toffel, M.W. (2013). How firms respond to mandatory information disclosure. *Strategic Management Journal*, 34(10): 1209–1231.

Dubbink, W., and Putten, F.P. van der. (2008). Is competition law an impediment to CSR? *Journal of Business Ethics*, 83: 381–395.

Dunphy, D., Griffiths, A., and Benn, S. (2003). *Organizational change for corporate sustainability*. London: Routledge.

Durach, C.F., and Wiengarten, F. (2017). Environmental management: The impact of national and organisational long-term orientation on plants' environmental practices and performance efficacy. *Journal of Cleaner Production*, 167: 749–758.

Dutton, J.E., and Jackson, S.E. (1987). The categorization of strategic issues by decision makers and its links to organizational action. *Academy of Management Review*, 12: 76–90.

Dyer, W.G., and Whetten, D.A. (2006). Family firms and social responsibility: Preliminary evidence from the S&P 500. *Entrepreneurship Theory and Practice*, 30: 785–802.

Eagly, A.H. (1987). *Sex differences in social behavior: A social-role interpretation*. Hillsdale, NJ: Lawrence Erlbaum Associates, Inc.

Eccles, R.G., Ioannou, I., and Serafeim, G. (2014). The impact of corporate sustainability on organizational processes and performance. *Management Science*, 60(11): 2835–2857.

ECEI (European Commission Enterprise and Industry). (2010). *SMEs and the environment in the European Union*. Denmark: Teknologisk Institut, http://ec.europa.eu/enterprise/policies/sme/business-environment/files/main_report_en.pdf [Accessed 17 May 2015].

Eisenberger, R., Rhoades, L., and Cameron, J. (1999). Does pay for performance increase or decrease perceived self-determination and non-financial motivation. *Journal of Personality and Social Psychology*, 77: 1026–1040.

El Ghoul, S., Guedhami, O., and Kim, Y. (2017). Country-level institutions, firm value, and the role of corporate social responsibility initiatives. *Journal of International Business Studies*, 48(3): 360–385.

Elkington, J. (1997). *Cannibals with forks: The triple bottom line*. Chicago: Capstone Publishing.

Elliot, K.A., and Freeman, R.B. (2001). *White hats or don quixotes? Human rights vigilantes in the global economy*. NBER Working Paper No. 8102. Cambridge: NBER.

Elster, J. (2007). *Explaining social behavior: More nuts and bolts for the social sciences*. Cambridge: Cambridge University Press.

ENSR. (2001). *ENSR enterprise study*, www.eim.nl/Observatory _7_and_8/en/ensr.html.

Etzioni, A. (1988). *The moral dimension: Towards a new economic*. New York: The Free Press.

European Commission. (2001). *Promoting a European framework for corporate social responsibilities, COM 366 final*. Brussels: European Commission.

European Commission. (2002). *European SMES and social and environmental responsibility*. Observatory of European SMEs, No. 4, https://op.europa.eu/en/publication-detail/-/publication/60177f21-1835-4c5e-bf29-6a47b5b0808f.

European Commission. (2007). *Opportunity and responsibility: How to help more small businesses to integrate social and environmental issues into what they do*, http://ec.europa.eu/enterprise/policies/sustainable-business/files/csr/documents/eg_report_and_key_messages/key_messages_en.pdf [Accessed 11 July 2014].

European Commission. (2011). *Communication from the commission to the European Parliament, the council, the European economic and social committee and the committee of the regions* (pdf), http://ec.europa.eu/enterprise/policies/sustainable-business/files/CSP/new-CSP/act_en.pdf [Accessed 24 July 2012].

European Commission. (2012). *EU SMEs in 2012: At the crossroads. Annual report on small and medium-sized enterprises in the EU*, http://ec.europa.eu/enterprise/policies/sme/facts-figures-analysis/performance-review/files/ supporting-documents/2012/annual-report_en.pdf [Accessed 24 July 2012].

Evan, W.M., and Freeman, R.E. (1988). A stakeholder theory of the modern corporation: Kantian capitalism. In Beauchamp, T.L., and Bowie, N. (Eds.), *Ethical theory and business* (pp. 75–84). Englewood Cliffs: Prentice Hall.

Ezzine-de-Blas, D., Corberac, E., and Lapeyred, R. (2019). Payments for environmental services and motivation crowding: Towards a conceptual framework. *Ecological Economics*, 156: 434–443.

Fainshmidt, S., Judge, W.Q., Aguilera, R.V., and Smith, A. (2018). Varieties of institutional systems: A contextual taxonomy of understudied countries. *Journal of World Business*, 53(3): 307–322.

Fassin, Y. (2008). SMEs and the fallacy of formalising CSR. *Business Ethics: A European Review*, 17(4): 364–378.

Fassin, Y., Van Rossem, A., and Buelens, M. (2011). Small-business owner-managers' perceptions of business ethics and CSR-related concepts. *Journal of Business Ethics*, 98: 425–453.

Ferenhof, H.A., Vignochi, L., Selig, P.M., Lezana, A.G.R., and Campos, L.M.S. (2014). Environmental management systems in small and medium-sized enterprises: An analysis and systematic review. *Journal of Cleaner Production*, 74: 44–53.

Fernández-Feijoo, B., Romero, S., and Ruiz-Blanco, S. (2014). Women in boards: Do they affect sustainability reporting? *Corporate Social Responsibility and Environmental Management*, 21: 351–364.

Fernández-Kranz, D., and Santaló, J. (2010). When necessity becomes a virtue: The effect of product market competition on corporate social responsibility. *Journal of Economics & Management Strategy*, 19(2): 453–487.

Ferreira Rino, C.A., and Salvador, N.N.B. (2017). ISO14001 certification process and reduction of environmental penalties in organizations in Sao Paulo State, Brazil. *Journal of Cleaner Production*, 142: 3627–3633.

Fey, C.F., and Denison, D.R. (2003). Organizational culture and effectiveness: Can American theory be applied in Russia? *Organization Science*, 14(6): 686–706.

Fiedler, K., Schott, M., and Meiser, T. (2011). What mediation analysis can (not) do. *Journal of Experimental Social Psychology*, 47: 1231–1236.

Filbeck, G., and Gorman, R. (2004). The relationship between the environmental and financial performance of public utilities. *Environmental and Resource Economics*, 29(2): 137–157.

Flammer, C. (2015). Does product market competition foster corporate social responsibility? Evidence from trade liberalization. *Strategic Management Journal*, 36(10): 1469–1485.

Flammer, C., and Kacperczyk, A. (2016). The impact of stakeholder orientation on innovation: Evidence from a natural experiment. *Management Science*, 62: 1982–2001.

Fligstein, N., and McAdam, D. (2011). Toward a general theory of strategic action fields. *Sociological Theory*, 29: 1–26.

Fombrun, C., and Shanley, M. (1990). What's in a name? Reputation building and corporate strategy. *Academy of Management Journal*, 33: 233–258.

Ford, R.C., and Richardson, W.D. (1994). Ethical decision making: A review of the empirical literature. *Journal of Business Ethics*, 13: 205–221.

Fraj-Andrés, E., López-Pérez, M.E., Melero-Polo, I., and Vázquez-Carrasco, R. (2012). Company image and corporate social responsibility: Reflecting with SMEs' managers. *Marketing Intelligence & Planning*, 30: 266–280.

Frankel, J.A., and Rose, A.R. (2005). Is trade good or bad for the environment? Sorting out the causality. *The Review of Economics and Statistics*, 87(1): 85–91.

Freeman, R.B., and Medoff, J.L. (1984). *What do unions do?* New York: Basic Books.

Frey, B.S. (1992). Pricing and regulation affect environmental ethics. *Environmental and Resource Economics*, 2: 399–414.

Frey, B.S. (1998). *Not just for the money: An economic theory of personal motivation*. Cheltenham: Edward Elgar.

Frey, B.S., and Jegen, R. (2001). Motivation crowding theory. *Journal of Economic Surveys*, 15: 589–611.

Frey, B.S., and Oberholzer-Gee, F. (1997). The costs of price incentives: An empirical analysis of motivation crowding out. *American Economic Review*, 87: 746–755.

Friedman, A., and Miles, S. (2001). SMEs and the environment: Two case studies. *Eco-Management and Auditing*, 8(4): 200–209.

Frondel, M., Horbach, J., and Rennings, K. (2007). End-of-pipe or cleaner production? An empirical comparison of environmental innovation decisions across OECD countries. *Business Strategy and the Environment*, 16(8): 571–584.

Fuller, T., and Tian, Y. (2006). Social and symbolic capital and responsible entrepreneurship: An empirical investigation of SME narratives. *Journal of Business Ethics*, 67: 287–304.

Gadenne, D., Kennedy, J., and McKeiver, C. (2009). An empirical study of environmental awareness and practices in SMEs. *Journal of Business Ethics*, 84(1): 45–63.

Galbreath, J. (2005). Which resources matter the most to firm success? An exploratory study of resource-based theory. *Technovation*, 25(9): 979–987.

Galbreath, J. (2011). Are there gender-related influences on corporate sustainability? A study of women on boards of directors. *Journal of Management and Organization*, 17(1): 17–38.

Gallego-Álvareza, I., and Ortas, E. (2017). Corporate environmental sustainability reporting in the context of national cultures: A quantile regression approach. *International Business Review*, 26: 337–353.

Gardberg, N., and Fombrun, C.F. (2006). Corporate citizenship: Creating intangible assets across institutional environments. *Academy of Management Review*, 31: 329–346.

Gilligan, C. (1982). *In a different voice: Psychological theory and women's development*. Cambridge, MA: Harvard University Press.

Gjølberg, M. (2009). The origin of corporate social responsibility: Global forces or national legacies. *Socio-Economic Review*, 7: 605–637.

Godfrey, P.C., Merrill, G.B., and Hansen, J.M. (2009). The relationship between corporate social performance and shareholder value: An empirical test of the risk management hypothesis. *Strategic Management Journal*, 30(4): 425–445.

Graafland, J.J. (2002). Sourcing ethics in the textile sector: The case of C&A. *Business Ethics: A European Review*, 11(3): 282–294.

Graafland, J.J. (2016). Price competition, short-termism and environmental performance. *Journal of Cleaner Production*, 116: 125–134.

Graafland, J.J. (2018a). Ecological impacts of the ISO14001 certification of small and medium sized enterprises in Europe and the mediating role of networks. *Journal of Cleaner Production*, 174: 273–282.

Graafland, J.J. (2018b). Does corporate social responsibility put reputation at risk by inviting activist targeting? An empirical test among European SMEs. *Corporate Social Responsibility and Environmental Management*, 25: 1–13.

Graafland, J.J. (2018c). Collective agreements and equal opportunities for women and disadvantaged groups. In Rijken, C., and De Lange, T. (Eds.), *Towards a decent labour market for low-waged migrant workers* (pp. 267–282). Amsterdam: Amsterdam University Press.

Graafland, J. (2020a). Family business ownership and cleaner production: Moderation by company size and family management. *Journal of Cleaner Production*, 255: article 120120.

Graafland, J.J. (2020b). Women in management and sustainable development of SMEs: Do relational environmental management instruments matter? *Corporate Social Responsibility and Environmental Management*, 27: 2320–2328.

Graafland, J.J. (2020c). Competition in technology and innovation, motivation crowding, and environmental policy. *Corporate Social Responsibility and Environmental Management*, 27: 137–145.

Graafland, J.J., and de Bakker, F.G.A. (2021). Crowding in or crowding out? How non-governmental organizations and media influence intrinsic motivation towards corporate social and environmental responsibility. *Journal of Environmental Planning and Management*, https://doi.org/10.1080/09640568.2021.1873110.

Graafland, J.J., and Bovenberg, L. (2020). Government regulation, business leaders' motivations and environmental performance of SMEs. *Journal of Environmental Planning and Management*, 63(8): 1335–1355.

Graafland, J.J., and Gerlagh, R. (2019). Economic freedom, internal motivation, and corporate environmental responsibility of SMEs. *Environmental and Resource Economics*, 74: 1101–1123.

Graafland, J.J., Hudson, P., and Werner, J. (2016). Does corporate social performance reduce greenhouse gas emissions at the macro level? *Journal of Environmental Planning and Management*, 59(2): 203–221.

Graafland, J.J., and Mazereeuw-Van der Duijn Schouten, C. (2012). Motives for corporate social responsibility. *De Economist*, 160: 377–396.

Graafland, J.J., and Noorderhaven, N. (2018). National culture and environmental responsibility research revisited. *International Business Review*, 27(5): 958–968.

Graafland, J.J., and Noorderhaven, N. (2020a). Technological competition, innovation motive and corporate social responsibility: Evidence from top managers of European SMEs. *De Economist*, 168: 1–22.

Graafland, J.J., and Noorderhaven, N. (2020b). Culture and institutions: How economic freedom and long-term orientation interactively influence corporate social responsibility. *Journal of International Business Studies*, 51(6): 1034–1043.

Graafland, J.J., and Smid, H. (2015). Competition and institutional drivers of corporate social performance. *De Economist*, 163(3): 303–322.

Graafland, J.J., and Smid, H. (2016). Environmental impacts of SMEs and the effects of formal management instruments: Evidence from EU's largest survey. *Corporate Social Responsibility and Environmental Management*, 23: 297–307.

Graafland, J.J., and Smid, H. (2017). Reconsidering the relevance of social license pressure and government regulation for environmental performance of European SMEs. *Journal of Cleaner Production*, 141: 967–977.

Graafland, J., and Smid, H. (2019). Decoupling among CSR policies, programs, and impacts: An empirical study. *Business & Society*, 58(2): 231–267.

Graafland, J.J., and Van de Ven, B. (2006). Strategic and moral motivation for corporate social responsibility. *Journal of Corporate Citizenship*, 22: 111–123.

Graafland, J.J., Van de Ven, B.W., and Stoffele, N.C.G.M. (2003). Strategies and instruments for organising CSR by small and large business in the Netherlands. *Journal of Business Ethics*, 47: 45–60.

Granovetter, M. (2000). The economic sociology of firms and entrepreneurs. *Entrepreneurship: The Social Science View*, 244–275.

Greening, D.W., and Turban, D.B. (2000). Corporate social performance as a competitive advantage in attracting a quality workforce. *Business & Society*, 39(3): 254–280.

Greer, D.F. (1992). *Industrial organization and public policy*. New York: Macmillan Publishing Company.

Grillos, T., Bottazzi, P., Crespo, D., Asquith, N., and Jones, J.P. (2019). In-kind conservation payments crowd in environmental values and increase support for government intervention: A randomized trial in Bolivia. *Ecological Economics*, 166: 106404.

Grinyer, P.H., and Yasai-Ardekani, M. (1981). Strategy, structure, size and bureaucracy. *Academy of Management Journal*, 24(3): 471–486.

Gubler, T., Larkin, I., and Pierce, L., (2016). Motivational spillovers from awards: Crowding out in a multitasking environment. *Organizational Science*, 27(2): 286–303.

Guerrero-Baena, M.D., Gómez-Limón, J.A., and Fruet, J.D. (2015). A multicriteria method for environmental management system selection: An intellectual capital approach. *Journal of Cleaner Production*, 105: 428–437.

Guerrero-Villegas, J., Sierra-García, L., and Palacios-Florencio, B. (2018). The role of sustainable development and innovation on firm performance. *Corporate Social Responsibility and Environmental Management*, 25: 1350–1362.

Guiso, L., Sapienza, P., and Zingales, L. (2006). Does culture affect economic outcomes? *Journal of Economic Perspectives*, 20(2): 23–48.

Gunningham, N., Kagan, R., and Thornton, D. (2004). Social license and environmental protection: Why businesses go beyond compliance. *Law and Social Inquiry*, 29(2): 307–341.

Gwartney, J. (2009). Institutions, economic freedom, and cross-country differences in performance. *Southern Economic Journal*, 75(4): 937.

Gwartney, J., and Lawson, R. (2003). The concept and measurement of economic freedom. *European Journal of Political Economy*, 19: 405–430.

Hafenbrädl, S., and Waeger, D. (2017). Ideology and the micro-foundations of CSR: Why executives believe in the business case for CSR and how this affects their CSR engagements. *Academy of Management Journal*, 60: 1582–1606.

Hair, J.F., Anderson, R.E., Tatham, R.L., and Black, W.C. (1998, 2010). *Multivariate analysis*. Englewood Cliffs: Prentice-Hall.

Hall, N., Lacey, J., Carr-Cornish, S., and Dowd, A. (2015). Social licence to operate: Understanding how a concept has been translated into practice in energy industries. *Journal of Cleaner Production*, 86: 301–310.

Haller, S.A., and Murphy, L. (2012). Corporate expenditure on environmental protection. *Environmental and Resource Economics*, 51(2): 277–296.

Halme, M., and Laurila, J. (2009). Philanthropy, integration or innovation? Exploring the financial and societal outcomes of different types of corporate responsibility. *Journal of Business Ethics*, 84(3): 325–339.

Hamann, R., Smith, J., Tashman, P., and Marshall, R.S. (2017). Why do SMEs go green? An analysis of wine firms in South Africa. *Business & Society*, 56: 23–56.

Hambrick, D.C., and Mason, P. (1984). Upper echelons: The organization as a reflection of its business leaders. *Academy of Management Review*, 9: 193–206.

Hamilton, J.T. (1995). Pollution as news: Media and stock market reactions to the toxic release inventory data. *Journal of Environmental Economics and Management*, 28(1): 98–114.

Hampden-Turner, C., and Trompenaars, F. (2000). *Building cross-cultural competence*. Chichester: John Wiley.

Han, H., Zhang, Z., Xia, S., and Li, H. (2018). The carrot or the stick: Individual adaption against varying institutional arrangements. *Journal of Environmental Planning and Management*, 61(4): 568–596.

Harackiewicz, J.M., and Manderlink, G. (1984). A process analysis of the effects of performance-contingent rewards on intrinsic motivation. *Journal of Experimental Social Psychology*, 20(6): 531–551.

Hart, S.L. (1995). A natural-resource-based view of the company. *Academy of Management Review*, 20(4): 986–1014.
Hartmann, J., and Uhlenbruck, K. (2015). National institutional antecedents to corporate environmental performance. *Journal of World Business*, 50: 729–741.
Harzing, A. (1997). Response rates in international mail surveys: Results of a 22-country study. *International Business Review*, 6(6): 641–665.
Hatch, M.J., and Schultz, M. (2002). The dynamics of organizational identity. *Human Relations*, 55(8): 989–1018.
Hawn, O., and Ioannou, I. (2016). Mind the gap: The interplay between external and internal actions in the case of corporate social responsibility. *Strategic Management Journal*, 37(13): 2569–2588.
Heckman, J.J. (1979). Sample selection bias as a specification error. *Econometrica*, 47: 153–161.
Heikkurinen, P. (2010). Image differentiation with corporate environmental responsibility. *Corporate Social Responsibility and Environmental Management*, 17(3): 142–152.
Heilman, M.E., Wallen, A.S., and Fuchs, D. (2004). Penalties for success: Reactions to women who succeed at male gender-typed tasks. *Journal of Applied Psychology*, 89(3): 416–427.
Held, V. (2006). *The ethics of care: Personal, political and global*. Oxford, England: Oxford University Press.
Helmig, B., Spraul, K., and Ingenhoff, D. (2016). Under positive pressure: How stakeholder pressure affects corporate social responsibility implementation. *Business & Society*, 55(2): 151–187.
Hemel, C., and Cramer, J. (2002). Barriers and stimuli for ecodesign in SMEs. *Journal of Cleaner Production*, 10: 439–453.
Hemingway, C.A., and Maclagan, P.W. (2004). Managers' personal values as drivers of corporate social responsibility. *Journal of Business Ethics*, 50: 33–44.
Hendry, J. (2006). Taking aim at business: What factors lead environmental non-governmental organizations to target particular firm? *Business & Society*, 45: 47–86.
Heras-Saizarbitoria, I., Dogui, K., and Boiral, O. (2013). Shedding light on ISO14001 certification audits. *Journal of Cleaner Production*, 51: 88–98.
Herrera-Echeverri, H., Haar, J., and Estévez-Bretón, J.B. (2014). Foreign direct investment, institutional quality, economic freedom and entrepreneurship in emerging markets. *Journal of Business Research*, 67: 1921–1932.
Hewitt-Dundas, N. (2006). Resource and capability constraints to innovation in small and large plants. *Small Business Economics*, 26: 257–277.
Hillary, R. (2000). *Small and medium-sized enterprises and the environment: Business imperatives*. Sheffield: Greenleaf.
Hillary, R. (2004). Environmental management systems and the smaller enterprise. *Journal of Cleaner Production*, 12(6): 561–569.
Hitt, M.A., Hoskisson, R.E., and Kim, H. (1997). International diversification: Effects on innovation and firm performance in product-diversified firms. *Academy of Management Journal*, 40(4): 767–798.
Ho, F.N., Wang, H.M.D., and Vitell, S.J. (2012). A global analysis of corporate social performance: The effects of cultural and geographic environments. *Journal of Business Ethics*, 107(4): 423–433.
Hodgson, G.M. (2006). What are institutions? *Journal of Economic Issues*, XL(1): 1–25.
Hofstede, G. (1980). *Culture's consequences: International differences in work-related values*. Beverly Hills, CA: Sage.

Hofstede, G. (2001). *Culture's consequences* (2nd ed.). Thousand Oaks, CA: Sage.

Hofstede, G., and Minkov, M. (2010). Long-versus short-term orientation: New perspectives. *Asia Pacific Business Review*, 16(4): 493–504.

Hofstede, G., Neuijen, B., Ohayv, D.D., and Sanders, G. (1990). Measuring organizational cultures: A qualitative and quantitative study across twenty cases. *Administrative Science Quarterly*, 35(2): 286–316.

Hossain, R., and Li, K. (2014). Crowding out in the labor market: A prosocial setting is necessary. *Management Science*, 60: 1148–1160.

Howard, L.W. (1998). Validating the competing values model as a representation of organizational cultures. *The International Journal of Organizational Analysis*, 6(3): 231–250.

Howard-Grenville, J.A., and Hoffman, A.J. (2003). The importance of cultural framing to the success of social initiatives in business. *Academy of Management Perspectives*, 17(2): 70–84.

Hull, C., and Rothenberg, S. (2008). Firm performance: The interactions of corporate social performance with innovation and industry differentiation. *Strategic Management Journal*, 29: 781–789.

Hummels, H., and Karssing, E. (2007). Organising ethics. In Jeurissen, R. (Ed.), *Ethics and business* (pp. 249–275). Assen: Van Gorcum.

Humphreys, P., McAdam, R., and Leckey, J. (2005). Longitudinal evaluation of innovation implementation in SMEs. *European Journal of Innovation Management*, 8(3): 283–304.

Hungerman, D.M. (2009). Crowd-out and diversity. *Journal of Public Economics*, 93: 729–740.

Hunt, R.A., and Fund, B.R. (2016). Intergenerational fairness and the crowding out effects of well-intended environmental policies. *Journal of Management Studies*, 53(5): 878–910.

Ibrahim, N.A., and Angelidis, J.P. (2011). Effect of board members' gender on corporate social responsiveness orientation. *Journal of Applied Business Research*, 10(1): 35–40.

Ingram, P., and Clay, K. (2000). The choice-within-constraints new institutionalism and implications for sociology. *Annual Review of Sociology*, 26(1): 525–546.

Ioannou, I., and Serafeim, G. (2012). What drives corporate social performance & quest; the role of nation-level institutions. *Journal of International Business Studies*, 43(9): 834–864.

Jackson, G., and Apostolakou, A. (2010). Corporate social responsibility in Western Europe: An institutional mirror or substitute? *Journal of Business Ethics*, 94: 371–394.

Jackson, G., and Deeg, R. (2008). Comparing capitalisms: Understanding institutional diversity and its implications for international business. *Journal of International Business Studies*, 39(4): 540–561.

Jamali, D. (2010). MNCs and international accountability standards through an institutional lens: Evidence of symbolic conformity or decoupling. *Journal of Business Ethics*, 95(4): 617–640.

Jamali, D., and Mirshak, R. (2007). Corporate social responsibility (CSR): Theory and practice in a developing country context. *Journal of Business Ethics*, 72(3): 243–262.

Jamali, D., Yianni, M., and Abdallah, H. (2011). Strategic partnerships, social capital and innovation: Accounting for social alliance innovation. *Business Ethics: A European Review*, 20(4): 375–391.

Jamali, D., Zanhour, M., and Keshishian, T. (2008). Peculiar strengths and relational attributes of SMEs in the context of CSP. *Journal of Business Ethics*, 87: 355–377.

Jenkins, H. (2004). A critique of conventional CSR theory: An SME perspective. *Journal of General Management*, 9(4): 55–75.

Jenkins, H. (2009). A 'business opportunity' model of corporate social performance for small- and medium-sized enterprises. *Business Ethics: A European Review*, 18: 21–36.

Jeppesen, S. (2006). Strengthening corporate social and environmental responsibilities in SMEs – strengthening developing countries? In Hunisch, M., and Pedersen, E.R. (Eds.), *Corporate citizenship in developing countries: New partnership perspectives* (pp. 89–112). Copenhagen: Copenhagen Business School Press.

Jiménez-Parra, B., Alonso-Martínez, D., and Godos-Díez, J.L. (2018). The influence of corporate social responsibility on air pollution: Analysis of environmental regulation and eco-innovation effects. *Corporate Social Responsibility and Environmental Management*, 25(6): 1363–1375.

Johnson, M.P. (2015). Sustainability management and small and medium-sized enterprises: Managers' awareness and implementation of innovative tools. *Corporate Social Responsibility and Environmental Management*, 22(5): 271–285.

Johnstone, N., and Labonne, J. (2009). Why do manufacturing facilities introduce environmental management systems? Improving and/or signaling performance. *Ecological Economics*, 68: 719–730.

Jones, D.A., Willness, C.R., and Madey, S. (2014). Why are job seekers attracted by corporate social performance? Experimental and field tests of three signal-based mechanisms. *Academy of Management Journal*, 57(2): 383–404.

Jones, M. (1999). The institutional determinants of social responsibility. *Journal of Business Ethics*, 20(2): 163–179.

Jones, T.M., and Wicks, A.C. (1999). Convergent stakeholder theory. *Academy of Management Review*, 24: 206–221.

Joyner, B.E., and Payne, D. (2002). Evolution and implementation: A study of values, business ethics and corporate social responsibility. *Journal of Business Ethics*, 41: 297–311.

Julian, S.D., and Ofori-Dankwa, J.C. (2008). Toward an integrative cartography of two strategic issue diagnosis frameworks. *Strategic Management Journal*, 29: 93–114.

Kanter, R. (1977). Some effects of proportions on group life: Skewed sex ratios and responses to token women. *American Journal of Sociology*, 82(5): 965–990.

Kaplan, D. (2009). *Structural equation modeling: Foundations and extensions* (Advanced Quantitative Techniques in the Social Sciences Series. Vol. 10). Newbury Park, CA: Sage.

Kaptein, M., and Wempe, J. (1998). Twelve Gordian knots when developing an organizational code of ethics. *Journal of Business Ethics*, 17: 853–869.

Karpoff, J.M., Lott, J.J.R., and Wehrly, E.W. (2005). The reputational penalties for environmental violations: Empirical evidence. *Journal of Law and Economics*, 48(2): 653–675.

Kassinis, G., Panayiotou, A., Dimou, A., and Katsifaraki, G. (2016). Gender and environmental sustainability: A longitudinal analysis. *Corporate Social Responsibility and Environmental Management*, 23: 399–412.

Katz, D., and Kahn, R.L. (1978). *The social psychology of organizations* (2nd ed.). New York: John Wiley.

Kim, A., Kim, Y., Han, K., Jackson, S.E., and Ployhart, R.E. (2017). Multilevel influences on voluntary workplace green behavior: Individual differences, leader behavior, and coworker advocacy. *Journal of Management*, 43(5): 1335–1358.

Kinderman, D. (2008). *The political economy of corporate responsibility in Germany, 1995–2008*. Mario Einaudi Center for International Studies Working Paper No. 5–8. Ithaca, NY: Cornell University Press.

Kinderman, D. (2012). Free us up so we can be responsible: The co-evolution of corporate social responsibility and neo-liberalism in the UK, 1977–2010. *Socio-Economic Review*, 10: 135–157.

King, A., and Lenox, M. (2002). Exploring the locus of profitable pollution reduction. *Management Science*, 48(2): 289–299.

King, A., Lenox, M., and Terlaak, A. (2005). The strategic use of decentralized institutions: Exploring certification with the ISO14001 management standard. *Academy of Management Journal*, 48: 1091–1106.

King, B.G. (2008). A political mediation model of corporate response to social movement activism. *Administrative Science Quarterly*, 53: 395–421.

King, B.G., and McDonnell, M.H. (2012). *Good firms, good targets: The relationship between corporate social responsibility, reputation, and activist targeting*, http://papers.ssrn.com/sol3/papers.cfm?abstract_id=2079227[Accessed 5 June 2014].

Kitazawa, S., and Sarkis, J. (2000). The relationship between ISO 14001 and continuous source reduction programs. *International Journal of Operations & Production Management*, 20(2): 225–248.

Kitzmueller, M., and Shimshack, J. (2012). Economic perspectives on corporate social responsibility. *Journal of Economic Literature*, 50(1): 51–84.

Klein, M., and Harford, T. (2004). Corporate responsibility: When will voluntary reputation building improve standards? In *Public policy journal*. Washington, DC: World Bank.

Kleinknecht, A., Oostedorp, R.M., Pradhan, M.P., and Naastepad, C.W.M. (2006). Flexible labour, firm performance and the Dutch job creation miracle. *International Review of Applied Economics*, 20(2): 171–187.

Kline, P. (2000). *The handbook of psychological testing* (2nd ed.). London: Routledge.

Koehler, D.A. (2007). The effectiveness of voluntary environmental programs – a policy at a crossroads? *Policy Studies Journal*, 35: 689–722.

Korhonen, J. (2003). Should we measure corporate social responsibility? *Corporate Social Responsibility and Environmental Management*, 10(1): 25–39.

Kuckertz, A., and Wagner, M. (2010). The influence of sustainability orientation on entrepreneurial intentions – investigating the role of business experience. *Journal of Business Venturing*, 25: 525–539.

Kurucz, E., Colbert, B., and Wheeler, D. (2008). The business case for corporate social responsibility. In Crane, A., McWilliams, A., Matten, D., Moon, J., and Siegel, D. (Eds.), *The Oxford handbook of corporate social responsibility* (pp. 83–112). Oxford: Oxford University Press.

Kusyk, S.M., and Lozano, J.M. (2007). Corporate social performance in small and medium-sized enterprises. SME social performance: A four-cell typology of key drivers and barriers on social issues and their implications for stakeholder theory. *Corporate Governance*, 7: 502–515.

Kwan, P., and Walker, A. (2004). Validating the competing values model as a representation of organizational culture through inter-institutional comparisons. *International Journal of Organizational Analysis*, 12(1): 21–37.

Lacey, J., and Lamont, J. (2014). Using social contract to inform social licence to operate: An application in the Australian coal seam gas industry. *Journal of Cleaner Production*, 84: 831–839.

Laforet, S. (2008). Size, strategic and market orientation effects on innovation. *Journal of Business Research*, 61: 753–764.

Lähdesmäki, M., Siltaoja, M., and Spence, L. (2019). Stakeholder salience in the local small business context: A social proximity perspective. *Journal of Business Ethics*, 158(2): 373–385.
Lamb, N.H., and Butler, F.C. (2018). The influence of family firms and institutional owners on corporate social responsibility performance. *Business & Society*, 57(7): 1374–1406.
Lambooy, T. (2011). Corporate social responsibility: Sustainable water use. *Journal of Cleaner Production*, 19: 852–866.
Laudal, T. (2011). Drivers and barriers of CSP and the size and internationalization of firms. *Social Responsibility Journal*, 7: 234–256.
Laufs, K., Bembom, M., and Schwens, C. (2016). CEO characteristics and SME foreign market entry mode choice: The moderating effect of firm's geographic experience and host-country political risk. *International Marketing Review*, 33(2): 246–275.
Laverty, K.J. (1996). Economic 'short-termism': The debate, the unresolved issues, and the implications for management practice and research. *Academy of Management Review*, 21: 825–860.
Laverty, K.J. (2004). Managerial myopia or systemic short-termism? The importance of managerial systems in valuing the long term. *Management Decision*, 42(7–8): 949–962.
Lavine, M. (2014). Paradoxical leadership and the competing values framework. *Journal of Applied Behavioral Science*, 50(2): 189–205.
Le Breton-Miller, I., and Miller, D. (2006). Why do some family businesses out-compete? Governance, long-term orientations, and sustainable capability. *Entrepreneurship Theory and Practice*, 30(6): 731–746.
Le Breton-Miller, I., and Miller, D. (2016). Family firms and practices of sustainability: A contingency view. *Journal of Family Business Strategy*, 7: 26–33.
Lee, J., Gemba, K., and Kodama, F. (2006). Analyzing the innovation process for environmental performance improvement. *Technological Forecasting and Social Change*, 73(3): 290–301.
Lee, L. (1983). Generalized econometric models with selectivity. *Econometrica*, 51: 507–513.
Leonidou, C.N., and Skarmeas, D. (2017). Gray shades of green: Causes and consequences of green skepticism. *Journal of Business Ethics*, 144: 401–415.
Lepoutre, J., and Heene, H. (2006). Investigating the impact of firm's size on small business social responsibility: A critical review. *Journal of Business Ethics*, 67: 257–273.
Leroy, H., Manigart, S., Meuleman, M., and Collewaert, V. (2013). Understanding the continuation of firm activities when entrepreneur exit their firms using theory of planned behavior. *Journal of Small Business Management*, 53(2): 400–415.
Lewellyn, K.B., and Bao, S.R. (2014). A cross-national investigation of IPO activity: The role of formal institutions and national culture. *International Business Review*, 23(6): 1167–1178.
Li, Y., and Zahra, S.A. (2012). Formal institutions, culture, and venture capital activity: A cross-country analysis. *Journal of Business Venturing*, 27(1): 95–111.
Lin, C.Y., and Ho, Y.H. (2011). Determinants of green practice adoption for logistics companies in China. *Journal of Business Ethics*, 98(1): 67–83.
Lin, H., Zeng, S., Wang, L., Zou, H., and Ma, H. (2016). How does environmental irresponsibility impair corporate reputation? A multi-method investigation. *Corporate Social Responsibility and Environmental Management*, 23: 413–423.
Lindell, M.K., and Whitney, D.J. (2001). Accounting for common method variance in crosssectional research designs. *Journal of Applied Psychology*, 86(1): 114–121.
Lindenberg, S. (2001). Intrinsic motivation in a new light. *Kyklos*, 54: 317–342.

Lindenberg, S. (2003). The cognitive side of governance. *Research in the Sociology of Organizations*, 20: 47–76.

Linder, S., and Foss, N.J. (2018). Microfoundations of organizational goals: A review and new directions for future research. *International Journal of Management Reviews*, 20: S39–S62.

Linnenluecke, M.K., and Griffiths, A. (2010). Corporate sustainability and organizational culture. *Journal of World Business*, 45: 357–366.

Linnenluecke, M.K., Russell, S.V., and Griffiths, A. (2009). Subcultures and sustainability practices: The impact on understanding corporate sustainability. *Business Strategy and the Environment*, 18: 432–452.

Lioui, A., and Sharma, Z. (2012). Environmental corporate social responsibility and financial performance: Disentangling direct and indirect effects. *Ecological Economics*, 78: 100–111.

Little, T.D., Card, N.A., Bovaird, J.A., Preacher, K.J., and Crandall, C.S. (2007). *Structural equation modeling of mediation and moderation with contextual factors*, http://quantpsy.org/pubs/little_card_bovaird_preacher_crandall_2007. pdf.

Locke, R.M., Qin, F., and Brausse, A. (2006). *Does monitoring improve labor standards? Lessons from Nike.* MIT Sloan Research Paper No. 4612-06. Cambridge: MIT Press.

Logsdon, J.M., and Wood, D.J. (2002). Reputation as an emerging construct in the business and society field: An introduction. *Business & Society*, 41: 365–370.

Lopez-Gamero, M., Molina-Azorin, J., and Claver-Cortes, E. (2009). The whole relationship between environmental variables and firm performance: Competitive advantage and firm resources as mediator variables, *Journal of Environmental Management*, 90(10): 1–12.

López-González, E., Martínez-Ferrero, J., and García-Meca, E. (2019). Corporate social responsibility in family firms: A contingency approach. *Journal of Cleaner Production*, 211: 1044–1064.

Lougee, B.A., and Wallace, J.S. (2008). The corporate social responsibility (CSR) trend. *Journal of Applied Corporate Finance*, 20: 96–108.

Luo, X., and Du, S. (2015). Exploring the relationship between corporate social responsibility and firm innovation. *Marketing Letters*, 26(4): 703–714.

Lurie, L. (2013). Can unions promote employability? Senior workers in Israel's collective agreements. *Industrial Law Journal*, 42: 249–280.

Lurie, L. (2015). *Do unions promote gender equality?* http://scholarship.law.duke.edu/cgi/viewcontent.cgi?article=1290&context=djglp [Accessed November 2016].

Luthar, H.K., DiBattista, R.A., and Gautschi, T. (1997). Perception of what the ethical climate is and what it should be: The role of gender, academic status, and ethical education. *Journal of Business Ethics*, 16: 205–217.

Lynch-Wood, G., and Williamson, D. (2007). The social license as a form of regulation for small and medium enterprises. *Journal of Law and Society*, 34: 321–341.

Lynch-Wood, G., and Williamson, D. (2014). Understanding SME responses to environmental regulation. *Journal of Environmental Planning and Management*, 57(8): 1220–1239.

MacGregor, S.P., and Fontrodana, J. (2008). *Exploring fit between CSR and innovation.* IESE/CBS Working Paper WP No. 759. Barcelona: IESE.

Madrid-Guijarro, A., Garcia, D., and Auken, H.V. (2009). Barriers to innovation among Spanish manufacturing SMEs. *Journal of Small Business Management*, 47(4): 465–488.

Mallin, C., Michelon, G., and Raggi, D. (2013). Monitoring intensity and stakeholders' orientation: How does governance affect social and environmental disclosure? *Journal of Business Ethics*, 114: 29–43.

Mandl, I., and Dorr, A. (2007). *CSR and competitiveness, European SMEs' good practice.* Consolidated European Report. KMU Forschung Austria, Austrian Institute for SME Research, www.bsocial.gva.es/documents/610767/716777/CSR_competitiveness_european.pdf/64db87c9-3062-4e76-bcbf-bc1bcace91b3 [Accessed 17 May 2015].

Mannix, E.A., and Loewenstein, G.F. (1994). The effects of interfirm mobility and individual versus group decision making on managerial time horizons. *Organizational Behavior and Human Decision Processes*, 59: 371–390.

Maon, F., Swaen, V., and Lindgreen, A. (2009). *Mainstreaming the corporate social responsibility agenda: A change model grounded in theory and practice.* IAG-Louvain School of Management Working Paper. London: Springer.

Marens, R. (2008). Recovering the past: Reviving the legacy of the early scholars of corporate social responsibility. *Journal of Management History*, 14(1): 55–72.

Marginson, D., and McAulay, L. (2008). Exploring the debate on short-termism: A theoretical and empirical analysis. *Strategic Management Journal*, 29: 273–292.

Margolis, J., Elfenbein, H., and Walsh, J. (2007). Does it pay to be good? A meta-analysis and redirection of research on the relationship between corporate social and financial performance. *Ann Arbor*, 1001: 48109–41234.

Marin, L., Martín, P.J., and Rubio, A. (2017). Doing good and different! The mediation effect of innovation and investment on the influence of CSR on competitiveness. *Corporate Social Responsibility and Environmental Management*, 24: 159–171.

Marino, S., Penninx, R., and Roosblad, J. (2015). Trade unions, immigration and immigrants in Europe revisited: Unions' attitudes and actions under new conditions. *Comparative Migration Studies*, 3(1), https://doi.org/10.1007/s40878-015-0003-x.

Marques, P., Presas, P., and Simon, A. (2014). The heterogeneity of family firms in CSR engagement: The role of values. *Family Business Review*, 27(3): 206–227.

Marquis, C., and Battilana, J. (2009). Acting globally but thinking locally? The enduring influence of local communities on organizations. *Research in Organizational Behavior*, 29: 283–302.

Marquis, C., Glynn, M.A., and Davis, G.F. (2007). Community isomorphism and corporate social action. *Academy of Management Review*, 32: 925–945.

Marquis, C., and Lee, M. (2013). Who is governing whom? Executives, governance, and the structure of generosity in large U.S. firms. *Strategic Management Journal*, 34(4): 483–497.

Marsiglio, S., and Tolotti, M. (2020). Motivation crowding-out and green-paradox-like outcomes. *Journal of Public Economic Theory*, https://doi.org/10.1111/jpet.12444.

Martín-de Castro, G., Amores-Salvadó, J., Navas-López, J.E., and Balarezo-Nuñez, R.M. (2017). Exploring the nature, antecedents and consequences of symbolic corporate environmental certification. *Journal of Cleaner Production*, 164: 664–675.

Martínez-Ferrero, J., Rodríguez-Ariza, L., and García-Sánchez, I.M. (2016). Corporate social responsibility as an entrenchment strategy, with a focus on the implications of family ownership. *Journal of Cleaner Production*, 135(1): 760–770.

Mason, E.S., and Mudrack, P.E. (1996). Gender and ethical orientation: A test of gender and occupational socialization theories. *Journal of Business Ethics*, 15(6): 599–604.

Masurel, E. (2007). Why SMEs invest in environmental measures: Sustainability evidence from small and medium-sized printing firms. *Business Strategy and the Environment*, 16: 190–201.

Mathiyazhagan, K., Govindan, K., NoorulHaq, A., and Geng, Y. (2013). An ISM approach for the barrier analysis in implementing green supply chain management. *Journal of Cleaner Production*, 47: 283–297.

Matten, D., and Moon, J. (2008). "Implicit" and "explicit" CSR: A conceptual framework for a comparative understanding of corporate social responsibility. *Academy of Management Review*, 33(2): 404–424.

Maxwell, J.W., Lyon, T.P., and Hackett, S.C. (2000). Self-regulation and social welfare: The political economy of corporate environmentalism. *Journal of Law & Economics*, 43: 583–617.

Mazereeuw, C. (2010). *Doing business for heaven's sake*. Dissertation. Tilburg: Tilburg University.

Mazzi, A., Toniolo, S., Mason, M., Aguiari, F., and Scipioni, A. (2016). What are the benefits and difficulties in adopting an environmental management system? The opinion of Italian organizations. *Journal of Cleaner Production*, 139: 873–885.

McBride, A. (2001). *Gender democracy in trade unions*. Aldershot: Ashgate.

McDonnell, M.H., and King, B. (2013). Keeping up appearances reputational threat and impression management after social movement boycotts. *Administrative Science Quarterly*, 58(3): 387–419.

McDonnell, M.H., King, B., and Soule, S. (2015). A dynamic process model of contentious politics: Activist targeting and corporate receptivity to social challenges. *American Sociological Review*, 80: 654–678.

McGuire, J., Dow, S., and Ibrahim, B. (2012). All in the family? Social performance and corporate governance in the family firm, *Journal of Business Research*, 65: 1643–1650.

McWilliams, A., and Siegel, D. (2000). Corporate social responsibility and financial performance: Correlation or misspecification? *Strategic Management Journal*, 21: 603–609.

Meijer, S. (2007). A survey on economic theories and field evidence on pro-social behavior. In Frey, B.S., and Stutzer, A. (Eds.), *Economics and psychology: A promising new cross-disciplinary field* (pp. 51–87). Cambridge: MIT Press.

Melo, T., and Garrido-Morgado, A. (2012). Corporate reputation: A combination of social responsibility and industry. *Corporate Social Responsibility and Environmental Management*, 19: 11–31.

Michailnova, S., and Hutchings, K. (2006). National cultural influences on knowledge. *Journal of Management Studies*, 43: 384–406.

Midtun, A. (2007). Corporate responsibility from a resource and knowledge perspective. Towards a dynamic reinterpretation of C(S)R: Are corporate responsibility and innovation compatible or contradictory. *Corporate Governance*, 7(4): 401–413.

Miller, D., and Le Breton-Miller, I. (2014). Deconstructing socioemotional wealth. *Entrepreneurship Theory and Practice*, 38: 713–720.

Miller, D., Le Breton-Miller, I., and Scholnick, B. (2008). Stewardship vs. stagnation: An empirical comparison of small family and non-family businesses. *Journal of Management Studies*, 45(1): 51–78.

Miller, T., and del Carmen Triana, M. (2009). Demographic diversity in the boardroom: Mediators of the board diversity – firm performance relationship. *Journal of Management Studies*, 46(5): 755–789.

Miska, C., Szőcs, I., and Schiffinger, M. (2018). Culture's effects on corporate sustainability practices: A multi-domain and multi-level view. *Journal of World Business*, 53(2): 263–279.

Mitchell, C.G., and Hill, T. (2009). Corporate social and environmental reporting and the impact of internal environmental policy in South Africa. *Corporate Social Responsibility and Environmental Management*, 16(1): 48–60.

Mittra, B., Lucas, N., and Fells, I. (1995). European energy. Balancing markets and policy. *Energy Policy*, 23(8): 689–701.

Moon, J., Brunn, C., Hardy, P., Slager, R., and Steen-Knudsen, J. (2012). *Analysis of the national EU policies supporting corporate social responsibility and impact*. IMPACT Working Paper No. 2, www.csr-impact.eu [Accessed 30 June 2014].

Mosey, S., Clare, J., and Woodcock, D. (2002). Innovation decision making in British manufacturing SMEs. *Integrated Manufacturing Systems*, 13(3): 176–183.

Muller, A., and Kolk, A. (2010). Extrinsic and intrinsic drivers of corporate social performance: Evidence from foreign and domestic firms in Mexico. *Journal of Management Studies*, 47: 1–26.

Murillo, D., and Lozano, J. (2006). SMEs and CSR: An approach to CSR in their own words. *Journal of Business Ethics*, 67(3): 227–240.

Naranjo-Valencia, J.C., Jiménez-Jiménez, D., and Sanz-Valle, R. (2011). Innovation or imitation? The role of organizational culture. *Management Decision*, 49(1): 55–72.

Nash, J., and Ehrenfeld, J.R. (2001). Factors that shape EMS outcomes in firms. In Coglianese, C., and Nash, J. (Eds.), *Regulating from the inside: Can environmental management systems achieve policy goals?* (pp. 61–81). Washington, DC: Resources for the Future.

Neubaum, D.O., and Zahra, S.A. (2006). Institutional ownership and corporate social performance: The moderating effects of investment horizon, activism, and coordination. *Journal of Management*, 32: 108–131.

Nguyen, Q.A., and Hens, L. (2015). Environmental performance of the cement industry in Vietnam: The influence of ISO14001 certification. *Journal of Cleaner Production*, 96: 362–378.

Niehm, L.S., Swinney, J., and Miller, N.J. (2008). Community social responsibility and its consequences for family business performance. *Journal of Small Business Management*, 46: 331–350.

North, D.C. (1991). Institutions. *Journal of Economic Perspectives*, 5(1): 97–112.

Nyström, K. (2008). The institutions of economic freedom and entrepreneurship: Evidence from panel data. *Public Choice*, 136(3–4): 269–282.

O'Boyle, E.H., Jr., Rutherford, M.W., and Pollack, J.M. (2010). Examining the relation between ethical focus and financial performance in family firms: An exploratory study. *Family Business Review*, 20: 1–17.

Ogawa, R.T., and Scribner, S.P. (2002). Leadership: Spanning the technical and institutional dimensions of organizations. *Journal of Educational Administration*, 40(6): 576–588.

Okhmatovskiy, I., and David, R.J. (2012). Setting your own standards: Internal corporate governance codes as a response to institutional pressure. *Organization Science*, 23(1): 155–176.

Oliveira, J.A., Oliveira, O.J., Ometto, A.R., Ferraudo, A.S., and Salgado, M.H. (2016). Environmental management system ISO14001 factors for promoting the adoption of cleaner production practices. *Journal of Cleaner Production*, 133: 1384–1394.

Oliveira, O.J., Serra, J.R., and Salgado, M.H. (2010). Does ISO14001 work in Brazil? *Journal of Cleaner Production*, 18: 1797–1806.

Oliver, C. (1991). Strategic responses to institutional processes. *Academy of Management Review*, 16: 145–179.

O'Mahoney, J. (2012). *Why did you do that? A methodological exploration of motive attribution*, http://ssrn.com/abstract=2108912.

Orlitzky, M. (2001). Does firm size confound the relationship between corporate social performance and firm financial performance? *Journal of Business Ethics*, 33: 167–180.

Orlitzky, M. (2008). Corporate social performance and financial performance. A research synthesis. In Crane, A., McWilliams, A., Matten, D., Moon, J., and Siegel, D. (Eds.), *The Oxford handbook of corporate social performance* (pp. 113–134). New York: Oxford University Press.

Orlitzky, M., Schmidt, F., and Rynes, S. (2003). Corporate social and financial performance: A meta-analysis. *Organization Studies*, 24(3): 403–441.

Ostman, A. (1998). External control may destroy the commons. *Rationality and Society*, 10(1): 103–122.

Padgett, R.C., and Galan, J.I. (2009). The effect of R&D intensity on corporate social responsibility. *Journal of Business Ethics*, 93: 407–418.

Palmer, J., and Van der Vorst, R. (1997). New recipe green reporting for small and medium-size enterprises. *Eco-Management and Auditing*, 4(2): 57–67.

Paolillo, J.G.P., and Vitell, S.J. (2002). An empirical investigation of the influence of selected personal, organizational and moral intensity factors on ethical decision making. *Journal of Business Ethics*, 35: 65–75.

Parisi, C., and Maraghini, P. (2010). Operationalising sustainability: How small and medium sized enterprises translate social and environmental issues into practice. In Taticchi, P. (Ed.), *Business performance measurement and management* (pp. 131–147). Berlin: Springer.

Park, H., Russell, C., and Lee, J. (2007). National culture and environmental sustainability: A cross-national analysis. *Journal of Economics and Finance*, 31(1): 104–121.

Patzelt, H., and Shepherd, D.A. (2011). Recognizing opportunities for sustainable development. *Entrepreneurship Theory and Practice*, 35(4): 631–652.

Paulrai, A. (2009). Environmental motivations: A classification scheme and its impact on environmental strategies and practices. *Business Strategy and the Environment*, 18: 453–468.

Pellerano, J.A., Price, M.K., Puller, S.L., and Sánchez, G.E. (2017). Do extrinsic incentives undermine social norms? Evidence from a field experiment in energy conservation. *Environmental and Resource Economics*, 67(3): 413–428.

Peng, Y.S., Dashdeleg, A.U., and Chih, H.L. (2014). National culture and firm's CSR engagement: A cross-nation Study. *Journal of Marketing and Management*, 5(1): 38–49.

Penninx, R., and Roosblad, J. (Eds.). (2000). *Trade unions, immigration, and immigrants in Europe, 1960–1993: A comparative study of the attitudes and actions of trade unions in seven West European countries*. New York and Oxford: Berghahn Books.

Pepper, A., and Gore, J. (2015). Behavioral agency theory: New foundations for theorizing about executive compensation. *Journal of Management*, 41(4): 1045–1068.

Perez Sanchez, D., Barton, J.R., and Bower, D. (2003). Implementing environmental management in SMEs. *Corporate Social Responsibility and Environmental Management*, 10(2): 67–77.

Perrini, F. (2006). SMEs and CSR theory: Evidence and Implications from an Italian perspective. *Journal of Business Ethics*, 67(3): 305–316.

Perrini, F., and Tencati, A. (2006). Sustainability and stakeholder management: The need for new corporate performance evaluation and reporting systems. *Business Strategy and the Environment*, 15(5): 296–308.

Perz, S.G., Brilhante, S., Brown, I.F., Michaelsen, A.C., Mendoza, E., Passos, V., Pinedo, R., Reyes, J.F., Rojas, D., and Selaya, G. (2010). Crossing boundaries for environmental science and management: Combining interdisciplinary, interorganizational and international collaboration. *Environmental Conservation*, 37: 419–431.

Peterson, M.F., Arregle, J., and Martin, X. (2012). Multilevel models in international business research. *Journal of International Business Studies*, 43: 451–457.

Peterson, M.F., and Barreto, T.S. (2018). Interpreting societal culture value dimensions. *Journal of International Business Studies*, 49(9): 1190–1207.

Pett, M.A., Lackey, N.R., and Sullivan, J.J. (2003). *Making sense of factor analysis: The use of factor analysis for instrument development in health care research*. Thousand Oaks, CA, London and New Delhi: Sage.

Petts, J., Herd, A., Gerrard, S., and Horne, C. (1999). The climate and culture of environmental compliance within SMEs. *Business Strategy and the Environment*, 8: 14–30.

Pirsch, J., Gupta, S., and Landreth Grau, S. (2006). A framework for understanding corporate social responsibility programs as a continuum: An exploratory study. *Journal of Business Ethics*, 70: 125–140.

Podsakoff, P.M., Mackenzie, S.B., Lee, J.Y., and Podsakoff, N.P. (2003). Common method biases in behavioral research: A critical review of the literature and recommended remedies. *Journal of Applied Psychology*, 88: 879–903.

Poksinska, B., Dahlgaard, J., and Eklund, J. (2003). Implementing ISO14001 in Sweden: Motives, benefits and comparison with ISO 9000. *International Journal of Quality and Reliability Management*, 20: 585–606.

Porter, L.W., and Lawler, E.E. (1968). *Managerial attitudes and performance*. Homewood, IL: Richard D. Irwin, Inc.

Porter, M., and Kramer, M. (2006). Strategy and society: The link between competitive advantage and corporate social responsibility. *Harvard Business Review*, 84(12): 78–92.

Porter, M., and Kramer, M. (2011). Creating shared value. *Harvard Business Review*, 89(1–2): 62–77.

Post, C., Rahman, N., and McQuillen, C. (2015). From board composition to corporate environmental performance through sustainability-themed alliances. *Journal of Business Ethics*, 130: 423–435.

Post, C., Rahman, N., and Rubow, E. (2011). Green governance: Boards of directors' composition and environmental corporate social responsibility. *Business & Society*, 50: 189–223.

Pouliakas, K., and Theodossiou, I. (2013). The economics of health and safety at work: An interdisciplinary review of the theory and policy. *Journal of Economic Surveys*, 27(1): 167–208.

Preacher, K.J., and Hayes, A.F. (2008). Asymptotic and resampling strategies for assessing and comparing indirect effects in multiple mediator models. *Behavior Research Methods*, 40: 879–891.

Preacher, K.J., Rucker, D.D., and Hayes, A.F. (2007). Addressing moderated mediation hypotheses: Theory, methods, and prescriptions. *Multivariate behavioral research*, 42(1): 185–227.

Prieto-Sandoval, V., Jaca, C., Santos, J., Baumgartner, R.J., and Ormazabal, M. (2019). Key strategies, resources, and capabilities for implementing circular economy in industrial small and medium enterprises. *Corporate Social Responsibility and Environmental Management*, 26(6): 1473–1483.

Puhani, P. (2000). The Heckman correction for sample selection and its critique. *Journal of Economic Surveys*, 14(1): 53–68.

Quinn, R.E., and Spreitzer, G.M. (1991). The psychometrics of the competing values culture instrument and an analysis of the impact of organizational culture on quality of life. *Research in Organizational Change and Development*, 5: 115–142.

Rabin, M. (1998). Psychology and economics. *Journal of Economic Literature*, 36: 11–46.

Rao, P., Singh, A.K., O'Castillo, O., Intal, P.S., Jr., and Sajid, A. (2009). A metric for corporate environmental indicators for small and medium enterprises in the Philippines. *Business Strategy and the Environment*, 18(1): 14–31.

Rao, K., and Tilt, C. (2016). Board composition and corporate social responsibility: The role of diversity, gender, strategy and decision making. *Journal of Business Ethics*, 138: 327–347.

Rappaport, A. (2005). The economics of short-term performance obsession. *Financial Analyst Journal*, 61: 65–79.

RARE. (2006). *Rhetoci and realities: Analysing corporate social responsibility in Europe*, www.rare-eu.net.

Redding, G. (2008). Separating culture from institutions: The use of semantic spaces as a conceptual domain and the case of China. *Management and Organization Review*, 4(2): 257–289.

Rehbein, K., Logsdon, J.M., and Van Buren, III, H.J. (2013). Corporate responses to shareholder activists: Considering the dialogue alternative. *Journal of Business Ethics*, 112: 137–154.

Reinhardt, F. (1999). Market failure and the environmental policies of firms: Economic rationales for "beyond compliance" behavior. *Journal of Industrial Ecology*, 3(1): 9–21.

Resh, W.G., Marvel, J.D., and Wen, B. (2019). Implicit and explicit motivation crowding in prosocial work. *Public Performance & Management Review*, 42: 889–919.

Rest, J., Narvaez, D., Bebeau, M.J., and Thoma, S.J. (1999). *Postconventional moral thinking: A neo-Kohlbergian approach*. Mahwah, NJ: Lawrence Erlbaum Associates, Inc.

Reuber, A.R., and Fischer, E. (2010). Organizations behaving badly: When are discreditable actions likely to damage organizational reputation? *Journal of Business Ethics*, 93(1): 39–50.

Revell, A., and Blackburn, R. (2007). The business case for sustainability? An examination of small firms in the UK's construction and restaurant sectors. *Business Strategy and the Environment*, 16(6): 404–420.

Revell, A., Stokes, D., and Chen, H. (2010). Small businesses and the environment: Turning over a new leaf? *Business Strategy and the Environment*, 19(5): 273–288.

Rhee, M., and Haunschild, P.R. (2006). The liability of good reputation: A study of product recalls in the US automobile industry. *Organization Science*, 17: 101–117.

Ribar, D.C., and Wilhelm, M.O. (2002). Altruistic and joy-of-giving motivations in charitable behavior. *Journal of Political Economy*, 110: 425–457.

Ringov, D., and Zollo, M. (2007). The impact of national culture on corporate social performance. *Corporate Governance*, 7(4): 476–485.

Rivera, J., Oetzel, J., deLeon, P., and Starik, M. (2009). Business responses to environmental and social protection policies: Toward a framework for analysis. *Policy Science*, 42: 3–32.

Roberts, P.W., and Dowling, G.R. (2002). Corporate reputation and sustained superior financial performance. *Strategic Management Journal*, 23(12): 1077–1093.

Roberts, S. (2003). Supply chain specific? Understanding the patchy success of ethical sourcing initiatives. *Journal of Business Ethics*, 44(2): 159–170.

Rode, J., Gómez-Baggethun, E., and Krause, T. (2015). Motivation crowding by economic incentives in conservation policy: A review of the empirical evidence. *Ecological Economics*, 117: 270–282.

Rogelberg, G., and Stanton, J.M. (2007). Understanding and dealing with organizational survey nonresponse. *Organizational Research Methods*, 10(2): 195–209.

Ross, W.D. (1930). *The right and the good*. Oxford: Oxford University Press.

Russo, A., and Perrini, F. (2010). Investigating stakeholder theory and social capital: CSR in large firms and SMEs. *Journal of Business Ethics*, 91(2): 207–221.

Russo, A., and Tencati, A. (2009). Formal vs. informal CSR strategies: Evidence from Italian micro, small, medium-sized, and large firms. *Journal of Business Ethics*, 85(2): 339–353.

Samuelson, P.A. (1980). *Economics*. New York: McGraw-Hill.

Sánchez-Medina, P.S., and Díaz-Pichardo, R. (2017). Environmental pressure and quality practices in artisanal family businesses: The mediator role of environmental values. *Journal of Cleaner Production*, 143: 145–158.

Schaper, M. (2002). Small firms and environmental management. Predictors of green purchasing in Western Australian pharmacies. *International Small Business Journal*, 20(3): 235–251.

Schneider, B., Ehrhart, M.G., and Macey, W.H. (2012). Organizational climate and culture. *Annual Review of Psychology*, 64: 361–388.

Scholtens, B. (2008). A note on the interaction between corporate social responsibility and financial performance. *Ecological Economics*, 68: 45–55.

Schons, L., and Steinmeier, M. (2016). Walk the talk? How symbolic and substantive CSR actions affect firm performance depending on stakeholder proximity. *Corporate Social Responsibility and Environmental Management*, 23: 358–372.

Schouten, E.M.J., and Remmé, J. (2006). Making sense of corporate social responsibility in international business: Experiences from Shell. *Business Ethics: A European Review*, 15(4): 365–379.

Schultz, M. (2012). Relationships between culture and institutions: New interdependencies in a global world? *Journal of Management Inquiry*, 21(1): 102–106.

Schumpeter, J.A. (1976). *Capitalism, socialism and democracy* (5th ed.). London and Boston: George Allen & Unwin.

Schwartz, D., Milfont, T.L., and Hilton, D. (2019). The interplay between intrinsic motivation, financial incentives and nudges in sustainable consumption. In Gangl, K., and Kirchler, E. (Eds.), *A research agenda for economic psychology* (pp. 87–103). Cheltenham: Edward Elgar.

Schwarz, B., and Tilling, K. (2009). 'ISO-lating' corporate social responsibility in the organizational context: A dissenting interpretation of ISO 26000. *Corporate Social Responsibility and Environmental Management*, 16: 289–299.

Schylander, E., and Martinuzzi, A. (2007). ISO14001 – experiences, effects and future challenges: A national study in Austria. *Business Strategy and the Environment*, 16: 133–147.

Scopelliti, M., Molinario, E., Bonaiuto, F., Bonnes, M., Cicero, L., and De Dominicis, S. (2018). What makes you a 'hero' for nature? Socio-psychological profiling of leaders committed to nature and biodiversity protection across seven EU countries. *Journal of Environmental Planning and Management*, 61(5–6): 970–993.

Segelod, E. (2000). A comparison of managers' perceptions of short-termism in Sweden and the U.S. *International Journal of Production Economics*, 63: 243–254.

Seiffert, M.E.B. (2008). Environmental impact evaluation using a cooperative model for implementing EMS (ISO14001) in small and medium-sized enterprises. *Journal of Cleaner Production*, 16(14): 1447–1461.

Sekaran, U. (2003). *Research methods for business: A skill building approach*. New York: John Wiley & Sons.

Setó-Pamies, D. (2015). The relationship between women directors and corporate social responsibility. *Corporate Social Responsibility and Environmental Management*, 22(6): 334–345.

Shah, K.U. (2011). Organizational legitimacy and the strategic bridging ability of green alliances. *Business Strategy and the Environment*, 20: 498–511.

Shapiro, C. (1989). The theory of business strategy. *The Rand Journal of Economics*, 20(1): 125–137.

Sharma, P., and Sharma, S. (2011). Drivers of proactive environmental strategy in family firms. *Business Ethics Quarterly*, 21: 309–334.

Sharma, S. (2000). Managerial interpretations and organizational context as predictors of corporate choice of environmental strategy. *Academy of Management Journal*, 43(4): 681–697.

Shi, H., Peng, S.Z., and Liu, Y. (2008). Barriers to the implementation of cleaner production in Chinese SMEs: Government, industry and expert stakeholders' perspectives. *Journal of Cleaner Production*, 16: 842–852.

Shrivastava, P. (1995). Environmental technologies and competitive advantage. *Strategic Management Journal*, 16(S1): 183–200.

Shrout, P.E., and Bolger, N. (2002). Mediation in experimental and nonexperimental studies: New procedures and recommendations. *Psychological Methods*, 7: 422–445.

Sims, R.L., and Keon, T.L. (1997). Ethical work climate as a factor in the development of person-organization fit. *Journal of Business Ethics*, 16: 1095–1105.

Singh, M., Brueckner, M., and Padhy, P.K. (2015). Environmental management system ISO14001: Effective waste minimisation in small and medium enterprises in India. *Journal of Cleaner Production*, 102: 285–301.

Škerlavaj, M., Štemberger, M.I., and Dimovski, V. (2007). Organizational learning culture – the missing link between business process change and organizational performance. *International Journal of Production Economics*, 106(2): 346–367.

Slawinski, N., and Bansal, P. (2009). *Short on time: The role of time in business sustainability*. Paper presented at AOM Annual Conference, Chicago.

Sliwka, D. (2007). Trust as a signal of a social norm and the hidden costs of incentive schemes. *American Economic Review*, 97(3): 999–1012.

Solomon, R.C. (1992). Corporate roles, personal virtues: An Aristotelian approach to business ethics. *Business Ethics Quarterly*, 2: 317–339.

Spence, J., and Helmreich, R. (1980). Masculine instrumentality and feminine expressiveness: Their relationships with sex role attitudes and behaviors. *Psychology of Women Quarterly*, 5(2): 147–163.

Spence, L.J. (1999). Does size matter? The state of the art in small business ethics. *Business Ethics: A European Review*, 8: 163–167.

Spence, L.J. (2016). Small business social responsibility: Expanding core CSR theory. *Business & Society*, 55: 23–55.

Spence, L.J., Schmidpeter, R., and Habisch, A. (2003). Assessing social capital: Small and medium sized enterprises in Germany and the UK. *Journal of Business Ethics*, 47(1): 17–29.

Steger, U. (2000). Environmental management systems: Empirical evidence and further perspectives. *European Management Journal*, 18(1): 23–37.

Steinhorst, J., and Klöckner, C.A. (2018). Effects of monetary versus environmental information framing: Implications for long-term pro-environmental behavior and intrinsic motivation. *Environment and Behavior*, 50: 997–1031.

Stewart, H., and Gapp, R. (2014). Achieving effective sustainable management: A small-medium enterprise case study. *Corporate Social Responsibility and Environmental Management*, 21(1): 52–64.

Stoian, C., and Gilman, M. (2017). Corporate social responsibility that "pays": A strategic approach to CSR for SMEs. *Journal of Small Business Management*, 55(1): 5–31.

Studer, S., Welford, R., and Hills, P. (2006). Engaging Hong Kong businesses in environmental change: Drivers and barriers. *Business Strategy and the Environment*, 15: 416–431.

Suchman, M.C. (1995). Managing legitimacy: Strategic and institutional approaches. *Academy of Management Review*, 20: 571–610.

Surroca, J., Tribo, J., and Waddock, S. (2010). Corporate responsibility and financial performance: The role of intangible resources. *Strategic Management Journal*, 31(5): 463–490.

Swanson, D. (1999). Toward an integrative theory of business and society: A research strategy for corporate social performance. *Academy of Management Review*, 24(3): 506–521.

Tabernero, C., and Hernández, B. (2011). Self-efficacy and intrinsic motivation guiding environmental behavior. *Environment and Behavior*, 43: 658–675.

Tang, A.K.Y., Lai, K.H., and Cheng, T.C.E. (2012). Environmental governance of enterprises and their economic upshot through corporate reputation and customer satisfaction. *Business Strategy and the Environment*, 21(6): 401–411.

Tang, J. (2006). Competition and innovation behavior. *Research Policy*, 35(1): 68–82.

Telle, K. (2006). "It pays to be green" – a premature conclusion? *Environmental and Resource Economics*, 35(3): 195–220.

Testa, F., Rizzi, F., Daddi, T., Gusmerotti, N.M., Frey, M., and Iraldo, F. (2014). EMAS and ISO14001: The differences in effectively improving environmental performance. *Journal of Cleaner Production*, 68: 156–173.

Thanetsunthorn, N. (2015). The impact of national culture on corporate social responsibility: Evidence from cross-regional comparison. *Asian Journal of Business Ethics*, 4: 35–56.

Thomas, J.B., and McDaniel, R.R. (1990). Interpreting strategic issues: Effects of strategy and information-processing structure of top management teams. *Academy of Management Journal*, 33(2): 286–306.

Tilley, F. (2000). Small firm environmental ethics: How deep do they go? *Business Ethics: A European Review*, 9(1): 31–41.

Tilley, F. (1999). The gap between the environmental attitudes and the environmental behaviour of small firms. *Business Strategy and the Environment*, 8: 238–248.

Tomarken, A.J., and Waller, N.G. (2005). Structural equation modelling: Strengths, limitations, and misconceptions. *Annual Review of Clinical Psychology*, 1: 31–65.

Torchia, M., Calabro, A., and Huse, M. (2011). Women directors on corporate boards: From tokenism to critical mass. *Journal of Business Ethics*, 102(2): 299–317.

Treviño, L.K., and Nelson, K.A. (1999). *Managing business ethics, straight talk about how to do it right*. New York: Wiley and Sons.

Treviño, L.K., Weaver, G.R., and Reynolds, S.J. (2006). Behavioral ethics in organizations: A review. *Journal of Management*, 32: 952–990.

Trianni, A., Cagno, E., Thollander, P., and Backlund, S. (2013). Barriers to industrial energy efficiency in foundries: A European comparison. *Journal of Cleaner Production*, 40: 161–176.

Tsoy, D., and Yongqiang, G. (2016). A cross-national study of the relationships between cultural determinants, sustainable governance and sustainable development. *International Journal of Management Science and Business Administration*, 2(4): 28–43.

Tudway, R., and Pascal, A.M. (2006). Corporate governance, shareholder value and societal expectations. *Corporate Governance*, 6: 305–316.

Turban, D.B., and Greening, D.W. (1997). Corporate social performance and organizational attractiveness to prospective employees. *Academy of Management Journal*, 40: 658–672.

Udayasankar, K. (2008). Corporate social responsibility and firm size. *Journal of Business Ethics*, 83: 167–175.

Ulrich, P., Lunau, Y., and Weber, T. (1998). Ethikmassnahmen in der Unternehmenspraxis. In Ulrich, P., and Wieland, J. (Eds.), *Unternehmensethik in der praxis: Impulse aus den USA, Deutschland und der Schweiz* (pp. 121–194). Bern: Verlag Paul Haupt.

UNIDO. (2006). *Responsible trade and market access: Opportunities or obstacles for SMEs in developing countries?* Vienna: UNIDO.

Valentine, S.V. (2016). Kalundborg Symbiosis: Fostering progressive innovation in environmental networks. *Journal of Cleaner Production*, 118: 65–77.

Van Beurden, P., and Gössling, T. (2008). The worth of values – a literature review on the relation between corporate social and financial performance, *Journal of Business Ethics*, 82(2): 407–424.

Van de Ven, B.W., and Jeurissen, R.M.J. (2005). Competing responsibility. *Business Ethics Quarterly*, 15: 299–318.

Van Gils, A., Dibrell, C., Neubaum, D.O., and Craig, J.B. (2014). Social issues in the family enterprise. *Family Business Review*, 27(3): 193–205.

Van Hoof, B., and Lyon, T.P. (2013). Cleaner production in small firms taking part in Mexico's sustainable supplier program. *Journal of Cleaner Production*, 41: 270–282.

Velasquez, M.G. (2011). *Business ethics: Concepts and cases.* New York: Pearson.

Vickers, J. (1995). Concepts of competition. *Oxford Economic Papers*, 47: 1–23.

Vogel, D. (2010). The private regulation of global corporate conduct: Achievements and limitations. *Business & Society*, 49: 68–87.

Vollan, B. (2008). Socio-ecological explanations for crowding-out effects from economic field experiments in Southern Africa. *Ecological Economics*, 67: 560–573.

Vries, G. de, Terwel, B.W., Ellemers, N., and Daamen, D.D.L. (2015). Sustainability or profitability? How communicated motives for environmental policy affect public perceptions of corporate greenwashing. *Corporate Social Responsibility and Environmental Management*, 22: 142–154.

Vroom, V.H. (1964). *Work and motivation.* Oxford: Wiley.

Waddock, S.A., and Graves, S.B. (1997). The corporate social performance-financial performance link. *Strategic Management Journal*, 18: 303–319.

Wagner, M. (2007a). Integration of environmental management with other managerial functions of the firm: Empirical effects on drivers of economic performance. *Long Range Planning*, 40(5): 611–628.

Wagner, M. (2007b). On the relationship between environmental management, environmental innovation and patenting: Evidence from German manufacturing firms. *Research Policy*, 36(10): 1587–1602.

Wagner, M. (2009). Innovation and competitive advantages from the integration of strategic aspects with social and environmental management in European firms. *Business Strategy and the Environment*, 18(5): 291–306.

Wagner, M. (2010). Corporate social performance and innovation with high social benefits: A quantitative analysis. *Journal of Business Ethics*, 94: 581–594.

Wagner, T., Lutz, R.J., and Weitz, B.A. (2009). Corporate hypocrisy: Overcoming the threat of inconsistent corporate social responsibility perceptions. *Journal of Marketing*, 73(6): 77–91.

Wakabayashi, M., and Arimura, T.H. (2016). Voluntary agreements to encourage proactive firm action against climate change: An empirical study of industry associations' voluntary action plans in Japan. *Journal of Cleaner Production*, 112: 2885–2895.

Waldman, D.A., Siegel, D., and Javidan, M. (2006). Components of CEO transformational leadership and corporate social responsibility. *Journal of Management Studies*, 43(8): 1703–1725.

Walker, M., and Mercado, H. (2015). The resource-worthiness of environmental responsibility: A resource-based perspective. *Corporate Social Responsibility and Environmental Management*, 22: 208–221.

Wang, H., and Choi, J. (2013). A new look at the corporate social-financial performance relationship: The moderating roles of temporal and interdomain consistency in corporate social performance. *Journal of Management*, 39: 416–441.

Wang, T.T. (2013). *So different yet so similar: Long-term orientation and CSP in new and mature companies*. Paper presented at AOM Annual Conference, Orlando.

Wassmer, U., Paquin, R., and Sharma, S. (2014). The engagement of firms in environmental collaborations: Existing contributions and future directions. *Business & Society*, 54(6): 754–786.

Weaver, G.R., Treviño, L.K., and Agle, B.R. (2005). "Somebody I look up to": Ethical role modeling in organizations. *Organizational Dynamics*, 34: 313–330.

Weaver, G.R., Treviño, L., and Cochran, P. (1999). Corporate ethics programs as control systems, Influences of executive commitment and environmental factors. *Academy of Management Journal*, 42: 41–57.

Welford, R., and Frost, S. (2006). Corporate social responsibility in Asian supply chains. *Corporate Social Responsibility and Environmental Management*, 13(3): 166–176.

Welsh, J., and White, J. (1981). A small business is not a little big business. *Harvard Business Review*, 59(4): 18–32.

White, J.C., Varadarajan, P.R., and Dacin, P.A. (2003). Market situation interpretation and response: The role of cognitive style, organizational culture, and information use. *Journal of Marketing*, 67(3): 63–79.

Whitehouse, L. (2006). Corporate social responsibility: Views from the frontline. *Journal of Business Ethics*, 63(3): 279–296.

Wickert, C., Scherer, A.G., and Spence, L.J. (2016). Walking and talking corporate social responsibility: Implications of firm size and organizational cost. *Journal of Management Studies*, 53(7): 1169–1196.

Widiss, D.A. (2012). Divergent interests: Union representation of individual employment discrimination claims. *Indiana Law Journal*, 87(1): 421.

Williams, G., and Zinkin, J. (2008). The effect of culture on consumers' willingness to punish irresponsible corporate behavior: Applying Hofstede's typology to the punishment aspect of corporate social responsibility. *Business Ethics: A European Review*, 17(2): 210–226.

Williams, L.J., Vandenberg, R.J., and Edwards, J.R. (2009). Structural equation modeling in management research: A guide for improved analysis. *Academy of Management Annals*, 3: 543–604.

Williams, M., and Polman, E. (2015). Is it me or her? How gender composition evokes interpersonally sensitive behavior on collaborative cross-boundary projects. *Organization Science*, 26(2): 334–355.

Williams, R.J. (2003). Women on corporate boards of directors and their influence on corporate philanthropy. *Journal of Business Ethics*, 42(1): 1–10.

Williamson, D., and Lynch-Wood, G. (2001). A new paradigm for SME environmental practice. *The TQM Magazine*, 13(6): 424–432.

Williamson, D., Lynch-Wood, G., and Ramsay, J. (2006). Drivers of environmental behaviour in manufacturing SMEs and the implications for CSR. *Journal of Business Ethics*, 67: 317–330.

Wohlfarth, K., Eichhammer, W., Schlomann, B., and Mielicke, U. (2017). Learning networks as an enabler for informed decisions to target energy-efficiency potentials in companies. *Journal of Cleaner Production*, 163: 118–127.

Wong, J.J., Abdullay, M.O., Baini, R., and Tan, Y.H. (2017). Performance monitoring: A study on ISO14001 certified power plant in Malaysia. *Journal of Cleaner Production*, 147: 165–174.

Wood, D.J. (1991). Corporate social performance revisited. *Academy of Management Review*, 16(4): 691–718.

Wood, D.J. (2010). Measuring corporate social performance: A review. *International Journal of Management Reviews*, 12(1): 50–84.

Yang, X., Wang, Y., Hu, D., and Gao, Y. (2018). How industry peers improve your sustainable development? The role of listed firms in environmental strategies. *Business Strategy and the Environment*, 27(8): 1313–1333.

Yong Oh, W., Chang, Y.K., and Martynov, A. (2011). The effect of ownership structure on corporate social performance: Empirical evidence from Korea. *Journal of Business Ethics*, 104: 283–297.

Young, S.L., and Makhija, M.V. (2014). Firms' corporate social responsibility behavior: An integration of institutional and profit maximization approaches. *Journal of International Business Studies*, 45(6): 670–698.

Yu, X. (2009). From passive beneficiary to active stakeholder: Workers' participation in CSR movement against labor abuses. *Journal of Business Ethics*, 87: 233–249.

Zammuto, R.F., Gifford, B., and Goodman, E.A. (2000). Managerial ideologies, organizational culture, and the outcomes of innovation. In Ashkanasy, N.M., Wilderom, C.P.M., and Peterson, M.F. (Eds.), *Handbook of organizational culture & climate* (pp. 261–278). Thousand Oaks, CA: Sage.

Zellweger, T., Nason, R., Nordqvist, M., and Brush, C. (2011). Why do family firms strive for nonfinancial goals? An organizational identity perspective. *Enterpreneurship, Theory & Practice*, 37(2): 229–248.

Zhang, A., Moffat, K., Lacey, J., Wang, J., Gonzalez, R., Uribe, K., Cui, L., and Dai, Y. (2015). Understanding the social license to operate of mining at the national scale: A comparative study of Australia, China and Chile. *Journal of Cleaner Production*, 108: 1063–1072.

Zhang, M., MacPherson, A., and Jones, O. (2006). Conceptualizing the learning process in SMEs: Improving innovation through external orientation. *International Small Business Journal*, 24(3): 299–323.

Zhang, Q., Oo, B.L., and Lim, B.T.H. (2019). Drivers, motivations, and barriers to the implementation of corporate social responsibility practices by construction enterprises: A review. *Journal of Cleaner Production*, 210: 563–584.

Zhao, X., Lynch, J.G., and Chen, Q. (2010). Reconsidering Baron and Kenny: Myths and truths about mediation analysis. *Journal of Consumer Research*, 37(August): 197–206.

Ziegler, A., and Nogareda, J.S. (2009). Environmental management systems and technological environmental innovations: Exploring the causal relationship. *Research Policy*, 38(5): 885–893.

Zientara, P. (2017). Socioemotional wealth and corporate social responsibility: A critical analysis. *Journal of Business Ethics*, 144: 185–199.

Zorpas, A. (2010). Environmental management systems as sustainable tools in the way of life for SMEs and VSMEs. *Bioresource Technology*, 101: 1544–1557.

APPENDIX 1

Survey Questions

Introduction to Respondents of the Survey

The concept of CSR was introduced to the respondents as follows:

> The topic of this survey is corporate social responsibility (CSR). CSR is the practice whereby enterprises integrate social and environmental concerns in their business operations on a voluntary basis, in order to contribute to public prosperity in the longer run. It concerns various environmental aspects (e.g. reduction of CO_2 emissions, energy consumption, water consumption and hazardous waste), but also social aspects (e.g. the provision of equal opportunities to women, job opportunities for disadvantaged people, training of employees, safe working conditions and contribution to social projects). You can interrupt answering the online survey at any time and return to it again whenever it suits you. If exact answers for your enterprise are not possible, please provide your best estimate. Thank you very much in advance.

TABLE A1.1 List of survey questions

No.	*Survey question*	*Answer options*
1	What is your position in the enterprise?	1 Director owner; 2 Director; 3 Manager; 4 Other
2	What is your age?	1 <30; 2 30–45; 3 46–55; 4 >55
3	Your company is:	1 fully owned by a family 2 partly owned by a family 3 not owned by a family
4	Your company is fully owned by a family and	1 fully managed by family members 2 partly managed by family members 3 not managed by family members
5	Your company is partly owned by a family and	1 fully managed by family members 2 partly managed by family members 3 not managed by family members
6	To whom do you sell your products and/or services?	1 Only enterprises; 2 Mainly enterprises; 3 Both enterprises and consumers; 4 Mainly consumers; 5 Only consumers
	How important are the following relationships for your enterprise?	Seven-point scale ranging from 1 'not at all' to 7 'very much'
7	Relations with shareholders and/or director owner	
8	Bank relations	
9	Employee relations	
10	Customer relations	
11	Supplier relations	
12	Relations with government bodies	
13	Local community relations	
14	Societal relations (like NGOs)	
15	Characterize your enterprise on the following scale. The scale concerns the organizational focus. This scale ranges from: 1 In our enterprise we focus on optimizing the internal organizational efficiency 7 In our enterprise we focus on adapting to the demands of the external environment	Select the answers on the seven-point scale here; 4 indicates an intermediate position

(Continued)

TABLE A1.1 (Continued)

No.	*Survey question*	*Answer options*
16	Characterize your enterprise on the following scale. The scale concerns the management style. This scale ranges from 1 In our enterprise we manage employees by supervision and strict compliance mechanisms 7 In our enterprise we stimulate employees autonomy and participative decision making	Select the answers on the seven-point scale here; 4 indicates an intermediate position
17	What is the average time horizon of the financial targets of your enterprise?	1 1 year or less; 2 2 years; 3 3 years; 4 4–5 years; 5 > 5 years
	How important are the following motives for your enterprise to engage in CSR?	Seven-point scale ranging from 1 'not at all' to 7 'very much'
20	It serves long-term financial interests of shareholders and/or director owner	
21	It helps to meet (future) government regulation	
22	It leads to innovation	
23	It reduces operational costs	
24	It limits reputational risks	
25	Your enterprise feels responsible for the planet and the society	
26	It creates personal satisfaction for the people in your enterprise	
27	Large customers ask for it	
28	It fulfils expectations of society	
29	CSR may demand extra financial resources. What is the average time horizon for these investments in your enterprise?	1 1 year or less; 2 2 years; 3 3 years; 4 4–5 years; 5 > 5 years
	To what extent does engagement in CSR influence the following aspects for your enterprise?	Seven-point scale ranging from 1 'not at all' to 7 'very much'
30	CSR makes it easier to attract investors	
31	CSR makes it easier to get credit from banks	
32	CSR improves inflow of highly qualified employees	
33	CSR motivates the employees	
34	CSR increases profit margins on products	
35	CSR increases turnover	
36	CSR helps meeting (future) government regulation	
37	CSR improves innovative capacity	
38	CSR improves profitability in the long term	
39	CSR limits reputational risks	

No.	*Survey question*	*Answer options*
40	To what extent did your enterprise face complaints (from inside or from outside the enterprise) about your enterprises social and/or environmental aspects?	Seven-point scale ranging from 1 'not at all' to 7 'very much'
41	Do industry and/or branch associations provide information on CSR?	Seven-point scale ranging from 1 'not at all' to 7 'very much'
42	Do NGOs and/or (social) media monitor your CSR?	Seven-point scale ranging from 1 'not at all' to 7 'very much'
	Which measures are realized in your enterprise?	1 Yes; 2 No; 3 Unfamiliar with this measure
43	Internal publication of a code of conduct	
44	External publication of a code of conduct	
45	Active dialogue with NGOs concerning CSR issues	
46	Cooperation with other enterprises in supply chain to meet CSR goals	
47	Partnerships with professional training institutes (technical schools, laboratories, etc.) to anticipate technological evolutions of products or services	
48	Participation in local initiatives (cooperation with local governments or social organizations) to meet social or environmental objectives	
49	Director/manager is answerable to CSR issues	
50	Remuneration of management is explicitly linked to CSR performance	
51	A confidential person or a confidential complaint procedure/whistle-blower procedure	
52	Ethics committee	
53	Training programme in (aspects of) CSR for employees and/or managers	
54	The use of a reference guide or external CSR tool to measure and verify your SR performance	
55	Use of global initiatives (like GRI and/or Global Compact) as a frame of reference	
	Which measures are realized in your enterprise?	1 Yes; 2 No; 3 Partially; 4 Unfamiliar with this measure
56	ISO 9001/9002/9003	
57	ISO 14001 and/or regulated by Eco-Management and Audit Scheme (EMAS) or Greenhouse Gas Protocol	
58	SA 8000	
59	Other (e.g. ISO 27001, FSC, etc.)	

(Continued)

TABLE A1.1 (Continued)

No.	*Survey question*	*Answer options*
	Indicate for each social issue below whether your enterprise actively improved it.	1 no; 2 on an ad hoc basis; 3 continuously
60	Share of women in board and/or executive positions	
61	Share of employees recruited from disadvantaged groups (e.g. ethnic minorities, people with disabilities, long term unemployed)	
62	Work–life balance	
63	Employee training	
64	Contribution to social projects (e.g. sponsoring)	
65	Reduction in workplace accidents and/or sickness absence rate	
66	Labour conditions of suppliers/subcontractors and/or respect of human rights	
	What was your enterprise's performance on the following social aspects in 2010?	%
67	Share of women in board and/or executive positions	
68	Share of employees recruited from disadvantaged groups (e.g. ethnic minorities, people with disabilities, long-term unemployed)	
69	Number of overtime hours as % of total FTEs	
70	Share of employees covered by collective bargaining agreement as % of total number of employees	
71	Sickness absence rate	
72	Share of permanent employment contracts as % of total number of employment contracts	
73	Contribution to social projects as % of net profit	
	Has your performance on the following social aspects increased, decreased or remained more or less the same in 2010 compared to 2007?	1 Decreased more than 5%: -3.0 2 Decreased by 3–5%: -2.0 3 Decreased by 1–3%: -1.0 4 Not changed very much: 0.0 5 Increased by 1–3%: 1.0 6 Increased by 3–5%: 2.0 7 Increased more than 5%: 3.0
74	Share of women in board and/or executive positions	
75	Share of employees covered by collective bargaining agreement	
76	Share of permanent employment contracts as % of total number of employment contracts	

No.	*Survey question*	*Answer options*
	Has your performance on the following social aspects increased, decreased or remained more or less the same in 2010 compared to 2007?	1 Decreased by more than 2% 2 Decreased by 1–2% 3 Decreased by 0.5–1% 4 Not changed very much 5 Increased by 0.5–1% 6 Increased by 1–2% 7 Increased by more than 2%
77	Share of employees recruited from disadvantaged groups as % of total inflow	
78	Number of overtime hours as % of total FTEs	
79	Sickness absence rate	
80	Contribution to social projects as % of net profit	
	Please indicate whether your enterprise has taken the following measures	1 We use methods to measure; 2 We use concrete targets; 3 We report on it; 4 None of these
81	Share of women in board and/or executive positions	
82	Share of employees recruited from disadvantaged groups (e.g. ethnic minorities, people with disabilities, long term unemployed)	
83	Work–life balance	
84	Employee training	
85	Contribution to social projects (e.g. sponsoring)	
86	Reduction in workplace accidents and/or sickness absence rate	
87	Labour conditions of suppliers/ subcontractors and/or respect of human rights	
88	What is the average length of contract in your enterprise?	In number of years
89	What are the average annual hours of training (course, education) per FTE that your enterprise fully or partly funds?	
	Indicate for each environmental issue below whether your enterprise actively improved it.	1 no; on an ad hoc basis; 3 continuously
90	Reduction of CO_2 emissions	
91	Reduction in energy consumption and/or increase in use of renewable energy	
92	Reduction in water consumption	
93	Reduction in waste and/or increase in recycling of waste	
94	Environmental conditions of suppliers/ subcontractors	

(Continued)

TABLE A1.1 (Continued)

No.	*Survey question*	*Answer options*
	Please indicate whether your enterprise has taken the following measures (multiple answers possible):	1 We use methods to measure; 2 We use concrete targets; 3 We report on it; 4 None of these
95	Reduction of CO_2 emissions	
96	Reduction in energy consumption and/or increase in use of renewable energy	
97	Reduction in water consumption	
98	Reduction in waste and/or increase in recycling of waste	
99	Environmental conditions of suppliers/subcontractors	
	Has your performance on the following environmental issues increased, decreased, or remained more or less the same in 2010 compared to 2007 (respective 2013 compared to 2010)?	1 Decreased more than 5%: -3.0 2 Decreased by 3–5%: -2.0 3 Decreased by 1–3%: -1.0 4 Not changed very much: 0.0 5 Increased by 1–3%: 1.0 6 Increased by 3–5%: 2.0 7 Increased more than 5%: 3.0
101	CO_2 emissions	
102	Energy consumption	
103	Use of renewable energy	
104	Water consumption	
105	Waste	
106	Share of waste that is recycled	
	Please indicate for each environmental aspect which of these causes contributed most to your improvement on that aspect	1 Voluntary initiatives by own enterprise 2 Collective initiatives in supply chain and/or industry 3 Legal requirements 4 Market pressure 5 Not applicable
107	Decrease in CO_2 emissions	
108	Decrease in energy consumption	
109	Increase in use of renewable energy	
110	Decrease in water consumption	
111	Decrease in waste production	
112	Increase in share of waste that is recycled	
	What was your enterprise's employment?	In FTE
113	In 2007	
114	In 2010	
115	What is the share of the skill level categories of employees?	as % of total FTEs
	Low skilled (no qualifications, O-levels, CSEs, GCSEs)	
	Medium skilled (A levels or BTEC equivalent)	
	High skilled (degree and post graduate level qualifications)	
116	What is the share of the age categories of employees?	as % of total FTEs
	<25 years	
	25–50 years	
	>50 years	

No.	*Survey question*	*Answer options*
119	Which of the following statements is most applicable to your enterprise? 1 many enterprises are selling products and/or services that have very similar characteristics (so-called perfect market) 2 many enterprises are selling products and/or services, but the product and/or services have slightly different characteristics (so-called monopolistic competition) 3 a few enterprises are active that provide 70% or more of the market (so-called oligopoly) 4 no other enterprise is active that sells a product and/or service that has similar characteristics as your product and/or service (so-called monopoly)	
120	What best characterizes the market position of your enterprise in the market for your main product or service?	1 Your enterprise is market leader 2 Your enterprise is following the market leader 3 Your enterprise operates on a level-playing field with many enterprises 4 Your enterprise is niche product supplier
	In the market for your main product or service, your enterprise is prone to	Seven-point scale ranging from 1 'not at all' to 7 'very much'
121	price competition:	
122	competition on quality and/or product innovation	
123	Has your enterprise introduced new or significantly improved products or services since 2007? (Exclude the simple resale of new goods and changes of a solely aesthetic nature.)	Seven-point scale ranging from 1 'not at all' to 7 'very much'
124	Has your enterprise introduced new or significantly improved production or organizational processes since 2007?	Seven-point scale ranging from 1 'not at all' to 7 'very much'
	How important are the following motives for your enterprise to innovate?	Seven-point scale ranging from 1 'not at all' to 7 'very much'
125	Increasing market share	
126	Reduction of production costs per unit output	
127	Meeting government regulation	
128	Improvement of health and safety of your employees	
129	Reduction of your environmental impact and/or your material and energy costs	

APPENDIX 2

Sample and Methods of Statistical Testing

Sampling Method and Survey Development

Sampling Method

To disentangle the complex relationships between institutions, internal environment, CSR implementation, CSR impacts, and other impacts, we needed an extensive databank. Empirical studies on CSR often use ratings from professional rating bureaus, such as KLD, Asset4, Sustainalytics, Calvert, FTSE4Good, DJSI, EIRES, or public data bases (Aravind and Christman, 2011). These data are typically only available for large companies (Testa et al., 2014) and not for SMEs. Although several researches have been done to CSR of SMEs, all these researches were based on samples that are limited to a small number of SMEs and often relate to one or a few countries and typically include only a limited number of variables to be analysed. These samples are too small for a wide econometric analysis of CSR by SMEs.

For this reason we set up an ambitious new data project that aimed at gathering data of CSR, its drivers, and its impacts for at least 1,000 enterprises in 12 European countries. The focus on European countries was due to data limitations – a larger geographical diversity could not be obtained within the limits of the financial means provided by the European Union. We therefore selected a sample of countries that is considered representative of the existing variety of political and economic institutions in Europe: Continental Western Europe (Austria, Germany, France, and the Netherlands); Scandinavia (Finland, Sweden, and Denmark); Mediterranean Europe (Italy, Spain); Central Europe (Poland and Hungary); and Anglo-Saxon Europe (the United Kingdom) (see Table A2.1).

TABLE A2.1 Response to SME survey in 2011 and 2014 per country

	2011			*2014*		
Country	*Invitations*	*Completed Responses*	*Response rate (%)*	*Invitations*	*Completed Responses*	*Response rate (%)*
UK	31,801	163	0.5	383	69	18.0
Italy	85,920	1,534	1.8	3,610	906	25.0
Spain	38,870	566	1.5	1,290	226	17.5
Denmark	8,431	358	4.2	633	141	22.3
Finland	6,039	240	4.0	433	83	19.2
Sweden	13,771	263	1.9	561	110	19.6
Austria	11,254	148	1.3	310	33	10.6
France	63,054	346	0.5	1,105	128	11.6
Germany	50,129	537	1.1	1,182	187	15.8
Netherlands	12,885	624	4.8	1,198	380	31.7
Hungary	12,155	223	1.8	492	94	19.1
Poland	30,693	315	1.0	1,125	141	12.5
Total	365,002	5,317	1.5	12,321	2,498	20.3

Our ambition could only be realized by using a high cost-efficient way of gathering information. For that purpose, we contacted CentERdata, a data research institute specialized in online data collection. CentERdata has much experience in cross-European data collection and uses an advanced Language Management Utility to coordinate questionnaire development in different languages. Because questionnaires can be filled in online, the marginal costs of distributing questionnaires are extremely low if contact addresses are available.

In 2011, the survey was set out by CentERdata. After the first invitation, we sent three reminders. In 2014, CentERdata repeated this survey among the companies that cooperated to the survey in 2011.[1] To fully benefit from the longitudinal character of the study, the questions used in the 2011 survey were also included in the new wave. A time interval of three years should be sufficient to monitor the evolution of CSR over time, as CSR policies of companies only gradually change. Companies from all industries participated in the survey (see Table A2.3 below).

In October and November 2011 we fielded the first wave of the survey. The e-mail addresses of companies were obtained from KOMPASS (www.kompass.com). The researcher personally contacted the representative of KOMPASS in his country and discussed the characteristics of the database to be delivered by KOMPASS. An advantage of the KOMPASS database is that it includes both large and small companies. The number of e-mails of enterprises per country was set proportional to the total number of enterprises in these countries. A number of e-mail addresses bounced and therefore were not useable. The survey was presented to 365,002 enterprises and 13,637 responded (3.7%), of which 5,317 completed the long survey. International mail surveys aiming at an industrial population have a history of very low response rates varying between 6% and 16% (Harzing, 1997). Since our survey targeted SMEs, was electronic, and took substantial effort to fill out, the response rate is even lower and in line with ex-ante expectations. Based on statistical criteria (Cochran's sample size using an alpha of 0.05),[2] this response is adequate to infer reliable research findings for the total population of companies in the 12 countries. In November 2014, the respondents who had participated to the first study were contacted again and invited to take part in the second wave. The questionnaire was sent to 13,634 e-mail addresses, of which 9.6% was bounced. Of the remaining 12,321 invitations, 2,498 companies completely responded. Using Cochran's sample size formula with alpha of 0.05, we find that this response, too, is adequate. Table A2.1 shows many responses from Italy. This is due to the large number of Italian SMEs. The response rate was highest for the Netherlands, Denmark, and Finland. In contrast, for the UK, Austria, and France, we received a relatively low number of responses.

In our survey, we focused on small and medium-sized companies. As reported in Table A2.2, the size of the SMEs in our survey is very different. A substantial number of companies are micro enterprises with 10 or less employees. Also small companies (between 10 and 50 employees) and medium-sized enterprises (50–25) are well presented in our survey. Finally, 7–10 % of the respondents represent large companies with more than 250 employees (in FTEs).

Table A2.3 reports the sector division. We distinguish 19 sectors based on the National Accounts classification. Most companies operate in manufacturing sectors, but a substantial part concerns service industries. In the two waves, the sector allocation slightly changes, but no major differences occur.

Trend in CSR from 2011 to 2014

Tables A2.4 and A2.5 indicate how CSR changed during the period 2011–2014. Table A2.4 reports the general organizational measures or instruments that can be used to integrate CSR in the company's organization. Table A2.5 presents issue-specific measures for five social and five environmental aspects of CSR.

The first two measures indicate the commitment of the enterprise to CSR. An internal code of conduct is quite common but externally published codes

TABLE A2.2 Company size (employees, FTE) (in %)

	Micro (<10)	*Small (10–50)*	*Medium (50–250)*	*Large (>250)*
2011	23	38	29	10
2014	35	36	22	7

TABLE A2.3 Sector division (in %)

	2011	*2014*		*2011*	*2014*
Agriculture, forestry and fishing	2.2	2.7	Electricity, gas and water supply	1.1	0.7
Mining and quarrying	0.6	0.5	Construction	7.2	6.6
Food products, beverages and tobacco	4.2	4.4	Trade and hotels and restaurants	8.7	8.2
Textile and leather	3.0	3.4	Transport	3.9	3.6
Paper, publishing and printing	2.2	2.2	Telecommunications and computer services	4.4	3.3
Oil and chemical industry	2.9	3.3	Finance	1.1	0.9
Metal industry	8.9	8.2	Real estate activities	0.8	0.7
Machine industry	9.0	9.3	Other services	18.0	17.2
Transport equipment	0.7	0.6	Other business activities	12.3	14.1
Other manufacturing	8.8	9.8			

TABLE A2.4 Application of general CSR measures in 2011 and 2014 (%)

	2011	*2014*
Internal code of conduct	48	52
External code of conduct	20	24
Dialogue with NGOs	17	18
Cooperation on CSR in supply chain	38	41
Partnerships with training institutes	35	38
Participation in local initiatives with regard to CSR	41	45
CSR remuneration management	7	7
CSR training programme	30	32
ISO 14001/EMAS/GHG protocol	16	18
Other certifications	17	21

of conducts are not. Comparing 2011 and 2014, the commitment to CSR is slightly growing in time. This trend is also present for other measures that foster external CSR relations, for example an active dialogue with NGOs, cooperation with other companies in the supply chain, partnerships with professional training institutes, and participation in local initiatives of governments or social organizations to achieve CSR objectives. During 2011–2014, particularly participation in local initiatives increased. The company can also employ various instruments to improve the CSR awareness within the firm. Examples are CSR training of managers and other employees and CSR-dependent remuneration schemes. Table A2.4 shows that linking the remuneration of managers to their CSR performance

TABLE A2.5 Trends in issue-specific implementation (in %)

	Efforts[a]		*Targets (%)*		*Reporting (%)*	
	2011	*2014*	*2011*	*2014*	*2011*	*22014*
Social aspects						
Share of women in board and/or executive positions	44	47	11	12	10	13
Share of employees recruited from disadvantaged groups	38	40	12	13	11	13
Reduction in workplace accidents and sickness absence rate	80	83	27	29	29	31
Employee training	75	77	35	37	29	31
Labour conditions of suppliers and respect of human rights	59	63	17	18	14	15
Environmental aspects						
Reduction in energy consumption and/or increase in renewable energy	68	71	25	28	20	23
Reduction in water consumption	61	63	18	21	18	20
Reduction in waste and/or increase in recycling of waste	79	81	28	32	23	25
Environmental conditions of suppliers	51	53	13	13	13	13

a Measured on a three-point scale ranging from 0 (no effort), 50 (incidental effort), to 100 (continuous effort).

was still very rare in 2014, whereas CSR training was more common and growing over time. The last category refers to management systems that foster CSR. Table A2.4 shows that environmental certifications were not very common but slightly growing. Furthermore, companies may apply sector-specific certifications. In the Dutch construction sector, for example, the VCA certification (which focuses on health and safety issues) is very common among SMEs.

Application of general instruments will allow companies to improve its CSR outcomes. But the link between general instruments and concrete CSR outcomes is mediated by measures at the issue-specific level. Table A2.5 presents three types of indicators of the implementation of CSR at the issue-specific level: the effort that companies spend on improving specific CSR issues, use of targets for improving the realization of the respective CSR aspects, and whether it reports the realization of the targets. Table A2.5 shows SMEs have put gradually more effort into improving their CSR. Between 2011 and 2014, the average effort increased for all issues investigated. Safety and health issues and employee training received most attention. However, improvement of labour conditions in the supply chain was also an important item; almost 50% of SMEs said that they put continuous effort in improving this issue. Least effort was put into fostering the presence of women in top management of the company and recruitment of employees from disadvantaged groups.

Only a small minority of SMEs attached such a high priority to improving CSR that they used concrete targets and report on realization of these targets to guide their policies, although the use of this kind of procedural measures was slowly increasing between 2011 and 2014. Only for health and safety, employee training and reduction in waste, targets, and reporting were more commonly used by SMEs.

Methodology of Survey Development

In developing the survey, we first analysed how CSR is measured by professional rating bureaus. We only considered generic measurements, not sector-specific variables. Second, we sought guidance from an SME consultant who specialized in advising SMEs on their CSR to establish the kind of indicators known to micro, small, and medium-sized companies, indicators that they could look up relatively easily when filling out the survey questions. We also discussed the survey questions in two rounds with a research team of 14 renowned CSR researchers from the 12 European countries where the survey would be sent, who participated in the IMPACT project of the FP7 programme of the European Union. Next, we pre-tested the survey by interviewing ten executives from companies. We used a convenience sample (Sekaran, 2003) by selecting companies from the local environment of the researcher. The companies were selected from both manufacturing and service sectors (food industry, construction, trade, ICT, insurance) as well as from different size classes (micro, small, medium-sized and large) to explore content validity in various different contexts. The executives were asked to fill in the survey before the interview was held. Then the researcher visited the company and discussed the survey questions and the company's responses in depth, to check whether the respondent fully understood the survey questions and whether the questions suited the CSR of the company. These interviews provided us with extensive feedback on the survey questions. Based on the outcomes of this pilot survey, we fine-tuned the cut-off values.

As the use of English-language questionnaires in cross-national surveys might subconsciously adjust the responses, the survey was translated by members of the IMPACT research team into their own languages for the 12 countries in which the companies were located. As all of them are experts in CSR research and well known with the survey questions because of their participation in the discussion on the content and formulation of the survey questions, translation back of the relative simple survey questions into English to ensure correspondence with the original survey was not necessary. For the coordination of the translations, CenterData used an advanced language management utility to ensure consistent content coverage.

Estimation Methodology

Measures to Remedy Common Method and Non-response Biases

Using surveys potentially can cause several types of method biases, such as common method bias and non-response bias, or attrition bias in the 2014 survey. Common method bias arises from common rater effects due, for example, to social desirability and positive (or negative) mood state (Podsakoff et al., 2003). To address the potential concerns of common method and non-response or attrition bias, we used several precautionary remedies and ex post tests that are recommended by Podsakoff et al. (2003) and Antonakis et al. (2010). First, to reduce the potential for social desirability bias, we explained in a covering letter to the respondents in both surveys that the study was confidential and to be used for research purposes only. Respondents thus had little reason to present a more favourable picture than they knew to be the case, and research has shown that there are strong correlations between self-reported and actual behaviours (Beaver and Prince, 2004). Second, item ambiguity was reduced by avoiding vague concepts and keeping the questions simple, specific, and concise, steering respondents to least effort genuine answers. CSR was measured by very concrete yes/no questions (e.g. does your enterprise have a public code of conduct? Etc.), which reduce influences from affective mood or social desirability. A third precautionary remedy recommended by Podsakoff et al. (2003) that we employed is temporal separation. When testing the influence of independent variables on the dependent variables, we used in some of the analyses three years lagged values. As a fourth precautionary measure, the scales of different variables often differed. This reduces common method biases caused by commonalities in scale endpoints and anchoring effects. Finally, to diminish the effects of consistency artefacts, we put the survey questions that enquire the dependent variables at the end of the survey, and the independent variables more up front, so that the respondents did not fill in their responses to the independent variables with their response to the dependent variables in mind (Muller and Kolk, 2010).

Besides these precautionary measures, we applied two ex post tests for common method bias (see Table A2.6). First, Podsakoff et al. (2003) recommend Harman's single factor test through an unrotated principal component analysis on all the variables included in the analysis. The basic assumption of this technique is that if a substantial amount of common method variance is present, either (a) a single factor will emerge from the factor analysis or (b) one general factor will account for the majority of the covariance among the measures. Second, in some chapters we also employed the marker variable technique (Lindell and Whitney, 2001). A marker variable is a variable that is theoretically unrelated to at least one of the variables being studied. The correlation between this

TABLE A2.6 Overview of estimation methods per chapter

Part	*Ch.*	*Common method*		*Non-response*			*Factor analysis*		*Estimation techniques*
		Harman	*Marker*	*Wave*	*Heckman*	*Attrition*	*EFA*	*CFA*	
I	2	+		+	+				OLS, logistic
	3	+		+	+	+		+	SEM, lags
	4	+		+	+	+	+		OLS, IV, lags
	5			+	+	+	+		IV, lags
II	6	+		+	+		+		OLS
	7		+	+				+	SEM
	8		+		+		+	+	SEM, IV
	9	+		+	+		+		OLS
III	10	+		+	+			+	SEM
	11		+		+		+		Bootstrap
	12		+	+					Ordered logit
IV	13	+		+	+			+	SEM
	14		+		+		+	+	SEM, IV
	15	+			+		+		CMP, IV
	16		+		+		+	+	SEM
	17				+		+		SEM
	18			+	+				SEM

marker variable and the theoretically unrelated variable is treated as an indicator of common method bias.

To evaluate the non-response and attrition bias, we used three ex post tests. First, wave analysis compares the scores on key variables in the survey for early respondents and late respondents, assuming that late respondents are more similar to non-respondents than early respondents (Rogelberg and Stanton, 2007; Lin and Ho, 2011). To apply this test, we constructed a wave variable with value 1 for respondents that responded after the first invitation to participate in the survey, value 2 for responses after the first reminder, value 3 for responses after the second reminder, and value 4 for responses after the third reminder. If late respondents differ from early respondents, it suggests some level of non-response bias exists. The wave variable was included as an additional control variable in the regression analysis to correct for possible non-response bias. We further controlled for non-response bias by using the Heckman two-step estimation procedure (Heckman, 1979; Lee, 1983; Puhani, 2000; Certo et al., 2016). Heckman developed a two-stage procedure to eliminate the non-response bias in the regression analysis that follows from a selective response. Heckman showed that non-response bias can be interpreted as omitted variable bias and that the non-response bias disappears if one includes the omitted variable, the so-called inverse Mills ratio, in the regression analysis as control variable. In the first step, a probit model as selection equation is estimated for the full sample of 365,002 companies explaining the response (0 for non-response; 1 for response) in 2011 by type of country, sector, company size, and the year the company started. As exclusion restriction we used the degree of feeling European as measured by the Eurobarometer because the invitation letter that requested companies to respond to the survey was signed by a representative of the European Union. It is expected that respondents who feel more European are more inclined to cooperate with the survey, independent of their interest in sustainability. The estimation results of the probit model supported this proposition and showed a highly significant positive effect on the response rate of feeling European ($p < 0.001$), controlling for sector, company size, and the year that the company started. From the regression result, we calculated the inverse Mills ratio. The inverse Mills ratio expresses the unobserved characteristics of the company that might affect the likelihood that a company responds to the survey as well as the dependent and independent variables (causing the omitted variable bias). Next, the inverse Mills ratio is included as additional control variable in the regression analysis of the dependent variable. By including the inverse Mills ratio as explanatory variable in the regression analysis, one removes the selection bias part from the survey from the error terms. For the second survey in 2014, we additionally tested for attrition bias (selection bias caused by loss of participants) by performing regression analysis for the dependent and independent variables on a dummy measuring the response to the 2014 survey for all respondents that responded to the 2011 survey.

Estimation Techniques

In order to ascertain the validity of the constructs of variables based on a cluster of survey items, we used exploratory and confirmatory factor analysis (see Table A2.6). If the proposed clustering is based on the literature and clearly related to the theoretical meaning of these variables, but there is no previous literature that establishes the relation between our expected factors, it is then common practice to use an exploratory factor analysis (EFA) to test our predictions about the factor decomposition of the survey questions. EFA is independent of the structural model; the factor elements are chosen purely on the basis of the subset of survey questions and free of any *a priori* assumed relationships. For the exploratory factor analysis, we used principal component analysis with Oblimin rotation. The confirmatory factor analysis (CFA) tests validity of the factors in the specific context of the structural equation model by the estimation of the measurement model. It is performed simultaneously with the estimation of the structural model.

For the regression analysis, we mostly used structural equation modelling (SEM) with maximum likelihood estimation that simultaneously estimates the structural paths and the measurement model (confirmatory factor analysis). Factor analysis and structural equation modelling are well-known estimation techniques in management literature (Williams et al., 2009). The SEM methodology has several advantages (Tomarken and Waller, 2005). First, it provides a convenient method to simultaneously estimate latent variables and their manifest indicators (the measurement model/confirmatory factor analysis) and the relationships among constructs (the structural model). The use of latent constructs represented by multiple indicators provides more valid and reliable measurements of the variables studied and corrects for biases attributable to random error and construct-irrelevant variance. This improves the ability to draw causal inferences because testing models with good data and cross-validation allow a better understanding of the phenomenon studied. Another commonly acknowledged strength of SEM is the availability of measures of global fit that provide a summary evaluation of the full model, in contrast to models that are estimated on an equation-by-equation basis. Finally, SEM provides an easy way to test for mediation by the estimation of direct and indirect effects (Bullock et al., 1994).

A possible weakness of the SEM methodology is that it cannot fully prove causality. Notwithstanding the several advantages discussed earlier, it can only offer tentative causal inferences (Bullock et al., 1994). For this reason, we additionally used in some chapters the instrumental variable (IV) approach to additional test causality. We employed the Hausman specification test (also known as the Hausman test of endogeneity or Hausman-Wu test) and the Sargan test to test for exogeneity of the dependent and instrumental variable. In some chapters, we also used lagged variables, which is also a precautionary method to diminish reverse causality in CSR research (Waddock and Graves, 1997; Surroca et al., 2010).

If we used SEM, it was easy to test for mediation by inspecting the significance of indirect effects. In Chapter 11, we employed the regression-based macro for SPSS of Preacher and Hayes (2008) to test for mediation, using 1,000 bootstrap samples and bias-corrected confidence intervals. Because the mediation effect is the product of parameters, its sample distribution is skewed, with a shorter, fatter tail to the end of the distribution closer to zero. This implies that the lower bound of the confidence interval has less than 2.5% of the true sampling distribution, meaning that the 95% confidence interval will often improperly include zero. The bootstrap test of Preacher and Hayes solves that problem by generating an empirical sampling distribution of the mediation effect by bootstrapping. The lower bound of the 95% confidence is at 2.5% on this cumulative distribution (Zhao et al., 2010).

In Chapter 15, we used the conditional mixed process (CMP) estimator. The CMP modelling framework is essentially that of seemingly unrelated regressions, but is more general. In particular, the individual equations need not be classical regressions with a continuous dependent variable. The dependent variables may also be binary, ordered, and categorical or based on interval measures. CMP can also estimate parameters in mixed-process simultaneous systems that are recursive, meaning that endogenous variables may appear on the right-hand side as observed variables in other equations. Conditional means that the individual model equations can vary by observation.

Furthermore, cross plots between dependent and the independent variables and box plots were used to identify heteroscedasticity and the occurrence of problematic outliers in our researches, respectively. We also tested for multicollinearity of the independent variables by examining the variance inflation factor (VIF) (Hair et al., 1998). For each variable we checked that the variance inflation factor was smaller than five. Given the fact that our sample is very large, normality does not pose problems.

Control Variables

In the regression analysis, we controlled for various external, internal company, and respondent factors (see Table A2.7). External control variables include sector, country or region, position in the chain, and intensity of price competition.[3] Obviously, the type of sector in which the company operates will have a major impact on the type of CSR issues that a company will focus on. The nature of the business in terms of production processes or products determines the extent of social and environmental externalities that a firm creates (Brown et al., 2010). For example, companies in the construction sector take particular care of the safety and health aspect of CSR because of the nature of the building process. For chemical industries environmental issues are very important. For textiles, child labour and other social issues in the supply chain are a focal point (Graafland, 2002). Also the incentive to pursue an active CSR policy may differ for different sectors, as the reputation mechanism varies among sectors. Brammer and Pavelin (2006) found that environmental performance affects reputation positively in none but the chemicals, consumer products, resources, and transportation sectors. Three of these sectors are commonly identified as industries with salient environmental issues. Furthermore, they did not find any influence of employee performance on reputation, except for the resources sector. In most chapters, eight sectors were distinguished, based on the Global Industry Classification Standard (GICS). In other chapters, we used the sector division reported in Table A2.3. Furthermore, we used dummies for the 12 countries as control variables, or, alternatively, five dummies for the region in which the company operates. Country/region is included because CSR is affected (but not determined) by the culture and wider institutional environment of the company (Matten and Moon, 2008). For the five regional dummy variables, we used the categorization developed by Albareda et al. (2007) and Moon et al. (2012) that is based on different types of capitalism and CSR policies of governments (Anglo-Saxon Europe (UK), Scandinavia (Denmark, Finland, Sweden), Continental Europe (Austria, Germany, France, the Netherlands), Central Europe (Hungary, Poland), and Mediterranean Europe (Italy, Spain)). Next, environmental outcomes may be dependent on the enterprise's position in the chain. Companies that operate in business-to-consumer (B2C) relations rather than business-to-business (B2B) relations may be more sensitive to public reputation (Hendry, 2006). The closer

TABLE A2.7 Descriptive statistics of control variables[a]

		Mean	*SD*			*Mean*	*SD*
External controls							
Regional	Scandinavia	0.14	0.35	Sector	Materials	0.16	0.37
	Continental Europe	0.31	0.46		Energy	0.03	0.18
	Central Europe	0.13	0.34		Industrials	0.17	0.37
	Mediterranean Europe	0.39	0.49		Consumer staple	0.04	0.19
	UK	0.03	0.16		Consumer discretionary	0.17	0.38
Other	B2C (6)	2.03	1.07		Financials	0.03	0.16
	GDP per capita (ln)	3.16	0.43		IT & com	0.03	0.18
					Other sectors	0.37	0.48
Internal controls							
Age (116)	<25 years	0.11	0.13		high skilled	0.25	0.28
	25–50 years	0.67	0.23				
	>50 years	0.22	0.21	Other	Tenure (88)	13.31	9.23
Skill (115)	low skilled	0.33	0.32		Company size (ln) (113)	3.51	1.82
	medium skilled	0.42	0.29		Company age (ln)	3.33	0.65
Respondent controls							
Function (1)	Director-owner	0.33	0.47		Other function	0.29	0.45
	Director	0.19	0.39				
	Manager	0.19	0.40	Other	Age of respondent (2)	2.76	0.91

a The numbers in brackets refer to the numbers of the survey questions reported in Appendix 1. Country and sector, and company age are taken from the KOMPASS data source. The descriptives per chapter vary due to sample differences caused by differences in availability of data per survey question.

a particular firm is to consumers in the supply chain, the more likely consumers would be familiar with that firm and the more likely NGOs could mobilize consumers to influence the firm. Finally, the intensity of price competition was controlled for. The more competitive the market environment, the lower profitability and, according to slack resource theory (Waddock and Graves, 1997), the less resources a company has available for investing in CSR.

For internal company factors, we used age structure, skill structure, tenure, company size, and company age. The age structure (measured by the share of young, middle-aged, and old employees), skill structure (low, medium, and high skilled), and tenure were included as control variables, since these have been shown to affect managerial beliefs, values, and actions and therefore might also

TABLE A2.8 Estimation results of control variables[a]

	External factors				*Internal factors*									*CSR implementation*				
	Pcom	*Tcom*	*NGO*	*CA*	*TH*	*ExtMot*	*InnMot*	*IntrMot*	*FBO*	*WM*	*EO*	*FO*	*EFS*	*EFE*	*TRE*	*RelIn*	*ISO14*	*IntIn*
Scandinavia	**−0.21**		**0.06**	**0.37**		**−0.09**		**0.09**	**−0.09**		**−0.10**	**0.09**	**−0.15**	**−0.09**		**−0.05**	**−0.09**	**−0.21**
Continental Europe	**−0.31**		**0.09**	**0.46**	**0.08**	**−0.18**	**0.12**	**0.13**			**−0.09**	**0.04**	**−0.13**	**−0.10**		**−0.06**	**−0.14**	**−0.11**
Central Europe	**−0.11**		**0.05**	**0.13**	0.03	**−0.21**	**−0.06**	**0.06**		**0.15**	**0.06**	**−0.10**	0.05				**−0.12**	**−0.14**
Mediterranean Europe	**−0.10**			**0.74**		**−0.16**	**0.15**	**0.13**					**−0.10**			**−0.12**	**−0.21**	**−0.18**
Materials			0.02	**0.08**					**0.08**	**−0.06**	**−0.03**		*−0.03*					
Energy			0.02	*0.03*	0.03	**0.03**	*0.03*	*0.03*	*0.06*		0.02			*0.03*	**0.04**		**0.07**	
Industrials	**0.08**			**0.04**	*−0.04*					**−0.12**		*0.03*		*−0.03*				
Consumer staples				*0.03*					*0.04*						0.02			
Consumer discretionary	**0.07**			*0.04*					**0.07**			*0.03*	*−0.03*					
Financials							*−0.03*	*−0.03*	*−0.05*			**−0.03**	**−0.04**	**−0.06**		*−0.03*	**−0.05**	
IT						*−0.03*						**0.04**		**−0.05**		−0.02	*−0.03*	**−0.03**
Medium skilled			0.03				*0.04*	**0.05**	*−0.06*		**0.05**	**0.06**	**0.07**					
High skilled	**−0.11**	**0.09**	0.03	**−0.12**			**0.11**	**0.13**	**−0.16**	**0.09**	**0.08**	**0.13**	**0.04**	**−0.05**		**0.06**		*0.03*
Young			**0.05**				*0.04*	**0.06**	0.05							**0.05**		**0.07**
Medium Aged				*0.04*			0.03	**0.05**				*0.03*	*0.03*					**0.05**
Tenure	**−0.05**			*0.04*	**0.08**							0.03						
B2C	**−0.07**	*−0.04*	**0.08**	*0.03*	0.03			*0.03*		**0.07**	**0.04**			*0.04*	−0.02	*0.03*	**−0.08**	
Director-owner	*0.05*	**0.06**	**−0.09**		*0.05*	**−0.05**		**0.09**	**0.23**	**0.07**					**0.08**			
Director	*0.04*	0.03	*0.04*		*0.04*		0.03	**0.07**		**0.05**			*0.03*		**0.08**	**0.04**	*0.03*	*0.03*
Manager	**0.08**							0.03	**0.06**						**0.06**	**0.04**	**0.07**	**0.05**

Company age (ln)		**−0.07**	**0.05**	**0.06**		**0.05**			*0.05*								
Age respondent	*−0.04*					**0.05**	*0.03*	**0.04**			**0.08**		*−0.03*	**0.04**		*−0.03*	
Inverse Mill's ratio	**−0.06**	**−0.06**	**0.07**	0.04	**−0.06**	**−0.06**	*−0.03*		**−0.08**	**0.11**		**0.13**	**−0.13**	**−0.14**	**−0.09**		*0.04*

a The reference dummy for region, sector, skill level, age, and function are for the UK, other, low-skilled, old and other function, respectively. Standardized coefficients. Normal: $p < 0.05$; Italics: $p < 0.01$; Bold: $p < 0.001$. For the meaning of the symbols, see Table 19.6 in Chapter 19.

TABLE A2.9 Indirect and total effects[a]

	Indirect effects						*Total effects*[b]					
	EFS	*EFE*	*TRE*	*RelIn*	*ISO14*	*IntIn*	*EFS*	*EFE*	*TRE*	*RelIn*	*ISO14*	*IntIn*
Scandinavia	**0.08**	**0.04**	**0.02**	**0.05**		**0.02**	*−0.08*	**−0.05**	**0.02**		**−0.09**	**−0.19**
Continental Europe	**0.11**	**0.07**	**0.03**	**0.10**		**0.03**		−0.03	**0.03**	0.04	**−0.14**	**−0.08**
Central Europe	**0.04**		0.01	**0.04**	*−0.01*		**0.09**		0.01	**0.03**	**−0.14**	**−0.13**
Mediterranean Europe	**0.12**	**0.06**	**0.04**	**0.07**	−0.01	**0.02**		0.06	0.04	*−0.04*	**−0.21**	**−0.16**
Materials		*0.01*		0.01	*0.01*		-0.02	*0.01*		0.01	0.01	
Energy	**0.02**	**0.02**	**0.01**	**0.02**	**0.01**	**0.01**	0.02	**0.04**	**0.05**	**0.02**	**0.07**	**0.01**
Industrials	−0.01		−0.00	**−0.01**	*0.01*	*−0.01*	**−0.01**	*−0.03*	−0.00	**−0.01**	*0.01*	*−0.01*
Consumer staples	*0.01*	*0.01*	0.00	0.00	−0.00		*0.01*	*0.01*	0.02	0.00	−0.00	
Consumer discretionary	**0.01**	*0.01*	0.00		0.00		*−0.03*	*0.01*	0.00		0.00	
Financials	**−0.01**	*−0.01*	−0.00	−0.00	−0.00	**−0.01**	**−0.05**	**−0.06**	−0.00	**−0.03**	**−0.05**	**−0.01**
IT	*0.01*		−0.00		−0.00	−0.00	*0.01*	**−0.05**	−0.00		**−0.04**	**−0.03**
Medium skilled	**0.02**	**0.01**	**0.01**	**0.02**	*0.01*	**0.01**	**0.10**	**0.01**	**0.01**	**0.02**	*0.01*	**0.01**
High skilled	**0.06**	**0.03**	**0.01**	**0.04**		**0.04**	**0.10**		**0.01**	**0.11**		**0.09**
Young	**0.02**	**0.02**	**0.01**	**0.02**	**0.01**	**0.02**	**0.02**	**0.02**	**0.01**	**0.07**	**0.01**	**0.06**
Medium Aged	**0.02**	**0.01**	**0.01**	**0.01**	0.00	**0.01**	**0.05**	**0.01**	**0.01**	**0.01**	0.00	
Tenure	**0.01**	**0.01**	0.00	**0.01**		−0.00	**0.01**	**0.01**	0.00	**0.01**		0.00
B2C	**0.03**	**0.02**	**0.01**	**0.03**		**0.02**	**0.03**	**0.06**			**−0.08**	**0.02**
Director-owner	**0.04**	*0.02*			*−0.01*	−0.01	**0.04**	*0.02*	**0.09**		*−0.01*	−0.01
Director	**0.03**	**0.02**	**0.01**	**0.01**			**0.06**	**0.02**	**0.09**	**0.05**	*0.03*	**0.04**
Manager	*0.01*	*0.01*			*0.01*	0.00	*0.01*	*0.01*	**0.06**	**0.04**	**0.07**	**0.05**
Company age (ln)	*0.01*	*0.01*	*0.01*	**0.02**	**0.01**	*0.01*	*0.01*	*0.01*	*0.01*	**0.02**	**0.01**	*0.01*
Age respondent	**0.02**	**0.01**		**0.01**		**0.01**		**0.05**				**0.01**
Inverse Mill's ratio	**0.04**			**0.03**	−0.01		**−0.09**	**−0.14**	**−0.16**	**0.03**		

a Standardized coefficients. Normal: $p < 0.05$; Italics: $p < 0.01$; Bold: $p < 0.001$.

b The total effects are equal to the direct effects on CSR implementation reported in Table 19.5 plus the indirect effects reported in the left part of Table 19.6.

affect environmental performance (Marginson and McAulay, 2008). Mannix and Loewenstein (1994) found that tenure affects investment choices in a manner consistent with managerial opportunism. The prospect of leaving one's present firm leads to a greater focus on short-term pay-offs. Furthermore, many studies found that CSR is positively related to company size (e.g. Graafland et al., 2003; Laforet, 2008; Yong et al., 2011; McGuire et al., 2012). Based on interviews with staff members of NGOs, Hendry (2006) showed that the magnitude of the consequences that particular firms were having on the natural environment was an important factor in deciding to target particular firms or industries. Besides, enterprise size can also directly affect market benefits and CSR. Larger enterprises can spread the costs of CSR over a substantial larger turnover. Firm size is measured by the (natural logarithm of the) number of employees (in FTEs).

At the respondent level, the function and the age of the respondent are controlled for, as directors may be more informed and able to answer the survey questions than a manager at a lower level in the organization may. Mazereeuw (2010) found that CSR in Dutch SMEs is positively related to the age of executives. This contrasts with the finding of Luthar et al. (1997) that younger executives are significantly more likely to believe that good business ethics lead to successful business outcomes.

Table A2.8 reports the estimation results for the control variables for the integrative model presented in Chapter 19. The effects of regional dummies are mixed. Particularly, the UK differs from other regions. Whereas the intensity of price competition and extrinsic motivation are higher for the UK, NGO monitoring, collective agreements, and intrinsic motivation are lower. Overall, the indirect effects are lower for the UK than for other regions, but this is compensated by higher direct effects on the implementation of CSR (see Table A2.9). At the sectoral level, companies from the energy sector are most actively engaging with CSR, whereas companies from the finance sector show the lowest CSR implementation. Furthermore, CSR implementation increases with the skill level and decreases with the age level of employees. Finally, CSR is highest for companies that exist for a long period and tends to increase with tenure, position in the chain, and age of the respondent.

Notes

1 The survey in 2011 was financed by the FP7 program of the European Union. The survey in 2014 was possible due to a grant from ING.
2 The total number of companies in the 12 countries equals 16091,476 (Source: EU, http://ec.europa.eu/enterprise/policies/sme/facts-figures-analysis/performance-review/index_en. htm# h2-1).
3 In some chapters, also market position (survey question 120) was used as control variable.

INDEX